A VARIORUM COMMENTARY ON THE
POEMS OF JOHN MILTON
Volume 5, Part 8 [*Paradise Lost,* Books 11–12]

A Variorum Commentary on the Poems of John Milton

GENERAL EDITOR:

P. J. Klemp

CONTRIBUTING EDITORS:

Archie Burnett
W. Gardner Campbell
Claudia Champagne
Stephen B. Dobranski
Cheryl Fresch
Edward Jones
Jameela Lares
John Mulryan
Stella Revard
Louis Schwartz

A Variorum Commentary on the Poems of John Milton

VOLUME 5, PART 8

Paradise Lost, Books 11–12

By

Jameela Lares

Edited by

P. J. Klemp

Duquesne University Press

Pittsburgh, Pennsylvania

Published in the United States of America by
Duquesne University Press
600 Forbes Avenue
Pittsburgh, Pennsylvania 15282

LCCN 70129962
ISBN 978-0-8207-0446-3

∞ Printed on acid-free paper.

This volume is supported, in part, by a grant from the Calgon Corporation.

For my peerless friend,
Linda C. Mitchell

Contents

Abbreviations of Milton's Writings

Animad	*Animadversions upon the Remonstrants Defence*
Apol	*An Apology against a Pamphlet*
Arc	*Arcades*
Areop	*Areopagitica*
Circum	"Upon the Circumcision"
CivP	*A Treatise of Civil Power*
ComBk	*Commonplace Book*
DDD	*The Doctrine and Discipline of Divorce*
Def 1	*Pro populo anglicano defensio*
Def 2	*Pro populo anglicano defensio secunda (The Second Defence)*
DocCh	*De doctrina Christiana*
Educ	*Of Education*
Eikon	*Eikonoklastes*
El	*Elegia*
Epistol	*Familiar Letters of Milton*
EpWin	"An Epitaph on the Marchioness of Winchester"
Hirelings	*Considerations Touching the Likeliest Means to Remove Hirelings Out of the Church*
HistBr	*The History of Britain*
HistMosc	*History of Moscovia*
Idea	"De Idea Platonica"
IlPen	*Il Penseroso*
L'All	*L'Allegro*
LetFr	*Letter to a Friend*

Log	*Art of Logic*
Lyc	*Lycidas*
Mask	*A Mask Presented at Ludlow Castle (Comus)*
Nat	"On the Morning of Christ's Nativity"
OAP	*Observations on the Articles of Peace*
Patrem	*Ad Patrem*
PE	*Of Prelatical Episcopacy*
PL	*Paradise Lost*
PR	*Paradise Regained*
ProdBom	*In Proditionem Bombardicam*
Prol	*Prolusions*
Ps	Psalm
RCG	*The Reason of Church-Government*
Ref	*Of Reformation*
REW	*The Readie and Easie Way*
SA	*Samson Agonistes*
SolMus	"At a Solemn Music"
Sonn	Sonnet
Tetr	*Tetrachordon*
Time	"On Time"
TKM	*The Tenure of Kings and Magistrates*
Vac	"At a Vacation Exercise"

Preface

P. J. KLEMP

A Variorum Commentary on the Poems of John Milton has been a work in progress for over half a century. Another step in bringing closure to that monumental work, this volume on books 11–12 of *Paradise Lost,* like the volumes on book 4 and on *Samson Agonistes* published by Duquesne University Press in 2009, is a tangible sign of the scholarly continuity that exists between a new generation of Miltonists and our esteemed predecessors. Commentary about Milton's poems extends back to his own time, when the first variorum edition of *Paradise Lost* appeared in 1749 and that of *Paradise Regained, Samson Agonistes,* and many of the shorter poems in 1752, both edited by Thomas Newton. While this current volume looks back to those landmarks of scholarship, our main goal is to continue and complete the *Variorum Commentary* published between 1970 and 1975 by Columbia University Press.

Although the *Variorum Commentary* appeared in the 1970s, its inception occurred fully two decades earlier, in 1949. Merritt Y. Hughes, the *Variorum Commentary*'s first general editor, explains the process by which that scholarly project took shape. Following a survey of the Modern Language Association's members conducted by J. Milton French, in December 1949 the "interested section" of that organization "commissioned" the new *Variorum Commentary.* The editors selected were some of the twentieth century's finest Milton scholars, starting with French, who conducted the initial survey and declined the offer to become general editor. The rest of the participants were of the same stature, many of them joining French in being named Honored Scholars of the Milton Society of America: Merritt Y. Hughes (assigned to annotate *Paradise Lost*), Walter MacKellar (*Paradise Regained*), William Riley Parker (*Samson Agonistes*), A. S. P. Woodhouse (the so-called minor English poems), Douglas Bush (the Latin and Greek poems), and James E. Shaw (the Italian poems). If this epic catalog of scholars shines so brightly as to intimidate future generations who toil in the variorum's fields, it soon grew shorter.

For this generation of Milton scholars faced mortality, some well before their time. The opening volume of the Columbia University Press *Variorum Commentary* refers to the deaths of James E. Shaw, whose work on the Italian poems was updated by A. Bartlett Giamatti, and of William Riley Parker, whose work on *Samson Agonistes* would be carried on by John Steadman and, decades later, by Stephen B. Dobranski and Archie Burnett. The second volume refers to more departures—including that of A. S. P. Woodhouse, whose commentary on the minor English poems was completed by Douglas Bush. In his preface to that volume, Bush expresses his grief over the death of Merritt Y. Hughes, the annotator of *Paradise Lost*, which would mark perhaps the greatest impediment to the completion of the *Variorum Commentary*. If some of the variorum's charter members left scholarly work for others to complete almost immediately, Hughes's work on *Paradise Lost* and Parker's on *Samson Agonistes* would need to wait for future generations.

Since no one except John Steadman had expressed any interest in completing the *Variorum Commentary*, the indefatigable Albert C. Labriola stepped in as general editor, prompted by his respect for the labors of Hughes and Parker, a respect that also motivates the new contributing editors. Having seen the *Variorum Commentary* languish in an unfinished state, Al first located the typescripts that had been collecting dust in boxes. With the help of John Steadman, who held the draft of Hughes's annotations to *Paradise Lost* (and had done some minor revising of them) as well as Parker's introduction and annotations to *Samson Agonistes,* Al gathered up these typescripts, facilitated the transfer of the publishing rights, recruited a new group of esteemed Miltonists to take over the research and compilation, and secured funding to allow the project to get underway. In mid-1997, the editorial process officially began when a delivery van brought seven boxes of this material to my doorstep. Fortunately, just before his death in early 2009, Al was able to see the appearance of the first volume of the new *Variorum Commentary* that he had initiated.

Because more than three centuries of scholarship have accumulated about Milton's poems, much of that scholarship rich and perceptive, no variorum commentary could synthesize and present all, or even the bulk, of it. The term *variorum*, as demonstrated by the original Columbia University Press volumes and *"Paradise Lost," 1668–1968: Three Centuries of Commentary* (2004), by Earl Miner, William

Moeck, and Stephen Jablonski, does not imply exhaustive coverage of scholarship. Indeed, by overwhelming readers and blurring key studies with exceedingly minor ones, such a goal would make the variorum unwieldy, unusable. Scholars working on the older volumes, like their counterparts working on the Duquesne University Press volumes devoted to *Paradise Lost* and *Samson Agonistes,* encountered the problem of making selections from a mountain of riches. In the preface to the first volume of the *Variorum Commentary,* Merritt Y. Hughes remarks that he had to look back almost two centuries to find his *Variorum*'s immediate predecessor, which was Todd's *Poetical Works* from 1801. In the world of Miltonic scholarship, those had been two busy centuries, as Hughes explains: "The bulk of Miltonic scholarship and criticism has grown so enormously since Todd... that his successors... are beset with problems of selection and annotation" (1:vi). Working to now complete the *Variorum Commentary,* the current *Variorum*'s 12 contributing editors—all of whom have been attempting to locate and synthesize the most significant Milton scholarship about *Paradise Lost* before 1970 (the cutoff date determined by the year when the original volumes started to appear)—face precisely the same problems that Hughes mentions.

As today's contributing editors work with material left behind by Merritt Y. Hughes and William Riley Parker, they deal with many other issues that the original compilers also had to address. When he inherited the "minor" English poems following A. S. P. Woodhouse's death, Douglas Bush found himself in the position that the new contributing editors occupy with respect to their predecessors, Hughes and Parker. Bush notes that Woodhouse "left a large but far from complete manuscript which was given to me to revise and finish. The work he had done was, as we should expect, substantial, precise, and judicious." However, "The manuscript was a first draft, ranging in various parts from approximately finished form to pencilled notes" (Hughes, *Variorum* 2:1:ix). The current *Variorum Commentary*'s contributing editors inherited something quite similar: a draft of Hughes's annotations (about 5,000 pages, many containing only one sentence) to *Paradise Lost,* up to book 11, line 613, with some revisions by John Steadman (Hughes did not begin work on an introduction), and Parker's annotations (about 2,000 pages) and nearly complete introduction (208 pages) to *Samson Agonistes.* The current contributing editors, who in the late 1990s received lightly edited versions of Hughes's annotations to *Paradise Lost* and Parker's introduction and annotations to *Samson Agonistes,* understand what it means to work in someone's shadow. Even Douglas Bush expressed uneasiness about this role in handling Woodhouse's manuscript:

> There has...been much to add in various places....Most small additions...have
> been made silently....While I have been very reluctant to change what he wrote, it
> has often seemed necessary, as the manuscript grew in bulk, to omit, condense, or
> otherwise alter....In general, the effort to revise and complete the work of another
> man...has involved endless difficulties. I cannot claim to have resolved them without
> various kinds and degrees of awkwardness; but I hope that my editorial operations
> have not blurred or misrepresented Woodhouse's insights and opinions. (Hughes,
> *Variorum* 2:1.ix–x)

Part of the current *Variorum Commentary*'s methodology, an act of historical
reconstruction that is analogous to Bush's treatment of Woodhouse's manuscript,
is to use as much of Hughes's and Parker's material as future readers will find valu-
able, incorporating it into the new material.

The *Variorum Commentary* on *Paradise Lost,* besides continuing the *Variorum*'s
philosophy about selective coverage, cutoff date, and respect for the work of
departed Milton scholars, also shares its view about presenting a text of the poetry.
If Hughes judged that it was "neither necessary nor feasible to include another text"
in 1970 (Hughes, *Variorum* 1:v), the recent proliferation of editions of Milton's
writings makes such an undertaking even less necessary as part of our *Variorum
Commentary.* Nevertheless, because the use of the *Variorum Commentary* on
Paradise Lost will inevitably result in closer scrutiny of the books of Genesis and
Judges, for example, and of Milton's poems, it is recommended that readers keep
these texts at hand.

Although the goals of a variorum commentary are largely consistent from generation to generation, the scholarly environment of the 1970s differs in many ways
from the one we inhabit in a new millennium. In his prefatory remarks, Hughes
articulated the goals of the *Variorum Commentary:*

> While the chief end is interpretative criticism, the larger part of a variorum commentary
> must necessarily be given to supplying information of all kinds, from the history and
> meaning of words to the history and meaning of ideas. Our object in this work is to
> furnish a body of variorum notes and discussions uniting all available scholarly illlu-
> minations [*sic*] of the texts on all levels from the semantic and syntactical to those of
> deliberate or unconscious echoes of other works in all the languages known to Milton.
> In notes on the longer passages we have considered their inner rhetorical organization
> and involvements in the design of the poem as a whole, in the backgrounds of the
> literary traditions of which they themselves are outstanding developments, and in the
> many aspects of Milton's interests—theological, cosmological, hexameral, historical,
> psychological, and so on. (1.vi–vii)

Today's contributing editors grew up with the *Variorum Commentary*'s values and assumptions in their consciousness, and with the volumes at their side. Whether or not the contributing editors fully endorse that volume's foundational values, it is worth noting that those unspoken assumptions include more than a hint of new critical interest in formal matters of poetic design, which would make poststructuralists uncomfortable; a thorough old historical privileging of Milton's text over any context (historical, literary, theological, and so forth), a hierarchy that new historicists would qualify; the veneration of Milton, his verse, and the canon in general, a view interrogated by those who work in multicultural studies or engage in debates about the canon; and a perspective that advances the significance of notes, marginal material that appears on the bottom of the page in most editions, but which *is* a variorum commentary from cover to cover. Those scholars working on the history of the book and those bibliographers interested in the material conditions under which texts are produced, exchanged, and consumed would grasp the scope of a Milton variorum, new or old, but only after its assumptions were thoroughly examined. Perhaps nothing better characterizes the difference in Hughes's scholarly environment and our own than this emphasis on continuous reflection, particularly about privileging and, to use the title of Adrian Johns's study, *The Nature of the Book,* which forms part of the new *Variorum Commentary*'s foundation.

After we have completed the *Variorum Commentary* on *"Paradise Lost,"* we hope to turn to an even more ambitious project, updating the entire *Variorum Commentary*—on the shorter English poems, Latin and Greek poems, Italian poems, *Paradise Lost, Paradise Regained,* and *Samson Agonistes*—to cover scholarship published from 1970 to 2000.

Acknowledgments

I am deeply grateful to those scholars who involved or sustained me in this project. The late John M. Steadman, former editor for both *Paradise Lost* and *Samson Agonistes*, and always supportive of my scholarship, very kindly recommended me as the contributing editor for this volume, and general editor Albert C. Labriola very firmly insisted that I take the position. Al encouraged me at every step of this project until his untimely death; I am sorry he will not see the finished version. I have been equally encouraged by general editor Paul J. Klemp, who from the first tentative draft has tirelessly and graciously provided detailed and useful editorial comments. The late John T. Shawcross provided not only his usual collegial encouragement but also helpful answers to any number of Milton-related questions. I am additionally grateful for the collegiality of all of the *Variorum*'s contributing editors, and especially to John Mulryan and Stella P. Revard for their perennial support of my work and for help with questions about Greek and Latin usage, for which I also thank John K. Hale. Special thanks also to Stephen B. Dobranski, whose published volume on *Samson Agonistes* served as my model for revisions.

Although I never met the original editor of this project, heartfelt thanks are due to Merritt Y. Hughes. He presided over my early Milton studies by means of his annotations in various editions of Milton, and I have made every effort to preserve his scholarship in this volume. Another important scholar I must mention here, one whom I will never sufficiently thank, is my mentor and friend, Lawrence D. Green. I hope that this volume is worthy of his scholarly benediction.

I also thank my colleagues at The University of Southern Mississippi for their ongoing support of my scholarship. Without the personal example and early encouragement of my one-time colleague Gary A. Stringer, now Distinguished Professor at East Carolina University, I might not have gotten involved in this project. I certainly would have had much more difficulty completing it without the sustained encouragement of my other English department colleagues, particularly longtime chairs Michael N. Salda and Michael Mays and now Eric Tribunella. I owe special thanks also to a number of careful research assistants who helped me assemble the bibliography for this volume and compile the needed documents—Scott Bailey, Marilyn Ford, Michael Howell, Sam Ruddick, and Gregory J. Underwood. Thanks also to some very special students, Armond J. Boudreaux, Leah Boudreaux, René Fleischbein, Corey Latta, and Hannah Ryan, for their encouragement at the last stages. Initial research for this project was undertaken thanks to an Aubrey K. and Ella Ginn Lucas Award and thanks to our British Studies Program, which always helped me to set time aside for research; thanks especially to program directors Douglas Mackaman and Kenneth Panton and to support staff Jessica Lamb and Philip and Frances Sudduth.

Indeed, I owe many thanks to individuals and institutions in Britain, such as to the Department of English and Drama at Loughborough University, where I was visiting professor during the academic year 2002–03, and especially to Elaine Hobby, Brian Jarvis, John Schad, and Nigel Wood. Numerous friends in Britain have offered their longtime encouragement in this project, including Robert and Susan Cockcroft, Thomas S. Freeman, Iain Murton, Geoffrey Rivett, and Heward and Francis Wilkinson. Special thanks to Sarah Hutton for her hospitality, friendship, and mentorship over the years. Special thanks also to Adrian Brink of James T. Clarke and the Lutterworth Press for many gracious years of friendship and support.

I could not have completed this project without the valiant assistance of numerous librarians at my university, including Karolyn Thompson (now retired), Nadine Phillips, and the staff of the University of Southern Mississippi Libraries Document Delivery System. Thanks also to the wonderful reader service personnel of the Bodleian Library, the British Library, the Cambridge University Library, the William Andrews Clark Memorial Library, and the Henry E. Huntington Library. So many thanks do I owe to people at these collections that I would surely overlook someone if I tried to name them all, but I will make special mention of Christopher Adde, Paul Hudson, Elisabeth Leedham-Green, and Suzanne Tatian.

Thanks to Duquesne University Press for its support of my scholarship and work, especially to director Susan Wadsworth-Booth, for a decade and more of encouragement; to the anonymous reader for many illuminating and encouraging comments; and to my copyeditor, Kathy Meyer, for her energetic dedication to accuracy. All residual errors are mine. Thanks as well to David Luljak, who prepared the index.

Finally, thanks to my family and friends, including my church family at the Episcopal Church of the Ascension in Hattiesburg, Mississippi. Linda C. Vance helped me by checking citations in the library. My brother, Charles W. Young, took care of all family business during a crucial time in this project. My son Robert Lares provided me a place to stay near the Huntington Library during my sabbatical in 2000, and later he and his partner Lisa Carroll provided much needed diversion with long-distance phone calls. My daughter and son-in-law, Julia and David Argueta, my granddaughter Zoe, and her other grandmother, Luz Maria Argueta (with all of whom I share a house) have been endlessly patient with me in the final stages. Julia also provided extensive research help, pinpointing relevant commentary in scores of books and articles.

Finally, I wish to thank my friend Linda C. Mitchell for all she has done to help me complete this project and, indeed, to be a human being. Since our graduate days together under Lawrence D. Green at the University of Southern California, she has been my best friend, study partner, travel companion, and secular life coach. This volume is dedicated to her.

A Note on the Annotations

As in other volumes in this series, all annotations for the last two books of *Paradise Lost* (hereafter *PL*) follow as closely as possible the lineation of various editors' notes. Long annotations are organized topically and, in one or two cases, chronologically within those topics. For consistency, longer sections beginning with the same line number precede shorter ones. References to sources have been kept simple. Passages from *PL* are accompanied by only as much information on book or line as necessary. The most complex citations are from Sylvester's translation of Du Bartas, for which I have indicated the volume in the Snyder edition along with page(s) and usually line(s). I have retained standard references for texts whenever possible, so that, for instance, poetry is cited by line number unless otherwise noted. I have also referred to standard modern editions of texts cited by commentators, although citations to the works of Josephus are from William Whiston's classic translation (1736), because his version is the one generally used by Milton's commentators and critics and indeed is still in general use. When no page numbers are indicated for an author, that entry refers to an edition of *PL*. Cross-references to commentaries identified with bold numbers are to the line-by-line entries in this book; numbers not in bold refer to pages within the scholarly writing there cited.

I have referred to the Authorized Version of the Bible (1611) as KJV (King James Version), the title by which it is known in the United States. My abbreviations for biblical books are the expanded ones recommended by *The Chicago Manual of Style*, 15th edition, so that, for instance, Deuteronomy is indicated by Deut. rather than Dt. I have followed Milton in using the term "saint" to refer to biblical authors (St. Paul, St. John), but not church fathers (Augustine, Jerome). I have cited both the 1877 and 1894 editions of R. C. Browne, the latter one including etymological notes revised by Henry Bradley. John Wesley's abbreviated version of *PL* (1763) is among editions cited, as it was surely influential in certain circles.

My references to the *Oxford English Dictionary* (*OED*) reflect an amalgam of the second edition online (1989) and updates. A definition followed by "so *OED*" indicates that the passage in *PL* is cited in this amalgamated edition. Milton's last two books are cited in hundreds of *OED* entries; I have only included the ones for which modern meanings are not immediately apparent or for which the *OED* entry is particularly illuminating.

All references to Milton's work in this commentary are from *The Works of John Milton*, ed. Frank Allen Patterson, 18 vols. in 21 (New York: Columbia University Press, 1931–38). In citations of Milton's *De doctrina Christiana,* I have lowercased the continuous uppercasing he employs in key sections.

I have endeavored to avoid sexist language except in cases where it is too idiomatic to avoid, as in the case of "inner man," a theological phrase from Eph. 3:16 that pervades theological discussions of Christian regeneration.

I repeat here my thanks to Merritt Y. Hughes, the original editor of the *Variorum* volume of *PL.* Although he only produced notes for various lines within 11.1–264 and for 11.395–96, 573–92, and 613, with none at all for book 12, Milton scholars will surely agree with me that his comments are important and influential. I have quoted these comments whenever possible under the title "Variorum." I have not, of course, quoted his mere citation of other critics.

Commentary
Introductory Note

Critical discussions of books 11 and 12 of *Paradise Lost* often focus on the entwined questions of whether the final two books are artistically equal to the preceding ten and what the books represent in themes, structures, or genres. Neoclassical critics initially complained that the ending was not happy enough for an epic, whereas some early twentieth century critics have complained that it was not disconsolate enough for the theology (Moore 1–34). Among the earlier critics, Addison complains that the vision/narrative disjunction between the final books is "as if an History Painter should put in Colours one half of his Subject, and write down the remaining part of it" (*Spectator* 3 [May 3, 1712]: 386). Dunster (in Todd) argues that the epic needed to conclude with the state of the postlapsarian world because Milton was "standing upon the earth" and writing to its inhabitants for their instruction as well as their delight (380). Johnson famously said of *PL* that "None ever wished it longer than it is" ("Milton" 196), though one cannot be sure he was referring specifically to the last two books. Coleridge, on the other hand, wished that *PL* were read and studied more carefully, "especially those parts which, from the habit of always looking for a story in poetry, are scarcely read at all,—as for example, Adam's vision of future events in the eleventh and twelfth books," and Dorothy Wordsworth wrote in her journal for February 2, 1802, "After tea I read aloud the eleventh book of *PL*. We were much impressed, and also melted into tears" (Wittreich 110, 245). McColley sees a sea change in attitudes toward the last two books since perhaps as late as 1750; earlier readers were far more interested in amplified paraphrases of biblical history ("*Paradise Lost*" [1939], 228–29). Good

compares book 11 with social criticism based on deviations from a state of innocence; Jean-Jacques Rousseau, the first great champion of such criticism, was a
student of *PL* (229). McColley also finds extensive structural similarities with Du
Bartas (*"Paradise Lost": An Account* 199). In his notes to *PL* 11.113–15 and 384,
Fletcher emphasizes the vision at the expense of the narration, claiming that epic
ends with a "grand apocalypse, or vision," just as the Bible ends with the book of
Revelation. Maurice Kelley, presenting a study of *DocCh* as a gloss upon the epic,
claims that much of book 12 is "a rapid blank-verse summary of the doctrines" in
DocCh 1.14–32 (Patterson, *Works* 15:257) and that the epic is as antitrinitarian as
the treatise, as for instance in there being no "full notice" of the Holy Spirit (i.e.,
the third person of the Trinity) until book 12 (193).

Another famous criticism is that of C. S. Lewis, who thinks that the last two
books represent one of Milton's few artistic failures, "an untransmuted lump of
futurity" at a "momentous part of the narrative" in writing that is "curiously bad"
(*Preface* 129), though as Madsen notes, Lewis does not offer any specific examples
of that badness ("Idea" 256). Lewis's comment has evoked much response, such
as that of Thompson, who argues that Milton chooses the details of his historical
survey poetically and orders them effectively, that the syntax is similar to the rest
of the epic, and that Michael's revelation of history affords Adam not only positive
assurance of God's justice but also some necessary experience of the world ("For
Paradise Lost" 376, 378).

Ross judges these last two books to be a historical "desert," since permanent
redemption can be imposed only from outside. In his reading, the Old Testament
saints are not types of Christ but rather moral signposts in that desert (*Poetry and
Dogma* 95–99). Muir finds the last two books poetically inferior, complaining
that "Michael's outline of history is too brief for any episode to be very effective
in itself, except the account of the Flood"; Muir nevertheless thinks the books are
necessary, or at least the last 200 lines that include the announcement of the *felix
culpa* in 12.469–78 (160). Whaler points out the relative paucity of similes in book
12 and explains that Milton could find no range of simile that would illustrate
post-Adamic history to Adam ("Compounding" 324–25).

The critical watershed of the theme/structure reconciliation is probably F. T.
Prince's 1958 argument that the two last books are integral to the design of the epic,
and that Milton's contemporaries had no difficulty either with their concentration
of dogma or with their length or scale, and certainly not with their elegiac sense
(38–52). Prince's argument had to some extent been anticipated. For instance,
in 1950 Mahood acknowledges that "some final rounding-off is necessary," and
although Milton's powers were somehow unequal to his purpose ("the verse

flags dismally"), that "the world's balance is restored in the poem's quiet close" (186–87). It is particularly after Prince, however, that discussions of the last two books develop ways to reconcile theme and structure.

Kurth finds the last two books "of prime importance in Milton's design…because they provide…the necessary context for Christian heroism" as demonstrated in biblical history; he denies that the two books are primarily theological; the details of the "cosmic drama" have already been supplied, and the dramatic situation requires that Adam and Eve be prepared for the Expulsion (123). Colie, who examines the theological tensions between foreknowledge and free will, remarks that these books demonstrate "the difference between the way God knows time and the way Adam must experience it," and also that the paradox linking Adam to each Christian makes all historical times seem immediate (132). Even more pointedly theological is the work of Sims, who traces Milton's use of the Bible in *PL* and *PR;* Sims demonstrates that even the clear references to Scripture in Milton's epics have been remarkably underglossed and concludes his study with a line-by-line index of biblical references (*Bible* 2–3, 259–78).

Watson stresses the importance of these books in justifying the ways of God to men, particularly how specific passages are symmetrically linked with cognate passages in the early books (148–55). Patrides characterizes the last two books as "Milton's magnificent survey of the course of human events from the first Adam to the second" (*Phoenix* 67) and can claim by 1967 that the last two books are seen as indispensable, both poetically and theologically ("*Paradise Lost*" 106). MacCallum insists that the technique in each of the two books is remarkably appropriate to its subject; book 11 focuses on the spiritual bankruptcy of fallen humanity and is thus episodic, but book 12 "has a beginning, middle, and end" because it focuses typologically on Christ, the real hero of the story ("Milton and Sacred History" 165–66).

Shumaker agrees that in these books "compression interferes with immediacy," yet nevertheless praises Milton's commendable restraint in taking only 1,077 lines to summarize millennia of events; his narration permits expressions of judgment, which add a sense of human warmth (*Unpremeditated Verse* 198, 213, 218). Daniells, arguing for the impact of mannerism on the epic, links Milton's powerfully focused control of space with his powerfully focused control of time; although Daniells characterizes the last two books as a "long monotonous historical forecast," he nevertheless sees them transformed by the paradox of the fortunate Fall together with the ideal of a paradise within (*Milton* 98–99, 122–23). Lawry identifies two additional, often overlooked explanations of why the last two books are necessary: Adam must repent "originally," not only for himself but also for all his sons, and also must be originally compassionate for them; and the last two books demonstrate how the unholy trinity of Satan, Sin, and Death are worked into their opposites in terms that we can understand from human history (*Shadow* 268–69).

Miner (43–54) insists that the last two books narrate the redemptive process in human history rather than the fortunate Fall that benefits relatively few of Adam's descendants. Radzinowicz, who also finds the fortunate Fall overstated, claims that "the great epic design is meant to reveal how individual free will interacts with historical necessity," blending the "double burden" of time's lessons, which are both ethical and political (36–38); cf. main discussion in **12.469–78**. Erskine had already implied this generic distinction in his claim that Adam and Eve became less insipid after their sin—they moved from epic allegories to tragic characters reaping the results of their actions; the epic becomes "livelier, more liberal, more sympathetic, more hopeful" (577–78, 81). Stoll rejects Erskine's reading, claiming that he ignores the human mixture of sorrow with joy; Milton's purpose is instead "to make the superhuman life in Eden slope down to the level of the life that men lead and have always led" ("Was Paradise" 431), a claim he repeats in 1933 ("From the Superhuman").

Sasek complains that "band wagon psychology" may have sustained misreadings of the last two books, such as reading them as the pictures on a shield in Homer, Virgil, and Tasso, whereas Milton's epic device has more in common with Du Bartas and dynamically links Michael's mission, biblical narration, and Adam's state of mind by cause-and-effect relationships (181–85). Sasek also explains the shift from vision to narration in dramatic and psychological terms: the visions allow Adam to understand God's scheme of salvation (192–93). In an earlier reading, Woodhouse downplays the influence of the shield motif; in fact, the shield itself disappears: the Messiah needs no defensive armor, and Satan's shield is a blank ("Pattern" 125).

One of the most positive treatments of the disjunction between vision and narration is Burden's; he maintains that Adam's shift from actor to spectator allows Milton to highlight paradoxical distinctions between epic and tragedy (187–201). Reesing devotes much of his discussion of *PL* to the last two books, finding them an "elaborate interweaving of psychological and theological subtleties" (54); in answer to C. S. Lewis, he calls the last two books a "terse, discriminating, economical condensation of huge masses of [biblical] materials," with regularly occurring passages of splendid poetry that support the rhetorical and thematic structure; the language sounds different because the shortened semantic units are more charged with meaning (80–81). Reesing even analyzes the last two books in terms of musical tempos and dynamics (89–104); see **11.1–21**.

By 1972, Waddington could report that a generation of readers had been convinced that Milton firmly controlled the structure and function of books 11 and 12, identifying the two most influential kinds of readings as psychological (Prince and Sasek) and typological (Lewalski), the litmus test for reading these books remaining the ability to explain the shift from vision to narration (Waddington 9). Nevertheless, Hughes identifies as "a prevailing opinion" Marshall's claim that Milton shifts from a dramatic system to an intellectual one as Satan is defeated ("Some Illustrators" 673). In Marshall's reading, the last two books provide Adam with "an explicit and complete revelation" of the intellectual meaning of the poem, but the statement of this meaning in *PL* 12.469–78 is anticlimactic because of the didactic requirement (17–19).

Some discussions of the arrangement of the last two books are quite detailed. Shawcross ("Balanced Structure" 696–718), who argues that *PL* is an intricately organized whole, explains how discrete sections of books 1–6 are answered by similar sections in books 7–12, so, for example, the morning and Eve's dream (5.1–135) find their analog in Eve's dream and evening (12.607–49), Raphael's visit (5.219–6.912) is answered by Michael's visit (11.238–12.605), and the Son's victory in heaven (6.669–892) by the Son's victory on earth (12.285–465). Shawcross asserts, "Milton is really concerned with Man in the Christian world, a world which will end with Judgment Day and the resurrection of the dead" ("The Son" 394). Moreover, he argues that books 11–12 replay the Exodus in successive stages of trial and purgation, and from specific and earthly to general and universal; the Exodus is also a birth metaphor, as is the Expulsion ("*Paradise Lost*" 3, 8–9, 22).

Other systems in the last two books are likewise traced. Arnold Williams argues that *PL* deals with the problem of evil in five great cycles that move from the ostensible triumph of evil to its discomfiture in the "greater good"; the second of the five cycles concludes in book 11 and the last three comprise book 12 ("Conservative Critics" 90–106); see **11.763–65** and **11.807–12**. Fox argues convincingly that the various episodes in the pageant of history represent the Seven Deadly Sins: envy (Cain's motive), gluttony (the "cave of death" or lazar-house), avarice (sons of Cain), lust (daughters of men), wrath (giants at war), sloth (age of Noah), and pride (Nimrod); Abraham then represents the beginning of redemption (2–3). Roland Mushat Frye claims that Adam's experience is repeated factually and parabolically in books 11–12, so that "the fall of Everyman is seen as the continuous fact of human history" (63).

Some critics identify perceptual structures in the epic. Summers asserts that the pattern of "secret consolation" in each of the six visions of book 11 represents a duality of vision, central to the final books, that integrates the mechanical separation of vision and consolation in the earlier proposed drama. The shift of vision to narration thus follows the audience's means of knowledge of both the sinful world, attained visually, and of ultimate redemption, an inward vision (*Muse's Method* 196–97, 206–08). Lewalski rejects Addison's judgment that the disjunction between the two books was caused by the difficulty of visualizing a complicated story, arguing instead that the shift "from vision to non-vision" is related to sight imagery throughout the two books that reflects the three root sins identified by traditional biblical exegesis: intemperance, vainglory, and ambition. Adam and Eve's ambition was traditionally associated with the "lust of the eyes" of 1 John 2:16 (25–28; cf. Addison, *Spectator* 3 [May 3, 1712]: 386). See also **11.368, 11.385–87, 11.412–18, 11.423, 11.429, 11.556, 11.638, 11.712, 11.840,** as well as Elizabeth Marie Pope's discussion of the traditional "triple equation" of Adam and Christ's temptations with the triad in 1 John 2:16 (51–69). Knott examines how Adam and Eve's relationship to topography changes with the Fall ("Symbolic Landscape" 53–54).

Although Ferry's argument that Milton's epic is built in a pattern of repeated cycles makes little mention of the final two books (*Milton's Epic Voice* 149–50, 165, 177), Mollenkott builds on Ferry's system to argue that a "cycle of sins" in book 11 resembles Dante's vision of hell. The first three visions elaborate the sins of Satan, Eve, and Adam, respectively, and the fourth and fifth elaborate the first and second, while the sixth vision of Noah's ark allows the book to close on an image of redemption (33, 38–39). Radzinowicz, who accounts for the difference in the two books by their opposing focus on destruction (book 11) and restoration (book 12), charts three pairs of visions in book 11 — Cain and Abel and the lazar-house, the actions of the unrighteous in peace and war, and Noah's two-part narration — to argue that lessons of time are both ethical and political (31–51).

Other structural readings include the traditional six ages of human history that parallel the six days of Creation, each to be followed by a Sabbath of rest. For instance, Whiting identifies everything from *PL* 11.429 to the end of that book as the first age of human history, the second being the postdiluvian world to the withdrawal of God's presence, the third from Abraham to the return of the Israelites to Canaan and their establishing of their worship, the fourth from the kingdom of David to the destruction of the temple, the fifth from the captivity of the Jews to the birth of the Messiah, and the sixth or last age of the world (*Milton* 185–89). Summers draws parallels between the last two books and the survey of sacred history in Heb. 11:1–40 (*Muse's Method* 198), as does MacCallum ("Milton and

Sacred History" 158), Rajan ("*Paradise Lost:* The Hill" 48), Radzinowicz (42–45), and Waddington (9–21). Muldrow understands the last three books to be a unit exemplifying what should happen to everyone—contrition in book 10 and contrite repentance and return to God in books 11–12 (105). The shift from vision to narration is appropriate, because once Adam is impressed by the consequences of the Fall in book 11 he needs positive teaching leading to conversion and the recovery of true freedom (92).

Following Bundy (127–52), some critics have interpreted the last two books as pedagogical, with the archangel Michael voicing Milton's theories enunciated in *Educ.* Pecheux also speaks of Adam's "education" ("Abraham" 367). Williamson uses the term *education* to mean doctrinal instruction in its broadest sense, in which the narration and narrator are didactic agents, so that *education* in books 11–12 serves first as the dramatic preparation for the catastrophe and then as the moral extension of its consequences (96–97). Fish claims that much of what is usually thought to be unsatisfactory in books 11–12 results from misunderstanding Milton's trial-and-error method of instruction of both Adam and the reader; vision is no longer necessary when progressively educated Adam no longer needs exposure to things he can see. Fish particularly defends the less ornamented style as intentional, since by the end of the epic the reader no longer needs practice in identifying ironies and subtleties (288, 290, 302, 304).

Typological criticism has also been productive. Pecheux argues that Abraham's faithful obedience in taking an unknown journey is a model for Adam through the last two books ("Abraham" 365–71); she also demonstrates how Old Testament events and persons appear in book 12 in their typological aspect ("Concept" 365) and how Eve's treatment in books 11–12 typifies the birth of the church ("Second Adam" 173–87). Trapp, examining lapsarian iconography, finds the redemption always present in illustrations of the Fall (226). Lieb asserts that in the last two books Adam participates in what Milton in *DocCh* 1.17 calls *fides historica,* or historical faith, "an assent to the truth of the scripture history, and to sound doctrine," which while "not in itself a saving faith" is "certainly necessary to salvation" (Patterson, *Works* 15:361, 363); for Milton, the essential function of history is soothing the mind and restoring its equilibrium (Lieb, "*Paradise Lost*" 30–32). Carnes claims that typology is necessary because the Fall breaks the order of divine time; she also finds Michael's language closer to God's than Raphael's, "much plainer, more didactic, less figurative, more overtly moral and sermonizing" (536–37).

Criticism of the last two books has additionally considered genre. Gilbert, looking for continuities with Milton's earlier dramatic drafts in the Trinity Manuscript, remarks that conversation in book 11 runs to nearly 190 lines and to nearly 75 in book 12; he draws attention to such dramatic conventions in the Trinity Manuscript as mutes in one projected plan and maskers in another (*On the Composition* 21, 24).

Critics have also commented on the perceived optimism or pessimism of the text. Rajan often finds the last two books "bleak and barren"; though he praises their "ground-swell of insistent courage" and argues that Milton's original audience would have found them far more congenial, Rajan judges that Milton's "clenched, spasmodic despair" intruded into the epic (*"Paradise Lost" and the Seventeenth Century* 79–80, 84–85, 89). Madsen remarks that although Rajan tries to rehabilitate the last two books, "his cure is perhaps worse than the disease" ("Idea" 259). Rajan, however, seems to find the two books less bleak 30 years later, when he remarks that the primary response they call for is joy (*"Paradise Lost:* The Hill" 45) and that the last two books "are not meant to be intimidating or dominated by the flaming sword of God's wrath" (47). Perhaps the bleakest reading has been that of Martz, who complains that the last two books, "with their darkly pessimistic view of human history, have offended and disappointed many readers, who have felt here a failure of imagination, a failure of human sympathy, and a consequent falling-off in Milton's poetical powers" (141); Martz particularly takes issue with what he identifies as the failure of an explicit contract to balance "supernal Grace . . . With sinfulness of Men" (141–67). Dick Taylor Jr., on the other hand, argues that the last two books are "strikingly compassionate and hopeful" in comparison to earlier hexameral works ("Milton's Treatment" 51). Daiches even argues that *PR* is necessary—as Thomas Ellwood suggested at the time of its composition—because the Christian scheme of redemption is not emotionally integrated into *PL* at all (59). Hughes denies that the last two books maintain on a poetic level the hope that the promised paradise should inspire, and judges that Milton chose, rather, to stress personal perfection than to rely on apocalyptic possibilities ("Beyond Disobedience" 197).

Paradise Lost, Book 11

The Argument: The second edition of 1674, which divided the original book 10 into books 11 and 12, also divided the original 1668 Argument between the two new books.

He makes intercession: cf. *DocCh* 1.15, which specifies Christ's intercession as, first, appearing on humanity's behalf before God and, second, "rendering our prayers agreeable to God" (Maurice Kelley 162; Patterson, *Works* 15:295); Adam and Eve's prayers are described in *PL* 11.14–32.

The Arguments were prefixed to the original ten books for the first time in the edition of 1669, producing several variants: 1669 *prayers,* 1674 *Prayers;* 1669 *and,* 1674 *but;* 1669 *Cherubims,* 1674 *Cherubim;* 1669 *signs,* 1674 *signs;* 1669 *happen,* 1674 *happ'n;* 1669 *Flood,* 1674 *Flood.*

1–21. In his analysis of the musical tempos and dynamics of the last two books, Reesing argues that book 11 begins *allegretto* and *piano,* dynamics that prolong the quietness of book 10's conclusion (89–90); see also **11.737, 11.763–86, 11.890–901; 12.79, 12.105–06, 12.115–20, 12.126–34, 12.176–90, 12.260–62, 12.267–69, 12.307–14, 12.419–35, 12.451–65, 12.473–78, 12.524–51, 12.561–73, 12.575–87, and 12.610–23.**

1–10. Burke, who argues that the choice of humility over pride is "Milton's inner crisis," finds that these ten verses represent a necessary clarification of that crisis (205).

1–4. Cope calls this passage "the fortunate fall in little," since descending grace enables Adam and Eve's prayers to fly up (143). Shawcross compares Milton's "alchemical transformation" here both to his *Ps 114,* 17–18, where water flows from rocks, and to the emblem on the title page to Henry Vaughan's *Silex Scintillans* of the stony heart being made flesh; he also contrasts the image to the "obdurate…hard'n'd" fallen spirits of *PL* 6.790–91 (*"Paradise Lost"* 19); see also Pharaoh's hardened heart in *PL* 12.192–94 and the law written in hearts in *PL* 12.489.

lowliest: "very lowly," a Latinate construction. R. C. Browne (1877) and others cite a similar use of the superlative in *PL* 10.859.

1–2. *repentant stood:* the sudden contrast to "kneel'd and fell prostrate" in the preceding line (*PL* 10.1099) has been variously explained. Bentley emends *stood* to *kneel'd,* also because of the "kneel'd and fell prostrate" of the preceding book, but the participles adjacent to *stood* encourage its interpretation in a way that discredits Bentley's emendation of it to kneeling (Hughes, "Variorum"). Pearce argues that *stood* has the sense of "were" (cf. "stand in arms" of *PL* 2.55, and *stetit* [Latin] and ἐσήκε [Greek]). The Richardsons read *stood* as "remained, continued"; Fowler also argues for "remained." Todd surmises that Milton may have thought of Mark 11:25 ("when ye *stand praying,* forgive"), and Keightley even suggests Milton may have been thinking of both the publican and the Pharisee, who stood while they prayed in Luke 18:11, 13. Joseph Hunter insists that Milton follows the Dissenters' preference for a standing posture in prayer (70). Montgomery thinks Milton may have meant *stood* literally, since 8–9 indicate dignified demeanor. Hughes (*"Paradise Lost," A Poem*) notes Adam standing to pray in *PL* 4.720. Le Comte refers to the *stood* of 14 and also to "the Puritan in *Christian Doctrine.*" In *DocCh* 2.4, Milton wrote that "no particular posture of the body in prayer was enjoyed even under the Law," citing such examples of standing prayer as 1 Kings 8:22, 2 Chron. 20:5, and Luke 18:13 as examples of standing to pray (Patterson, *Works* 17:90); this passage is also noted by Maurice Kelley (187); cf. 11.150. In "Standing Prostrate," an article dedicated to the passage, Parish argues that the confusion between stances is intentional, and links it to the paradox that only by humbling himself can postlapsarian humanity rise. Kirkconnell lists an analogue in Avitus, "Together on the earth they fell in prayer; / Then rose, and entered on an empty world" (17), though that prayer occurs after the Expulsion. Sims references the standing position of the repentant Israelites in Neh. 9:2 (*Bible* 269).

2–7. Whaler, arguing that *PL* is informed by complex mathematical patterns, cites these lines as an example of a pattern he calls "E 4-3 2-1," which occurs frequently in Milton's blank verse and always "stresses or implies an idea of negation, imperfection, disorder, ruin, impotence, ignorance, hate, malice, abasement, or deadly sin" (*Counterpoint* 56); see also **11.14–21** and **12.562–65**.

2. *Mercie-seat:* located beneath the two cherubim on the Ark of the Covenant, first mentioned in Exod. 25:17–22; see also Heb. 9:5, *PL* 12.253, and the attendant cherubim in *Ref* (Patterson, *Works* 3:60). The sanctity of the mercy seat in Hebrew faith and worship is asserted by many invocations, such as in Ps. 80:1: "O Shepherd of Israel,... thou that dwellest between the cherubims" (Hughes, "Variorum").

3. *Prevenient Grace:* from Latin *preveniens* ("coming before"), anticipates and assists repentance. Fowler glosses the theological meaning of *prevenient* as "antecedent to human action" (so *OED* 2), explaining that "Prevenient grace precedes the determination of the human will.... It is the condition and initiation of all activity leading to justification"; he also links the doctrine to such biblical passages as Ps. 59:10: "The God of my mercy shall prevent me." Hume cites both Zech. 12:10 ("the spirit of grace") and 2 Tim. 1:9 ("called us... according to his... grace... before the world began"). Wesley glosses as "preventing grace," and Bush as "anticipating and promoting repentance." The theological meaning of *prevenient grace* informs the Collect for the seventeenth Sunday after Trinity ("We pray thee that thy grace may always prevent and follow us"), which Verity cites rather than biblical proof-texts; the concept is much more theological than biblical (Hughes, "Variorum"). "*Prevenient Grace* is used in the full theological sense of grace which anticipates repentance" (Hughes, *Paradise Lost*). Patrides (*Milton* 203, 204) cites the term's use by Melanchthon, Musculus, Thomas Sutton, Donne, and also William Perkins, who explained the term as God in mercy enlightening the mind and redirecting the will; it is prevenient grace that causes Eve to ask pardon from Adam in *PL* 10.910–13 instead of protesting or replying in kind (Patrides, *Milton* 211).

Besides defining *prevenient grace,* critics also dispute its theological sources. Hutchinson insists that for Milton's "sturdy individualism," prevenient grace is not irresistible, as it was for Calvinists, but merely persuasive; there is room for the human will to respond and cooperate, and also for Milton "to safeguard his freedom even in receiving divine assistance" (183). Grierson similarly states that Milton rejected the doctrine of complete depravity — humanity is so fallen that it cannot even desire to be saved — and instead found the cooperation of the believer to be necessary (*Poems* 101–02), while Dick Taylor Jr. argues that for Milton grace is a result of human effort: "Adam has done his part on his level first before grace descends and Christ intercedes" ("Grace" 73). Boswell, arguing against both Grierson and Taylor, cites heavily from *PL* and *DocCh* to argue that Milton regarded repentance strictly as a gift of grace, even though *PL* 11.3 is the only explicit mention of prevenient grace in the epic (84). On the other hand, Eastland sees "no Calvinistic tenets explicit in 10.1097–1104" (47). Another position is taken by Patrides, who rejects its "close analysis," quoting Henry More's warning that "these things are safelier felt than spoken" (*Milton* 204), while Fish points out the contrast between God's view of the repentance of Adam and Eve and the self-contained human view, which "is itself a rhetorical deception" (19–20). The Richardsons refer to the *motions* in *PL* 11.91 preceding any act of Adam and Eve. Di Cesare claims it to be thematically necessary that Eve not remain divided from Adam; prevenient grace miraculously heals their rift; the poetry also embodies that grace in terms of life — fruit, opposed to stoniness — recalling the life-giving Spirit brooding in *PL* 1.21 (20). Collett finds that this passage combines poignant Edenic myths with historical "fables" about fallen angels to create a mythical imagery that both transcends and is anchored in history (95). Sims cites James 4:6: "God resisteth the proud, but giveth grace unto the humble" (*Bible* 269).

4–5. *stonie:* figuratively, "hard, insensible, or unfeeling, as if consisting of stone; hardened, obdurate" (so *OED* 5a). The *stonie* metaphor makes explicit the fulfillment of God's prophecy in *PL* 3.189–93; in the background is God's promise in Ezek. 11:19 and 36:26 to change the "stony heart" of the Hebrew nation into "an heart of flesh" (Hughes, "Variorum"). Keightley objects to the combination "hearts [or flesh]...breathed." Stroup argues that this passage adumbrates the Lord's Supper, citing the priest's invitation to confess sins "with an humble, lowly, penitent, and obedient harte to the end that we may obtain forgivenes of the same by his infinite goodnesse and mercie" (40), also noting that prevenient grace, by taking away the "stonie from thir hearts," has already begun to impart some of the "benefits of [Christ's] Passion," as noted in the "Prayer of Humble Access" familiar to Milton's contemporaries (43).

4. *& made:* 1667 *and made.*

5–7. Many commentators cite St. Paul's comment, "The Spirit also helpeth our infirmities: for we know not what we should pray for as we ought: but the Spirit itself maketh intercession for us with groanings which cannot be uttered" (Rom. 8:26). Milton alludes to the verse in *Eikon* 16 (Patterson, *Works* 5:224).

 Unutterable: Sprott cites this word and *miserable* in 11.500 as examples of Milton's preserving the secondary accent and eliding the final syllables (91), pronounced "unuttr'able" and "mis'rable." Muldrow (75) glosses the "vague term *Spirit of Prayer*" with Milton's explicit definition of *petition* in *DocCh* 2.4 as "that act whereby under the guidance of Holy Spirit we reverently ask God for things lawful" (Patterson, *Works* 17:81), also noted by Maurice Kelley (108), as is the specification that prayer can be silent, whispered, groaned, or exclaimed inarticulately (187; Patterson, *Works* 17:87). Cf. the "sighs though mute" of 11.31 and "short sigh of humane breath" of 11.147.

5. *Regenerate:* "in religious use: Spiritually re-born" (so *OED* 2). 1667 *Regenerat.* Milton sometimes elides the unaccented syllable before an *l* or *r*, but not always; cf. *PL* 12.351 (Darbishire, *Poetical Works* 1:xxix). The opening of *DocCh* 1.18 describes the process of regeneration as creating the inner man afresh and infusing "new and supernatural faculties" from above (Maurice Kelley 168; Patterson, *Works* 15:367).

6–10. *prayer…Pair:* these lines rhyme with three intervening lines (Purcell 172), a rhyme category also mentioned by Diekhoff but not for these lines ("Rhyme" 542).

8–14. *yet thir port / Not of mean suiters:* Wesley omits 8b–14b. Newton argues that the "yet" refers back to "repentant stood" in line 1 and that all the intermediate lines should be read as a parenthesis. Cf. "Their port was more then human, as they stood" (*Mask* 295).

 Port: "bearing." Hughes cites *PL* 4.869, where the word is applied to Satan's arrogant mien; here the context implies modest but self-respecting demeanor ("Variorum"). Himes (*Paradise Lost: A Poem*) notes the paradox: "in the very act of humbling themselves they are exalted (Luke 18:11–14)."

Of Themis stood devout: commentators have much to say about the underlying mythology and its relation to the biblical account of the Flood (Gen. 6:6–9:17). In Ovid, the tale of the Thessalian king and queen, Deucalion and Pyrrha, runs about 100 lines (*Metamorphoses* 1.313–415); the two pray to the goddess of Justice, Themis, and the nymphs of the mountain Parnassus, where their little boat has grounded after a vast flood (1.320–21). The resemblances led many Ovidian commentators and Renaissance mythographers to treat Deucalion's myth as a pagan version of Noah's Flood (Allen, *Mysteriously Meant* 196, 228). But, as noted by Hughes ("Variorum"), there had been other traditional floods, and chronology raised difficulties; in his *Historie of the World,* Sir Walter Raleigh dated Deucalion's flood close to the Exodus of the Israelites from Egypt, or about 782 years after Noah's Flood (1.7.3). Even if historically disparate, they might morally be associated if Deucalion's myth is understood allegorically as a spiritual repeopling of the world, as in Natale Conti, *Mythologiae* 8.18. According to Starnes and Talbert (248–49), Milton may have known Conti's five-column version of the story (1581), along with the more compact accounts in the dictionaries of Charles Stephanus (1553) and Ambrosius Calepine (1609). Newton defends Milton's "frequent allusions to the heathen mythology and his mixing fables with sacred truths" as usually only being in similitudes. Gillies adds that Milton resembled Bezaleel, the talented biblical artisan who made furnishings for the tabernacle out of Egyptian (i.e., pagan) gold. Radzinowicz, who argues that the lessons of time are both ethical and political, asserts that here "the peculiar complexity of the historical stage is most carefully set," since Adam and Eve, not only before the Crucifixion but before the biblical Flood and also Ovid's later metaphoric flood, are "praying and free while three stages of time in separate circles wait upon their acts" (37–38). Shumaker compares the close "rational and affective implications" of the two scenes (*Unpremeditated Verse* 200). Dunster (in Todd) surmises that Ovid was a favorite poet of Milton's partly because so many of his subjects were related to scriptural events: Creation, Deluge, and final destruction of the world by fire. Bentley rejects this entire passage as an editorial interpolation, but the Richardsons note that the church fathers often referred to biblical stories as *fables* (*fabulae*) without suggesting that they were unhistorical, as Jerome (*Commentariorum* 26:609) ("Longum est universa Judicum gesta percurrere, et totam Samson fabulam" [It would take too long to run through all the deeds of the Jews, and the whole fable of Samson]), also quoted by Zeno (*Tractatus* 11:516n2).

Indeed, according to Collett, "Deucalion and Pyrrha were almost universally interpreted in the Renaissance as types of Noah and his wife" (95). St. Maur lists their flood as historical (405), placing it 15 years before the Exodus. Ussher's chronology reports, in 1556 BCE (*Annals* 12), the growth of Greek miraculous tales—including Deucalion's flood, which occurred at about the time of Moses, according to Eusebius (*Praeparatio Evangelicae* 10.9). Fowler finds a parallel in Sandys's *Ovid's Metamorphoses* 33 between Ovid's transformation of the stones of Mt. Parnassus into men and John the Baptist's assertion that "God is able of these stones to raise up children unto Abraham" (Matt. 3:9). Verity remarks that Milton's couple "stood," whereas in *Metamorphoses* 1.375–76 the two fell down prone on the earth. Himes (*Paradise Lost: A Poem*) finds the mention of Deucalion and Pyrrha to "eminently fit" here, since with sacrifices they signal a new covenant with God, just as Noah and his wife did. Osgood (28) thinks that Milton's citation of the legend, though primarily based on Ovid, may also refer to Apollodorus's comment (*Bibliotheca* 1.7.2) that Pyrrha was the first mortal woman. Hughes (*Paradise Lost*) thinks that Milton is contrasting *prayers* with the "fruits / Of painful superstition and blind zeal" of the Limbo of Vanity in *PL* 3.451–52. Northrop Frye ("*Paradise Lost*") points out that Deucalion and Pyrrha repopulated the earth by throwing stones behind them, which carries on the metaphor of the stony heart in *PL* 11.4. Shumaker identifies a blend of images: Adam and Eve have just begged pardon, "with tears / Watering the ground" (10.1101–02), and Deucalion and Pyrrha also approached a wet shrine (*Unpremeditated Verse* 199). Empson judges that in this passage Milton compares Christian and pagan views of life as equally solid and possible (*Some Versions* 179–80). St. Maur glosses Deucalion's name as "calling upon God," and Pyrrha's as "fire," because of her singular piety, zeal for the gods, and chastity (362–63). As Hume remarks, Deucalion was a son of Prometheus, and Pyrrha the daughter of his brother; they were linked—according to Ovid—not merely by blood but also by the threat of extinction ("Then flesh was joined; now danger itself joins them" [Deinde torus junxit; nunc ipsa pericula jungunt]; *Metamophoses* 1.353). Extinction is a threat that Adam and Eve have also been contemplating.

Themis: Greek θέμις: "fit" or "right," to which St. Maur links the Hebrew *tham* or *thummim* ("just" or "right"), adding that Themis had an oracle on Parnassus (363). *Themis* has been variously glossed by commentators. Hume explains that the Greek goddess Themis supposedly prompted appropriate prayers and prospered oracles and public assemblies. According to Osgood (82),

Themis is "really a personification of justice," organizing meetings among men or gods in Homer (see *Odyssey* 2.68, *Iliad* 20.4). Cf. *Homeric Hymn* 23, where Zeus whispers words of wisdom to Themis. Fletcher (*Complete Poetical Works*) identifies Themis as "a Titaness, a form of the earth goddess of the law and arrangement of physical phenomena." Cann claims that Themis was said to be the first deity to whom the inhabitants of the earth raised temples (234). Lieb finds that Milton thematically connects the destructive Fall with the Flood, from which there is a new birth, and via Themis with God's own justice, which paradoxically allows new birth through the Son (*Dialectics* 211).

8. *Oratorie:* "effective public speaking"; Hume: "the art of speaking well and readily."

11. *less ancient:* Fowler complains that Bentley and Empson "perversely" construe this phrase to imply that Genesis is also a fable and thus discredited as an explanation of origins.

14–125. The opening scene in heaven recalls the parallel scene in book 3; God's justice is again shown, but God's tone is milder in view of Adam and Eve's repentance (Ogden 17).

14–38. Cf. *DocCh* 1.15, which identifies Christ's intercession as appearing on our behalf before God and "by rendering our prayers agreeable to God" (Maurice Kelley 162; Patterson, *Works* 15:295).

14–21. Most commentary on this passage concerns its sources or metaphoric coherence. Beginning with Newton, commentators note the familiar classical poetic claim that unanswered prayers and vows were dispersed by the wind, a claim often associated with avian imagery; see, for instance, Virgil's *Aeneid* 11.794–95, where Phoebus gives part of a prayer to the birds ("partem volucris dispersit in auras") and Ovid's *Metamorphoses* 10.642, where the amicable breeze brings Venus prayers ("Detulit aura preces ad me non invida blandas" [It brought to me charming prayers which were not disdained]). Hume finds a parallel in the urgent prayers of Iulus for Nisus and Euryalus in *Aeneid* 9.312–13: "sed aurae / Omnia discerpunt, et nubibus inrita donant" (but the breezes / Rent and gave them, useless, to the clouds). In Fairfax's translation of Tasso's *Jerusalem*

Delivered, the swift, winged prayers of the starving crusaders are answered, as Godfrey's "Prayers just, from humble heart forth sent, / Were nothing slow to climb the starry sky, / But swift as winged birds themselves present / Before the Father of the heavens high" (Tasso 13.72.1–4). In William Browne's *Britannia's Pastorals* (83), "Swift are the prayers, and of speedy haste, / That take their wing from hearts so pure and chaste"; Dunster (in Todd) also observes that "winged prayers" and "winged sighs" occur in Sylvester's Du Bartas. Cf. *Eikon*, where Milton rejects Anglican prayer "flying up in hast on the specious wings of formalitie" (Patterson, *Works* 5:223) and also *Sonn 14*, 10–11.

Most early commentators on this passage cite the apocalyptic vision of Rev. 8:3, in which an angel stands at the heavenly altar, offering with a censer full of incense the prayers of all saints. Commentators also sometimes note the biblical analogues in Ps. 141:2 and Ezek. 20:40–41, but Addison sees all of 14–20 as referring to the vision of saints' prayers in Rev. 8:3–4 (*Spectator* 3 [Apr. 26, 1712]: 358). Broadbent argues that the Revelation passage is derived "from the Jewish temple direct" rather than through "a Roman cathedral" (*Some Graver Subject* 157).

Himes (*A Study*) sees 14–20 as a Trinitarian statement; 20 years later, in his edition of *PL*, he claims the prayers succeed because Adam and Eve have complied with the conditions of effective prayer, humbling themselves (Luke 18:9–14) and agreeing with each other (Matt. 18:19). Broadbent, however, finds that by this time the dramatic narrative of Adam and Eve's fall has been separated from its earlier heroic context, especially without a new invocation for book 11, and complains that the "great antistrophe of their penitence has gone quaint" (*Some Graver Subject* 267). He also claims that Milton wavers between apocalypse and emblem (157), but Fowler contends that if we accept Milton's initial premise about the corporeality of spirits, his heaven is appropriate and consistent. Although Keith finds the imagery curiously inconsistent—the personified prayers are also offerings laid on an altar (405), Hughes counters that the sighs of Adam and Eve are not personified by the metaphor "wing'd for Heav'n" ("Variorum"); cf. Yerkes 129. Empson complains that here, as well as in *PL* 5.140, 12.41, and 12.50, Milton's process of employing concrete images for abstractions is "caught half-way"; he finds it irritating to have "prayer…found to be as solid as angels" (*Some Versions* 154–55).

Dimentionless: "without dimension or physical extension…of no (appreciable) magnitude; extremely minute…without dimensions" (so *OED* 1), which Bush glosses as "incorporeal" and Wesley as "being of a Spiritual Nature." This word has particularly attracted comment. Bentley, who emends *heav'nly* to *solid* (17), complains that the word is either redundant or ill-chosen, to which the Richardsons answer that the prayers are dimensionless because spiritual, and Newton suggests Milton may have been alluding to the fable of Menippus's Jupiter shutting the trapdoor of heaven when unwilling to hear further petitions. Todd notes that in Milton's text, the Son himself performs the angel's task. Himes (*Paradise Lost: A Poem*) thinks *Dimentionless...doors* may refer to God's ability to hear sincere prayers made in "closets" (Matt. 6:6–8). Hughes (*Paradise Lost*) remarks, "extensionlessness and incorporeality were the terms by which Descartes defined spiritual things." Hughes ("Variorum") also refers to Yahweh's pleasure with the "sweet savour" (Hebrew, *reyach*) of the incense, which Yerkes declares was a feature of "every fire rite" on record in the Old Testament (129), so that without the symbolic surcharge of the perfume of the burning incense, the *Dimentionless* (incorporeal) prayers would be archetypally less acceptable than their ectypes in traditional worship. Ryken includes the *Golden Altar* as an example of how Milton pictures heaven by combining "visual splendor and textual rigidity" and *incense* as an example of how olfactory images are sensible but not substantial and visual (85, 224). Cf. Glanvill's observation in *Vanity of Dogmatizing* that although most people agree that the soul and angels have no dimensions, they still imagine for them a definitive place (100). Not all commentators have difficulty with the passage. Whaler claims that the metrics of these lines can be graphed as a spiral, just as in Adam and Eve's evening prayer in *PL* 4.720–35, which "gyres heavenward on wings" (*Counterpoint* 139–40); see **11.2–7**.

    nor...frustrate: "not lost in the Paradise of Fools (3.444–97)" (Bush).

    vagabond: "roaming or wandering from place to place without settled habitation or home; leading a wandering life; nomadic" (so *OED* A1).

    Wesley omits 15b–16a.

18–20. *Intercessor:* "the Son of God, who Milton says, citing Heb. 9:24, makes intercession by 'appearing in the presence of God for us' and by 'rendering our prayers agreeable to God'" (Hughes, "Variorum"; cf. *DocCh* 1.15; Patterson, *Works* 15:294–95). Robert Thyer (in Todd) prefers Milton's allegorical description of repentant prayer to Ariosto's prayer of Carlomagno (*Orlando Furioso* 14.73–74) and Tasso's prayers of Raimond and Godfrey (*Gerusalemme liberata* 7.79, 13.72). Peter claims that "we are shocked" that despite Adam and Eve's standing "in lowliest plight repentant" (*PL* 11.1), the Son must still intercede before the Father will hear their prayers (147). Svendsen categorizes the epithets *great Intercessor* and *glad Son* as the fourth of five major sets of characteristics of the Son in the epic ("Epic Address" 199–200).

Them the glad Son: Bentley emends to "Them *glad the* Son," presumably to preserve the meter.

20–21. Sims cites Heb. 7:24–25 and 12:2, which mention the Son's interceding role, and also cites the Son's enthroned position in Rev. 3:21 (*Bible* 269).

22–30. Cf. the idea of "implanted grace" in God's decree in *PL* 3.173–82. Patterson (*Student's Milton*) understands these lines on Christ's intercession to indicate that "even the Son says that the Fall was a good thing," whereas Broadbent (*Some Graver Subject* 269) complains that the "first fruits" prayer is swelled into a 15-line conceit (22–36) because of Milton's "timid" reliance in books 11 and 12 on biblical metaphor and repetitious dogma. Muldrow thinks that this passage "hints at the possibility of man's fall being a fortunate one" (75). Miner, arguing that Milton's view has been oversimplified because the Fall is fortunate for only a few, observes that the final two books begin as well as end with a preference for Adam and Eve's new state (45). Kurth judges that for Providence to bring greater good out of evil's apparent victory, the Fall should be viewed as beginning a larger heroic action rather than as ending a tragedy, so that Milton now portrays Adam and Eve as repentant and submissive to show they are beginning to understand their act in relation to larger issues of good and evil (7). Empson thinks that the "implanted Grace" of 11.23 and God's curse both work biologically, since each grows after being planted; although Milton came to insist against the Calvinists that fallen human nature was not totally corrupt, he still apparently thought we could do good only by divine grace (*Milton's God* 168). Huntley says that after the Fall, the Father and the Son enter into a kind of husbandry that did not exist previously: the fruit of disobedience is created in mothers' wombs and supported by the sweat of the fathers' brows, while Death holds the pruning shears ("Before and After" 5). C. H. Collins Baker judges that E. F. Burney's 1799 illustration of Christ as intercessor is probably novel, as distinct from Christ returning to heaven in book 3 and rendering judgment in book 10 (4). Madsen argues that this passage, which combines the garden ("fruits," "implanted," etc.) and Old

Testament ceremonialism to enact the ascent "from shadowy Types to Truth" (*PL* 12.303), is not metaphoric because Milton uses the words in their primary sense—Christ is the only king, the only true priest, and the supreme sacrifice (*From Shadowy Types* 105–06); see **12.302–03**.

22–25. In 1943, Ross comments, "In spite of his typical Puritan hatred of Catholicism, Milton's heaven when it is not an armoury is a Catholic cathedral…never…the conventicle" (*Milton's Royalism* 104), but he later cites these lines as an example of Milton's complete rejection of ritual and therefore of analogy, a rejection that permits him "imagistic structures and relationships quite beyond the reach of traditional Christian art," even verging on the anti-Christian (*Poetry and Dogma* 224).

22–23. *What first-fruits:* "the frequently restated principle of God's right to the sacrifice of all *first fruits* is first asserted in Exod. 23:19" (Hughes, "Variorum"). In the Son's joy, his intercession for transgressions, and the fruits of redemption, Himes (*Paradise Lost: A Poem*) sees a reference to Isa. 53:11 ("He shall see of the travail of his soul, and shall be satisfied"). Patrides traces Milton's exposition of prevenient grace from its "implanting" here, to its "motions" in 11.91, its "strength added from above" in 11.138, its struggle with sinfulness in 11.359–60, and its victory in 12.478 (*Milton* 214).

23–49. These lines primarily reflect biblical texts. Sims (*Bible* 269) cites Ezek. 20:41 ("I will accept you with your sweet savour") and Heb. 4:14, which identifies Jesus as the "great high priest."

24–25. Edmundson, who argues that Milton found much of his material in Vondel's *Adam in Ballingschap* (1613), includes as evidence how the council of heaven in Vondel's version concludes with the Son "offering up a prayer / To Heaven, as from a golden censer filled with incense" (104). Cf. *DocCh* 1.15, which specifies that Christ "has always made, and still continues to make intercession for us" (Maurice Kelley 161; Patterson, *Works* 15:291).

24. *Censer:* "a vessel in which incense is burnt; a thurible" (so *OED* 1).

26–44. "In the metaphor of the fruit of the seed which God has sown in the contrite hearts which are no longer 'stony,' there is a glance back both to 11.3–4 and to Adam's practical manuring (literally, tending or cultivating with his own hands) of the trees of the garden in 4.624–28" (Hughes, "Variorum"). Keightley finds that the phrase "Fruits of more pleasing savour" is also a play on words. Whaler, who argues that Milton tightly controls animal similes, lists this passage as one of the seven plant-life similes in *PL* of over two lines, the others being 1.292–94, 302–04, 304–06, 612–15; 4.980–85; 8.212–16 ("Animal Simile" 534, 542n24). Di Cesare (20) compares "his own hand manuring all the Trees" in *PL* 11.28 with "Least therefore his now bolder hand / Reach also of the Tree of Life, and eat" in 11.93–94. Martz, though generally disappointed by the poetry of the last two books, nevertheless judges that in these lines, book 11 opens well (143). Lieb asserts that Milton employs growth metaphors here to equate prayer with the "offspring" of penitence, "created as a result of God's having impregnated man with divine grace" and to assert that God prefers the state of contrition to that of innocence, because the latter relies directly on his grace rather than man's "cultivating practices" (*Dialectics* 212). Madsen argues that Christ's ability to use language in this way depends on a human act performed at the beginning of history, since only because of the Fall could the garden become a type of the spiritual life ("Earth" 524).

B. A. Wright finds this passage a "more authoritative statement of the *felix culpa* doctrine" than Adam's outburst in 12.469–73 (*Milton's "Paradise Lost"* 193).

26–29. See **12.543–47** on seed imagery. Fowler views the passage as a combination of the parable of the sower in Mark 4:14–20 and the "sacrifice" of verbal praise in Heb. 13:15.

26–27. *Sow'n with contrition in his heart:* Sims (*Bible* 269) cites Mark 4:20, where the good harvest results from seed being sown in good "ground," or listeners.

26. *savour:* as noted by Fowler, the "sweet savour" of acceptable sacrifice is a biblical commonplace. Cf. *PL* 5.84, 401; 9.741.

30–44. The remaining speech is a reminder to the reader, if not to God, that the Son has already accepted this function (Muldrow 76). Summers denies that the words of the speech actually matter: "only the position, the attitude, the state of the heart are important" ("Voice" 1088; see also *Muse's Method* 184).

31. *his sighs though mute:* Dunster (in Todd) traces "mute sighs" to a description of extreme affliction in Statius's *Thebaid* 11.604: "Tandem muta furens genitor suspiria solvit" (Both mute and furious the father let loose sighs). Montgomery hears a liturgical echo to "Him who despiseth not the sighing of a contrite heart." See comments on varieties of prayer in **11.5–7.**

32–44. Fowler states that the emphatic repetition of *me* (an example of what classical rhetoricians called *ploce,* or repetition of the same word) links this passage to Christ's earlier offer of atonement in *PL* 3.236–49. Hughes ("Variorum") adds that the Son's confirmation of that offer is interwoven here with explicit scriptural affirmation of his service from humanity's point of view: "'we have an advocate with the Father, Jesus Christ the righteous: And he is the propitiation for our sins' (1 John 2:1–2)." Darbishire observes that the *mee* was changed from the unemphatic *me* on an uncorrected sheet (*Poetical Works* xiii).

32–35. Cf. *DocCh* 1.15, which specifies that Christ's mediatorial office was "at the special appointment of God the Father" (Maurice Kelley 161; Patterson, *Works* 15:285). Patrides, arguing that Eve's asking for Adam's forgiveness is motivated by prevenient grace, finds the occurrences of *mee* here reminiscent of *PL* 10.930–36 (*Milton* 212).

Newton glosses 32–34 as, "Let me interpret for him unskilful with what words to pray for himself, me, his advocate and propitiation."

unskilful: "ignorant of something" (so *OED* 2b, obsolete). Cf. Rom. 8:26, where the spirit of God aids those who do not know how to pray.

32. *pray, let mee:* some editions of 1667 omit the comma.

35–44. Hughes links the emphasis on faith rather than works to Christ's parable of himself as a vine of which his disciples are the branches (John 15), echoed by the Son in *PL* 3.257–94, and also to one of St. Paul's frequent gardening images, in this case a great olive tree, the severed branches of which may be regrafted "if they abide not still in unbelief" (Rom. 11:23); cf. James 1:21, "receive with meekness the engrafted word." Here, as in *PL* 3.337–41, the horticultural imagery supports a vision of Joy and Love and Truth triumphing through "golden days, fruitful of golden deeds," when the Son is one with his disciples and when "God shall be All in All," fulfilling the plea of Jesus: "Holy Father, keep through thine own name those whom thou hast given me, that they may be one, as we are [John 17:11]" ("Variorum").

36. *for these my Death shall pay:* cf. *DocCh* 1.14, which specifies that Christ's redemption was made "at the price of his own blood"; Maurice Kelley includes among numerous biblical illustrations Acts 20:28, "purchased with his own blood," and 1 Cor. 6:20 and 7:23, "bought with a price" (158; Patterson, *Works* 15:158).

38–40. Peter objects that the thought and syntax are both obscure (161), but Ricks finds the passage "characteristically good" and "characteristically Miltonic" because "it exactly fits Mr. Empson's unforgettable account of 'the sliding, sideways, broadening movement, normal to Milton' " (*Milton's Grand Style* 35).

38. *smell of peace:* Hume cites Lev. 3:5 and 4:31, describing the Levitical peace offering as being of "a sweet savour," and also St. Paul's description of Christ's sacrificial death as "our peace" (Eph. 2:14). Cf. the "scent . . . Of carnage" that draws Death toward earth after the Fall (*PL* 10.267–69). R. C. Browne (1877) cites the "sweet savour" of Noah's sacrifice (Gen. 8:21). Cf. also the "savour" of Christ's knowledge (2 Cor. 2:14–16). Sims (*Bible* 269) also cites the "sweetsmelling savor" of Christ's sacrifice (Eph. 5:2). Lawry explains, "As before, the Son pleads in part to understand God's design. His prayer seeks the production of greater good out of temporary evil, life 'more abundant' after the evil of death, a 'life' [*PL* 11.42] made one with God as all in all" (*Shadow* 271).

39–40. *his days / Numberd:* "his appointed time, short and sad," i.e., until death (Hume). "Since death at a distant, determinate date has been pronounced among the punishments of Adam's sin (10.208), his days are not to be countless, but providentially limited to a certain number" (Hughes, "Variorum"). Cf. **11.84–98**. Fowler notes that in the Bible, the elect are often numbered, as in Exod. 30:12, though this numbering may also refer to numerological symbolism governing the days of the poem's action. Cf. also Ps. 90:12: "So teach us to number our days, that we may apply our hearts unto wisdom."

Doom: "judgment"; cf. *PL* 9.763. On God's control of man's longevity, see **11.553–54.**

days / Numberd, though sad: see similar language in *PL* 12.602–03.

40–43. Sims (*Bible* 269) cites Phil. 1:21, 23, which declares that being with Christ is better than living on earth.

40–41. Cf. *PL* 10.76–77.

44–46. *one…son:* a case of rhyme after an intervening line, missed by Diekhoff ("Rhyme" 540), but noted by Purcell (171).

44. *Made one with me as I with thee am one:* cf. Christ's prayer in John 17:11: "that they may be one, as we are." This line is glossed in *DocCh*'s chapter on the "Son" (1.5), which explains that "one" can have a variety of meanings, that although God and the Son speak as one their essence is not one, and that the Son's union with the Father is the same that we have (Maurice Kelley 87; Patterson, *Works* 14:209).

45. *without Cloud:* Fowler glosses as "without darkening of his countenance," citing *OED* 10a, and also alludes to the "clouds of mystery from which God speaks to angels or to men," as in Num. 11:25 and Mark 9:7, as well as *PL* 3.378–79 and 6.28. B. A. Wright wants the stress on the first syllable of *without* to prevent "a flat, pointless rhythm" ("Stressing" 203). Though God resides "amidst / Thick clouds and dark" (*PL* 2.263–64), the Son has foretold his final entry into heaven with redeemed humanity to find his Father's face visible, "wherein no [metaphoric] cloud / Of anger shall remain, but peace assur'd, / And reconcilement" (3.262–64; Hughes, "Variorum"). See also *PL* 12.202.

46–47. *All thy request…was my Decree:* cf. 1 Pet. 1:20, where Christ's redemption is "foreordained before the foundation of the world," and also *DocCh* 1.14, which specifies that Christ's redemption was conformable "to the eternal counsel of God" (Maurice Kelley 158; Patterson, *Works* 15:253). Sims (*Bible*

269) cites a parallel in Job 42:8–9, where the friends must have Job pray that their sins be forgiven.

46. *accepted:* in a survey of *a-* words that have been unreported, unglossed, or incorrectly glossed by Milton's editors, B. A. Wright defines this past participle as "acceptable, approved, favoured" ("Note" 145); see also **11.324–26, 11.433, 11.542, 11.661, 12.12, and 12.239–40**.

47–49. Wesley reduces these three lines to two, "Obtain, but in that Paradise to dwell, / The Law I gave to Nature him forbids."

47. *Decree:* cf. *PL* 3.115. Keightley: "Everything related to Man had been already determined by the Divine decree."

48–57. Various editors cite God's words in Lev. 18:25: "The land is defiled…and the land itself vomiteth out her inhabitants." The metaphor expresses moral loathing of Israel's carnal sins, but the law of nature is also at work here, anticipated in Nature's reaction to its "wound" by Eve and Adam in *PL* 9.782 and 1001. The "high Passions" (9.1123) are reflected in the climatic distemper (10.1065). Physical diseases and atmospheric disturbances are alike due to imbalances or distempers in what should be the temperate nature of all bodies and all climates; the first two *OED* definitions for *distemper* are respectively medical and meteorological. The *incorrupt elements* of Eden are expelling distempered humanity as surely as Belial warns the devils that if they again assault heaven, its "Ethereal mould, incapable of stain," will automatically "purge" them off (*PL* 2.141; Hughes, "Variorum"). Eastland struggles with defining Milton's concept of "law of nature"; it is the unwritten law of God, originally given to Adam; it is also conscience; it is also right reason (44). Peter claims that God's speech "maintains its serenity only with an obvious effort, quickly breaking down again into what seems to be its natural choler," as evidenced here (16); "what is far more striking is the almost obsessive craving he displays to justify his own part in the Fall" (145). Reesing, on the other hand, reads both of God's speeches (11.46–71, 84–125) sympathetically, claiming, "there is no bluster at all" (89). Madsen sees man's expulsion as being as inevitable as Satan's; they both deliberately chose to misread the book of nature, despite—on Adam's part—Raphael's long recital on the nature of reality ("Idea" 253–54). Cf.

Beatrice's comments in *Purgatorio* 30.74–75 about the earthly paradise being happy (Samuel, *Dante* 219).

49. *The Law I gave to Nature:* cf. "Nature's Law" (*PL* 10.805). Maurice Kelley notes that Milton rejects "nature or fate" as a power in itself in *DocCh* 1.2 (73; Patterson, *Works* 14:27). "God's mercy operates through his grace and not by abrogation of his law of nature" (B. A. Wright, *Milton's "Paradise Lost"* 51).

50–57. According to Hume, the elements were mixed so perfectly in Eden that they would have preserved Adam incorruptibly until his translation to heaven. Cf. the impossibility of mixing evil with blessedness in *PL* 7.56–59. Lieb cites this passage as an example of Milton's lexical linking of "corrupting" with "distempering," changing order back to chaos rather than the "tempering" of bringing order from chaos (*Dialectics* 212–13). The decree in this passage is reversed in the discussion of the resurrection in 1 Cor. 15:53–54, where "this corruptible must put on incorruption" (Weidner). Empson interprets 11.50 to mean that before the Fall, Adam and Eve had a much less crude metabolism; almost all details about food in the epic are consistent with the great chain of being; this passage suggests that Adam and Eve were "perhaps actually better fitted to eat with Raphael than with ourselves" (*Milton's God* 149). Ryken cites "no unharmoneous mixture foule…incorrupt" as an example of how Milton describes the prelapsarian garden as transcendental by denying empirical qualities (100).

51. *gross:* Bentley emends to *dross,* since Milton has *gross* again in line 53, but as Pearce argues, dross is proper to metals, not to pure elements.
   unharmoneous: "not exhibiting harmony or agreement" (so *OED* 2).

52–57. *Eject him tainted now….at first with two fair gifts:* Ryken finds a similar then/now pattern in *PL* 9.1137–39 (48). Williamson, stressing the didactic role of the epic, relates this passage to Adam's earlier instruction in the "book of God's works," which could lead to the sin of pride (97, 106).

52–53. Allen claims that this is the only time in *PL* that God slips into a poetic figure; he does not need the comparatives of metaphor and simile to express Creation (*Harmonious Vision* xi).

53. *As a distemper, gross to aire as gross:* Pearce and Newton reject Bentley's punctuation that renders the distemper itself as gross. Montgomery claims that putting the comma after *gross* is "Milton's own punctuation." Cf. the "purer air" of paradise in 4.153.

54. In Eden Raphael has explained that he can relish "Mans nourishment" (5.483) and encouraged Adam and Eve to hope that their "bodies may at last turn all to Spirit" (5.496–97) though at present they know only "corporal nutriments." The flowers of Eden diffuse "ambrosial smell" (9.852) even on the bough that Eve has cut on her way to tempt Adam to join her in the original mortal sin. This reminder of Raphael's reference to the celestial food, known to humans only by its "Ambrosial odours," is possibly ironic (Hughes, "Variorum," 2.245).

55–56. *dissolution wrought by Sin, that first / Distempered all things:* cf. *SolMus* 19–20: "Till disproportion'd sin / Jarr'd against nature's chime."
    dissolution: "dissoluteness and eventual death" (Ricks, *"Paradise Lost"*).
    Distempered: refers to a disordered proportion of cold and heat (Hume). "Dissolution was thought to be held at bay only by a proper tempering of conflicting qualities, so that decay and death were physical consequences of sin" (Fowler). So *OED* 5 for "distemper," "To disorder or mar the condition of; to derange, confuse, put out of joint."

56. *of incorrupt:* i.e., "from being incorrupt," as in similar constructions in *PL* 4.153 and 9.563 (R. C. Browne [1877]); Verity also cites 10.720 and 12.167.

57–62. The words are no mere self-defense; since we come to them "fresh from Adam's midnight agonies," we are prepared to accept them as genuine proof of God's "Eternal Providence" (Evans 291). The words are clearly related to Adam's fear of "deathless pain" in 10.775. Several commentators had seen a physical immortality of pain for Adam as the supreme punishment. Its remedy can be the only one that God must now provide—death on the terms that Michael will declare (Hughes, "Variorum"). The contradiction between Death being fathered by Satan but also being provided by God is resolved by Erskine, who refers to the four degrees of death in *DocCh* 1.12–13 (guiltiness, spiritual death, death of the body, and eternal death or damnation [Patterson, *Works* 15:203, 205, 215, 251]); the death from God is the third, the sleep of the soul between this life and the resurrection, which was finally seen by Milton the poet—as opposed to Milton the theologian—as a heaven-sent release after a long and exhausting life, a conviction from which he would not later vary and would merely elaborate in *SA* 575–76 (573, 575–76, 582). Stoll counters that no resolution of the contradiction is needed, since we know that death is both a penalty and a relief ("Was Paradise" 432). See also **11.467–69** and **11.705–07** on death. *DocCh* 1.13 indicates that just as before sin entered the world all man's parts were alike immortal, they have since all become equally subject to death (Maurice Kelley 133; Patterson, *Works* 15:229).

57–59. *two fair gifts...Happiness / And Immortalitie:* according to St. Paul the restored endowments of Eden are righteousness and eternal life (Himes, *Paradise Lost: A Poem*); cf. Rom. 5:17–21. Kermode claims that whatever escape is offered here by Death, the text does not suggest that the offer makes up for the loss of these gifts (119). Moore argues that although this passage does contradict earlier statements about the origin and nature of death, those contradictions are "imposed upon Milton by his creed and his own narrative attempts to render the paradox intelligible" (28). Milton often describes Adam and Eve's condition in conceptual rather than visual terms (Ryken 197).

59. *fondly:* foolishly. Cf. *PL* 9.999.

60. *eternize:* Verity glosses as "make everlasting," but also claims that in 6.374 the word has its more common Elizabethan sense of "to immortalize," especially with poetry. "To make eternal, i.e. everlasting or endless; to give endless nature or duration to" (so *OED* 1).

61–66. Miner observes that God's reply to the Son's long speech emphasizes the sterner subjects of the poem: justice and knowledge (45).

61–62. *I provided Death:* Gillies infers a reference to 1 Cor. 3:21–22: "all things are yours; Whether...life, or death, or things present, or things to come."

62–66. "Paradoxically, rather than negation, Death becomes man's 'final remedie,' a means of new birth" (Lieb, *Dialectics* 213).

63–64. *DocCh* declares that works must be the test and consequence of truly saving faith (Maurice Kelley 171–72; Patterson, *Works* 16:37, 39); see also *PL* 12.408–10 and 12.426–27. Michael's warning to Adam in 12.427 occurs in a passage resonant of Scripture (Hughes, "Variorum"). In the Judaic tradition as shaped by Philo, "faith (piety) was a primary intellectual virtue," basic in "the psychological integrity of thought, word, and deed," and in "the Platonic unity of the virtues" (Stein, *Heroic Knowledge* 20). Here and in 12.427 ("Faith not void of workes"), Milton indicates his qualified assent to the doctrine of justification by faith (Hughes, *"Paradise Lost": A Poem*). Fowler identifies this moment in the "long progression of stages in regeneration" when faith has been achieved.

63. *Tri'd in sharp tribulation:* "God's words quickly point up the irony of Adam's earlier complacency of prospect" (Burke 207).

refin'd: Hume refers to *PL* 3.337, and also, from its concrete connection with metallurgy, to Prov. 17:3 and additionally, because of its abstract connection to purification by trial, to Luke 12:49.

tribulation: "a condition of great affliction, oppression, or misery" (so *OED* 1).

65. *Wak't in the renovation of the just:* Sims (*Bible* 269) cites Dan. 12:2 ("And many of them that sleep in the dust of the earth shall awake, some to everlasting life, and some to shame and everlasting contempt") as well as the corresponding prophecy in Matt. 25:31–46 and the promise of "the resurrection of the just" in Luke 14:14. See also the reference to "put[ting] off…the old man" in Eph. 4:22, 23 and to the renovation of our mortal bodies in 1 Cor. 15:53. Since the renovated must first die, "death ironically becomes in part redeemer" (Lawry, *Shadow* 271–72). Wesley omits this line.

66. Cf. 2 Pet. 3:13 ("we, according to his promise, look for new heavens, and a new earth") and also *PL* 10.638. Patrides traces other key passages in *PL* that stress a conflagration and renewal at the end of time: 3.334–35; 10.647; 11.900–01; 12.463–65, 548–51 ("Renaissance and Modern Thought" 181–82).

67. *But let us call to Synod:* cf. Gen. 1:26, "Let us make man," etc. On "synod," cf. *PL* 2.391, 3.60, 5.583–85. In his prose Milton used the word *Synod* in its broadest etymological sense of "an assembly, convention, or council of any kind" (*OED* 2), as he does in 2.391 and 6.156, where the devils are convened, and in 10.661, where astrological *Synod unbenigne* (apparent malignant conjunction of the planets) signifies a general disaster (Hughes, "Variorum"). These are large assemblies met to be informed, rather than to consult. Many commentators note that Themis summoned the gods to a council prior to the final exploit of Achilles (*Iliad* 20.4–11). Edward Chauncey Baldwin, finding Milton's elaborations of the biblical Fall paralleled in Jewish tradition, quotes a Midrash—Bereshith Rabba 20—that God convened a full Sanhedrin of 71 angels as soon as sin entered the world ("Some Extra-Biblical Semitic Influences" 386).

68–71. *DocCh* 1.9 asserts that good angels do not know all of God's secrets (Maurice Kelley 137; Patterson, *Works* 15:107). Empson judges this passage to verge on propaganda: "He will not admit that they were not firm; but says it was right to make them firmer" (*Milton's God* 175–76). Hamilton finds a "monstrous incongruity between Christian doctrine and the hard insensitivity of this heaven," since "All-power is only to be justified by All-love, and Milton's imagination creates an Almighty who is not first and foremost a King of Love" (34–35).

69. *proceed:* in the rare sense of "to treat or deal with a person, esp. judicially; to take action with regard to a person" (so *OED* 1d).

70. *peccant:* "sinning," from Latin *peccare,* to offend. 2 Pet. 2:4 refers to "the angels that sinned" (Sims, *Bible* 269).

73–76. According to Hughes ("Variorum"), the trumpet call to Michael's *Powers Militant* in heaven (6.60–61) anticipates the sound on Mt. Sinai when God's voice was preceded by the "voice of the trumpet exceeding loud" (Exod. 19:16–19; cf. Heb. 12:19); the *Minister* on watch in line 73 is the archangel who St. Paul declared in 1 Thess. 4:16 would descend from heaven with "the trump of God" at the Day of Judgment (the "general Doom" of line 76, in contradistinction to the "renovation of the just" in line 65 [Fowler]); according to some traditions recorded in the *Jewish Encyclopedia* (8:537), the archangel Michael will sound the trumpet (Hughes, "Variorum"); cf. *Nat* 156–58. Many commentators are careful to note the "perhaps," as it is not clear whether the two biblical trumpets are the same. Hume and others refer to both God's appearance on Sinai (Exod. 20:18) and the Second Coming (Matt. 24:31, 1 Thess. 4:16, and elsewhere). Gillies links Exod. 19:19 ("the voice of the trumpet sounded long") with 1 Cor. 15:52 ("The trumpet shall sound"). Dunster (in Todd) asserts that the "perhaps" does voice doubt about "the events themselves, of the dispensation of the law and the final judgement" and about the identity of the trumpet; he also cites Wakefield's observations on Alexander Pope's *Temple of Fame* (306). Edward Chauncey Baldwin notes that in the Apocalypse of Moses, Michael blows a trumpet (*shofar*) to summon the angels to heaven, after Adam and Eve have sinned, to hear God's judgment on the pair (*Paradise Lost* 385), and also that Eve relates in the Life of Adam and Eve, "In that same hour we heard the archangel Michael blowing with his trumpet" ("Some Extra-Biblical Semitic Influences" 386). Gage adds that in the Apocalypse of Moses, "Michael is recognized as the angel of humanity, and his instructions to Adam and Eve play an important part in the book" (112). Cf. the "ethereal trumpet" of *PL* 6.59–64 that sounds the march against Satan's host (Verity). Himes (*Paradise Lost: A Poem*) finds it significant that in book 6 Michael directed the trumpet to signal judgment without mercy on the fallen angels, but here it is directed by the merciful Son. In "The Plan," Himes argues that the epic, particularly books 11 and 12, follows the plan of the seven trumpets of the Apocalypse. Radzinowicz judges that Milton's single image of the trumpet reminds his audience of the shifting location of the epic in time (38). MacCaffrey claims that in these compact lines, "history is shut in a span as the three points for its circumference are indicated" (124).

hee blew: Johnson includes these two words among those he finds inharmonious because their break with the rest of 73 allows no "associate sounds to make them harmonious," whereas he praises the "full and solemn close" of *To sound at general Doom* in line 76, typical of a phrase stopping after the sixth syllable of a line (*Rambler* 4 [26 Jan. 1651]: 112, 115); see also 11.133.

Oreb: Paterson glosses the Hebrew *Oreb* (also *Horeb* or *Choreb*) as "dryness," noting that Horeb is part of Mt. Sinai on the west side; Strong glosses it as "desolation" (43). Beeching notes a similar spelling of "Ebrew" for *Hebrew* in *SA* 1308. Cf. "Oreb" (or Sinai) in *PL* 1.7.

76–77. C. H. Collins Baker remarks that among John Martin's 1824–26 mezzotint illustrations of *PL,* the new subjects include "The Angelick blast fill'd all the regions" from book 11 (5, 111, 113).

76. *blast:* "the sending of a continuous puff of breath through a wind-instrument, so as to make it sound" (so *OED* 3a).

77–80. "The *waters of Life* are the *Rivers of Bliss* of 3.358" (Hughes, *"Paradise Lost": A Poem*). Empson sees the angels' leisure as a sign that the ambiguously "jealous" God is "noticeably jovial" about the angels' "sexual" unification, their joining of two divine natures being but one step for making "one individual soul" with God (*Milton's God* 107–08).

   By the waters: Sprott claims that both the first and second syllables are stressed (104).

77. *regions:* Verity glosses as "realms of air." Scientific thinking in Milton's time divided the atmosphere into three regions, including the "middle air" of 1.516 (Fowler). Cf. *Nat* 103 and see *PL* 7.425.

78. *amaranthine:* "of or pertaining to amarant(h), of everlasting flowers, fadeless" (so *OED* 1). Cf. "Amarant" in *PL* 3.353. The flower is a type of immortality, because ἀμάραντος means "unwithering" (Verity). According to Allen, the presence of the flower in heaven is partly explained by Clement of Alexandria's *Paedagogus* 2.2, where, in contrast with the crowns of athletes and the garlands of banqueters, he praises the Christian's "fair crown of amaranthus, the flower which earth cannot bear, and which grows only in heaven," and partly perhaps by *Laus Serenae* by the late Latin poet Claudius Claudianus ("Milton's Amarant" 256–58). Tuve cites this line in her discussion of the "Amaranthus" of *Lyc* 149 ("Bid Amaranthus all his beauty shed") as a "symbol of the flawless world before the Fall," and—as repeated in *PL*—as a slowly growing idea, or a "revealing (Invention, uncovering)" gained from invoking a heavenly muse (104–05n18).

79. *By the waters of Life, where ere they sate:* Bridges claims that the iambs are inverted into trochees in both the first and second feet (43). Cf. "the river of Bliss" in *PL* 3.358 and references to the waters, fountain, or river of life in Rev. 7:17, 21:6, and 22:1, 17.

80. Cf. the "sweet Societies" of heaven in *Lyc* 179 and the implied definition of fellowship as participation in "All rational delight" in *PL* 8.391. Todd also lists

Drummond's *Poems* ("The fellowship of God's immortal train") and Dante, *Paradiso* 24.1–2 ("O elect sodality, at the great Supper / Of the blessed Lamb"). Himes (*Paradise Lost: A Poem*) points to the image of the Israelites spread out in Balaam's gaze (Num. 24:5–6), with "families" changed to "fellowships" to distance the sexual implications.

   Sons of light: Sims (*Bible* 269) cites references to belonging to the "light" in John 8:12, Eph. 5:8, and 1 John 1:5b.

81. *resorting:* "to proceed or go to (or toward) a place; to respond to a call or summons (so *OED* v¹7). Hume glosses as "to issue forth," from French, *ressortir*. If so, Milton may be suggesting a connection between the "Sons of Light" (80) and "the waters of Life" (79), since the former would more properly issue forth. Allen cites the "Sons of Light" passage as one proof that Milton's major imagery rests on light and its derivative manifestations (*Harmonious Vision* 102).

82. *And took thir Seats:* Bentley emends *Seats* to *Stand,* since Milton's angels do not sit elsewhere (5.595, 11.221). Pearce suggests that Bentley is thinking of the scholastic maxim *sola sedet Trinitas* ("only the Trinity sits"), which Pearce rejects in favor of Rev. 4:4 and 11:16, where the 24 elders are seated around God's throne. The Richardsons suggest that the ever-reverent angels are here being allowed a "filial freedom" and that accordingly God calls them sons. William Greenwood (in Todd) also asserts that angels called to a synod would properly sit. Keightley claims that Milton may have had Homer in view. R. C. Browne (1877) also cites Matt. 19:28 in answer to Bentley.

   Throne supream: cf. *PL* 10.28. Oras, examining Milton for signs of earlier and later style, reports that after book 4 of *PL* the word *stress* clearly coincides with the metrical stress and compares this line and the "sovran Throne" of 5.656 with the metrically suspect "supreme Throne" of Milton's "On Time," line 17 ("Milton's Blank Verse" 172–73).

84–98. Cf. the briefer biblical referent in Gen. 3:22–24. Various issues in this passage have occasioned critical discussion, including ones on tone. According to Hume, all Genesis interpreters expound *like one of us* ironically, as referring to the false promises of Satan in the serpent, and Milton more or less subscribes to this reading with *let him boast / His knowledge* (86–87). But Hume also thinks Milton has partly followed Hieronymus Oleaster's opinion that the biblical lines were spoken to the still unfallen angels in heaven, to confirm them in their obedience (11.71). Saurat finds this passage one of the two places where God tempers his divine irony with humaneness, the other being his assurance to Adam that his eternal existence is without loneliness (*PL* 8.398–406); there could be a Mephistophelian irony to God's portrayal if Milton had the intellectual agility, perfect tact, and deep bitterness of feeling necessary to such a picture (192–93). Empson links this passage to a larger puzzle about whether God actually wants his angels to have an individuated existence apart from him; the comment "certainly has a mysterious tone of connivance" (*Milton's God* 107–08). Fowler acknowledges Empson's comment but prefers Burden's explanation (7–8) that Milton makes God speak even more ironically to eke out the meaning in the biblical text. Both Fowler and Patrides (*Milton* 105) quote from the early seventeenth century author Andrew Willet, who agrees with Calvin and Mercerus that God is speaking ironically. Brooks claims that Milton is not putting a sneer into the Genesis account but rather demonstrating that God's self-consciousness, as understood by Western tradition from Aristotle onward, is too great a burden for Adam to assume ("Eve's Awakening," 296–97). Cf. *PL* 11.547–52, 598–602.

Other analyses of this passage focus on warning and punishment. According to Hughes ("Variorum"), no possibility of earthly survival could be literally consistent with the divine warning that Adam would die on the day he ate from the forbidden tree, yet by adding banishment from Eden to the punishment, the warning implied an indefinite survival. Time will reveal that the death of the body is implied in the corruption of the soul, as Milton declares in *DocCh* 1.13; Patterson, *Works* 15:217. As Burden observes, any hope of escaping it that Adam and Eve might entertain is a mere fantasy (8). Theologians had agreed that the ironic result of their sin had been to know good by evil, because as Sir Francis Bacon said in the beginning of *The Advancement,* they sought knowledge "with an intent in man to give a law unto himself and to depend no more on God's commandments" (*Works* 6:92). Brooks thinks that the knowledge of good and evil includes a self-consciousness that only God's perfect omniscience is able to bear ("Eve's Awakening" 296–97), and Babb finds it illogical that the inhabitants of heaven seem to know both good and evil (10). Cf. Gen. 3:22–24. Rajan includes this passage as one of many accumulating repetitions that inescapably stress disobedience issuing in *hubris;* the various sins of Satan, Adam, and Eve all "riot from a common stem of disobedience" (*"Paradise Lost" and the Seventeenth Century* 44–45). Although Gen. 3:15 informs many of the traditional accounts of Adam seeing his descendant through angelic vision or narration, other accounts depend on Gen. 3:22 or 5:1 (Steadman, "Adam" 214–15). Dick Taylor Jr. argues that this passage explicitly denies that the Fall was in any way fortunate ("Milton" 51). "The temper…of the deity at this juncture is admirably represented…in his justice there is no harshness, while in his forgiveness there is no complacency towards man's sins. He is eminently a god whom the wicked fear and the righteous trust" (Himes, *A Study* 231–32). Maurice Kelley traces in this passage a number of issues raised in *DocCh:* angels are called the sons of God because of their similar holiness, we know good only by knowing evil because of the Fall, and the tree of knowledge is not itself a sacrament but rather either a symbol of eternal life or the nutriment that sustains that life (135, 141; Patterson, *Works* 15:35, 115).

Tschumi (154) suggests an antithesis between this exclusionary congress resulting from the wrong use of nourishment and the inclusive banquets of Plato's *Symposium* and the *gran cena* or "great dinner" of Dante's *Paradiso* 24.1–3.

84. *one of us:* Banks claims that Milton never has God use the "plural of excellence"; here he means the angels ("Meaning" 451).

85–86. *defended:* "forbidden" (so *OED* 1, obs.). Cf. "defends" in *PL* 12.207 and *PR* 2.370. Hume and the Richardsons cite the *Prologue* to Chaucer's *Wife of Bath's Tale,* 59–60: "Where can you say in any manner age / That ever God defended Marriage?" The word often occurs in this sense in old statutes, a remnant of Norman French (Keightley). Wesley reduces this passage to a single line, "To know both Good and Evil; but let him boast," which no longer scans.

87. *His knowledge of good lost and evil got:* cf. *PL* 9.1071–73. Le Comte compares 7.543; 9.697, 723; see also 4.222; 8.324.

88–89. *to have known / Good by it self, and Evil not at all:* critics differ on the import of these lines. According to Samuel, they express Milton's "considered opinion of the value of experiencing evil" ("Milton" 714n9); cf. James Ussher's catechetical discussion of the tree of knowledge (*Body of Divinity* 125–26). Hughes claims that Adam's mood at the end of the poem would have been no different had he known about God's solemn declaration here ("Some Illustrators" 676). Miner asserts that these two lines prohibit any easy application of *felix culpa* "because they show that the oxymoronic character of the expression depends upon a prior assumption of *infelix culpa*" (46). According to Bøgholm, discourse had to take the place of intuition more extensively after the Fall (39).

90–96. Critics vary in their reception of this passage. Himes finds God's judicial temper to be "akin to the human pity of a tender judge" (*A Study* 232). MacCallum compares the "too explicit account of the mechanics of grace" to Milton's distinction in *DocCh* 1.17 between natural and supernatural renovation ("Milton and Sacred History" 161); see Patterson, *Works* 15:345. Peter complains that God's reasoning here is "too indecisive to be convincing…and his claim that their contrition is due to his 'motions' in them rather than their own volition seems downright unfair" (145). Sasek asserts that fallen human nature is not only a theological concept but is acted out, such as Adam's unstable joy at the beginning of book 11 and Eve's preference for material over spiritual (186–87).

90–93. *motions:* "working[s] of God in the soul" (*OED* 12b). The word may be charged with a similar meaning in *SA* 1382; if Adam's heart were left to itself after it responded to divine grace, only God knows how inconstant it might be (Hughes, "Variorum"). Bentley finds "no sense at all" in *longer then they move* and emends it to *should they cease to move,* and Keightley ends line 91 with an ellipsis, indicating a break in sense. Verity, however, glosses the line as "I know man's variableness after my influences have ceased to work in him." Cf. the biblical distrust of human hearts in Jer. 17:9 and John 2:24–25. Fowler finds the delay mimetic; his gloss is, "I know his heart will outlast these impulses to good, and I know how variable and vain it will become if left to itself." On Milton's exposition of prevenient grace, including *motions,* see **11.22–23.** Cf. *DocCh* 2.1, "Hence may be easily discerned the vanity of human merits; seeing that…our good actions are not our own, but of God working in us" (Maurice Kelley 186; Patterson, *Works* 17:21).

90. Cf. *contrite* in 10.1091. According to Verity, the accent for Milton is always on the last syllable, showing the influence of the Latin. In *DocCh* 1.19, contrition is the next step after conviction of sin (Patterson, *Works* 15:385); see **11.141.**

91. *My motions in him:* see Patrides' comment in **11.22–23.**

92–95. Empson is puzzled about this fruit's mode of action, since unlike the forbidden tree it is not an intoxicant; he assumes that both trees have magical properties, though Milton seems to deny it, and he concludes, "the text was pretty difficult to handle" (*Milton's God* 188–89).

92. *His heart I know, how variable and vain:* Bridges believes that the elision should be between *–ble and* rather than making *–ria* a single syllable (31); see a similar case in *PL* 12.582.

　　variable: said of thought or conduct that is "liable or apt to vary or change; (readily) susceptible or capable of variation; mutable, changeable, fluctuating, uncertain" (so *OED* 1b).

93. *Self-left:* i.e., left to himself. Warton (208) cites this line as an example of Milton's fondness for "self-" in compounds, along with *PL* 1.634; 3.130; 5.254, 860; 7.154, 242, 510; 8.572; 9.183, 1188; 10.1016; and 11.203.

95–96. *dream at least to live / For ever:* Rupertus assumed that Satan was unaware of the power of the tree of life, or he would have urged Adam and Eve to eat of it, to render their misery perpetual (Hume). Milton's explanation is more coherent in 11.57–62 regarding God's fear of Adam's touching the tree of life (N. Frye, *"Paradise Lost"*). Bush notes that Milton adds the reinterpretive "dream" to the Genesis passage.

95. *And live for ever:* citing Gen. 3:22. Hume quotes Francisco Valles's opinion, "Homo qui mortalis erat, & redigi naturaliter poterat, in suum cinerem voluntate Dei viveret semper, nisi peccatum obstitisset; non est itaque per peccatum factus mortalis, sed qui cùm erat innocens voluntate Dei servabatur, ob peccatum traditus est suae mortalitati" (sin does not render man mortal but rather betrays God's preservation of his natural mortality; otherwise he could have lived forever by the will of God in his ashes) (Valles, *De iis* 114). The "forever" of Scripture and its synonyms do not denote eternity, but rather a long time (cf. Gen. 49:26, Deut. 15:17, Dan. 3:9, 1 Cor. 8:13), as Adam would eventually have been translated to heaven. Renaissance commentators disagreed over whether the promise of immortality should be interpreted literally or merely ironically (Arnold Williams, *Common Expositor* 136).

96–108. Reesing judges that these "most official moments" of the Father's speech bear the complex feeling of "a person who has made something infinitely beautiful for another's joy, only to see it trampled and profaned in sheer malice" and "a father working to shield his disappointing child from a really vicious danger" (89).

98. As explained in 11.48–57, Adam will find the soil outside Eden less fertile than the ecologically "pure immortal Elements" within. The curse on the ground that God pronounces in Gen. 3:17 is a fit punishment for his sin (Hughes, "Variorum"). Fowler cites Norman Powell Williams (363) to suggest that Milton alludes to the scholastic distinction between *donum supernaturale*, Adam's superadded original righteousness, and *pura naturalia*, the ordinary properties of human nature itself, including the dust from which Adam was taken.

99. Much of the commentary on this line concerns how appropriate it is for Michael to escort the pair out of the garden. Michael, "of Celestial Armies Prince" (*PL* 6.44), is to use none of the violence with which he expelled from heaven the rebel angels; for them, the "fear / Of…the Sword of Michael" was still dreadful (2.293–94). Satan dares not approach Michael, who—as Fletcher recalls—was the traditional "superintendent of Eden" (*praepositus paradisi*) (Hughes, "Variorum"; cf. Fletcher, *Milton's Rabbinical Readings* 250). Dunster (in Todd) also argues that Michael would otherwise lack his due share of the epic action. Keightley expands on this idea; since book 6 was only episodic, Michael has not yet appeared "as an actor" in the poem. Montgomery adds that Gabriel would not have done, as he conveys "good tidings" to humankind. Edward Chauncey Baldwin remarks that in every instance in the Apocalypse of Moses and the Life of Adam and Eve, it is Michael who after the pair's condemnation comes to them with messages of comfort or of admonition ("Some Extra-Biblical Semitic Influences" 389). Fletcher thinks it especially fitting that Michael carry out the decree of banishment, as he embodied the principle of God's justice, and also is the kind of angel announced in Exod. 23:20–23 to guide the chosen throughout history (*Milton's Rabbinical Readings* 250–51). Peter cites various lines in the last two books to argue that our regard for Michael, once established, "continues more or less intact until the end"; his status, though inferior to the Son's, is not altogether different (29–30). Fowler thinks that Michael's presence here is fitting because he is the angel of the Apocalypse, and the visions shown to

Adam "are essentially apocalyptic visions of history." Fowler also reports that Michael's name occurs in the Trinity Manuscript of Milton's first draft of a tragedy on the Fall. Reesing finds that Michael's role becomes more personal in book 12 because his own speech must mediate the revelation (54). On the choice of Michael, see also *PL* 11.239–40.

101–03. "The view that there is a calculated progressive decay of Satan is not upheld by this passage" (Empson, *Some Versions* 165).

101. *Thy choice of flaming Warriours:* cf. the "ministers" of Ps. 104:4, described as "flaming," and the "ministering spirits" of Heb. 1:14, also reflected in *PL* 6.102, 9.156, and *Circum* 1. Milton, citing Luke 10:18, links the angels with lightning in *DocCh* 1.7, adding that the name of seraphim is thus derived (Maurice Kelley 135; Patterson, *Works* 15:35); the Hebrew root *saraph* denotes burning (Strong). As noted by both West (*Milton and the Angels* 134) and Gage (15), Milton's names for angels are too fluid to be schematized into any consistent ranking; further angelic names appear at 11.126, 220–21, 230–32, 296–97, 598, 759, 884; 12.2, 574, 590, 626–28. According to Hughes, the duty of the cherubim emerges in 11.127–28 and 12.625–28 ("Variorum").

102–03. *or to invade / Vacant possession:* Keightley glosses *invade* as to enter on (*invado*) the property that was lying unguarded; the language is partly legal. *OED* 1c cites Nathan Bailey's 1730 definition for "vacant effects" as "such as are abandoned for want of an Heir, after the Death or Flight of their former Owner"; Fowler judges that the passage "continues the ironic tone of the previous paragraph." Cf. the "vacant interlunar cave" in *SA* 89. Hughes ("Variorum") thinks *invade* may mean to "usurp, seize upon, take possession of" (*OED* 4b).

102. *in behalf of Man:* Bentley objects that the phrase suggests philanthropy in Satan, and emends God's words to *in despite to Us,* but Pearce glosses it as "on account of Man" and adds that had Milton meant *despite,* he probably would have used *of* instead of *to,* since in 12.34 he says, *in despite of Heav'n.* The Richardsons explain the phrase as "not out of Friendship to him, but as being his Subject or Ally Now, and part of his New Acquisition." Robert M. Adams (119) quotes *OED*'s explanation of the phrase as meaning "as concerns" or "with regard to" (1d).

104. *Hast:* the archaic reflexive use of "has" (so *OED* 2).

105. *remorse:* "sorrow, pity, compassion" (so *OED* 3a). Milton uses *remorse* six times in *PL,* five of them–including this one–with the old sense of sympathy or tender regard. The other instances are in *PL* 1.605, 4.109, 5.134, and 5.566; only the usage in 10.1098 is doubtful. Cf. Shakespeare's similar use of the word in *Richard III* 3.7.211 and *Othello* 3.3.369, as cited by the semi-anonymous "N.O." (77). Verity likewise cites Shakespeare's "usual sense of 'pity, tenderness of heart,'" as in *Merchant of Venice* 4.1.20: "show thy mercy and remorse." Himes (*Paradise Lost: A Poem*) maintains that Michael in many ways resembles Achilles, whose name he claims means "without pity" (αχίλεος). Ricks (*"Paradise Lost"*) glosses *remorse* as "compunction"; since neither Raphael nor Michael *could* feel fallen remorse, its very inapplicability highlights their goodness (Ricks, *Milton's Grand Style* 116). Burden argues that pity would be wrong here, because it would imply that God was unjust (36). Michael must not yield to *remorse* in the sense of "sorrow" or "signs of tender feelings" that Raphael confesses in 5.564–68, since proper respect for God's justice obliges him to exercise self-control (Hughes, "Variorum").

106–08. *denounce...to thir Progenie / Perpetual banishment:* cf. *DocCh* 1.11, which denotes the effects of the Fall on Adam and Eve's progeny (Maurice Kelley 147; Patterson, *Works* 15:183); see also 11.423–26, 12.285–86, 398–400.
    denounce: announce, proclaim, with the notion of hostility or menace (Verity). Cf. *OED,* "to proclaim, announce, declare; to publish, promulgate an event about to take place: usually of a calamitous nature, as war or death" (1b) and "to announce or proclaim in the manner of a threat or warning (punishment, vengeance, a curse, etc.)" (3). Cf. similar uses at *PL* 2.106–07 and 11.815.

108–133. Cf. God's promise of revival for the contrite in Isa. 57:15.

108–17. Martz argues that despite these initial statements, Michael's sentence is "rigorously urged, and terror...emphasized, not hidden, in his history of the world," and that this passage thus serves to indicate "how far Milton has failed...to measure up to the great achievement of his first ten books" (166). Miner claims that joy and tragedy in these lines are carefully modulated (46).

108. *faint:* in the archaic sense of "to lose heart or courage, be afraid, become depressed, give way, flag" (*OED* 1).

109–17. Dick Taylor Jr. claims that God's pronouncement "reveals sympathy and sadness as well as sternness"; his requirement that Michael encourage, strengthen, and instruct them particularly reveals "profound solicitude" ("Milton's Treatment" 75).

109. Wesley omits this line.

110. *softn'd:* 1667 *soft'nd.* Cf. "soften," "To render more impressionable or tender; to affect emotionally" (so *OED* 2a).

111. *Bewailing thir excess, all terror hide:* Baumgartner, arguing that blindness and the Restoration were responsible for a change in Milton's temperament, lists this passage as one of 17 significant mentions of patience after Milton's sonnet on blindness (204–05, 210); see also **11.314, 355–64; 12.562–64, and 582–83**.

    excess: "extravagant violation of law, decency, or morality; outrageous conduct" (*OED* 4a); cf. "vengeful Justice bore for our excess" (*Circum* 24). Hume links *excess* (Latin, a going beyond [our duty to God]) with *transgression,* as do the Richardsons, who also cite *PL* 4.879. Bentley finds *excess* "too soft a word" and thinks Milton intends the word *offense,* but Pearce counters that *excess* is aptly soft, since "all that God here says, has the marks of Pity in it." Cf. "th'inabstinence of Eve" (11.476). *Excess* agrees with God's command to Michael, "all terror hide" (Newton). Ricks (*"Paradise Lost"*) glosses *excess* as "violation" and Fowler as "transgression, outrage." "Compare this once common use of *excess* with Milton's axiomatic view of sin as 'alwaies an excess' in *Tetr*" (Hughes, "Variorum"; Patterson, *Works* 4:159).

112–13. *If patiently thy bidding they obey, / Dismiss them not disconsolate:* critics differ on the import of these lines. The Richardsons find them a good example of Milton's verbal economy, showing that obedience gains not only God's favor and acceptance but comfort as well. Parish argues that Milton's extension of the Genesis narrative, which follows a long tradition, both preserves the epic device of the hero seeing his future offspring and allows Adam to become a Christian ("Pre-Miltonic Representations" 1–24). As here, the revelation is meant to console, as in Reuchlin's somewhat parallel account in *De arte cabalistica* (Steadman, "Adam" 222–25). Pecheux argues that the sentence of banishment is Adam's first crucial test after the Fall; the greater revelation depends on how he responds ("Abraham" 365). Kirkconnell reports that in Serafino della Salandra's *Adamo caduto* (1647), Mercy meets and consoles the penitent Adam and Eve, while in Pordage's *Mundorum explicatio* (1661), it is Christ himself, as Love, who sends Michael with the command, "tell man not to fear" (Kirkconnell 346, 432). In Andreini's *L'Adamo* (1613), Michael is not consolatory in 3.8, but later is described by Adam as "pietoso" (compassionate) (5.9).

113–17. Cf. Milton's notes for his draft of "Adam unparadiz'd" in the Trinity Manuscript: "the Angel is sent to banish them out of paradise but before causes to passe before his eyes in Shapes a mask of all the evills of this life & world he is humbl'd relents, dispaires. at last appears Mercy comforts him promises the messiah, then calls in faith, hope, & charity, instructs him he repents gives god the glory, submits to his penalty" (Patterson, *Works* 18:232); see **11.477–93**. Cf. *DocCh* 1.14: "There was a promise made to all mankind, and an expectation of the Redeemer, more or less distinct, even from the time of the fall" (Maurice Kelley 159; Patterson, *Works* 15:257) and *PL* 12.232–35. Fish finds Michael's voice and tone far less varied or intrusive than "the epic voice, that great amphibian"; Michael's performance is controlled by the divine command here (288).

114. *what shall come in future dayes:* cf. Michael's similar introductory phrase in Dan. 10:14. Edward Chauncey Baldwin says that a revelation following Adam's penitential prayer was a common rabbinical tradition ("Some Extra-Biblical Semitic Influences" 391).

115–16. *intermix / My Cov'nant in the womans seed renewd:* the promise that Christ would bruise the head of the serpent and that it would bruise his heel (Gen. 3:15) is announced in *PL* 10.179–81 and revisited in 10.498–99, 1031–32, and 11.155. As commanded, Michael makes it the theme of his discourse, repeating it in 12.148–50, 233–34, 311–12, 327, 378–79, 543, 600, 623; see Patrides, " 'Protevangelium' " 19–30, and *Milton* 123–28; and also Steadman, *Milton's*

Epic Characters 77–79. According to *DocCh* 1.26, the covenant of grace itself, on the part of God, is first declared in Gen. 3:15 (Patterson, *Works* 16:99). John Boys, a well-known divine of the earlier seventeenth century, said that this verse generated all sermons ("all that is said by Christ and his blessed Apostles in the New Testament, is summarily nothing else, but a repetition and explanation of that one prophecy" [242]), and in Vondel's *Lucifer* of 1654, the "firm consolation" of fallen man is linked to the "woman's seed," Christ, and his redeeming contest with the devil (Kirkconnell 419–20). For the extension of *seed* to Abraham, see 12.125–26. God's prophecy that Eve's descendants shall "bruise the serpent's head" is regarded as a covenant of grace with man no less binding upon God than his explicit covenants with Noah (*PL* 11.867, 892, 898), with the Israelites (12.252), and with David (12.346–47). All God's covenants of both grace and works with man are perpetual as the "covenant of... Redemption" of which Milton speaks in *Ref* as perpetuated by "the quickning power of the Spirit" (Hughes, "Variorum"); see Patterson, *Works* 3:3. Fowler glosses *Covenant* as, initially, "the bond between the God of Israel and his people" that resulted in physical offerings and later as the spiritual bond, "wherein righteousness, made perfect by the gift of grace, was the offering."

115. *As I shall thee enlighten:* "in one sense, the divine inspiration is Milton's credo concerning the truth of the Bible; but dramatically, it suggests that his words... come more directly from God than Raphael's earlier discourses" (Sasek 187).

    enlighten: "to supply with intellectual light; to impart knowledge or wisdom to; to instruct" (so *OED* 5).

116. *womans:* 1667 *Womans.*

117. *So send them forth, though sorrowing, yet in peace:* cf. 12.603–05. "Even this early, Milton is preparing for the marvelous close of the poem" (Patterson, *Student's Milton*). This divine injunction controls the tone of Michael's directions to Adam in 12.594–605 (Fisch 42). Rajan claims this requirement "is scarcely to be avoided except by those who seem to think that Adam should leave Eden in a state of blurred elation, inebriated, as it were, by the *felix culpa*" (*"Paradise Lost:* The Hill" 47); see 12.469–78. Stoll complains that Erskine (580) "does violence to the text" by making Adam and Eve overly eager to leave Eden, whereas "mood

and metre both breathe the spirit" of the words in this passage, where Milton represented life as we know it, "a mingled web, good and ill together" ("Was Paradise" 433); see also **12.641–48**. Joseph, arguing that the theology of *PL* is in conformity with the Roman Catholic Church, takes this passage as proof of the efficacy of prayer, as the Father's command is immediately contiguous with Adam and Eve's sense of new strength (282); cf. *PL* 11.137–38.

118–20. *on the East side…Cherubic watch, and of a Sword the flame:* cf. Gen. 3:24, "So he drove out the man; and he placed at the east of the garden of Eden Cherubims, and a flaming sword which turned every way, to keep the way of the tree of life," and also Balaam's encounter with the angel in Num. 22:31 and David's in 2 Sam. 24:17. The weapons of Gabriel's "Angelic Guards" at the gates of the garden were aflame "with Diamond…and with Gold" (*PL* 4.550–54), but they are transcended by "the brandisht Sword of God [that] blaz'd / Fierce as a Comet" (12.633–34, 643) before Michael's guard of cherubim" (Hughes, "Variorum"). The Richardsons identify *of a Sword the Flame* as a Hellenism imitated by such Latin writers as Horace: "Cecidit tremendae / Flamma Chimerae"; "He slays of a terrible Chimera the flame" (*Odes* 4.2.15–16). Thomas Warton cites this passage as one example that the "Cherub Contemplation" of *IlPen* 54 is not a cupid (76). Cf. the "cherubic watch" in *PL* 9.68, and their descriptions in 12.590–93 and 626–36. McColley claims that this passage, along with 11.377–78, 12.637–40, and five others from books 4 and 8 represent a link to Mt. Amara drawn from Heylyn and Purchas and representing a composition year of 1652–53 (*"Paradise Lost": An Account* 314).

flame: Paterson supplies an unlikely Latinate etymology from "flash of fire," not attested in *OED*, to propose that the line suggests "the wide-waving flame of a sword, by a figure of rhetoric." Cf. Heb. 1:7, where angels are identified as both "ministers" (i.e., servants) and "a flame of fire."

121. *fright:* "to scare away" (so *OED* 2b).

122. *passage:* "an opportunity to pass; the power, permission, or right to pass" (so *OED* 4a).

123. *receptacle:* as Fowler notes, the stress is on the third syllable. Cf. the obsolete meaning of "A place into which a person, animal, ship, etc., is received and sheltered; a haven" (*OED* 5a).

124–25. Wesley omits these lines.

126. *th'Archangelic Power:* on the fluidity of Milton's names for angels, see **11.101**, s.v. *Thy choice of flaming Warriors.*

127. *Cohort:* "a body of [Roman] infantry…of which there were ten in a legion, each consisting of from 300 to 600 men…applied (later) to bodies of cavalry" (*OED* 1); "a similar division of other armies" or "a band of warriors in general" (so *OED* 2). Both Hume and the Richardsons identify a Roman *cohors* as 555 infantry and 66 cavalry, ten of which constituted a legion. "Michael is bringing even better protection with him than Gabriel had in his 'Angelic Squadron'" (Collett 95); cf. *PL* 4.977.

128–33. Wesley reduces this passage to a single line, "Of watchful Cherubim [descend]. Mean while."

129. *like a double Janus:* Janus is "the name of an ancient Italian deity, regarded as the doorkeeper of heaven, as guardian of doors and gates, and as presiding over the entrance upon or beginning of things; represented with a face on the front and another on the back of his head; the doors of his temple in the Roman Forum were always open in time of war, and shut in time of peace" (so *OED* 1a). Cf. Virgil, *Aeneid* 7.180, 610, and Ovid, *Fasti* 1.43–44, as well as the four-faced cherubim in Ezek. 1:6 and 10:14, which also inform the chariot of paternal deity in *PL* 6.749–59. Numerous early commentators supply details on Janus, a legendary Roman king in whose court Saturn took refuge and for whose wisdom he was enrolled among the gods. His image in the temple built for him by Numa Pompilius had two faces; some commentators find a reference to Noah, having seen one world destroyed and another restored, and per-haps—because of his drunkenness in Gen. 9:20–21—for being associated with Roman wine offerings, as in Cato, *Of Agriculture* 134. The month of January was named for him, as having seen both the old and new year. Bentley supposes that Milton's editor may have conflated several myths, and emends *PL* 11.128–35 to the brief, "four fac'd were each, / And all their shape spangled with Eyes. Mean while / Leucothea wak'd." But as noted by Gilbert ("Double Janus" 1027–30) and earlier commentators, including Verity, there was a lesser-known four-faced Janus, a *Janus quadrifrons* or *Janus geminus* to which Milton may be referring; Gilbert supplies citations from Macrobius, Pierius Valerianus, and others, also remarking that Calvin interpreted Ezekiel's four-faced cherubim as signifying God's providential rule over the four quarters of the world and that Ben Jonson, in his entertainment for King James's coronation, refers to Janus as "the deity who respecteth all climates and fills all parts of the world with his majesty." T. W. Baldwin adds that although *Janus geminus* was established as an official phrase by such Renaissance compendia as that of Robert Stephanus, the necessity of doubling an already twinned image led to some ambiguity (583–84). As Osgood (47–48) notes, this figure is referred to in Macrobius, *Saturnalia* 1.9.13: "Thus, among us too, Janus looks toward the four quarters of the world...and [is] quadriform, to show that his greatness embraces all the regions of the world." This Janus presided over daybreak under the title of Matutinus, and his two faces probably represented morning and evening. He also ruled the year's opening, the first month being named after him, and his four faces represented the seasons (Himes, *Paradise Lost: A Poem*). Collett points out that only Gyraldus among Renaissance mythographers mentions a double Janus, which represented the four seasons; the four beasts of the biblical passages were commonly taken to represent the four Gospels, so that Michael's cohort prefigures the Christian revelation he will deliver (96), but Thomas De Quincey argues that the four-faced Janus became the standard one under the Caesars (De Quincey cited in Wittreich 492). Fowler finds the use of the double Janus particularly appropriate, since the four heads of Janus were interpreted as the four seasons, and "man is going out into a world of change, seasonal and historical." Cf. Milton's reference to the "two controversal faces" of Janus in *Areop* (Patterson, *Works* 4:347) and also **11.209**.

130–31. *eyes more numerous then those / Of Argus:* Argus was a shepherd with 100 eyes, whom Juno charged with guarding the cow into which Jupiter had transformed his paramour Io (Ovid, *Metamorphoses* 1.622–29); see also *Iliad* 24.343, Apollodorus, *Bibliotheca* 2.1.2–3, Virgil, *Aeneid* 7.791. As Dunster remarks (in Todd), Dante compares the eyes in the wings of cherubim to those of Argus (*Purgatorio* 29.95–96); cf. Ezek 1:18. Milton cites Argus's "hundred eyes of jealousie" in *Ref* (Patterson, *Works* 3:38). Edmundson (100) thinks Milton took this image from Vondel's *Adam in Ballingschap*. Argus, like Janus, was a temporal or astronomical symbol (Fowler).

131. *more wakeful then to drouze:* Bentley finds this expression ridiculous, but Pearce argues that it must be considered against the powerful soporifics mentioned in the next two verses. Himes (*Paradise Lost: A Poem*) contrasts the wakefulness of God, who shall "neither slumber nor sleep" (Ps. 121:4). Verity points out that Milton's use of the comparative *more wakeful* with *than* and the inifinitive *to drowse* is similar to the Greek construction of ἤ ὥστε, the comparative implying a negative answer; cf. Liddell and Scott under ὥστε, B.2.

drouze: "to be drowsy; to be heavy or dull with or as with sleep; to be half asleep" (so *OED* 2).

132–33. *Charm'd with Arcadian Pipe, the Pastoral Reed / Of Hermes, or his opiate Rod:* see also *Arc* 28, 95 and *Mask* 341. Much of this passage refers to an episode in Ovid's *Metamorphoses* in which Mercury (Hermes) charms Argos asleep with his pipe and rod and then beheads him (1.713–19), having told the story of Pan creating the shepherd's pipe, Syrinx, from the transformed nymph he loved (1.689–712). It may seem fantastic to link the cherubim with the 100-eyed Argus, but Io was allegorized as the horned moon, and Natale Conti recorded many commentators who regarded the 100 eyes of her supervisor as signifying the stars, which never cease to maintain their watch upon the earth (8.18) (Hughes, "Variorum").

opiate Rod: Mercury's *caduceus,* olive wood entwined by two serpents, is said to confer sleep (*Odyssey* 24.2–4); cf. Spenser's *Faerie Queene* 2.12.40–41, where the Palmer's staff is made from the same material.

opiate: the word may be derived from the *medicata* of Ovid's *Metamorphoses* 1.716 (Verity).

Arcadian: "belonging to Arcadia; ideally rural or rustic" (so *OED*). Arcadia is the Greek region mythically associated with pastoral poetry.

133. *Mean while:* Johnson includes these two words among those he finds inharmonious because their break with the rest of the line allows no "associate sounds to make them harmonious" (*Rambler* 4 [Jan. 26, 1751]: 112); see also *PL* 11.73–76.

134–35. *To resalute the World with sacred Light / Leucothea wak'd:* critics supply extensive information on *Leucothea* (Greek, "white goddess"), the earliest morning, preceding Aurora, which is purple or gold. See Lucretius, *De rerum natura* 5.656. The term is *matuta* in Latin; cf. *PL* 11.175. Wesley glosses Leucothea as "Dawn of Day." Leucothea was admired by Apollo, who could not save her from death and who sprinkled nectar and ambrosia on her tomb, from which grew the tree that bears frankincense (Cann 238). Keightley, who correctly identifies Leucothea as Ino, the daughter of Cadmus, complains that "the Latins rather strangely identified her with their Mater Matuta, whose name also signifies *Bright-goddess,* but who was really the goddess of the Dawn. . . . Milton stands alone in giving the office of Matuta to Leucothea." Hughes (*Paradise Lost*), however, finds this identification in Ovid's *Fasti* 6.545: "Leucothea Grais, Matuta vocaberis nostris" (You will be called Leucothea by the Greeks, and Matuta by us). Fowler adds that she belongs here because, according to Ovid, *Fasti* 6.481–82, "She keeps handmaidens afar from the threshold of her temple" (famulas a limine templi / arceat); Fowler additionally claims that Milton's *embalmed* is sinister now, since humankind is decaying. Himes (*Paradise Lost: A Poem*) claims that in *Odyssey* 5.346–47, the veil that Leucothea supplies Odysseus is of "heavenly woof."

Critics also comment on temporal issues in this passage. Although Addison reports that the action of the poem on earth comprises ten days (*Spectator* 3 [May 3, 1712]: 391), Newton thinks that this final morning marks the eleventh day, though he cautions that Milton's chronology is somewhat obscured. Cope specifies that this morning is the last temporal shifting of the light and dark setting he traces; it will last — properly — until Adam's eyes have been truly opened in book 12 (142). Stapleton (734–48), arguing that Milton's use of narrative time in the final four books pushes the narrative forward and enlivens some of its most memorable passages, identifies this passage as part of a careful temporal sequence that comprises 9.58–67, 399–403, 1188; 10.92–95, 329, 342–44, 845–46; 11.134–35, 204, 252–55; 12.1–2, 463–67, 471–73, 553–57, 588–94, and 629–32. Similarly, Knott compares the tentative expectations of this daybreak ("joy, but with fear yet linkt" [11.139]) with Adam's delight at the prospect of the daybreak of Christ's Resurrection described by Michael in *PL* 12.420–23 ("Pastoral Day" 178–79). Le Comte compares this passage with the dawning in 9.192.

135. *fresh dews:* cf. 1.771.

136–207. B. A. Wright finds this scene, with Adam and Eve's optimistic longing to stay in the garden, to be an effective introduction to all that follows; it is pathetic, and it clearly shows their need for instruction (*Milton's "Paradise Lost"* 194).

137. *ended now thir Orisons, and found:* cf. the customary morning orisons, or prayers, of 5.145. 1667 has a comma after *found*.

138–39. *but with fear yet linkt:* Stoll, arguing that the end of the epic represents the human condition, a "mingled web, good and ill together," cites this passage as one of the continual preparations for that end ("From the Superhuman" 14); see also *PL* 11.290–91, 553–54; 12.473–78, 614–19. Burden links this passage with Adam's expression of doubt in 12.473; in both places, joy and woe are subtly balanced (199).

138. *Strength added from above:* the Richardsons link the natural progression of regeneration to the progression of dawn. On Milton's exposition of prevenient grace, see Patrides' comment in **11.22–23**.

139. Some copies of the first edition have a comma after *linkt* and some a semicolon.

140. *Which thus to Eve his welcome words renewd:* Keightley glosses this line as "which feelings of hope and joy his words 'renewed' in, brought back to, the mind of Eve," but Verity has "which feeling [of joy] made him address Eve again." Joseph judges that Adam's subsequent eloquence results from his impressive peace of heart (282); see also Joseph comment in **11.117**.

141–79. This "brief drama … indicates the reciprocal responsibilities, powers, and duties of man and wife" and finds that their hopes vary with their personalities: Adam's is rational, Eve's good but delusional, with "the right tone of penitence but the wrong deduction" (Radzinowicz 39).

141–61. Roland Mushat Frye claims to find a "three-fold reconciliation" implicit in this passage, to match three alienations suffered by fallen humanity—persuasion, peace, reorientation—and that will abrogate Satan's conquest (84–85).

141–50. Benson (58) praises the prosody of this passage: the soft beginning caused by the assonance of *Eve* and *easily* and the alliteration of the next five words on the same vowel, *a* (though the vowel sounds actually vary between /e/,

/ae/, and /a/); the solemn pause after *But* in 143 with the caesura on *us* in the same line and *yet* in 146, and the placement of *Kneel'd* in 150, which suggests the action. Samuel claims a similar willingness of heaven to be influenced in *Purgatorio* 6.28–42 and *Paradiso* 20.94–99 (*Dante* 247).

141–48. Wesley notes this passage as among those particularly excellent.

141. *easily may Faith admit:* on unclear grammatical grounds, Bentley wants "easily *it* may Faith admit." Todd emends *may* to *my.* Fowler claims that this mention of *Faith* indicates a new phase in Adam's regeneration; on contrition, see **11.90**.

142. *good...from Heav'n descends:* according to James 1:17, "Every good gift and every perfect gift is from above." There is no period in 1667 after *descends,* which is flush to the margin.

143–46. *But that from us ought should ascend to Heav'n...Hard to belief may seem:* as Himes (*Paradise Lost: A Poem*) points out, the second part of faith is to believe that God "is a rewarder of them that diligently seek him" (Heb. 11:6).

144–45. *the mind / Of God:* cf. *PL* 5.117.

144. *prevalent:* both Hume and Bush gloss this word as "powerful." Fowler supplies "efficacious, influential, powerful," citing *OED* 1b.

146–48. Stoll, arguing for a modulated descent to the human at the close of the epic, claims that even the speeches of God and the Son are less exalted than earlier ("From the Superhuman" 14).

146. *Hard to belief may seem; yet:* Fish claims that this sequence of words "contains all the linguistic signs of faith, the independence of belief from what seems logical and from appearances ('may seem'), and the willingness to break out of the visibly relevant to another level of discourse ('yet')" (277).

147. *short sigh of humane breath:* see varieties of prayer in **11.5–7**.

148–53. Keats notes this passage in his copy of Newton's edition of *PL* (Wittreich 545).

148–52. Citing Ps. 38:15 and 86:7, the Richardsons remark that God is swift to answer prayer for pardon and acceptance.

148. *the Seat of God:* cf. the *Mercie-seat* of *PL* 11.2. Buff (36) claims a reference here to Homer's θεῶν ἕδος, "abode of the gods"; cf. *Iliad* 5.868.

150. *Kneel'd and before him:* on prayer postures, see **11.1–2**. Wesley omits this line.

151–52. *placable and mild, / Bending his eare:* MacCallum finds Adam's "wishful, partially vain, optimism" a sign that the humans' change of heart has been inconclusive, as is Eve's in 11.180; their attitude, though it arouses pity and even respect, is both unrealistic—ignoring the new reality they have caused—and also terribly insecure, as it easily leads to despair ("Milton and Sacred History" 161).
  Placable: "appeasable" (Wesley).

152–58. Because Adam is convinced that God is placable and mild, he can conjecture on matters less certain (Fish 277).

152. *Bending his eare:* Patrides underscores the role of hearing, both God's and man's, in redemption (*Milton* 208–09).
  perswasion in me grew: cf. *DocCh* 1.20, where "saving faith" is equated with "a full persuasion operated in us through the gift of God, whereby we believe…that whatsoever things he has promised in Christ are ours" (Maurice Kelley 169; Patterson, *Works* 15:393). This passage is also noted by Lewalski (30), who argues that according to that section of the treatise, Adam's faith here is not yet "saving" but "implicit," which can be a stage in the faith of "novices or first converts…[who] believe even before they have entered upon a course of instruction" (Patterson, *Works* 15:397).

153–54. *peace returnd / Home to my Brest:* cf. *PL* 9.1125–26.

154–58. *memorie...thee:* Purcell notes that these lines rhyme with three intervening lines (172), a rhyme category also mentioned by Diekhoff ("Rhyme" 542) but without specifics.

154. *Brest:* 1667 *brest.*

155. *thy Seed shall bruise our Foe:* for the oft-repeated promise of Gen. 3:15, see **11.115–16.** In 1953, Parish marks these verses as the "final step in solving the riddle of the curse" ("Pre-Miltonic Representations" 24), though in 1959 he places the recognition moment just before *PL* 12.469 ("Milton" 246–47); he also identifies similar uses of dramatic irony in Sophocles' *Oedipus the King,* since in both texts the audience immediately understands the ambiguous oracle, though to opposite effect, since in the Greek play increased understanding means increased horror, whereas in *PL* it means mounting joy ("Milton" 241).

156. *Which then not minded in dismay:* Bentley wants "*less* minded," since Adam did in fact mind it in *PL* 10.1030, but Pearce argues that the earlier passage speaks of remembering it later, not minding it then.

157–58. *the bitterness of death / Is past, and we shall live:* a Hebraism for "bitter death" (Hughes, *Paradise Lost*). Adam's short-lived assurance will quickly be dashed (182–98), undercut by his echoing the words that the Amalekite king Agag spoke immediately before being slain by the prophet Samuel (1 Sam. 15:32–33), as various commentators note. Brisman finds Adam's desire for quick resolution typical of both his fallen state and his youthfulness, while Eve tries not to rush the consummation (273–74). Reesing links Adam's false conclusion to his earlier discovery of prayer's efficacy and argues that this moment is the first in the "detailed local pattern of Adam's experience from now on," that of "a new insight, from which he moves to a false conclusion, which then has to be corrected, which in turn starts the sequence over again" (54). Summers points out the touching ironies: "Everything that Adam says is true, but none of it true in the sense which he imagines. The 'bitterness of death' is truly past, but not the fact of death; they will live, but not as Adam thinks" (*Muse's Method* 192).

158–59. *Whence Haile to thee, / Eve rightly call'd, Mother of all Mankind:* this passage has occasioned much comment. Adam calls his wife Eve (Hebrew, *chavvah,* "life-giver") in Gen. 3:20, whereas in Gen. 2:23 he had initially called her *ishshah* (Hebrew, "woman") because taken out of *ish* (Hebrew, "man"), as in *PL* 8.496. Newton claims that Milton called her Eve earlier in the epic "in anticipation," apparently assuming that Milton intended to observe the biblical timetable of naming. Milton follows most biblical commentators who argue that the name is not ironic but a response to the redemptive promise of Gen. 3:15 (the "seed" of the "woman"). Eve is called *Mother of human Race* in 4.475, and Raphael hails her as "mother of mankind" in 5.388, a name also used by the narrator in 1.36. Adam's words to Eve directly after "the bitterness of death is past" recall the angel Gabriel's annunciation to the Virgin Mary in Luke 1:28; as a seventeenth century Protestant, Milton characteristically implies that the Virgin is no more important than Eve in the plan of salvation (Parish, "Pre-Miltonic Representations" 24). Stroup, linking the epic to Christian liturgy, calls this passage Adam's "Ave Eva" (44–45). Kermode (89–90) is reminded of Lucretius's *Venus genetrix,* "per te quoniam genus omne animatum / concipitur" (for by thee all living things are conceived); cf. *De rerum natura* 1.4–5. Hutcherson points out that *Mother of all Mankind* is Adam's last epithet for Eve in the epic (260). Steadman traces "the validity and significance of titles" as primary considerations in Milton's argument of nobility; Eve's epithet is earned, but not the empty titles of the giants in 11.793 or Nimrod's in 12.33–35 or of the "wolves" who succeed for teachers in the church in 12.515–16 (*Milton's Epic Characters* 272). Summers finds the *Hail* startling, as it embodies what Adam knows but also shows his ignorance of how many centuries will follow before the second Eve (*Muse's Method* 192). Ryken includes epithets for Adam and Eve as one of Milton's means of distancing them from the reader, as he does for *our Ancestor* in 11.546 (183).

160–61. Wesley omits these lines.

161. *all things live for Man:* Todd cites John Bowle's reference to Zanchius's *De operibus sex dierum* (1632), "Dicamus de homine cujus causâ reliqua omnia, praesertim vero visibilia, creata esse creduntur" (We say it must be believed that for the sake of man were created all that is, especially visible things) (602) and "Omnia hominis causâ facta et condita sunt" (For the sake of man all things were made and founded) (604).

162–71. Pecheux argues that Milton fuses "with consummate skill" the first Eve with the second (the Virgin Mary); Eve "glides easily from her literal role as the one who 'first brought Death on all' to her typical role as one who 'grac't / The sourse of life.'" Pecheux describes this Eve passage as the second of three milestones "on the inner journey from innocence to regeneration," the first being Eve's offer to bear the punishment alone in 10.914–36, and the third being her "lead on" in 12.614 ("Concept" 364).

162. *sad demeanour meek:* this phrase exhibits Milton's favorite word order (Verity).

164–65. *thee ordaind / A help:* cf. Gen. 2:18 and also the *help* in 8.450 and the *meet* in 8.448. Fletcher links Eve's comment to Milton's other attempts to show the full meaning of the Hebrew phrase translated "help meet" (*Milton's Rabbinical Readings* 173–75).

164. *transgressour:* "one who transgresses; a law-breaker; a sinner" (so *OED*).

166. *distrust:* "the fact of being distrusted; loss of credit" (so *OED* b).

167. *dispraise:* "disparagement; blame, censure" (so *OED* 1).

168–69. *am grac't / The sourse of life:* i.e., have received the grace or favor to be (Keightley). Cf. "grace," "to name or designate honourably" (so *OED* 5b). Kermode finds Eve's statement to be "a paradox more central to the mood of the poem than the famous *felix culpa*" (120); cf. **12.469–78.** Shawcross finds three occurrences of the spelling *sourse* (the others being in 10.832 and 12.13 [*sours*]) against one of *source* in 4.750 ("Orthography" 132).

171–72. *But the Field / To labour calls us now:* Himes (*Paradise Lost: A Poem*) sees Eve's concern for labor as a first sign of her penitence, citing St. Paul's exhortation to women in 1 Tim. 5:14, yet Eve fell not in the course of what Himes calls "idle wanderings" but rather through just such a concern with their agricultural tasks.

172. *with sweat impos'd:* Fowler reminds us that agricultural labor is the curse of Adam; cf. *PL* 10.205 and Gen. 3:19.

173–75. *the Morn, … Her rosie progress smiling:* many commentators from Newton have cited Lucretius, *De rerum natura* 5.656–57, where the white morning gives way to rose, "roseam Matuta per oras / aetheris auroram differt" and also *1 Henry 4:* "the heav'nly-harnass'd team / Begins his golden progress in the east" (3.1.218–19). Osgood (14–15), who notices that Milton also uses *rosy* to describe morning in *PL* 5.1 and 6.3, compares the *rosie progress* of the morning to Night's *gloomy progress* driven away by dawn in *Orphic Hymn* 77.4. Ricks finds tension in these lines; Milton is partly reviving a dead metaphor, but partly also reminding us of the ominous possibilities—the apples brought back by fallen Eve in 9.851 also *smil'd* (*Milton's Grand Style* 58–59).

    Rosie: "having the crimson or pink colour of a rose; rose-coloured, rose-red" (so *OED* A1a).

    Progress: "onward movement following a prescribed course, in a specific direction, or towards a particular place" (so *OED* 6b).

176. *I never from thy side henceforth to stray:* Pecheux claims that Eve means this both literally and metaphorically, since Adam's side had been her native home, as dust was Adam's ("Abraham" 366). Eve's sincerity here contrasts with the duplicity of her proposal to Adam in 9.214 that they divide their labors (Tillyard, *Studies in Milton* 17).

177–78. Wesley omits these lines.

178–79. *while here we dwell, / What can be toilsom:* Eve corrects what she has just said about the day's labor, supposing that the toil would be alleviated by the charms of paradise (Keightley). Eve's response to exile is human, while Adam's is theological (Williamson 106).

    toilsom: "characterized by or involving toil; laborious, tiring" (so *OED* 1).

178. *droop:* with the sun, day, etc., "to decline, draw to a close" (so *OED* 2, now poetic).

180. *Here let us live, though in fall'n state, content:* cf. Adam's misplaced optimism above and **11.151–52**. Summers finds that this scene anticipates the characteristic pattern of Adam's too easy reconciliation to the present moment as the final end (*Muse's Method* 193).

content: Sims (*Bible* 270) cites Phil. 4:11: "I have learned, in whatsoever state I am, therewith to be content."

181–86. This passage demonstrates Milton's consistent spelling of *-d* for the preterite and *-t* for the participle; he uses spelling in his intricate sentences to help distinguish verbal forms (Darbishire, *Poetical Works* 1:xxxi–xxxii).

181–84. *So spake...short blush of Morn:* Benson cites these four lines to demonstrate the superiority he claims English poetry has over French, as French would require the addition of nine particles: *le, la, des, les, les, le, le, un, du* (75).

182–90. *Nature first gave Signs:* this passage has occasioned extensive commentary. Addison praises it for combining "great and just Omens" with the enmity now produced in nature and having the sun's eclipse prepare for the brilliant angelic light in the west (*Spectator* 3 [Apr. 26, 1712]: 359). Himes (*Paradise Lost: A Poem*) claims that in Job 9:26 "the eagle that hasteth to the prey" represents the shortness of life, and the hunt of the "fierce lion" (Job 10:16) God's judgment on sin. Edward Chauncey Baldwin lists this passage as the last of four in which Milton has nature express crucial parts of the epic action, the others being the consummation of Adam and Eve's marriage in 8.511, Eve's transgression in 9.782, and Adam's transgression in 9.1000 ("Some Extra-Biblical Semitic Influences" 377). Bøgholm claims that while an omen in the classical epic was an uncorrelated fact, in *PL* it becomes a "sympathy" in the etymological sense, a suffering enveloping humanity and nature in one condemnation (83–84). Verity thinks that Wordsworth alludes to this passage in "The Redbreast Chasing the Butterfly" ("Could Father Adam open his eyes / And see this sight beneath the skies, / He'd wish to close them again" [12–14]). Bush judges that "these first signs of nature red in tooth and claw" also anticipate the expulsion of Adam and Eve. Cf. the natural changes already announced in *PL* 10.651–715; similar changes in nature occur in Andreini's *L'Adamo* 4.4 (101–04). Butler cites this passage in his discussion of Milton's "formidable" way of ascribing sentience to nature; the "pathetic fallacy," though distrusted by New Critics, is common in earlier English poetry (269–72, 275); see also **11.336–37**. Ferry links the signs in nature's wheel to the broken circle of divinely established moral order, as "terms in a single metaphor" (*Milton's Epic Voice* 164–65).

Gardner praises Milton's first illustrator, Medina, for his background details in the plate to book 11 (*Reading* 127–28); the "finely filled in" background shows the "Signs, imprest / On Bird, Beast, Aire" (*PL* 11.182–83), the low-ering sky, the eagle diving down on two birds, and the lion pursuing the two hinds ("Milton's First Illustrator" 34); see also **11.239–40** and **12.643–44**. C. H. Collins Baker complains that Richard Westall's 1794–95 illustration for book 11, "The Change in Nature," makes "the smallest use" of its topic; Baker also notes that in Tonson's 1720 edition of *PL,* the "tail-piece" to book 11 (i.e., the ornament at its ending) is "Strife among Birds and Beasts" by Chéron and Gucht (5, 13, 109). Peter, who finds unsatisfactory the presentation of the Deity in the last books, also claims that "the eagle and the lion are obviously meant to symbolize God, and it is noteworthy that Milton should represent his justice so harshly, as something predatory and cruel" (146). Svendsen points out that the movement of the prey is downward, "even as Adam and Eve were hastened by Michael to the subjected plain" (*Milton and Science* 159). Unlike many of his contemporaries, Milton did not generally assume that all apparent disorders in the earth presaged evil, though if they were clearly from God he accepted them as divinely purposed (Patrides, *Milton* 79). Fowler asserts that in all three signs, "the sovereign of a realm of creation"—i.e., sun, eagle, lion—"displays his power in a changed and grimmer form," that the lion's pursuit recalls Satan's stalking his prey in 4.402, and that the two pair of beasts correspond to the human couple. Empson praises the "imaginative stroke" of Milton's having Adam see the animals of paradise begin to eat each other, the first sign of the harm he has done to the world, before he is told the harm he has done to all his descendants (*Milton's God* 190).

182. *Subscrib'd not:* i.e., assented not. "*Subscribere,* to underwrite, thence to agree to.... Milton often uses words according to the Latin idiom" (Newton). Cf. Angelo in *Measure for Measure:* "Admit no other way to save his life, / As I subscribe not that" (2.4.88–89). Cf. Milton's "Hope would fain subscribe" (*SA* 1535). Peter says that this is one place where Milton makes an effort to palliate the impression left by God, since here he attributes his inflexibility to "Fate" (148).

183. *Aire suddenly eclips'd:* Bentley finds this phrase "unwarrantable" and emends to "Aire suddenly *obscur'd.*" But Pearce observes that Milton uses *Eclipses* in *PL* 2.667 for *grows dark* or *appears dark.* Hughes (*Paradise Lost*) judges that Milton is at the point of narrating the blight on Edenic life consequent to the postlapsarian "influence malignant" of heavenly bodies (10.662). Cf. Milton's own use of eclipse as ill omen in *PL* 1.597, *Lyc* 101, and *HistBr:* "The same year was seen an Eclips of the Sun in May, followed by a sore pestilence" (Patterson, *Works* 10:169). Northrop Frye (*Paradise Lost*) glosses *eclips'd* as "darkened by pollution," citing 10.413. Cf. the darkened sky of the fallen world in Avitus, where "The day itself grows dim" (Kirkconnell 17).

184.   *blush:* "a rosy colour or glow, as that of the dawn" (so *OED* 5).

    nigh in her sight: since Adam was also present, Bentley wants "nigh in *their* sight." Newton argues that it is only afterward, in 11.191 that *Adam observ'd.*

185.   *Bird of Jove:* "eagle" (so *OED* 7), well known as sacred to Jupiter (cf., e.g., Shakespeare's *Cymbeline* 4.2.348, 5.3.42, and 5.4.113, 115). It is also a bird of ill omen (Homer, *Iliad* 12.200–09 and *Odyssey* 15.160); in Virgil's *Aeneid* 12.247–56, the eagle gives false hopes.

    stoopt from his aerie tour: commentators since Hume have noted that *stoop* is a term from falconry. Todd cites Latham, *Booke of Falconrie* (1615): "Stooping is when a hawk, being upon her wings at the height of her pitch, bendeth violently down to strike the...prey." Wesley glosses *aerie tour* as "whirling about in the air." Keightley and Verity have all argued for *tower* instead of *tour* (wheel), Verity doing so at some length, educing the lofty flight of the eagle, the similar "watch-tower" of the lark (*L'All* 43), and Milton's own irregular spelling in first editions (*PL* 2.635 has "touring high," and *PR* 2.280 has "high towring").

186–189.   *Two Birds...Hart and Hinde:* Keightley compares the omen to the two groups of swans in Virgil's *Aeneid* 1.393–401, but that omen is a happy one. Thompson, arguing that the last two books of the epic are necessary partly because Adam needs some experience before he goes into the world, cites this passage as one example of this experience; until the ravages of the bird and the beast of prey and the slaying of Abel, Adam has no conception of death ("For *Paradise Lost*" 378). The transformation of the eagle and the lion into hunters anticipates the change in human society that begins with Nimrod in *PL* 12.24–37 (N. Frye, *Paradise Lost*).

187.   *the Beast that reigns in Woods:* i.e., the lion, king of beasts. "The Lion Hunting" is one of five illustrations for book 11 in Tilt's 1843 illustrated edition of Milton's *Poetical Works* (C. H. C. Baker 116); see also **11.366–68, 445–47, 582**, and **855–60**, as well as **12.1–5** for a list of book 12's illustrations from Tilt.

188–91. *brace…chase:* one of the 52 instances of rhyming lines with two intervening nonrhyming lines (Diekhoff, "Rhyme" 541–42); see Purcell for additional instances (172).

188. *hunter:* 1667 *Hunter.*

190. *Direct to th'Eastern Gate was bent thir flight:* as Newton observes, these signs also foreshadow Adam and Eve being "driven out" at the eastern gate of paradise.

193–95. Patrides (*Milton* 79) argues that Adam's observation here is distinctly more cautious than Raphael's earliest assurance that the natural order is "the Book of God" (*PL* 8.67).
   by these mute signs in Nature: Hume links this passage to augury because of the flight of birds, one focus of ancient fortune-telling.

196. *too secure:* i.e., feeling too certain of (Verity). "Over-confident" (Fowler). "Cf. *secure* as God applies it to Adam in 5.238" (Hughes, "Variorum").

199–200. *we are dust / And thither must return:* cf. Gen. 3:19, "Dust thou art, and unto dust shalt thou return." Sims (*Bible* 270) also cites Eccles. 3:20: "All go unto one place; all are of the dust, and all turn to dust again."

200. *and be no more:* Adam did not yet know about the soul's immortality, though he feared it in 10.782–866.

203–41. Michael's gradually unveiled arrival portrays "apocalypse through distance" (Ryken 159–60).

203–07. Wordsworth's marginal comment on these lines records that Gray, by making his bards "vanish in a bright track instead of a murky cloud," has "lost that contrast which is so striking in Milton's." Moreover, since Gray was describing "a grisly band with bloody hands," a troubled, gloomy sky would have been more appropriate (Wittreich 107).

203. *the self-same hour:* in Matt. 8:13, the centurion's servant was healed "in the selfsame hour" (Sims, *Bible* 270).

204–06. *light…white:* one of 45 instances found by Diekhoff in the epic where two lines rhyme with one intervening nonrhyming line; he also notes *sight* in 201 ("Rhyme" 540). See Purcell for additional instances (171).

204–05. *Morning light / More orient in yon Western Cloud:* Todd suggests that Milton may have been thinking of masques performed during his youth, such as Carew's *Coelum Britannicum,* presented at Whitehall on February 18, 1633, with music by Henry Lawes, and including the descent from heaven in "a pleasant cloud, bright and transparent," after which more clouds appear in which are seated Religion, Truth, and other allegorical characters. Milton may have known Carew's poems, several of which were set to music by Lawes (Keightley), though Montgomery finds the imagery commonplace in both drama and poetry. Keightley also observes that Michael enters paradise from the west, as Adam would be sent out at the east. "The brightness in the west emanates from Michael's 'Cohort bright / Of watchful Cherubim' (11.127–28). Their glory is brighter than dawn, as Michael's is in Tasso's *Gerusalemme liberata* (18.92.3–4) when he appears to Godfrey 'In pure and heav'nly armour richly dress'd, / Brighter than Titan's rays in clearest skies'" (Hughes, "Variorum").

orient: "brilliant, radiant, resplendent" (*OED* 1b; obsolete, chiefly literary and poetic). Wesley glosses *more orient* as "more bright." Fowler records the pun on *orient* as "eastern," which is here paradoxical, as the light comes from the west.

204. *Darkness ere Dayes mid-course:* various commentators pick up Hume's citation of Ovid, *Metamorphoses* 1.602–03, where Jupiter by clouds creates night in day to hide Io, and several commentators since Todd have cited Marino's *Adone* 2.67, which describes the descent of the three goddesses upon Mt. Ida. Todd, after Bowle, also cites Isa. 16:3, "make thy shadow as the night in the midst of the noonday," which as a call for merciful hiding of fugitives might be relevant.

Cope compares "the ambiguous confusion of light and darkness" here to the analogous confusion that closes the poem at the eastern gate of paradise (144). Stapleton sees the darkness as a telling sign to Eve that morning is not a signal to return to their customary labor (745); see **11.134–35**. MacCaffrey compares this darkness brought by an unfallen angel to the earlier "pitchy cloud / Of Locusts" (1.340–41); that "darksome cloud" will return in 12.185. Ferry sees it as "the shattering of nature's cycle, the transformation of benevolent order into frightening unpredictability" (*Milton's Epic Voice* 165).

208. *He err'd not:* Fish finds the narrator's comment increasingly ironic in retrospect, given how many times Adam is wrong in the following episodes (277).

209. *Down from a Skie of Jasper:* the light from this gem figures in biblical similes for heaven: the one seated on heaven's throne looks like jasper in Rev. 4:3, and the heavenly city has a light like jasper in Rev. 21:11; the pavement of heaven is like a "sea of jasper" in *PL* 3.363. Since the modern-day jasper, a variety of quartz, typically ranges from brick to dark red, some other stone is probably meant. Collett thinks that Milton's mention of a gem further links Michael's coming to the "wheels / Of Beril" (*PL* 6.755–56) in the chariot of paternal deity and thus with the "double Janus" (96); see **11.129**.

    lighted: "descended" (*OED* 6a), but also, as Fowler supplies, "shone."

210. *made alt:* Addison has *halt* (*Spectator* 3 [Apr. 26, 1712]: 360), as does Wesley, though the Richardsons call the usage nonsense, identifying this phrase as "pure Italian" (*far alto*, "to stop," military). The usage, now obsolete, is attested in *OED alt*[1], from the French *faire alte*.

211–12. *glorious Apparition…doubt / And carnal fear that day dimm'd Adams eye:* Bentley thinks *fear* must be *film*, as in *PL* 11.412, but Pearce contrasts *carnal fear* with the "godly fear" of Heb. 12:28 and also insists that *doubt* works better with *fear* than with *film;* cf. the filial fear of 12.305–06. Burke adds that doubt must be replaced by faith (211). The speaker's sight and judgment are truer than Adam's fallen perceptions and are therefore the measure of meaning in the epic (Ferry, *Milton's Epic Voice* 48–49). Fowler glosses *carnal fear* as "fleshly fear; the animal's terror of the spiritual." Milton links "carnall feare" to "carnall desires" in *Animad* and contrasts to "spirituall valour" (Hughes,

"Variorum"); cf. Patterson, *Works* 3:110. Appearances of the term *carnal* in the KJV, all from the Greek *sarx* or *sarkikos* (fleshly), refer to physical and therefore unregenerate human nature; see Rom. 7:14, 8:7, 15:27; 1 Cor. 3:1, 3, 4; 9:11; 2 Cor. 10:4; Heb. 7:16, 9:10.

214–20. Though careful not to claim that Milton used rabbinical sources, William B. Hunter reports that the medieval Jewish commentator Maimonides mentions both the Mahanaim and Dothan episodes when discussing prophecy ("Prophetic Dreams" 281). Martz argues that since these allusions to divine power foreshadow Michael's assurance of God's omnipresence, they serve proleptically to moderate Adam and Eve's horror at the news of their expulsion (144). Milton also includes Jacob's earlier dream vision of the "guardians bright" (*PL* 3.512).

Mahanaim: in Gen. 32:1–2, Jacob sees God's angels sent to protect him from his brother Esau; he calls the place *Mahanaim* (Hebrew, "two camps"). It was later a city located east of the Jordan and north of the river Jabbok (Gilbert, *Geographical Dictionary* 181). Twenty years earlier, Jacob had dreamed of angels (Gen. 28:12), as noted in *PL* 3.510–15; "Jacob's guardian angels are encamped like th'Angelic Throng' encamped in 'Pavilions numberless' and 'sudden reard, / Celestial Tabernacles' (5.650–64)" (Hughes, "Variorum"). Milton may also intend here to signify God's mercy in judgment, since King David, fleeing his murderous son Absalom, was hospitably received in Mahanaim rather than languishing in the wilderness (2 Sam. 17:27–29). The Mahanaim simile, by following that of Dothan, creates a pairing similar to Homeric practice (Whaler, "Compounding" 317).

Guardians bright: Milton does not espouse the Catholic idea of guardian angels; Jacob's angels are not treated as though theirs was a routine assignment (West, *Milton and the Angels* 132).

Dothan: a city about ten miles north of ancient Samaria (Gilbert, *Geographical Dictionary* 106). Cf. 2 Kings 6:17, where Elisha's servant sees the mountain full of angels sent to protect the prophet from the Syrian army sent solely against him. To Milton's "Bible-wise generation" *Dothan* would have evoked an entire segment of 2 Kings, which evocation Milton "controls and concentrates" in the following lines to satisfy readers' memories and permit them to return to the main tale (Whaler, "Miltonic Simile" 1059–60).

215. *The field Pavilion'd:* i.e., tented. Wesley glosses as "cover'd with tents." Todd, after Bowle, cites Shakespeare: "And lie pavilioned in the fields of France" (*Henry V* 1.2.129). Verity judges that Milton is repeating his own paraphrase of Ps. 3, where David "fled from Absalom," who was "encamping round about…pitch[ing] against me their Pavilions" (17–18; cf. the phrasing of Ps. 3:6 in the KJV: "ten thousands of people…have set themselves against me round about"). The parallel may be significant, as David was camped in Mahanaim at the time (2 Sam. 17:27).

216. *flaming Mount:* cf. *PL* 5.598.

218–20. Wesley reduces this passage to a single line: "Against the Syrian King. The Hierarch," glossing *Hierarch* as "The Holy Prince."

219. *One man:* cf. the *one just man* of 11.818.
  Assassin-like: Bush glosses as "treacherously" and B. A. Wright as "in the manner of a treacherous attacker" ("Note" 148).

220–21. *Warr unproclaim'd:* Newton cites William Warburton's notion that Milton was referring to the war against Holland and to Whig protests that the English took the Dutch fleet at Bordeaux before war was proclaimed.
  unproclaim'd: so *OED;* cf. "proclaimed," "Publicly and officially announced; publicly declared; designated in a proclamation" (*OED* 1).
  Hierarch: according to Gage, "In the singular, 'hierarch' refers to a member of the higher orders; in the plural to the host as a whole" (18). Cf. 5.468, 591, 692; 7.192; 11.220. Raphael is called the "winged Hierarch" in 5.468.
  stand: "station (military)" (Ricks, *"Paradise Lost"*). "Cf. the *stand* of the angelic guards overlooking Eden with Satan's 'loftie stand on that high Tree' (4.395), i.e., 'The middle Tree and highest there that grew' (4.195), to survey all Eden" (Hughes, "Variorum"). Fowler asserts that although *stand* primarily refers to "station" (*OED* 11), its meaning in falconry, "the elevated resting place of a hawk" (*OED* 14) may also be grimly relevant. Cf. "the post or station of a soldier, sentinel, watchman, or the like" (*OED* 12a).
  his Powers: on Milton's names for angels, see **11.101**.

221–22. *to seise…Possession:* Keightley notes that these are legal terms. "To put in possession, invest with the fee simple of" (*OED*).

223. *find:* 1667 *finde.*

225. *Visitant:* "one who pays a visit to another; a visitor….applied to supernatural beings or agencies, etc., esp. as revealing themselves to mortals" (so *OED* 1b).

226. *Eve, now expect great tidings:* Summers points out the irony, since the angel comes to announce exile and to recount sin and death: "Adam will not hear fully the tidings of 'great joy' until he has heard fully those of sorrow" (*Muse's Method* 193).

227. *determine:* i.e., make an end of us (Verity). "To put an end to (in time); to bring to an end; to end, conclude, terminate; now chiefly in law" (*OED* 1).

228. *New Laws:* cf. *PL* 5.679–80.

229. *From yonder blazing Cloud that veils the Hill:* cf. the blazing cloud that veiled Mt. Sinai when God descended to give the law in Exod. 19:18; cf. also the "secret top" of *PL* 1.6 (Richardsons). Ryken identifies this statement as the most explicit among the host of techniques Milton uses to distance his apocalyptic vision from ordinary reality (174).

230–32. *and by his Gate / None of the meanest…Potentate:* Milton stresses the old idea that a man's gait revealed much about him (Todd); cf. the Apocrypha (Ecclus. 19:30), *Aeneid* 1.405, *King Lear* 5.3.176–77 ("Methought thy very gait did prophesy / A royal nobleness"). Cf. also how Eve shows her superiority above all female descendants by her "gate" surpassing "Delia's self" (*PL* 9.388–89) and how with his "gate / And fierce demeanor" Satan—called a "Potentate" in 5.706—revealed himself in 4.870–71 as "Prince of Hell" (Hughes, "Variorum"). Diekhoff lists *Gate/Potentate* as one of the 17 actual couplets in the epic ("Rhyme" 539–40), a number with which Purcell more or less concurs (171). While it is tempting to consider *Potentate* as a synonym for one of the traditional hierarchical divisions of angels, it apparently is only a general term for the higher orders or for any one of them (Gage 18); cf. *PL* 5.363, 749, and 7.198. On Milton's names for angels, see **11.101**.

230. *the heav'nly Host:* cf. *PL* 2.824.

232–36. *such Majestie / Invests him coming…solemn and sublime:* cf. the Lord "clothed with majesty…clothed with strength" in Ps. 93:1; Michael's clothing described in *PL* 11. 240–48 suggests aspects of divinity (Fowler). Compared with Raphael's "easy condescension and free communication," Samuel Johnson finds Michael "regal and lofty, and, as may seem, attentive to the dignity of his own nature" ("Milton" 185); cf. "sociable" Raphael (5.221).

233. *Invests…yet not terrible:* Bentley thinks *not* must be *nor*, as working better with the syntax. Bayly approves Milton's use of *invests* here and in 3.10 and 7.372 but not in 1.208, since he insists that the Latin term always refers to dressing or adorning with glory and authority (278). *OED*, however, attests pejorative English usages of *invest* before Milton, as Davies's "with brutish forms invest" in 1592.

   1667 *coming;* 1672 *coming?*

236–37. *whom not to offend, / With reverence I must meet, and thou retire:* Eve's presence would be indecent without the innocence that allowed her to wait naked on Raphael, as she did in *PL* 5.383–85 (Hume). Peter apparently rejects such a reading, as he credits Michael's readiness to overlook the misogyny attributed to him (29).

   Retire: "to withdraw, go away, remove oneself" (so *OED* 3a). Cf. **11.267**.

238–50. Addison finds the person, port, and behavior of Michael suitable to a spirit of the highest rank, and thus an example of how properly Milton also suits his parts to his actors (*Spectator* 3 [Apr. 26, 1712]: 360). Clements cites this passage as an example of how Milton distinctly and individually renders his main angelic characters, though they do not fit easily into any scheme or classification (292–93). "The term 'archangel' is used of good angels generally in *Paradise Lost*.…[and] frequently applied to the dignitaries of Satan's realm and to Satan himself" (15); the helping angel who appears in 2 Macc. 11:7–10, clad in white clothing with armor of gold and shaking his spear, is a nearer approximation of Milton's Michael here than to Raphael in the book of Tobit, "or any other angel whom mortals might conceivably entertain unawares" (Gage 103); cf. Heb. 13:2. Gardner praises Milton's first illustrator, Medina, for his fidelity to Michael's description and other details from book 11 (*Reading* 127; "Milton's First Illustrator" 34). C. H. Collins Baker also notes that "Michael Comes to Paradise" is the book 11 illustration for a 1758 Italian illustrated edition of *PL;* "Michael Greets Adam" is H. Richter's first 1794 illustration of the two for book 11, "Adam and Eve See Michael Coming" is William Hamilton's illustration for an 1802 edition, and "Adam Descries Michael" is John Martin's design of 1825–27 (17, 19, 102, 113).

238. Wesley indents this line.

239–40. *Man / Clad to meet Man:* cf. Raphael's appearance in his "proper shape" in 5.276. Gage argues that the choice of Michael is "undoubtedly dictated" by the biblical reference to Michael as prince of the Hebrew people (Dan. 12:1), since even though Gabriel is named as an earlier messenger in Dan. 8:16, Michael is the linen-clothed "man" in Dan. 10:5 who explains a vision to Daniel (75–76). Lawry compares Michael to Christ; both appear in the character of king and judge, but also incarnate in order to become redeemer (*Shadow* 274). Cf. the far less humane Michael in Andreini's *L'Adamo,* who comes as "punisher of all / Who disobey our Lord" and has thus put on his "brightest and most dreadful arms" so as to be "resistless" (Kirkconnell 259). Fowler sees the contrast between Raphael's earlier appearance (wings of regal purple, gold, and blue) and Michael's manlike shape as indicating that Michael has come to talk about "terrestrial matters...fallen mundane history" and to prepare Adam for a lowlier role. Hughes ("Variorum") contrasts this picture with the practice of most *PL* illustrators to show him winged, "e.g., L. Chéron (1720), F. Hayman (1749), J. Martin (1823), J. M. W. Turner (1835), and G. Doré (1885). The first illustrator, J. B. Medina (1688) drew him wingless, but in the expulsion scene (12.636–69) gave him a conspicuous pair of wings spread above a most unmilitary robe, and an inappropriately flaming sword. The wingless Michael of J. Isaacs's reprint of the 1667 text is draped in what seems to be a robe of chain mail spangled with flashing discs or eyes (Golden Cockerel Press, 1937). Most illustrations have been in black and white or mezzotint, with no attempt at anything like living color." See also **11.182–90** and **12.643–44.**

239. *shape Celestial:* Ryken identifies "celestial" as the qualifier used most frequently in Milton's description of apocalyptic reality (56–57).

240. *lucid:* "bright, shining, luminous, resplendent" (so *OED* 1). Bush and Ricks (*"Paradise Lost"*) both gloss as "bright," as does Wesley.

241–42. *of purple…Livelier then Melibœan:* Melibœa (modern Kastri), a Thessalian port at the foot of Mt. Ossa, was famous for a purple dye which Lucretius described (*De rerum natura* 2.500) and Virgil (*Aeneid* 5.250–51) as enriching the double border of a magnificent robe (Hughes, "Variorum").

    Livelier: i.e., more vivid (Verity). In Vondel's biblical epic, it is Lucifer who has a "military vest / Of glowing purple with a lustrous sheen" (Edmundson 70). Fletcher (*Complete Poetical Works*) cites the definition of *purpura* in *New World of Words* by Edward Phillips, Milton's nephew: "A Purple Garment, or Scarlet Robe," but in at least the 1658, 1671, 1678, 1696, and 1700 editions, Phillips's only gloss for *purple* (also *purpure*) is "In Heraldry, that color which we commonly call red," which entry is also found in his earlier *New World of English Words* in the 1658, 1662, and 1663 editions.

242–44. Wesley omits these three lines.

    graine: "dye in general, esp. a fast dye; colour, hue. Now only poetic" (*OED* 11). Cf. Raphael's *colors dipt in Heav'n* and *Sky-tinctur'd grain* (5.283, 285) and *Mask* 750–51.

    Sarra: the Latin name for Tsor or Tyre, the Phoenician seaport, known for its purple dye. Cf. Juvenal, *Satires* 10.38–49, Virgil, *Georgics* 2.506 (where "Sarrano" denotes "Syrian purple"), Lucretius, *De rerum natura* 2.500–01, and Pliny, *Natural History* 9.60–65. It might also recall the Tyrian King's promise to Solomon to send "'a man…skilful to work…in purple…and fine linen' to help furnish the temple at Jerusalem (2 Chron. 2.14)" (Hughes, "Variorum"). Himes (*Paradise Lost: A Poem*) says that *sar* is the name of the fish from which the dye was made, but the usage is attested in neither *OED* nor *Oxford Latin Dictionary*, and in Hebrew "sar" means "prince" or "leader."

    Woods finds in the descriptions of angels "a delightful hint of Milton's native love of colour and splendour, a love intensified rather than dulled by his blindness" (65).

243–44. *worn by Kings and Hero's old / In time of Truce:* cf. Raphael's *regal Ornament* (5.280). Robes of state were costliest in peacetime (Montgomery).

Himes notes the mingling of war and peace in Michael's appearance. Purple was both the color of peace and the bloody stain of war; the helmet and sword suggest war, but they are "unbuckled" or sheathed, and the spear is used as a sceptre (*Paradise Lost: A Poem*). Cf. Milton's mention in *Log* 1.11 (Patterson, *Works* 11:97) of Dido's hunting attire, including "Sidonia chlamys, purpurea vestis" (Sidonian cloak and purple clothes). Sidon was a city neighboring Tyre; cf. Virgil, *Aeneid* 4.137–39. Ross argues that Milton is using positive examples to avoid the appearance of inconsistency with his previous descriptions of worldly pomp (*Milton's Royalism* 106).

244. *Iris had dipt the wooff:* the rainbow had dyed the threads before weaving. Iris, the rainbow, was the daughter of Thaumas (wonder) and Electra. Cf. the descent of Iris in Virgil's *Aeneid* 4.700–01 and also of the "mighty angel" in Rev. 10:1 with "a rainbow [ἶρις or iris in Greek]...upon his head." Cf. also "Th'enameld Arras of the Rainbow" in *Nat* 143 and "sky robes spun out of Iris' woof" in *Mask* 83. If there were rain before the Flood, there must have been a rainbow; it was only afterwards that God made it the sign of his promise never again to drown the earth (St. Maur 372). The Iris of Milton, Homer, and the Bible is red, not many-colored, as the translation "rainbow" would imply (Himes, *Paradise Lost: A Poem*). Verity claims probable Miltonic borrowings ("glittering textures," "Dipt," and "tincture of the skies") in Alexander Pope's *Rape of the Lock* 2.63–68.

245–46. *His starrie Helme unbuckl'd shew'd him prime / In Manhood:* the Richardsons note that *starry* is often used by classical poets for anything glittering, but also sometimes to indicate youthfulness, such as Valerius Flaccus's description of Jason's "siderea juventa" (starlike youth) (8.26). Cf. *PL* 5.708, and also the description of Hermes in Homer's *Iliad* 24.347–48 and *Odyssey* 10.278. Himes (*Paradise Lost: A Poem*) cites *Iliad* 19.381–83, where the helmet of Achilles "glittered like a star."

247–48. *the Sword, / Satans dire dread:* cf. 6.250–53, 320–27. The poet Wordsworth's marginal comment points out that either the sword cannot be the huge one that "felled squadrons at once" (6.251) or that angels may also control the size of their swords, which seems to do "to[o] great violence even to the imagination. In fact Milton is perpetually entangled in difficulties respecting the armour he has chosen to give his Angels" (Wittreich 107).

247. *a glistering Zodiac:* the Richardsons claim that the oblique circle of the zodiac was in the form of a shoulder belt generally worn in Milton's time. Hughes (*Paradise Lost*) adds that it also suggests the splendor of the celestial zodiac and the constellations. Fowler rejects such a reading, asserting that the zodiac is mentioned because the belt, like the helm, is *starry,* and also because as the zodiac corresponds to the postlapsarian course of the sun, so Michael's mission relates to the new order of things. Hughes finds that "the cosmic symbolism of Michael's belt is as imposing as the power of his sword, at whose memory the rebel angels trembled in hell (2.294); here the sword, which is the terror of evil angels, is also the attribute of the champion of man who is ready to 'melt with ruth' (*Lyc* 163)" ("Variorum"). Wesley glosses *Zodiac* as "a broad Circle on the Celestial Globe, which marks out the yearly course of the Sun."

248. *and in his hand the Spear:* the Richardsons defend the potential beauty of this passage even while agreeing that it is difficult to know whether the spear was held loosely in Michael's hand, as it is not always clear in *PL* whether verbs govern one noun or more. Keightley names the phrase a *zeugma,* thus arguing for more than one. The absent verb is "a classical and not uncommon ellipsis" (Montgomery). On the mannerist presentation of Michael, see **11.298–300**.

249–50. *hee Kingly from his State / Inclin'd not:* i.e., Adam has bowed, but Michael does not, from the now rare sense of *state* as "dignity of demeanor or presence" (*OED* 18a). Cf. Adam's prelapsarian kingly state in 5.350–57; Adam also bows on that occasion, "as to a superior nature" (5.360).

hee Kingly: B. A. Wright praises the emphatic pronoun followed by an emphatic capital, "doing between them what could not be done so neatly or precisely in any other way" (*Milton's Poems* xxxii).

Inclin'd: Todd cites Bowle at length on this "perfectly Italian" expression, also occurring in, e.g., Spenser's *Faerie Queene* 5.9.34.

251–62. Michael's tone is "exactly right: terse, non-committal, but devoid of all hostility" (Peter 29). Adam spoke first (5.361) in the earlier meeting with Raphael (Fowler).

251. *Heav'ns high behest no Preface needs:* J. R. Brown thinks Milton owes the archaic "high behest" to Spenser, who uses the phrase four times (425).

252–55. *Death / Then due by sentence when thou didst transgress, / Defeated of his seisure:* death in these lines is both personified and abstract (Montgomery). Keightley points out that the terms in lines 253–54 are all from English law.

Defeat: "to do a person out of something expected, or naturally coming to him; to disappoint, defraud, cheat" (so *OED* 7). Cf. "*Law.* To render null and void, to annul" (*OED* 6). Fowler glosses *Defeated of his seisure* as either "frustrated, cheated in his attempt to seize" or "deprived, dispossessed of what he had seized, his seisin." On *seisure,* see **11.221–22.** Stapleton lists the news that Adam has been granted more days of life as structurally and thematically connected to other mentions of time in the last four books (745–46); see **11.134–35.**

252. *Sufficient that thy Prayers are heard:* cf. Isa. 38:5, "Thus saith the LORD…I have heard thy prayer," cited by Gillies and which concerns a penitent whose life has temporarily been spared.

256–57. *one bad act with many deeds well done / Mayst cover:* though Adam is exposed to the effects of original sin, he could still be redeemed by keeping the divine law perfectly (Rom. 10:5; Luke 10:27–28), as is perhaps exemplified by the translation of Enoch and Elijah (Himes, *Paradise Lost: A Poem*). Saurat glosses this passage to mean "Adam himself was saved, having expiated his fault" (148). Sims (*Bible* 270) cites 1 Pet. 4:8 ("charity [i.e., love] shall cover the multitude of sins"), also noted by Fowler.

258. Fowler glosses *quite* as either "completely" (an adverb) or "free, clear, rid of" (an obsolete adjective), i.e., the primary meaning could be either "redeem you completely from death" or else "redeem you as one clear of death." Hughes ("Variorum") argues that "since *quit* and *quite* were alternative spellings for the predicative adjective meaning 'free, clear' (*OED* 1a) of any incurred suffering or legal obligation or claim, it seems better to interpret *quite* as the adjective rather than as the adverb meaning 'completely, wholly, entirely' (*OED* A1)."

260. *Permits not:* i.e., "is not permitted." So glossed by Wesley. Cf. *OED* 5, "To leave undone; to let pass, omit," now obsolete.

261–62. As Newton points out, these lines are taken verbatim from 11.97–98, just as Homer repeats messages in the very words in which they are given, yet here only the last two lines are repeated, and 11.48 is echoed in line 259; Milton thus avoids some of Homer's tediousness, although he must repeat these particular words, since the catastrophe of the poem depends on them." R. C. Browne (1877) cites Homer's twofold repetition of Jupiter's words in *Iliad* 2.11, 28, 65. Bayly translates the syntax as "temper joy and pious sorrow with fear" (295). Peter finds Milton's portrayal of Michael far more coherent than that of God, including how he explicitly follows orders here — "he has a claim on us simply because no specious claims are made on his behalf" (29). Hughes hears an echo of "loss of Eden" (*PL* 1.4), "which has been the overshadowing theme of the poem thus far" ("Variorum").

262. *The ground whence thou wast tak'n, fitter Soile:* Adam was created outside of paradise (8.296–99). The poet Wordsworth asks in a marginal comment why the ground outside paradise was considered fitter than that within (Wittreich 107–08).

263–67. Thyer (in Marchant) finds a contrast between the two reactions; Adam's sorrow is "silent and thoughtful," while Eve's is "loud and hasty." Similarly, B. A. Wright finds the reaction of the pair to be characteristic, since Adam reacts as he did in 9.888–94, and Eve cries out (*Milton's "Paradise Lost"* 194). Bøgholm sees a tendency in Eve to "itching ears" (129); cf. 2 Tim. 4:3.

264. *Heart-strook:* "smitten with mental anguish or dismay" (so *OED* b).
   gripe: "the 'clutch' or 'pinch' of something painful. . . . Spasms of pain, pangs of grief or affliction" (*OED* 2a). Verity glosses as "seizure, spasm." Fowler points out that *gripe* can also mean "tenacious seizing," a sense that Milton uses in *Educ* to describe "all the Locks and Gripes of Wrastling" (Patterson, *Works* 4:288; so *OED* 1a); cf. Adam's earlier stunned astonishment at Eve's fall (9.889–94) as well as Virgil's *Aeneid* 3.259–60, where Aeneas's men have a similar blood-chilling reaction to the harpy Celaeno, and *Aeneid* 4.279–82, where pious Aeneas reacts in horror to the message of Mercury. Todd claims the word *gripe* was "usually" combined with *grief* or *sorrow* in the English Renaissance, as in the "griping grief" in the song from *Romeo and Juliet* (4.5.126), or "gripes of sorrow" in William Browne's *Britannia's Pastorals* (1.3). Sasek finds it "consistent with dramatic decorum" that Adam not express his grief, while Eve can "without impropriety," adding that while Adam weeps later in the epic, it is for

others' griefs and not his own (187). Summers sees Adam's reaction—chilling anxiety extending to horror and despair, numbness and blankness—as a true anticipation of death (*Muse's Method* 193–94).

265–67. Pecheux, arguing that Abraham is a model for Adam through the last two books, draws a parallel with Sarah laughing in her tent (Gen. 18:9–15), especially given the parallels between Gen. 18 and the arrival of the other angel, Raphael, in book 5 ("Abraham" 370).

265. *That:* Bentley thinks *which* would be "less ambitious."

267. *retire:* a substantive for *retirement* (Todd). "Retirement; withdrawal from the world or the society of others" (so *OED* 1, now rare). Milton initially had "solitarie sweet *retire*" (as noun) in *Mask* (Trinity Manuscript) but changed it to "sweet retired solitude" (Verity). Fowler glosses the word as "withdrawal." See **11.236–37**, s.v. *Retire*.

268–85. *Must I thus leave thee Paradise:* Addison praises Eve's lament for expressing not only sentiments appropriate to the subject but also for being particularly "soft and womanish" (*Spectator* 3 [Apr. 26, 1712]: 360). Lauder claims that Milton plagiarized a similar passage in Latin from Grotius's *Adamus Exul* (68–71), but Lauder is not himself to be trusted; see **11.388–411**. Todd thinks Milton had in mind the farewell of Sophocles' title character to his cave in *Philoctetes* 1453–63. Todd also repeats Benjamin Stillingfleet's claim that it is proper that Adam and Eve are initially silent: the awful judgment and its suspension "rendered all words improper"; as Seneca said, "Light cares speak, great ones stupefy" (*Hippolytus* 607). Early commentators have noted a parallel with Euripides' *Alcestis* 244, though as Verity observes, "speeches of farewell are apt to have a family likeness." Hazlitt (in Wittreich) cites this passage as an example of how Milton constructs his poem with numerous passages of "the highest intellectual passion, with little dramatic interest," a pattern he identifies as the poem's reason for excellence (373–74). Eve's claim that the flowers will not grow elsewhere is no figure of speech; the immortal amaranth that bloomed there was a plant of heaven itself (Himes, *A Study* 237); cf. *PL* 3.353–59. Keith claims that the poet's mood here gives consistency and power to the personification (406). Morris judges that the finest among John Christopher Smith's songs for his

1760 setting of *PL* represent Eve's realization that she must leave the garden
(153). Summers points out the underlying and finally comforting naïveté of Eve's
lament, since *bred up* and *rear ye* announce a mother's lament for her children,
but those children are only flowers; moreover, she identifies her human love
with a place—*nuptial bower*—rather than her husband (*Muse's Method* 194).
Dick Taylor Jr., arguing that Milton's epic does not present a fortunate Fall,
cites this passage as proof that Adam and Eve's labor in the garden is positive
and functional ("Milton" 45–46). He also compares Milton's treatment of the
Expulsion to that in preceding hexameral works, which stressed Adam and Eve's
fear of what they faced, whereas "Milton emphasizes the full and beautiful life
that they are leaving behind" ("Milton's Treatment" 76). Ferry sees Eve's lament
as an echo of Milton's own lament for his loss of the world of pastoral nature:
"Adam and Eve, like the fallen reader and the blind poet, are irrevocably cut
off from the light of Eden, the true pattern of pastoral nature, and are forced to
'wander down' into the world of chance and change" ("Bird" 193–94). Wesley
notes this passage as among those particularly excellent.

270. *native Soile:* Eve was born in the garden, being taken out of Adam's side after
he was placed there (Hume); cf. 11.292. Newton cites a Latin tag, "Nescio qua
natale solum dulcedine tangit / Humanos animos" (I do not know how native
soil sweetly touches human souls) without attribution; he is probably referring
to Ovid, *Ex Ponto* 1.3.35–36, "Nescioqua natale solum dulcedine cunctos /
ducit et inmemores non sinit esse sui" (I do not know by what sweetness our
native soil draws us all and does not allow itself to be forgotten).

   these happie Walks and Shades: B. A. Wright records numerous uses of *shade* for
tree in *PL,* in imitation of *umbra* (shade) for *arbor* (tree); that such substitution
is fairly common in Milton's time, and "Milton is only idiosyncratic in his fondness for it" (*Milton's "Paradise Lost"* 70–72). "The overwhelming impression of
the last two books is that man cannot look for any real refuge in the wilderness
of this world...after the Fall" (Knott, "Symbolic Landscape" 54).

271. *happie Walks and Shades, / Fit haunt of Gods:* this line is one of many where
the term *gods* refers to angelic beings rather than to classical gods, as in 11.696
(Banks, "Meaning" 450). Bush points out the unconscious irony of Eve's words,
in view of her former ambition. Ryken finds that Milton often combines the
conceptual term *happy* with a physical description of paradise (200).

272–73. *respit of that day / That must be mortal to us both:* Hughes (*Paradise Lost, A Poem*) glosses as "the remainder of the time granted by God's reprieve of the sentence of physical death."

   Respit: "time granted to one until the coming of a certain date" (so *OED* 5, obsolete). Fowler cites the more general "delay, extension" (*OED* 1).

275. *visitation:* i.e., visit. "The object of a visit" (so *OED* 2b). "Another example of Milton's use of the abstract for the concrete, whether actively or passively (as here)" (Verity). Hughes (*Paradise Lost*) glosses as "objects of visit."

276. *with tender hand:* Bentley insists that Milton wanted the word *tending.*

277. *gave ye names:* cf. God's directing Adam to name all birds and beasts in 8.343–44.

278. *Who now shall reare ye to the Sun, or ranke:* Bentley thinks *or* should be *who,* as being more pathetic.

   ranke: "to arrange (things) in a row or rows; to set in line; to put in order" (*OED* v¹2a). Verity cites the Genius of the Wood in *Arc* 58–59: "I . . . Number my ranks, and visit every sprout."

279. *water from th'ambrosial Fount:* Fowler points out that the fountain of Eden "ran nectar" in 4.240, and provides further instances in visual art where the river or fountain of Eden was conflated with the biblical references to the four rivers of Eden (Gen. 2:10–14) and "living water" (John 4:10).

   ambrosial Fount: cf. a similar fountain in the gardens of the Hesperides (Euripides, *Hippolytus* 742–51). In Milton's "modified empiricism," an empirical noun is modified by an "apocalyptic" adjective (Ryken 56).

280. *Thee lastly nuptial Bowre, by mee adornd:* cf. 8.510. Todd thinks these lines recall Euripides' *Alcestis* 248–49, where the title character looks for the last time on familiar scenes. B. A. Wright (*Milton's Poems* xxvii) judges that the *mee* does not require an emphatic spelling.

   With what to sight or smell was sweet: cf. the sensual description of Eve's preparation of the repast for Raphael (5.337–49).

281–85. Cf. Avitus's description of Adam and Eve's dismay: "Yet ugly seems the world when they compare / Its best with Paradise" (Kirkconnell 17). MacCaffrey (191) finds that Milton's adjectives evoke already established archetypes in the poem: *obscure* (further removed from the fountain of light and the illuminating planets), *wilde* (nature is now hostile), and *Less pure* (loss of brilliant paradise). "Falling floral imagery" such as in 9.892–93 recurs in this passage (Cope 138). Neither Eve nor Adam understands that they already inhabit the lower world because they chose to eat death (Lawry, *Shadow* 274).

281. *wander:* Pecheux links this word with the metaphoric confusion of book 10 after the Fall: *evasions…through Mazes* (829–30), *find no way* (844), *wand'ring vanity* (875), and *words…erroneous* (969); cf. *Wandring that watrie Desert* in 11.779 and *long wanderd man* in 12.313 ("Abraham" 366). Fish (140–41) claims that although wandering at first seems to denote exile and hopelessness, here and in 11.779, the meaning is ultimately transformed and Christianized in book 12 by such means as Abraham, who is *Not wandring poor* (12.133), the *Wandring* of the Ark of God itself (12.333–34), and Adam and Eve's final faithful movement into the world with *wandring steps and slow* (12.648). Ryken contrasts the negative connotation of *wander* after the Fall with its unfallen meaning of mere meandering, and also the postlapsarian *wilde* with its innocent prelapsarian uses (65–66).

283–84. *to this obscure / And wilde:* Bentley finds this phrase ambiguous and prefers *Obscure to this / And wilde.* Keightley points out that Milton also uses *to this* to mean *compared to this* in *Mask* 506. Bush and Fowler similarly gloss *to* as "compared with." Cf. also the "darksom house" of *Nat* 14 and the "dim spot" and "pinfold" of *Mask* 5, 7.

284–85. *how shall we breathe in other Aire / Less pure, accustomed to immortal Fruits:* cf. 11.50–54. Montgomery conjectures that the logical remainder of Eve's clause is interrupted by the angel. Bentley thinks some words were "dropped out" and supplies "How shall we breathe in Air Less pure? *What eat,* accustomed to immortal Fruits?" Pearce counters that both the future consumption of mortal fruit and of breathing air less pure could well make Eve concerned. Empson argues that the real effect of Bentley's emendation is to make Eve's pathos into a declamatory piece of argument, whereas Milton's Eve makes an argument that trails away, as if paradise were already distant (*Some Versions* 162). Fowler adds that Milton may have intended this nostalgia as a test of reader discrimination, since if she were exclusively accustomed to *immortal* fruits, she would not be now leaving paradise, and Michael's interruption may be provoked by her insensitive mention of *fruit.* Ryken cites this comparison as an example of Milton's construction of the apocalyptic state by contrast, either quantitatively or qualitatively, with ordinary reality (48).

286–92. Michael's response is perfectly tempered, firm but mild; "the poem, it seems, is to end in a delicate poise, a balance of attitudes, where the sense of immense loss is subtly qualified by a sense of gain" (Martz 145). "Michael is even milder than God's instructions have obliged him to be" (Peter 29). Hughes (*"Paradise Lost," A Poem*) finds a remote parallel with Henry More's interpretation of the Expulsion from paradise as "a descent from an 'aerial' to a terrestrial world," the loss of a "wholly etherial" original state, "an happy and joyful condition of the Spirit." Michael reminds Eve that she will achieve maternal fulfillment—and tragedy—outside the garden; she has not been asked to abandon love (Summers, *Muse's Method* 194).

286. *Whom thus the Angel interrupted milde:* Emma identifies the "whom" at the beginning of the sentence as a "resumptive" or "continuative"; it is one of the main linking devices that Milton uses in both *PL* and *PR,* at least in Emma's rather restricted sample (57–58).

287–89. *resigne . . . thine:* one of 45 instances found by Diekhoff in the epic where two lines rhyme with one intervening nonrhyming line ("Rhyme" 540). See Purcell for additional instances (171).

287. *patiently:* cf. the goal of *True patience* in *PL* 11.360–61.

289. *over-fond:* two words without a hyphen in 1667.

290–91. *Thy going is not lonely:* Stoll cites this passage as one of the continual preparations for the final human condition ("From the Superhuman" 14); see

11.138–39. Maurice Kelley cites *DocCh* 1.10, where the husband's rule over the wife was increased after the Fall (142; Patterson, *Works* 15:121).

going: "departure" (so *OED* 1b).

292. *Where he abides:* Hume cites the lines "Comitemque virumque sequenti / Omne solum nuptae Patria est," which Hughes (*Paradise Lost*) glosses as the Roman maxim (attributed to Pacuvius) that wherever a man's true good is, there is his *native soil*. Cf. Andromache's speech in *Iliad* 6.413–430 and noted by Himes (*Paradise Lost: A Poem*): though she has been deprived by Achilles of parents, brothers, and home, she finds all made up to her in Hector.

296–333. According to Addison, Adam's lament abounds with thoughts that are as moving as Eve's, "but of a more masculine and elevated turn" (*Spectator* 3 [Apr. 26, 1712]: 361). Newton asserts, "There is the same propriety in these speeches of Adam and Eve, as the critics have observed in the speeches of Priam and Hecuba to dissuade Hector from fighting with Achilles [in *Iliad* 22]."

296–98. Himes (*Paradise Lost: A Poem*) refers these lines to Michael's various biblical titles "one of the chief princes" (Dan. 10:13), "the great prince" (Dan. 12:1), as well as being commander of the heavenly armies (Rev. 12:7). Milton identifies Michael as possibly the chief good angel in *DocCh* 1.9 (Maurice Kelley 137; Patterson, *Works* 15:105).

Highest: Bush glosses as "Seraphim." Fowler claims that Adam worries only after the Fall about the "social status" of angels. On Milton's names for angels, see **11.101**.

297. *such of shape may seem:* Bentley contends that the context requires *may'st* as a direct address to Michael. Pearce thinks the syntax reads differently and thinks *may* is appropriate as a general statement. Keightley glosses the phrase as "such in shape; or one of such a shape."

298–300. Daniells (*Milton* 40–41) notes that Michael, who *gently* delivers his message here and will be "mov'd" by seeing Abel's death (11.453), still bears the sword that is "Satan's dire dread" (11.248); indeed, this mannerist conflation of opposites makes it possible that the "two-handed engine" of *Lyc* 130 may be Michael's sword, since not long after its mention, the angel is exhorted to turn homeward and weep (*Lyc* 163).

which might else in telling wound: Bentley finds *wound* "too little for the Poet's Notion" and supplies *stound*. Cf. the Messenger's delicacy toward Manoa in *SA* 1565–68 (Le Comte).

301. *dejection:* "depression of spirits; downcast or dejected condition" (so *OED* 3).

303–04. *this happy place:* the phrase echoes *PL* 4.562 and 5.364. Ogden argues that the "Paradise within thee, happier far" of 12.587 is meant to contrast with Adam's reference here to Eden, rather than enunciating an unquestioning belief in a fortunate fall (18).

Recess: "place of retirement, a remote and secluded spot, a secret or private place" (*OED* 5a). Cf. "the sweet recess of Eve" (*PL* 9.456).

306–07. *Inhospitable ... desolate, / Nor knowing us nor known:* "the bitter knowledge that he must become a type for Cain, the wanderer upon earth, was also 'tasted' in the forbidden fruit" (Lawry, *Shadow* 275).

Bridges extends his "rule of L" to include the elision of *Inhospitable appear* (30); see **12.201–03** and **12.332–34**. Sprott includes this line in his comment that the *l*-elision coming before *-ble* is the most interesting (90).

307–14. Wesley notes this passage as among those particularly excellent.

307–08. *if by prayer / Incessant I could hope to change the will:* Fowler lists Adam's claim here as "the first of many errors in his dialogue with Michael," since we know that prayer can be effectual from the parable in Luke's gospel (18:5–7).

309. *him who all things can:* here, *can* has the old sense of "to know how to" rather than being an auxiliary, indicating perhaps "him who is powerful in all things" (Verity). "To know or have learned ... to have practical knowledge of" (*OED* B1a); Hughes (*Paradise Lost, A Poem*) compares a line from Richard Lovelace: "Yet can I music too."

would: Wesley changes to *could*.

310–14. Darbishire (*Poetical Works* 1:xx–xxi) cites this passage to illustrate Milton's use of colons to mark steps in a logical argument.

310. *wearie:* "to tire the patience of; to affect with tedium or ennui; to satiate" (*OED* 5). Hughes (*Paradise Lost, A Poem*) has "importune."

    Assiduous: Wesley glosses as "constantly repeated." Cf. the wearied unjust judge of Luke 18:5–7, in contrast to God who is eager to answer prayer, and the *preca qua fatigent* ("wearying prayers") of Horace's *Odes* 1.2.26. The supposition that the God of *PL* could be so wearied strikes Peter as "a plausible criticism" (19).

311–13. *But prayer against his absolute Decree...Blown stifling back on him:* cf. *vagabond or frustrate* prayers of *PL* 11.15, as well as the "absolute decree" in 3.115. Sensitivity to the movement and quality of the air is virtually a new feature in Milton's late poems (Banks, *Milton's Imagery* 135). Broadbent cites this passage along with *PL* 12.193 as examples of the "sturdy, everyday" icons of the last two books (*Some Graver Subject* 271). This passage is one of the rare cases where Milton uses an individual simile to illustrate a generalization; see also *PL* 7.126–28, 8.605–06, and 11.535–37 (Whaler, "Compounding" 313n2); in this complex simile the power and efficacy of Man's prayer are compared with God's decree, as breath to wind (Whaler, "Miltonic Simile" 1064).

313. Wesley omits this line.

    stifling: cf. "stifle," "to affect with difficulty of breathing, produce a choking sensation in" (so *OED* v¹ 1b).

314. *to his great bidding I submit:* Dunster (in Todd), sees an echo of *Macbeth* 3.3.127–28: "How say'st thou that Macduff denies his person / At our great bidding?" See Baumgartner comment on patience in **11.111**.

    I submit: Adam's submission here and in *PL* 11.526 continues that begun in book 10, and stands in direct opposition to Satan's continued defiance (Toole 31).

315–33. Wesley notes this passage as among those particularly excellent. Hazlitt finds Adam's reflections to be in "different strain" than Eve's, "and still finer" (in Wittreich 374).

315–16. *This most afflicts me...from his face I shall be hid:* cf. Cain's similar lament in Gen. 4:14 and David's plea that God not hide his face (Ps. 27:9); the sentiment is echoed in *SA* 1749. Edward Chauncey Baldwin finds a similar fear that expulsion from the garden is expulsion from God's presence in *The Life of Adam and Eve* ("Some Extra-Biblical Semitic Influences" 389–90). Pecheux, who identifies Adam's tone here as humbly grateful, sees a connection to faithful Abraham, who was promised God's presence if he obeyed God's injunction, "Walk before me, and be thou perfect" (Gen. 17:1); in *PL* 12.562–63, Adam claims to have learned "to walk / As in [God's] presence" (Pecheux, "Abraham" 366–67). Corcoran demonstrates how Milton locates the significance of Eden—a favorite theme for Christian exegetes—in Adam himself: "If the garden was a sacred place to him, it was so only because of the holiness of its inhabitants" (30–33).

319. *Presence Divine:* cf. *PL* 8.314.

320–33. *On this Mount he appeerd:* cf. *PE:* "with lesse fervency was studied what St. Paul or St. John had written then was listen'd to one that could say here hee taught, here he stood" (Patterson, *Works* 3:93). As noted by Todd, see also the interest voiced in Cicero's *De legibus* about the earlier Athenians as to "where they lived, where they sat, where they were wont to dispute; I desire to contemplate even their graves" (2.2.4), and a similar comment about where Pythagoras lived, ate, and sat (*De finibus* 5.2.4). In this one of Milton's best passages, Adam is Everyman, "filled with wonder at created things and their Creator, moved by gratitude yet nostalgic at his incapacity for adoration or communion" (Burke 212). This passage suggests that Adam was in the garden longer than often reckoned; even if God proceeded directly to Creation after Satan was driven from heaven, it would have taken Satan 27 days at the earliest to have reached paradise (Gilbert, *On the Composition* 148–49). The phrasing of Adam's lament suggests God's continued presence, since Moses and Elijah will both hear God's voice on a mount, the angel of the Lord will appear to Gideon under an oak and to Zechariah under a myrtle tree, and the woman of Samaria will speak to Jesus at a well (Martz 146); see Exod. 3:1–6, Judg. 6:11–12,1 Kings 19:1–9, Zech. 1:8–13, John 4:5–7. Shumaker, arguing that Milton offers images as well as ideas, concludes an analysis of imagery from *PL* 11.151 to this section (*Unpremeditated Verse* 201–02).

321–22. *visible...voice...heard:* although Milton often anthropomorphizes parts of God's action (eyes, ears, hands, etc.), this synecdoche never encourages one to visualize God as a total human form; God's presence in the garden is further veiled by representing him as invisible voice, and it often is not clear whether the action is being performed by the Father or by the Son (Ryken 131, 152, 173).

323–27. *grateful Altars...Offer:* Milton often uses postlapsarian religious terms and imagery to describe Adam and Eve's prelapsarian relationship with God (Ryken 148). Ricks cites this passage as an example of how ingratitude, "the great theme of the poem," occasions some of its most moving passages: while *grateful* primarily indicates gratitude, *lustre* and *sweet smelling* indicate that the altars will also be pleasing, a distinction indicating "the infection of the Fall" (*Milton's Grand Style* 113). Cf. the "grateful steame" of *PL* 11.442.

324–26. Cf. *PL* 5.391 and also the rustic altar "of grassie sord" in 11.432–33.

    and pile up every Stone...in memorie, / Or monument to Ages: Bentley wants to rewrite this passage as *From the brooks in memory. / A monument,* since there is not enough difference in *memory* and *monument* to separate them with an *or.* Pearce differentiates the two: a sign to remind Adam of a prelapsarian past, but a monument to his sons who could have no memory of it. Wesley similarly differentiates between them. Verity, citing cases in *SA* 182 and 545 noted by Todd, thinks the conjunction beginning in *PL* 11.326 has been corrupted, possibly through eye-skip, and that passage should read *in memorie, / And monument.* Hazlitt echoes this passage in reference to Milton's own desire to raise a poetic monument "of equal height and glory" to the "mighty models of antiquity" (Wittreich 380). On the building of altars where God has appeared, cf. Gen. 12:7, 13:4, and 35:7.

    Ages: B. A. Wright defines this word as "future generations" ("Note" 146); see **11.46**.

327. Burnt offerings would not be appropriate for paradise, but Cain also makes an unacceptable offering of "fruit" in Gen. 4:3 (Fowler).

    Gumms: plant secretions "employed as drugs or perfumes, or for burning as incense" (so *OED* 2).

and Fruits: 1667 *& Fruits,* probably because the line is otherwise too long for the margin.

329. *foot step trace:* 1667 *footstep;* some editions of 1672 have *step-trace.*

330. *though I fled him angrie: angrie* modifies *him* (Bush).

331. *promisd Race:* probably the offspring implied by God's statement to Eve in 10.179–81 and 193–95.

332–33. *Gladly behold though but his utmost skirts / Of glory, and farr off his steps adore:* cf. *PL* 3.380 and Jehovah's shielded glory in Exod. 33:22. The second clause recalls Statius's advice at the close of the *Thebaid*, "sed longe sequere et vestigia semper adora" (but always follow at a distance the footsteps in adoration) (12.817), cited by Bentley, Newton, and others. In the Augustinian tradition, the *vestigia*, or traces, of the steps of God are everywhere apparent (Martz 146). Cf. "for God forbid that we should . . . turn this day from following the LORD" (Josh. 22:29), the Vulgate for which is "eius vestigia non relinquamus" (that we would not follow his footsteps).

335–52. Hughes (*Paradise Lost*) explains that several biblical passages are joined here, notably Christ's warning to the woman of Samaria against worshiping God only "in this mountain" (John 4:21) and God's question, "Can any hide himself in secret places that I shall not see him? . . . Do not I fill heaven and earth?" (Jer. 23:24); cf. the expression of God's omnipresence in Ps. 139:7–12. As Maurice Kelley notes, Milton includes omnipresence as one of God's attributes in *DocCh* 1.2 (75; Patterson, *Works* 14:47). Barker finds in Michael's words a "sounder perspective" on the continuity of human experience than that of Raphael in *PL* 5.496–503, which can be misread as an immaterial Neoplatonic ascent ("*Paradise Lost*" 63–64). Sister Margaret Teresa Kelley sees a parallel in Dante's *Paradiso* 1.4–12, where the speaker has seen more of the vision of God than his memory can retain (68). "The bounds Adam would set on God correspond to the area his own consciousness is aware of" (Fish 277). Hutchinson describes Milton's own experience as typically Puritan in its biblicism and intolerance of any ceremonial form of worship, and not only anticlerical but anti-ecclesiastical

(185). Fowler claims that local devotion and superstition also seem in Milton's work to be associated with depression of spirits. Wesley identifies this passage as among those particularly excellent.

335–40. *all the Earth,… No despicable gift:* "this is another demonstration of God's favor even within the Fall" (Lawry, *Shadow* 275).

335. The comma after *Earth* is often either missing or faint in 1667.

336–54. Patrides cites this passage as an example, in the Renaissance and earlier, of God's omnipresence being figured as a circle (*Milton* 14–15).

336–37. *his Omnipresence fills… and every kinde that lives:* Bentley emends to *and every Creature lives,* since otherwise Milton would be saying that God's omnipresence fills every living kind. Pearce thinks an easier emendation would be to read the statement about omnipresence as a parenthesis. Newton, arguing with Bentley, points out that the phrase agrees with Acts 17:28 ("in him we live, and move, and have our being") and suggests as well that Milton may have been thinking of Lucan's *Pharsalia* 9.578–80: "Estne dei sedes, nisi terra, et pontus et aer, / Et coelum et virtus? superos quid quaerimus ultra? / Iuppiter est, quodcumque vides, quocunque moveris" (Are not these seats of God—earth, sea, air, sky, and its excellence? What do you seek beyond these? Whatever you see, whatsoever you do, is God). Newton also finds similar sentiments in Alexander Pope's *Essay on Man,* 267–80. Cf. statements on God's omnipresence in Ps. 139:7, Jer. 23:24, Acts 17:24, and also *PL* 5.590 and 7.168–69. As Masson indicates, line 336 ("Not this rock onely; his Omnipresence fills") has an extra syllable. Fowler claims, citing R. H. Charles on the Old Testament Apocrypha and pseudepigrapha, that tradition ascribed Ps. 139 to Adam himself; cf. Charles 2:17n28. Butler cites this passage in his discussion of Milton's "formidable" way of ascribing sentience to nature, arguing that though it is distrusted by New Critics, the "pathetic fallacy" is common in earlier English poetry (269–72, 275); see **11.182–90.** Burke thinks that the passage may well reflect an orthodox, creaturely understanding of heaven rather than a form of pantheism (17). The aliveness of the universe was—despite its underemphasis in Christian theology—"a congenial and necessary postulate" (MacCaffrey 148).

336.   *this rock:* Fish interprets Milton's diction as a shock tactic meant to prepare us for Eden's eventual destruction and its meaning (*PL* 11.834–38); in the "hard literalism of 'Rock,' " we are urged to seek the spirit whose presence gives physical objects their value (307). Fowler surmises that Milton's substitution of *rock* for Christ's "mountain" in John 4:21 attacks the Roman Catholic claim that St. Peter was the "rock" on which Christ built his church (Matt. 16:18).

338.   *Fomented:* "filled with life-giving heat" (Hughes, *Paradise Lost*). "To cherish with heat, to warm. Always in conjunction with another word, as *chafe, heat, warm*" (*OED* 2, obsolete); cf. *PL* 4.669.

   virtual: Ricks renders as "inherently life-giving"; cf. *OED* 1a, "Possessed of certain physical virtues or capacities; effective in respect of inherent natural qualities or powers; capable of exerting influence by means of such qualities. Now rare." Northrop Frye (*Paradise Lost*) glosses *virtual* as "filled with energy," and Fowler as "potent, exerting influence."

   Wesley omits this line.

339–46.   Cf. the "gave to rule" of *PL* 1.736 (Le Comte). This passage amplifies 8.338–39 (Corcoran 50). Milton's unlost paradise could have been a heaven on earth, whereas Dante's earthly paradise on Mt. Purgatory served only as a departing place for heaven (Samuel, *Dante* 218). Pererius and other Renaissance commentators on Genesis tended to restrict the size of paradise, making the spread of mankind inevitable (A. Williams, *Common Expositor* 100).

340–41.   *surmise not then:* Fish (291) traces Adam's rapid progress from the understanding that called forth this "benign reproof" to Michael's praise for Adam's speech in *PL* 12.561–73.

   Surmise: "to suppose, imagine (that a thing is so); to expect" (so *OED* 3, obsolete).

343–46.   *Perhaps thy Capital Seate:* helped by Michael to imagine what might have been, Adam might also be able to imagine what changes can still be made in human society by applying the rules of temperance (Hughes, "Beyond Disobedience" 193). Lewis suggests that a descendant's visit to such an unfallen Adam would have meant "the almost terrifying honor of coming at last, after long journeys and ritual preparations and slow ceremonial approaches, into the very presence of the great Father, Priest, and Emperor," and argues that "no useful criticism of the Miltonic Adam is possible until the last trace of the *naïf*, simple, childlike Adam has been removed from our imaginations" (*Preface* 114). Empson judges Michael's action here as "nagging" (*Milton's God* 173).

344. *and had hither come:* Bentley cites this as *thither*, and wants *hither*, since the speech is spoken in paradise. Pearce reports that the first edition actually had *hither*; it was only *thither* in the later ones. Newton emends it back to *hither*.

345. *From all the ends of th'Earth:* cf. *PL* 5.586.

346. *great Progenitor:* cf. *PL* 5.544.

347. *thou hast:* "with a classical precedent Milton permits elision of a vowel before an initial *h* which is followed by another vowel, as if in pronunciation the *h* were completely silent" (Sprott 86–87); on *h*, see also **11.583–86.**

348. *To dwell on eeven ground now with thy Sons:* although Adam has lost his patriarchal preeminence, "the parallel of the incarnate second Adam lends radiance even to that 'descent'" (Lawry, *Shadow* 276).

349–62. Michael's desired stance is one of poise and "temper"; a similar balance occurs in the great windows of University College, Oxford, where between the panels showing the Expulsion and the labors of Adam and Eve and their offspring, a center panel shows Abraham entertaining the angels (Martz 147). Michael's promise is the consolation produced by Adam's submission: "wherever God's will prevails, God himself must be" (Thompson, "Theme" 117).

349–54. Patrides asserts that Milton's God is far more loving and less impatient with humans in the Expulsion than the legalistic God of Milton's contemporaries (*Milton* 178).

349–50. *in Vallie and in plaine / God is as here:* cf. God's claim of omnipresence in 1 Kings 20:28 in response to the Syrians, who said he was God of the hills, but not of the valleys.

349. *plaine:* 1667 *Plaine.*

350–58. Michael makes the assertion, startling to a modern reader, that the following pageant of world history will prove God's omnipotence, but a vision of horrific human depravity was commonplace in Milton's England (Rajan, *"Paradise Lost" and the Seventeenth Century* 81).

351–54. *signe…Divine:* one of the 52 instances of rhyming lines with two intervening nonrhyming lines (Diekhoff, "Rhyme" 541–42); see Purcell for additional instances (172).

351–52. *his presence many a signe / Still following thee:* Milton often portrays God in the epic as a presence not located precisely in space; Milton's combination of sensory with conceptual images evokes a world that transcends the senses (Ryken 153–54, 198).

352–53. *still compassing thee round / With goodness:* cf. Ps. 5:12.

352. *compassing:* 1667 *compassing.* 1674 *compasting.*

353–54. Wesley omits these lines.

354–55. *the track Divine. / Which:* Darbishire (*Poetical Works* 1:xx) cites this line to illustrate Milton's use of a period before *which* used conjunctively (xx).

354. *Express:* "of an image or likeness: truly depicted, exactly resembling, exact" (*OED* I10, which adds that the modern usage chiefly recalls the description of the Son in Heb. 1:3 as "the express image of [God's] person."

355–64. "Instead of disappointing the expectations he has aroused, the angel remains faithful to his announced syllabus" (Fish 288–89). See Baumgartner comment on patience in **11.111**.

355. *that thou mayst beleeve, and be confirmd:* Fowler links this statement to the progressive steps of regeneration leading to the final "perseverance of the saints" detailed in *DocCh* 1.25 (Patterson, *Works* 16:67–69), claiming "Faith is the theme of book 11, as repentance was the theme of book 10."

confirmd: 1667 *confirmd,*

356–66. This passage has produced much varied comment. Michael echoes God's charge in 11.114; cf. 6.502. Cf. also the biblical vision of "what shall befall thy people in the latter days," granted by Michael in Dan. 10:14, and the long epic tradition of such visions, including Aeneas's vision of the future of Rome in Virgil's *Aeneid* 6.788–886 and Britomart's vision of her descendants in Spenser's *Faerie Queene* 3.3. Bush claims that the vision is integral to Milton's theme because "it binds the sin of Adam and Eve firmly to history and shows the continual re-enactment of the Fall, the eventual means of salvation through Christ, and the necessity of patient trust in Providence." Verity cites Alexander Pope's Mount of Vision, in which Bays surveys the realms of Dulness (*Dunciad*, book 3) as one of his most elaborate Miltonic parodies. Hughes (*Paradise Lost*) thinks the vision device may owe something to the Apocalpyse of Moses and almost certainly something to the great series of visions of biblical history in Du Bartas's *Divine Weeks*, from *The Handicrafts* to *The Decay*, which Hughes (*Paradise Lost, A Poem*) identifies as "Milton's closest precedent"; cf. the series of visions in Du Bartas 1:380–2:767. The Jerusalem Bible (Ezek. 40:3n) remarks that angelic interpreters are a feature of late prophetic (i.e., apocalyptic) biblical literature, citing such examples as Dan. 8:16, 9:21–23, 10:5–11; Zech. 1:9 and 2:1–4. Lawry contrasts Michael's method to Satan's by citing words from *Nat:* "Something like the reality of hell, its 'dolorous mansions' open to the 'peering day,' will now appear, utterly stripped of the rhetoric permitted to Satan" (276).

Muldrow highlights the scope of Michael's task; he must not only cover the six eras of history but also announce the drama of the soul's redemption, and thus he must reveal both doctrinal and ethical truths (79–80). "Michael's presentation of the future ... for all its most skillful use of example, makes more use of precept than any other portion of the poem except possibly the end of the passage which recounts the warning visit of Raphael" (Diekhoff, *Milton's "Paradise Lost"* 135); cf. *PL* 11.515–18, 547–48, 553–54, 634–36, 884–85; *PL* 12.561–73, 581–85. Key words in this passage—*true patience, fear, pious sorrow*—are synonyms for *catharsis, fear, and pity,* and thus identify Milton's concern with tragedy (Burden 188–89). In his long overture, Michael "makes the moral of his sermon plain" (Rajan, *"Paradise Lost" and the Seventeenth Century* 80). Patrides (*Phoenix* 61–62; *Milton* 259–60) asserts that although a vision of the future is conventional in epic poetry, Milton's has a different purpose, as set forth by Michael; a similar purpose of recounting scriptural history from Adam to Christ, noting both sins and faults of some and rewards of others, was enunciated in an English translation of John Chrysostom published in 1542. C. H. Collins Baker advises that in Tonson's 1720 edition of *PL*, the "head-piece" to book 11 (i.e., ornament at its beginning) is "Michael Foretells the Future" by Chéron and Gucht, also an illustration by Hayman in 1749 that was further copied by Alexander Anderson in 1815; "Michael Shews the Future" is also the book 11 illustration for Frederick Schall's 1792 edition as well as for R. Westall's 1794 illustration for book 11, for H. Richter's 1794 second illustration for the book, and for M. Craig's 1804 design (13, 15, 18, 19, 103, 108).

358–60. Cf. "My spirit shall not always strive with man" (Gen. 6:3), and also "supernal grace" in *PL* 7.573 and Patrides' comment in **11.22–23.** Hutchinson contrasts Milton's occasional acceptance of the human need for grace with his much greater emphasis, almost Pelagian, on one's ability to work out one's own salvation by the reasonable control of passion (126). Fixler characterizes Michael's history as less of a spiritual progression than an outwardly indecisive struggle; humankind is helpful without a mediator (232). Fish argues that this phrase, which contrasts supernal grace and sinfulness, is finally a better description of the epic, which has little to say about "Man's First Disobedience," other than that it happened (289). Martz accepts this passage as Milton's explicit contract to provide equal representations for grace and sin (146–48). Rajan reads these lines, along with *PL* 9.1121–31 and 12.79–101, as adumbrating Michael's announcement of "the paradise within" of 12.587; in the epic's "endless involvement in a web of meaning and consequence," these lines indicate that "the arena of combat is now the mind and history becomes the collective result of the individual struggle for moral transformation" (*"Paradise Lost:* The Hill" 44–45).

    contending: referring to "the strife of natural forces, feelings, passions, etc." (so *OED* 2b).

360–64. Cf. the exhortation to earthly kings to "rejoice with trembling" (Ps. 2:11). William Chappell, Milton's first Cambridge tutor, proposed a sermon type that was based on the *epanorthosin* ("correction" in the KJV) of 2 Tim. 3:16 and balanced reprehension and consolation (20–21). This passage reflects the heavenly pattern in 12.295–306 of the Father's tempering his justice with the Son's mercy (Huntley, "Before and After" 12). "It is as though the seed of *PR* were already germinating in the poet's mind" (Peter 151). Rajan demonstrates that this passage is carefully balanced on three caesuras in successive lines, varying in position just enough to "avoid a deadweight"; though the insistence on tempering in line 361 might make us hurry over the seemingly frigid counsel and miss that joy is the emotion called for by the last books (*"Paradise Lost: The Hill"* 45).

360–61. *thereby to learn / True patience:* Burden cites Calvin, *Institutes* 3.8.8, where true Christian patience is contrasted with Stoicism's apathetic "shadow of patience" (189). According to Fowler, this patience is "to be distinguished from the false stubborn philosophical patience of 2.569 and 9.920." Both Fowler and Hughes (*Paradise Lost, A Poem*) claim that *moderation* was itself a Stoic and Aristotelian principle assimilated by early Christianity.

363. *By moderation either state to beare:* cf. the biblical counsel to remarkable moderation, "known unto all men" (Phil. 4:5). The phrasing suggests the title of Petrarch's treatise *On the Remedies of Both Kinds of Fortune* (i.e., of good and bad).

364. *Prosperous:* as Oras mentions, the meter requires this word to have three full syllables (*Milton's Editors* 316).

365–66. *endure / Thy mortal passage when it comes:* cf. biblical counsels to "endur[e] to the end," in Matt. 10:22 and elsewhere. Bentley wants *final passage*, since *mortal passage* would refer to the whole of life, but Pearce argues that *mortal passage* is not an established epithet for that meaning. Robert M. Adams cites this passage as one proof that Thyrsis's mention of "mortal change" in *Mask* 10 refers to death rather than some transcendental experience in life, as if Milton were a nineteenth century Romantic poet (30). Pecheux links *mortal passage* to the exile-journey motif ("Abraham" 366). The ensuing action will clearly constitute a moral lesson; it has been introduced dramatically, and given Adam's moods thus far, one can expect he will respond dramatically to subsequent revelations (Sasek 188).

366–68. *Ascend / This Hill; let Eve (for I have drencht her eyes) / Here sleep below:*
this passage has occasioned much commentary, one issue being Eve's exclusion
from the vision. Edward Chauncey Baldwin remarks that in The Apocalypse of
Moses Michael also shows a vision of the future to Adam but not Eve (*"Paradise
Lost"* 385). Thyer (cited by Marchant) argues that although Eve also needed
the vision, Milton continues the earlier decorum of having Eve retire from
angels, also supposing that her tender female mind could not bear the upcom-
ing shocking scenes. Douady judges that Eve could not view the funereal and
revolting scenes to follow without perhaps challenging anew the decrees of God,
whereas man "accept, excuse, il est faible, il est philosophe" (accepts, excuses,
he is feeble, he is philosophical) (198). Webb has a female interlocutor, Aspasia,
comment on this passage: "So it is you men deal with us; you cut us off from
the means of knowledge, and then wonder at our ignorance. Good sense you
have appropriated, by calling it manly. Taste, indeed, you allow us; but you keep
it in subjection to your superior genius" (61); see also **11.411–12**. Traditional
Christian commentators typically located a lengthy exposition about mankind's
future history in Adam's dream while Eve is being formed; Milton postpones
the exposition to the epic's end, but still links it to a dream (Evans 291–92).
Northrop Frye shows how Milton preserves the symmetry of Eve's having an
earlier dream coincide with the angelic visit, but also reminds us that we are
not given any information about her later dreams; we are told (*PL* 12.595–96,
610–14, 620–23) only that they are about the serpent's defeat by her redeemer-
descendant, and otherwise they represent a revelation that is distinctly hers
and, Frye suggests, a God-given feminine independence of thought and being
("Revelation" 19–20, 47). "Eve Asleep" is one of five illustrations for book
11 in Tilt's 1843 edition of Milton's *Poetical Works* (C. H. C. Baker 116); see
11.187 and **12.1–5**.

Other commentary cites patristic discussions of the prospect. Peck (*New
Memoirs* 195) cites a Latin passage from Cyprian's *Epistle to Donatus:* "For a
brief space conceive yourself to be transported to one of the loftiest peaks of
some inaccessible mountain, thence gaze on the appearance of things lying below
you.... Consider the roads blocked up by robbers, the seas beset with pirates,
wars scattered all over the earth with the bloody horror of camps. The whole
world is wet with mutual blood"; see Migne, *Patrologiae... Latina* 4.204B. Cf.
also Jerome, *Epistle* 60.18: "Oh, if we could ascend into such a watch-tower as
would give us a view of the whole world spread beneath our feet! Then I would

show you a universe in ruins, peoples warring against peoples, and kingdoms shattered on kingdoms" (Peck, *New Memoirs* 307; Migne, *Patrologiae...Latina* 22:601–02).

Still other commentary considers the significance of sleep. Hume points out that Milton's Latin translator confuses *sleep* with *weep* ("Lachrymarum fundere rivum"), a misreading also corrected by Thomas Warton (258), who cites the drenching with "Elysian dew" of *Mask* 996. Himes (*Paradise Lost: A Poem*) refers to Christ's Transfiguration, where like Eve his disciples were heavy with sleep (Luke 9:32) but nevertheless saw the vision (Matt. 17:9). Pecheux sees in Mary's sleep a typological birth of the church ("Second Adam" 181).

Radzinowicz includes this moment of the epic when she asserts that the restoration of peace and amity to Adam and Eve's marriage in book 10 precedes the restoration of free will in their prayers; the double mood of remorseful contrition continues to the close of the epic (40).

367. *drencht:* Fowler cites "administered medicine to" (*OED* 1). Cf. "to steep, soak, saturate" (*OED* 4) or "to drown, immerse, plunge, overwhelm" (*OED* 6). Hume sees *drencht* as referring to medicine.

368. *while thou to foresight wak'st:* Fletcher claims that this foresight is result of the Fall (*Milton's Rabbinical Readings* 203). Fowler sees a typological correspondence with Adam's "conscious dream" of Eve's creation in 8.452–78, since Adam is now to see the race leading up to the second Eve. Stillingfleet (in Todd) judges that the engaged mind is properly represented as waking, as in "Awake to righteousness" (1 Cor. 15:34) but when ignorant, stupid, or sinful as sleeping. Lewalski (26, 30–31) traces throughout book 11 the emphasis on Adam's purged and exercised physical sight, which includes visions of Abel, Enoch, and Noah, even though in Heb. 11:1 these are examples of a faith defined as "evidence of things not seen," because Adam's heightened bodily vision symbolizes the restoration of his marred faculties of reason and will, enabling him to perceive and be guided again by the law of nature; cf. 11.379–80, 385–87, 412–18, 423, 429, 556, 638, 712, 840, 901; 12.128, 141–59, 271–74, 276–77, 375–85, 553–57, 572–73.

foresight: "the action of looking forward...also, a look forward (at some distant object)" (so *OED* 2a).

369. *As once thou slepst, while Shee to life was form'd:* cf. 8.452–77. Lieb identifies the language of generation associated with Michael's "indoctrination" of the couple, which he also links to the "brooding" of meditation or inner speculation in 12.587–89 and 12.604–05 (*Dialectics* 214).

370–76. Adam's ascent is almost a rehearsal for the final Expulsion; Adam's resignation and confidence are part of a complex pattern closely linked with the exile-journey motif (Pecheux, "Abraham" 366). Although humanity can escape disaster because rescue is offered to Adam, he displays a "certain Pelagian tendency to self-dependence" (Reesing 77).

371–73. *Ascend, I follow thee, safe Guide…However chast'ning:* Summers compares Adam's words accepting a difficult vision with Eve's "Lead then" (*PL* 9.631) to the serpent's easy vision of godlike knowledge and power (*Muse's Method* 196).

373. *However chast'ning, to the evil turne:* Bentley claims *evil* is one syllable, and emends as "to the evil *I* turne." As Burke points out, Adam's uninformed consent here may be termed "academic" (212).

  chast'ning: "correcting, chastising; purifying, refining, subduing" (so *OED*, ppl. a.).

374. *obvious:* Keightley glosses *obvious* as "opposing, going against" from the Latin *obvius,* but that word also has the sense of "accessible." Wesley glosses the word as "ready to meet it," and Verity as "turned to meet the evil." Cf. *OED* 3, "exposed or open to; liable." Hughes (*Paradise Lost*) cites the literal Latin meaning, "in the path," that is, situated so as inevitably to be met; cf. *Oxford Latin Dictionary* 1. Le Comte has "literally, lying in the way."

374–75. *arming to overcom / By suffering:* cf. Nautes' assurance in *Aeneid* 5.710 that fortune is overcome by bearing whatever she brings.

375–76. *rest from labour won, / If so I may attain:* these lines blend Heb. 4:11 ("labour…to enter into that rest") and Phil. 3:11 ("If by any means I might attain unto the resurrection") (Fowler).

377–78. *It was a Hill / Of Paradise the highest:* Buff identifies this abrupt beginning of a landscape description, also found in *PL* 1.670, 9.69, and 10.547, as a typically epic pattern (31–32). Harding (*Club of Hercules* 38) finds an implied comparison with *Aeneid* 6.754, where the hero likewise has his vision from a *tumulus,* or hill. Milton had apparently rejected a current theory that God created the earth as a perfectly smooth globe (Babb 35). Eve's earlier dream includes such a prospect; for her now to be placed on a lower level to dream is another example of the "curious antithetic symmetry" pervading the poem (N. Frye, "Revelation" 25). See **11.118–20**, s.v. McColley. This mountain recapitulates "the theme of the holy mountain with which Milton opened the epic" and which he draws not from Exodus but from 2 Esdras 14:4–5, since it indicates that Moses on Mt. Sinai not only received the Law but also saw "the secrets of the times, and the end"; the two mountaintop tableaux in *PL* and the one in *PR* summarize the theological history of humankind: Adam the sinner, Moses the lawgiver, and Christ the redeemer (Mollenkott 33–34).

377. *In the Visions of God:* a biblical phrase for a revelation, as in Ezek. 8:3, 40:2, and 2 Chron. 26:5, as well as "visions of God" without the preposition in Ezek. 1:1. Dunster (in Todd) remarks that Ezek. 8:3 in particular introduces an ascent followed by a series of visions. Hughes (*Paradise Lost, A Poem*) adds that the vision in Ezek. 40:2 is upon "a very high mountain" and the temptation of Christ in Matt. 4:8 upon an "exceeding high mountain." Addison cites Adam's vision as an example of how much greater a poem is *PL* than the *Iliad* or *Aeneid;* although Aeneas is given a vision of all who will descend from him, Adam's vision is not confined to a particular human tribe but comprehends the entire species (*Spectator* 3 [Apr. 26, 1712]: 361–62). Since all other epic poems celebrated national glories, Milton would have celebrated the English Reformation had he not been disappointed in recent political events (Newton). Keightley complains about the grammar of the phrase, insisting that the preposition rendered *of* in English would have the meaning of *to* in the Hebrew, and that "so good an Hebrist" as Milton may have so understood it. Here and in 12.128, Sister Margaret Teresa Kelley (116) finds a suggestion of the intuitive, angelic mode of reasoning with which Dante invested Cacciaguida and Beatrice in *Paradiso* 15.40–72.

379–80. *in cleerest Ken / Stretcht out to the amplest reach of prospect:* cf. the Father's prospect (*PL* 3.77), the "prospect wide" of Eve's dream (5.88), and "all the Coast in prospect" before Christ at heaven's gate (10.89). MacCaffrey identifies this view as the stage from which all "the moralities and interludes" of books 11–12 are enacted, with Michael first as chorus and then as narrator (61). Fowler questions the idea of tableaux, seeing the following episodes more as brief tragedies (see **11.429–65**). Ferry (*Milton's Epic Voice* 84–85) demonstrates how this passage suggests that the world is glorious, far vaster than the "narrow bounds" of Eden (*PL* 11.341); this impression is produced not only by such words and phrases as *Stretcht out* and *reach* (which connote animation and power) and *amplest* (a superlative of scope and abundance), and by the double sense of *prospect* (extensive view, future hope) but also by the reminder in 11.381–84 that Christ will redeem the future. Nicolson relates the "sensation of the sudden view of far distance" to Milton's interest in the telescope ("Milton and the Telescope" 94). Sister Margaret Teresa Kelley's general comment applies here: "Milton's imagination of space is formed [not by Virgil, Ariosto, and Tasso, but] rather by St. John's in the Apocalypse, Homer's and Dante's. . . . When John, Homer and Dante look down on the earth, we feel not a 'deus ex machina' but 'ex cathedra,' an authority accustomed to the heights" (143–44). Prince identifies here one of Milton's characteristic devices: setting himself or his characters on a high place, from which they can see the world or history spread out below, a device appearing intermittently in the early poems and reaching its greatest development in the two great epics (44). Giamatti (348) claims that we only know what was lost when the future of the human race is stretched out in this prospect, because we then see the loss of "true Libertie" (*PL* 12.83–84). Shumaker argues that because Adam's view includes no close-ups, no faces, no clenched fists, and no praying hands, the technique results in a "certain coolness" (*Unpremeditated Verse* 203). Milton's curious distortion of space maintains the known world at the center of the map rather than picturing a globe and allowing "the intense axial organization of a moral universe . . . to dissolve" (Daniells, *Milton* 89–90). Lewalski traces Adam's purged and exercised physical sight throughout book 11 (26); see **11.368**.

    Ken: "range of sight or vision" (*OED* 2).

    the amplest: 1667 *amplest*. B. A. Wright, following Miltonic tendencies of elision, has *th'amplest* (*Milton's Poems*). Grierson insists that the 1674 reading is one that every editor accepts or should accept (*Poems* 2:xl–xli); see also **11.551–52, 11.651, 12.191, and 12.237–38**. Shawcross, on the other hand, thinks that *the* is a compositor's error ("Orthography" 149).

381–84. Cf. *PR* 3.251–440. The traditional location of Christ's temptation in the wilderness (Matt. 4:1–11; Luke 4:1–13) was Mt. Quarentana, between Jerusalem and Jericho, but Milton puts it on Mt. Niphates ("snow mountain") in the Taurus range of Armenia (Gilbert, *Geographical Dictionary* 210). Lerner reports the stylistic suggestion that the simile does not end in line 384; it is possible that the commanding eye in the next line refers not to "Adam being shown future empires by Michael, but Christ being shown present empires by Satan.... The whole passage in fact is a gloss on 'our second Adam'" (307). Rajan finds the carefully stated link between the first and second Adams to be dramatically different, since Adam views the results of his sin that he is powerless to modify, while the Son in *PR* is offered the means to change them but appears detached and seemingly indifferent ("Jerusalem" 65). Wesley omits these four lines.

381. *higher:* as B. A. Wright records, a monosyllable; "*h* does not count as a consonant" (*Milton's Poems* xiv).

382–84. *second Adam:* Christ is identified as the "last Adam" in 1 Cor. 15:45; cf. also Rom. 5:14, which identifies Adam as "the figure of him that was to come." Whereas MacCallum claims that Milton's typology is mainly located in people rather than objects, dominated by the "Pauline and Augustinian emphasis on the men of faith as prefigurements of Christ" ("Milton and Sacred History" 158), Waddington specifies that the two Adams form the primary typological scheme of the concluding books (10). Svendsen categorizes *second Adam,* along with such epithets as *one greater Man,* as the fifth of five major sets of characteristics of the Son in the epic ("Epic Address" 199–200). Patrides links Milton's *second Adam* to the "recapitulation theory" of the atonement, which sometimes includes Mary ("Milton" 7–10; see also *Milton* 130–42).

385–87. Adam's actual vision is of "nobler sights" (*PL* 11.411), but his potential vision here of cities and civilizations known to Renaissance geographers may be an example of the doctrine of "uniformitarianism," i.e., that the world and human nature are unchanging, which Herbert Weisinger lists as one of the six assumptions of Renaissance historiography; according to French theologian Pierre Charron (1541–1603), the contemplation of the world's essential homogeneity can lead to mature acceptance of reality (Weisinger, "Ideas" 429–30).

Lewalski (26) traces Adam's purged and exercised physical sight throughout book 11; see **11.368**.

386. *City of old or modern Fame:* Milton's listing of cities follows civilizations from early times to the present, implying that the present ones will also decay (Cawley 135).

387–88. Leigh Hunt includes these lines in his praise of the "variety and loftiness of modulation" in Milton's proper names (Wittreich 436–38).

388–411. Milton's geographical survey has elicited various responses. Bentley dislikes this passage and assumes it is an editorial addition: "If Milton would have spent six Lines in painting that Prospect; he would have contented himself with Continents, Seas, Islands, *Terrasque tractusque maris* [and lands and tracts of sea].... But our Editor would not lose the good occasion to shew...that he had perus'd a Sixpenny Map." Empson judges Bentley's complaints about Milton's pedantry here more rousing than what he finds to be sometimes unreasonable attacks by Bentley's detractors (*Some Versions* 152). Though Newton thinks the passage has been done "more with an ostentation of learning, than with any additional beauty to the poem," Thyer (in Newton) says that "such little sallies of the Muse agreeably enough diversify the scenes" and also that Tasso has much the same description in *Gerusalemme liberata* canto 15. Lauder initially claimed that Milton borrowed "almost the whole passage" from an encomium to marriage by Staphorstius (149); Douglas counters that Lauder has failed to cite either edition or line numbers, that he has misquoted Staphorstius in several places, and that the only eight lines bearing any resemblance to Milton's were not in Staphorstius but rather in the Latin translation of *PL* itself (29–33, 84–85); Lauder later confessed to imposture. Johnson believes that Milton's occasional long lists of proper names are motivated only by the poet's conviction that English was unfit for smooth versification, such as in *PL* 11.408–11 (*Rambler* 4 [Jan. 19, 1751]: 101). Wesley omits the entire geographical section, splicing 387a with 411b to produce the single line, "Of mightiest empire: but to nobler sights." Stebbing argues that the knowledgeable reader will recognize by the city names "some of the most brilliant passages of history," the simplest narrative account of which would be far too long. Joseph Hunter rejects the idea of Milton's supposed ostentation, claiming that a single book, Heylyn's

Cosmography, could have supplied Milton with most of the material (70–71). Masson thinks that Milton delighted in "the poetry of proper names"; Moody similarly remarks on Milton's delight in "the sonority and dim but gorgeous suggestiveness of proper names." Himes (*Paradise Lost: A Poem*) thinks that the list is also "remarkable" for omitting all Christian kingdoms, including Britain, Germany, Holland, and Scandinavia. Milton has similar lists in *PL* 1.396–411 and 582–87 (Verity). Thompson claims that the passage clearly proves the tenacity of Milton's memory for names ("Milton's Knowledge" 160), though Milton could certainly have checked the spellings later. McColley briefly revisits the issue in a footnote reference to Joseph Beaumont's geographical catalog in *Psyche* of 1648 (*"Paradise Lost"* 229n235); this catalog, however, is far more general, with the five-line stanza (16.100–04) describing the general characters of Asia, Europe, and Africa, and one describing the "strange, untutored" New World.

The most famous modern comment is T. S. Eliot's complaint that because Milton overemphasized the auditory imagination to the point of occasional "levity," this passage "is not serious poetry, not poetry fully occupied about its business, but rather a solemn game" ("A Note" 38–39). Eliot's comment has generated numerous responses. Tillyard counters, with some heat, that Milton must succinctly provide "the impression of great spaces of the earth and great epochs of history" (*Miltonic Setting* 92–93). Robert M. Adams also insists that Milton includes the place names to display large vistas of space and history, and for their sound, and cites this passage against modern critics who "think poetic ornament is bound to be 'organically' functional" (187–88). Bowra (238–39) argues that Milton follows good epic precedent; in *Os Lusiades,* Camoëns has Venus show Gama the whole world that he has opened for future generations, and geography would also be important to Milton's contemporaries not only for its romance but also because they expected poetry to be encyclopedic. Milton obviously borrows from Camoëns (see **11.399**) but also changes the significance of the geographic vision, since Gama sees the world as the stage of Portuguese exploits, but Adam is shown the havoc his descendants will make of it. Prince judges that Eliot has belletristically trivialized Milton's project: "if we accept the poetic instrument for the magnificent thing it is, and for the magnificent uses to which he puts it, we can see that this prelude sets the scene for a series of far-sweeping visions" (44). Martz praises "the gorgeous roll of names, with Milton manifesting all the power of his high style, recalling in one final burst of grandeur the epic panoply of the opening book" and putting all of the obvious excess to good thematic effect, since it highlights the "glories" of the fallen world and prepares for the "nobler sights" to follow (148–49). Bryan claims that every line of the passage is informed by the two ancient concepts of *translatio imperii* and *translatio studii,* that human history was a westward movement of civilized empire and of humane learning; in Adam's vision, however, sin and corruption rather than art, learning, and empire have moved from east to west (199–201). Ferry, who insists that the Fall was necessary for humanity to learn about goodness, finds the catalog both positive, "a list of places and rulers associated with the splendor and power of our history," and negative, since "it is our past, for these empires are fallen, their wealth dispersed"; she also claims that the *Eye* of line 385 could be either Adam's or Christ's (*Milton's Epic Voice* 85–87). Sasek doubts that the passage is a "tour de force of versification and sound effects" but finds it crucial to the story, as it enlarges the scope of action to the entire world, the stage for the playing of the biblical drama (189). Fish finds the studied virtuosity of the roll call of cities and empires to be a parody of Milton's earlier spectacular effects (301–02). Broadbent, noting that paradise itself ceases to be a locus of action in the last two books, judges that the descriptive method of Milton and his contemporaries was inflexible ("Milton's Paradise" 173–75).

387. *destind Walls:* because not yet built (Fowler).

388. *Cambalu, seat of Cathaian Can:* alternative name for Pekin (Beijing), Milton's "Paquin" of 11.390; cf. also the description of China in *HistMosc* (Patterson, *Works* 10:344–48). Many of Milton's contemporaries preserved the notion that Cathay and China were two different countries, with Cambalu and Pekin as their respective capitals; Milton follows this distinction in 11.388 and 390 but not in 3.437–39, where he identifies the Chinese with the inhabitants of Cathay (Gilbert, *Geographical Dictionary* 77–78). Chang reports that knowledge of Chinese geography was still incomplete in Milton's time (493–98).

    Can: cf. *khan,* "the specific title . . . given to the successors of Chingz Khan, who were supreme rulers over the Turkish, Tartar, and Mongol tribes, as well as emperors of China, during the Middle Ages" (so *OED* a). St. Maur glosses the word as "*Cham,* or *Chan,* Tat. i.e. *The Great Lord or Emperor;* as St. Maur also records, Milton's survey of the Eastern Hemisphere moves roughly from east to west (377). Verity reports that the name *Cambaluc* (emphasis on the second syllable) is a corruption of the Mongolian *Kaan-Baligh,* "the city of the Khan," built by Kublai Khan and capital of his China from ca. 1264 to 1368, and was further corrupted in English texts to *Cambalu* (emphasis on the first syllable) via Italian versions of Polo's travels. See Polo, *Travels* 2.4–8, 17, 27 (Weidner). Milton may have been stimulated by seeing, years before, the map by Ortelius on which Cambalu is "marked by several tents, in one of which the hero himself is sitting, scepter in hand," under an inscription reading, "Magnus Cham, maximus Asie princeps" (Great Cham, great prince in Asia) (Thompson, "Milton's Knowledge" 160).

389. *And Samarchand by Oxus, Temirs Throne:* Samarkand was the lavish capital and burial place of Timur (Tamerlane, 1336–1405), who Hume says brought into it 8,000 camels laden with the spoils of Damascus alone. Cann calls Samarkand "the chief city of Zagathaian Tartary" (242). Thompson points out that on Ortelius's map, Samarkand is indicated by several spires and the inscription, "Samarchand magni Tamber; quondam sedes" (Samarkand, once the seat of great Tamurlaine) on the river Oxus ("Milton's Knowledge" 160).

   Oxus: Greek, "swift," because of the river's descent from high mountains (St. Maur). The Oxus (now known as Amu Darya) is a large Asian river flowing into the Aral Sea, though maps in Milton's time showed it flowing into the Caspian Sea; mapmakers also often placed Samarkand on a tributary river of the Oxus, though the two do not actually join (Gilbert, *Geographical Dictionary* 224, 252–53). The Oxus is now about 150 miles distant from Samarkand, though there is evidence that the river has changed its course and that historically it did flow into the Caspian.

390. *Paquin:* i.e., Peking (Beijing), the Chinese capital, as written in Hexham's *Mercator;* Heylyn writes it "Pequin, or Pagnia, in the middle of the province so named" (3:185).

   Sinæan: a rare adjective for Chinese (so *OED*). Hume claims that China was called *Sinarum Regio* (realm of Sinaeans) to his day. Verity guesses the word is a corruption of *Tsin,* the great dynasty that gave the country its name *Tsina* or China, but according to *OED,* the etymology of *China* is debated, and is in any case not a native Chinese word. Ortelius places Pekin just inside the Great Wall of China (Thompson, "Milton's Knowledge" 160).

391. *Agra and Lahor of great Mogul:* both once rich capitals of the Mogul empire. Purchas describes them at length (Gilbert, *Geographical Dictionary* 12–13,

168–69). Keightley not only specifies their location precisely (Agra on the Jumnah River south of Agra in Central India, Lahor in the Punjab [i.e., present-day Pakistan]), but also insists—perhaps to correct Milton's implied iambic accent—that *Mogul* is correctly accented on the first syllable. The Moguls ruled India before and after Milton's lifetime; the Taj Mahal, built in Agra by the fifth Mogul emperor, Shah Jahan (1592–1666), was completed in 1648.

392–93. *where / The Persian in Ecbatan sate:* according to Xenophon, Ecbatana (its Greek name) was the summer residence of Persian kings (Gilbert, *Geographical Dictionary* 109) until the Greek conquest in ca. 330 BCE, Susa being the winter residence (Verity), and is the same city as what the KJV calls Achmetha, where Darius found an important scroll (Ezra 6:2). It is now Hamadan in west central Iran. Cf. *PR* 3.286. Heylyn reports the city's importance (Cawley 10).

392. *Chersonese:* Greek, "peninsula," originally the Thracian peninsula west of the Hellespont, now mostly poetic or rhetorical (so *OED*), but here intending either what is now Sumatra or the Malay peninsula.

    golden: Purchas (5:492–92) argues that although Ptolemy had called the region "aureate," the name must refer to Sumatra, as there is no gold in what was then called Malacca (see also Purchas 1.32). Josephus thought the region to be Ophir (*Antiquities* 8.6.4) along with later authors including Sir Thomas Browne (*Vulgar Errors* 2.2), and the Bible translators Junius and Tremellius identify Solomon's direction as the golden Chersonese (*ad auream Chersonesum*), citing Josephus as their authority (1 Kings 9:28n), as also noted by Purchas (5:491–92); see **11.400**. Milton mentions the peninsula in *PR* 4.74, where his spelling (*Chersoness*) avoids a rhyme with *these* in the preceding line (Bush). Fowler finds a pattern in Milton's arrangement of the nine Asian kingdoms; this kingdom, which occupies "the central position of sovereignty" in the list, is nevertheless the one without visible ruler, a pattern to be repeated for the African kingdoms (**11.396–407**).

393–94. *or since / in Hispahan:* Ispahan, or more properly Isfahan, a city in central modern Iran, was also a Persian capital, having become so in 1598 under Shah Abbás the Great (1586–1628), for whom the Englishman Sir Robert Shirley directed a major army reform. The city was greatly celebrated in the seventeenth century, many European merchants and artificers settling there. John Cartwright, visiting Persia in 1603, describes the circumference of Isfahan's walls as a day's journey on horseback, whereas Heylyn reports the walls' circumference as nine miles. Cawley claims that the change from Ecbatana in one line to Hispahan in the next would represent a vast change in time for Milton's contemporaries, since Ecbatana was associated with ancient Persian history and Hispahan with contemporary commerce (133–34). Hughes (*Paradise Lost*) assumes that *Hispahan* is a printer's error for *Ispahan*, since "Milton usually avoided aspirates."

394–95. *where the Russian Ksar / In Mosco:* Gilbert reports that Anthony Jenkinson, whose narratives are reflected in Milton's *HistMosc*, also furnished its correct latitude, acknowledged by Mercator in his new map (*Geographical Dictionary* 197; cf. Hakluyt, *Principal Navigations* 1.513). Masson claims that Moscow was considered in the seventeenth century to be part of Asia. The bounds that Milton sets for Russia at the beginning of *HistMosc* are considerably less than the modern ones (Gilbert, *Geographical Dictionary* 249).

   Ksar: also "tsar, czar," historically "the title of the autocrat or emperor of Russia" (so *OED* a).

395–96. *or the Sultan in Bizance / Turchestan-born: Bizance* is Byzantium, the former name of Constantinople, which became Istanbul after it fell to the Turks in 1453 CE and thence the seat of the Ottoman Empire ruled by the Sultan. Weidner says of Byzantium, "in ancient geography, a Greek city built on the eastern part of the site of Constantinople, in which it was merged in 330 A.D." Sandys spent four months there in 1610 and describes it at length. "By calling the Sultan 'Turchestan born,'Milton refers to the origin of the Turks in central Asia" (Gilbert, *Geographical Dictionary* 304). Keightley complains that *born* should be *descended,* since the Turks had left Turkestan centuries earlier.

   Sultan: "the sovereign or chief ruler of a Muslim country; specifically . . . the sovereign of Turkey" (so *OED* 1). "Of all the Turkish sultans who reigned in *Bizance* (ancient Byzantium, Constantinople), the reader would be likeliest to think of Solyman the Magnificent, in whose reign (1520–66) Turkish conquest was carried as far as the walls of Vienna, the frontiers of Persia, and many of the islands and cities of the Mediterranean as far as Algiers and Nice. Cf. 10.457" (Hughes, "Variorum").

396–407. Fowler finds the arrangement of nine African kingdoms to correspond with the nine Asian ones, with Ophir and its Solomonic associations in the center; he ekes out the list, however, with Rome (*PL* 11.405), which Milton explicitly puts in Europe.

397–98. *Th'Empire of Negus to his utmost Port / Ercoco:* Arkiko, a port on the western shore of the Red Sea, formerly belonged to the extensive empire of Negus, or Ethiopia. Milton's reference to the city as the "utmost Port" of the Negus empire suggests a passage in Purchas (Gilbert, *Geographical Dictionary* 116). Keightley notes, variously, that *Negus* means "king" in Ethiopian (i.e., Amharic), that Heylyn identifies Ercoco as the Adulis of Ptolemy, and that Mercator's map has it as *Arquico,* its name in Portuguese, as in *Os Lusiades* 10.52.5–6. A medieval legend identifies the Negus of Ethiopia with the legendary Prester John.

398–99. *and the less Maritim Kings / Mombaza, and Quiloa, and Melind:* cf. *Os Lusiades* 1.54.4, "De Quiloa, de Mombaça, e de Sofala." Both Mombaza and Melind (modern Mombasa and Malindi, in Kenya) were small kingdoms on the coast of East Africa. Melind was an ally of the Portuguese, but both Mombaza and Quiloa (modern Kilwa Kisiwani, in Tanzania) resisted them, and both were ransacked of plentiful gold, silver, pearl, and rich fabrics; the three names appear together in Purchas (2:1024) and several times in Camöens's *Os Lusiades* (1.54, 99, 103; 2.56–59, 70, 73, 94; 5.45, 84; 10.26–27, 39, 96) (Gilbert, *Geographical Dictionary* 186–87, 195–96, 241). The Richardsons find the substitution of *Kings* for "kingdoms" to be "elegantly poetical." Keightley complains that Milton mispronounces Quiloa, which should be disyllabic (Kíl wa), and Sofála, "as they are both pronounced by Camöens." Verity judges that East Africa may have had greater epic associations at the time due to the 1655 translation of *Os Lusiades* by Sir Richard Fanshawe (1608–66), whom he describes as "Milton's Cambridge contemporary and successor in the post of Latin Secretary," but Fanshawe supported the royalist side during the civil war and Interregnum, and thus could not have succeeded Milton.

398. *Maritim:* 1667 *Maritine.* Both forms were current until the eighteenth century; the 1672 word is stressed on its second syllable (Fowler).

400. *Sofala thought Ophir:* Sofala was a small East African trading port held first by Arabs, then by the Portuguese; it was identified by some as Ophir, an unidentified location from which King Solomon obtained gold (Gilbert, *Geographical Dictionary* 272). Cf. 1 Kings 10:11 and 2 Chron. 8:18. Heylyn (4:62) rejects that association, which he attributes to Ortelius, both because the biblical person named Ophir (Gen. 10:29) settled in the opposite direction and because the port was much too near Palestine for Solomon to have spent three years reaching it. The Portuguese took the port in 1505, and it remained part of their colonial province of Mozambique until independence in 1975. Starnes and Talbert note an expanded entry on Ophir in the 1638 edition of Charles Stephanus's *Dictionarium* (301). Fowler lays great emphasis on the Ophir connection, finding in it an absence of human sovereignty and instead the "unseen sovereignty of Christ," based on mentions of Ophir in Ps. 45:9 and Isa. 13:12–13, verses that are sometimes interpreted messianically. Milton referred to the "mines of Ophir" in *Ref* as proverbial sources of wealth (Patterson, *Works* 3:78). Josephus spoke of "the land that was of old called Ophir, but now the *Aurea Chersonesus*" (*Antiquities* 8.6.4; cf. *PL* 11.392).

401. *Of Congo, and Angola fardest South:* in Milton's time, Congo included most of western Africa south of Guinea, though Hume calls it "a little Kingdom on the Western Shoar of Africa...south of which is Angola." In *ComBk* 114, Milton cites Sir Walter Raleigh on the negative impact of polygamy on Christian conversion there (Patterson, *Works* 18:158). Purchas reports that the king of Angola was originally a deputy of the Congo, but had become independent and eventually conquered the surrounding countries (2:995). Milton wrote to the king of Portugal asking for compensation under treaty for an English captain who lost ship and cargo in either Angola or Brazil (*State Papers* 149; Patterson, *Works* 13:461, 463).

402. *thence from Niger Flood to Atlas Mount:* the Niger is a river of West Africa. Atlas, also known as Atlantis, is actually a high mountain range in North Africa, supposed in classical myth to be a giant holding up the sky (e.g., *Aeneid* 4.246–51). Verity claims *thence* indicates a move northward from the western coast of Africa. Cf. *Epistol* 20, where Milton puns on Atlas and a map book. Cf. also *Idea* 24, *PL* 4.985–89, and *PR* 4.115. Hume thought Milton referred to Atlas Minor, or Errif, the border between the kingdoms of Fez and Morocco.

403. *The Kingdoms of Almansor, Fez and Sus:* there were several rulers named Mansur or Al-Mansur; Milton is probably referring to Abu Amir al-Mansur

(939–1002 CE), a powerful Muslim ruler of Andalusia and most of North Africa north of the Atlas who was known as Almanzor by medieval Latin and Spanish writers and not, as Masson claims, to the second Abbasid Caliph, because that Al-Mansur died several centuries earlier (775 CE) far to the east in Mecca. The confusion accounts for Keightley's complaint that Milton's account is spatially misleading. Fez was both a city and region in what is modern Morocco, south of the straits of Gibraltar. Sus, a region of southwestern Morocco, was also described by Leo Africanus (Gilbert, *Geographical Dictionary* 122–23). An additional Almansor, reported by Cann, was emperor of Morocco who at the invitation of the Moors invaded Spain with 60,000 horses in 1158 CE and then usurped the territories of his allies, only to be slain by Christians at the siege of Santarem in Portugal. Thompson thinks Milton may have learned of Al-Mansur from Heylyn's *Cosmographie,* where Al-Mansur is the only personal name in the passage ("Milton's Knowledge" 160). Fowler glosses the Arabic name *Mansur* as "victorious" (245).

Verity (cf. *thence* in *PL* 11.405) claims that *Sus* or Susa is Tunis, but although there is such a city on the Mediterranean south of Tunis, and there have indeed been cities by that name elsewhere, the context suggests the Moroccan one.

404. *Marocco and Algiers, and Tremisen:* city-kingdoms of northwestern Africa in Milton's day. Morocco is described by Leo Africanus as "one of the greatest cities of the whole world," and Algiers as a beautiful town of many buildings and space for all trades and occupations (Gilbert, *Geographical Dictionary* 16). In *Animad,* Milton cites the Remonstrant's use of Constantinople and Morocco to denote Islam (Patterson, *Works* 3:169).

Tremisen: modern Tlemcen in Algeria. In Milton's day, it was another city-kingdom (Gilbert, *Geographical Dictionary* 302). Ortelius's map has Tremisen marked on the northern coast of Africa, exactly as Milton spelled it, a spelling shared by Heylyn in his *Cosmographie* (Thompson, "Milton's Knowledge" 160). Chaucer's Knight had been at "Tramyssene" (*General Prologue* 62).

405. *On Europe thence:* Fowler claims that the placement of Barbary and Rome in a position similar to Byzantium (New Rome) and Turkestan in *PL* 11.395–96 could imply an uncomplimentary analogy between papal empires (i.e., controlled by the pope) and Saracen ones (i.e., controlled by Muslims), since true power in Milton's mind did not lie in external *sway* but in "the power of the invisible incorruptible 'true Church.'"

On: Fenton (in Todd) has *Or* (725).

406. *in Spirit perhaps he also saw:* the Western Hemisphere would be invisible from any vantage point in the Eastern. Todd cites Joseph Cooper Walker on a similar series of revelations in Marino's *Gerusalemme distrutta*, beginning in 7.27.

407. *Rich Mexico the seat of Motezume* [*sic*]: i.e., Mexico City, described by Francis Lopez de Gomara at the end of Cortes's entry as a city of some 60,000 thousand houses (Gilbert, *Geographical Dictionary* 191). The Aztec emperor Moteuczoma (Spanish: Montezuma) was subdued by the Spanish general Cortez in 1519–20 (Verity).

408–11. Johnson cites this passage in his claim that Milton indulges only in occasional lists of proper names because he was convinced that English was unfit for smooth versification and that such names "add little but musick to his poem" (*Rambler* 4 [Jan. 19, 1751]:101).

408. *Cusco in Peru:* i.e., Cuzco, the capital, conquered by Pizarro in 1533. Verity notes that Cuzco is in the center of Peru and repeats the popular derivation; Cuzco is thought to mean "center" or "navel." Gilbert cites Purchas's report that the city had been worshiped as if a god. He also notes that in Milton's time, writers often called the entire continent Peru, as Milton seems to do in *Patrem* 94 (Gilbert, *Geographical Dictionary* 232).

409–10. *Atabalipa:* the son, along with his brother Guascar, of the Peruvian king Guainacapa; their strife allowed Pizarro—whom Hume calls an "Ignoble Hogherd"—to kill the first, then ransom out but still execute the second. Sir Walter Raleigh rehearses the Spanish accounts of these events (8.398). Gilbert cites the report that Atabalipa was able to fill an entire house with gold to pay his own ransom (*Geographical Dictionary* 232–33).

yet unspoil'd / Guiana, whose great Citie Geryons Sons: Guiana was a region in the northern part of South America, of greater extent that the present country of that name (Gilbert, *Geographical Dictionary* 134); Hume calls it the most fruitful part of Peru, and St. Maur reports that the people are long-lived (389–90). Verity specifies its location as between the Amazon and Orinoco rivers, now divided by Venezuela and Brazil. In Greek mythology, Geryon was a legendary Catalonian king overcome by Hercules, who carried off his oxen (*Aeneid* 8.202–03); the Spanish are thus his "sons." Joseph Hunter thinks the Geryon reference may have been suggested by Spenser in *Faerie Queene* 5.10.9, a connection Fowler finds probable, since Spenser "had built up Geryon as a type of political tyranny"; Fowler also links the three-headed Geryon to the three New World territories (Mexico, Peru, and El Dorado) mentioned here, and asserts that Guiana would have been of interest in 1667, when the English colony in Guiana was ceded to the Netherlands in exchange for New York. In contrast to *unspoil'd / Guiana,* cf. Sir Walter Raleigh's comment that the Spanish king Charles V "had the maidenhead of Peru" (8.388). Northrop Frye (*Paradise Lost*) explains *yet unspoil'd* as "not yet discovered."

411. *El Dorado:* Spanish, "the gilded." "The name of a fictitious country (according to others a city) abounding in gold, believed by the Spaniards and by Sir Walter Raleigh to exist upon the Amazon within the jurisdiction of the governor of Guiana" (so *OED*). Raleigh reported that Manoa, the imperial city of Guiana, which the Spaniards called El Dorado, exceeded all other cities in the world for size, riches, and position (8:398); Raleigh sought the city in 1595. Hakluyt's account of Guiana include Raleigh's claim that "The country hath more quantity of gold by manifold, then the best partes of the Indies, or Peru" (3:628). Diego Ordus, one of Cortez's companions, claimed to have entered it (Hume).

411–12. *but to nobler sights / Michael from Adams eyes the Filme remov'd:* cf. Pallas clearing Diomedes' eyesight in *Iliad* 5.127–28, imitated by Virgil in *Aeneid* 2.604–06. Michael does the same for Geoffrey in Tasso's *Gerusalemma liberata* 18.93, so that he may see the angelic hosts come to his aid, and as noted by Dunster (in Todd), a similar action occurs in Giangiorgio Trissino's lesser-known epic, *Italia liberata dai Goti* (1547–48), when an angel clears Belisario's eyes from the visual imperfections of the Fall before showing him visions of the future (9.185–97). Michael's *nobler sights* will include the principal actions of men to the final consummation of things (Newton). Webb has a female interlocutor, Aspasia, comment about this passage: "Such advantages were not intended for us poor women; even Angels are partial, as you represent them" (60); see also **11.366–68.**

412–20. Cope links this passage not only with Adam's later cry in 12.270–7 that he has been enlightened, but with the poem's pervasive images of falling and rising in the poem, conceptualized metaphors that are so transferred to the spiritual realm that the reader need not recognize their literal resonances (87–88).

412–18. Lewalski traces Adam's purged and exercised physical sight throughout book 11 (26); see **11.368**.

413–15. Wesley reduces this passage to a single line: "Which that false Fruit had bred; then purg'd the Nerve."

413. *that false Fruit that promis'd clearer sight:* cf. 9.705–09 and 1011.

414. *Euphrasy:* "a plant, *Euphrasia officinalis* (family *Scrophulariaceæ*), formerly held in high repute for its medicinal virtues in the treatment of diseases of the eye" (so *OED* 1); *Rue* is "a perennial evergreen shrub of the genus *Ruta,* esp. *Ruta graveolens,* having bitter, strong-scented leaves which were formerly much used for medicinal purposes" (so *OED* 1). Euphrasy is the herb eyebright; both euphrasy and rue were used for sharpening vision, and rue also to counteract poisons. Todd cites John Swan's *Speculum Mundi* for the claim that rue purges sight when taken internally ("Ruta comesta recens oculos caligine purgat" [248]) but does not include the potentially relevant second line of the Latin distich, "Ruta viris coitum minuit, mulieribus auget," which Swan renders in English as "It makes men chaste, and women fills with lust," i.e., because women are cold and moist (Swan 248–49). Hughes (*Paradise Lost, A Poem*) reports the mention of euphrasy or "eyebright" in Gerard's *Herball* (1597), which claims that euphrasy or eyebright "preserveth the sight, increaseth it, and being feeble and lost it restoreth the same" (Gerard 537). Rue was called the "herb of grace" because it was used in exorcisms (Montgomery). In Lawry's reading, these two herbs symbolize the dual action of the undervalued last two books of the epic, in which Adam's new perceptions represent not only the *anagnorisis* and *peripeteia* of classical tragedy (the rue of tragic suffering for error) but also the blessing of Christian repentance and reconciliation; the Greek word *euphrasy* means "delight or enhancement of heart or mind" ("'Euphrasy and Rue'" 3–5). Himes (*Paradise Lost: A Poem*), linking this delight to the bitterness of rue, finds some correspondence to the angel's bittersweet disclosure of the world's history in Rev. 10:10–11, whereas Fowler identifies the combination of "joy" and "pious sorrow" that Michael counseled Adam to temper in 11.361–62. Svendsen claims that although euphrasy and rue were noted to have the properties that Milton ascribes to them, they were usually joined in herbals by fennel; Milton probably avoided this herb because of its association with serpents and with Satan's speech in 9.581 (*Milton and Science* 130). Otten argues that rue is identical to the moly of the *Odyssey* (10.287–303; cf. *Mask* 629–41) and that Michael parallels Hermes not only in supplying rue to Adam, but in being his enlightener, a role assigned to Hermes in the Orphic hymns; rue is also linked in the Neoplatonic tradition to *paideia* or instruction; Otten reports that euphrasy was usually taken dissolved in water, and finds Milton's clinically specific three drops of water to be echoed in alchemy (361–72). Bentley objects to the use of euphrasy and rue at all, since if Adam could have seen America in spirit (11.377), he could have seen the rest in spirit as well. Verity, citing Sir Thomas Browne's remark that the medicinal efficacy of a plant or mineral was supposedly indicated by its similarity in color or shape to the part of the diseased body, points out that the euphrasy flower has an eyelike mark; Verity also claims that eyesight metaphors came naturally to Milton, citing *Ref,* "If we will but purge with sovrain eyesalve that intellectual ray which God hath planted in us" (Patterson, *Works* 3:33), and *RCG,* "some eye-brightning electuary of knowledge, and foresight" (Patterson, *Works* 3:231).

416. *of Life:* Ps. 36:9 connects "light" with the "fountain of life"; see also the "river of water of life" of Rev. 22:1.

    three drops: cf. *Mask* 912–13. Fowler links these three drops to three structural stages in the last two books; see **12.5** and **12.467**.

    instill'd: "introduce[d] drop by drop or in small quantities" (so *OED* 1).

417. *So deep the power of these Ingredients pierc'd:* Keightley supposes that attempts of this kind had probably been made on Milton's own eyes.

418. *mental sight:* cf. the "shine inward" of *PL* 3.51–55 and also the "inward eyes illuminated" of *SA* 1689. Wesley glosses as "the eye of the mind."

    Adam as the one seeing is partly tragic hero, partly prophet, partly all-seeing "Grand Parent," and partly the representative man indicated by his very name (Lawry, *Shadow* 277).

420. *Sunk down and all his Spirits became intranst:* cf. Adam's trance in 8.453. Pecheux uses the similarities in the trances to argue that the last two books partly typify the birth of the church ("Second Adam" 181–82).

421–22. *by the hand / Soon raised:* cf. the pattern in some biblical narratives of vision, where the fainting human agent is explicitly or implicitly raised to his feet before the vision is continued or explained (Ezek. 1:28–2:2, 3:23–24, 37:10; Dan. 8:17–18, 10:8–11; Acts 26:16; Rev. 1:17; see also the human agent waking from sleep or as from sleep in 1 Kings 19:5; Zech. 4:1; and Luke 9:32); see **11.758–59**. McColley claims that the motif indicates that Milton is influenced by the extrabiblical *Book of Enoch* ("Book" 38).

423–28. Coleridge cites this passage as an example of the doctrine of original sin being "excellently described" by "our English poets" (Wittreich 253–54). Cf. *DocCh* 1.11, which denotes the effects of the Fall on Adam and Eve's progeny (Maurice Kelley 147; Patterson, *Works* 15:183–89); see also *PL* 11.106–08; 12.285–86, 398–400.

423. *now ope thine eyes, and first behold:* as Samuel notes, the phrasing repeats Beatrice's bidding, "Apri gli occhi, e riguarda" nearly word for word (*Dante* 223), though the Italian lacks *first;* cf. *Paradiso* 23.46. Trapp reports a sixteenth century triptych depiction of the Fall in which the centerpiece is Adam, the serpent, and the tree, and the two wings the resultant evils of drunkenness and war/strife (264); these two sins account for most of the episodes in book 11. Fowler identifies this line as the beginning of the second major episode in *PL,* the first beginning the war in heaven in books 5 and 6, and cites Johnson's judgment that "both are closely connected with the great action; one was necessary to Adam as a warning, the other as a consolation" (Johnson, "Milton" 187). Lewalski traces Adam's purged and exercised physical sight throughout book 11 (26); see **11.368**.

425. *who never touch'd:* Burden notices here the same collapsing of Adam and Eve into a single sinning unit as in 3.130–32. Eve, not Adam, touched the tree, just as Eve, not Adam, was deceived (77).

426. *Th'excepted Tree:* "a traditional phrase for the Tree of Knowledge" ('excluded, forbidden')" (Ricks, *Paradise Lost*). The past participle of "except," "To leave out, to exclude from a privilege, to leave out of account or consideration" (*OED* 1).

427–28. *Nor sinn'd thy sin, yet from that sin derive / Corruption:* for the biblical phrase "to sin a sin"; see, e.g., Exod. 32:30 and 1 John 5:16. Newton says the idiom is also used by the best classical authors. Montgomery perhaps indicates a different audience when he specifies "scriptural as well as classical." Shawcross links Adam's sin to Israel's in Exod. 32; both of them will "wander" ("*Paradise Lost*" 10). For the generalized effect of Adam's sin, see Rom. 5:14.

    1667 *that sin derive:* 1674 *that derive.*

429–65. *His eyes he op'nd:* the episode of Cain and Abel (lines 429–47; cf. Gen. 4) is the first of six visions in book 11, the others being the lazar-house (477–93), the intermarriages between Cain and Abel's offspring (556–627), succeeded by scenes of sin in war and Enoch's translation (638–73), then scenes of sin in peacetime and Noah's unwelcome preaching, culminating in the Flood (711–53), and then the survival of Noah and his family, with their exit from the ark and the rainbow (840–69). Many commentators have compared the visions to the various scenes on Achilles' shield in *Iliad* 18.483–607. The Richardsons claim that while both vision and narration in books 11–12 are analogous to the description of Achilles' shield, they are also essential to *PL*, not only because of the power of the descriptions, but also because they serve to equip Adam for all good works (cf. 2 Tim. 3:17) and fully comfort him. Douady judges that Michael does not dare—except in ambiguous terms—identify Cain and Abel as Adam's own sons (198). Lawry claims that this encounter of opposing human choices is first because "typic" (*Shadow* 278). Martz cites this passage as one example of an imbalance he finds in the last two books: lengthy, vivid, and relentless descriptions of horror with only brief and abstract statements of countering grace; "theologically, the design may be said to work; poetically, it is a disaster" (150). Good identifies the sin Milton depicts here as religious envy, "which needed only to be magnified to national proportions to produce an Inquisition" (227). Radzinowicz reads this scene and the next as typological, since a type prefigures something to come, and "the history of the world is explainable as the type of the man of faith prefigures Christ, as the old Adam prefigures the new, as the

perfect life of the redeemed prefigures the perfect development of the state";
she argues that the purpose of the first two visions is to prepare Adam to take
death quietly, and death is finally stripped of its horror in the "sleep…gentle
wafting" of *PL* 12.434–35 (41–42); see also **11.515–25**.

429. *His eyes he op'nd, and beheld:* Lewalski traces Adam's purged and exercised
physical sight throughout book 11 (26); see **11.368**.

430. *arable and tilth:* Hume has "plowed and sown."
    tilth: "labour or work in the cultivation of the soil; tillage, agricultural work,
husbandry" (*OED* 2). Hughes (*Paradise Lost, A Poem*) has "land under cultivation." Verity claims that *tilth* is active in sense, denoting husbandry and
cultivation, citing Cotgrave's definition of "labouring, ploughing, or breaking
up of the ground."

431. *sheep-walks:* cf. the singular, "a tract of grass-land used for pasturing sheep"
(so *OED*).

432–60. Hughes (*Paradise Lost, A Poem*) claims the symbolic importance of
Cain's murder; Augustine makes it an example of the danger of envy in *City of
God* 15.5.

432–33. *Ith'midst an Altar as the Land-mark…ofgrassie sord:* cf. the altar Adam
proposed to raise from "grassie Terfe" in lines 323–24. Bridges cites *Ith'midst*
as the only use of the Shakespearean contraction; see also *i'th'midst* in *PL* 1.224
(37). Fowler judges that the spelling "probably gives a correct indication of the
necessary elision"; the *Altar* is not only a landmark because it is prominent, but
because it represents the Law and the covenant. Newton judges that Milton
makes the brothers share the same altar, since the word *brought* in Gen. 4:3,
retained by Milton in *PL* 11.434, supposes some common place of worship.
    sord: Hume believes the word to either be a misspelling for *sod* or a synonym
for *turf,* from the dark (swart) color of the earth. Bentley emends the spelling to
swerð (the Anglo-Saxon word means "skin or surface" [Verity]). Pearce objects
that *sord* replicates a common pronunciation, as in *Green-sord* and *sord of Bacon.*
Spelled as "sward," "the surface of soil covered with grass or other herbage;

turf" (so *OED* 2b). Newton and also William Aldis Wright note that "Fenton's edition," i.e., the twelfth edition with an added biography by Elijah Fenton (1725) has *sod.* Keightley cites the First Folio's "greene-sord" in *Winter's Tale* 4.3.157. Todd claims that *sord* is Milton's word, whereas Hughes (*Paradise Lost*) claims that *sord,* meaning "sward" or "green turf," did not become a dialectical form until the nineteenth century, though the perplexity of earlier Milton critics would seem to belie this claim. Wesley glosses *grassie sord* as "green Turf" and *Rustic* as "rough, unadorned."

433. *anon:* B. A. Wright defines this adverb, here and in 11.861 and 12.150, as a loose usage for "soon," now literary ("Note" 147); see **11.46.**

434–38. Fowler claims that the omission of names for *Reaper* and *Shepherd* is doubtless to mask the murderer's identity from his father.

434. *sweatie:* "laborious, toiling" (so *OED* 2b). Shumaker cites this passage as an example of how in the vision section we can "see meanings," e.g., *sweatie* Cain has worked hard, and he does not choose carefully; Shumaker also postulates that in order to render Cain's lack of respect visible, Milton borrowed the flame from heaven from biblical paintings (*Unpremeditated Verse* 203), but see **11.441–42.** George Coffin Taylor suggests that *sweatie,* a word used nowhere else by Milton, may have been suggested by Du Bartas's "sweating Tubal," a descendant of Cain he mentions immediately after this incident (*Milton's Use* 113); see *PL* 11.565–73.

435. *First Fruits:* "the fruits first gathered in a season; the earliest products of the soil; especially with reference to the custom of making offerings of these to God or the gods" (so *OED* 1).

436. *Uncull'd:* the opposite of *culled,* that is, "chosen, picked, selected; gathered, plucked" (so *OED*). Cf. Abel's *Choicest* in line 438 (Hughes, *Paradise Lost*). Cf. also the biblical requirement to bring the best and choicest of both animal and plant in Exod. 22:29–30 and Lev. 3:1.

439. *The Inwards and thir Fat:* i.e., the entrails and fat, a sacrificial practice echoing Lev. 3:3–4, though the Richardsons claim that Milton follows Homer and that this sacrifice is not typological but rather a tribute of acknowledgment and gratitude. St. Maur also claims it is "a Sacrifice of Thankfulness" (392). The poet Wordsworth finds fault with the line as "inelegant" and reminiscent of "a Butcher's stall," adding, "it is the more to be lamented as the rest of the description [11.429–47] is a pattern of simplicity; it is the language which seems lost, to modern tongues" (Wittreich 108). Verity cites a similar use of *inwards* for "inner parts" in *Othello* 2.1.297. *OED* lists only *inward* as the substantive.

   strew'd: past tense of "strew," "to cover … with something loosely scattered or sprinkled" (so *OED* 2).

440. *cleft Wood:* MacCallum claims that Milton's events and figures gain in significance by their typological suggestiveness; the wood of Abel's sacrifice ultimately denotes the sacrifice of Christ ("Milton and Sacred History" 154).

441–42. *propitious Fire from Heav'n / Consum'd with nimble glance:* fire from heaven was the common patristic gloss on "the LORD had respect unto Abel and to his offering" in Gen. 4:4 (Hume). Fire from heaven consumes offerings in Lev. 9:23–24, Judg. 6:21, 1 Kings 18:38, 1 Chron. 21:26, and 2 Chron. 7:1. Broadbent finds the earlier portion of the Cain-Abel sequence to be stylistically relaxed but complains that in these two lines "the language climbs back onto Homeric stilts" (*Some Graver Subject* 271). Fowler glosses *nimble* as "swift"; cf. *OED* 4a, "quick or ready to do something," and *OED* 3, "quick and light in movement or action; agile; active"; cf. *PL* 6.73.

   glance: "a swift oblique movement or impact" (*OED* 1a).

442. *grateful steame:* Ricks, noting the "the infection of the Fall" indicated in 11.323, also asks whether the steam of Abel's sacrifice is pleasant as well as thankfully received (*Milton's Grand Style* 113); see also *PL* 11.864.

   steame: "an odorous exhalation or fume" (so *OED* 1b).

443. *for his was not sincere:* Milton's extrabiblical explanation is added to justify God's ways (Le Comte). Whiting finds similarities between Milton's statement and the commentary in the Geneva Bible ("Before the Flood" 74–75) and that the ideas expressed there may have been traditional (*Milton* 137). In Serafino della Salandra's *Adamo Caduto* of 1647, Cain questions the existence of God and asserts that everything has its source in chance and nature (Kirkconnell 347). Cf. *DocCh* 2.4: "true worship is that by which God is worshipped with sincerity after the form and manner which he has himself prescribed...hypocritical worship, in which the external forms are duly observed, but without any accompanying affection of the mind" (Patterson, *Works* 17:75–77).

sincere: Ricks (*Paradise Lost*) notes that the word includes the literal sense of "pure, uncontaminated"; cf. *OED* 3: "Containing no element of dissimulation or deception; not feigned or pretended; real, true."

444. *hee inlie rag'd:* McColley (*"Paradise Lost": An Account* 189) wants to see parallels with Du Bartas's account (1:388–89.293–316), not only in Cain's concealed anger, but also in its visual focus. B. A. Wright doubts that *hee*, here and in line 453, is emphatic; it rather avoids elision (*Milton's Poems* xxvii).

rag'd: cf. "rage," "to show signs of madness or frenzy; to rave in madness or fury; to act or speak wildly or furiously; to storm" (so *OED* 2).

445–47. The first two lines are "wonderfully efficient and tonally correct," but the last is "too literary, with its noisy alliteration and assonance, falling rhythms, reference to Hebrew psychology" (Broadbent, *Some Graver Subject* 272). Maurice Kelley claims that book 11 contains four of the sins enumerated in *DocCh* as results of the Fall; this one is parricide (149); see also **11.472–77**, **11.630–32**, and **11.641–47**. "Murder of Abel" is one of five illustrations for book 11 in Tilt's 1843 illustrated edition of Milton's *Poetical Works* (C. H. C. Baker 116); see further lists of Tilt's illustrations in **11.187** and **12.1–5**.

445. *Smote him into the Midriff with a stone:* Hume claims that Milton here has followed "the most probable opinion" as to Abel's manner of death and, citing 1 John 3:12, that Abel's pure contribution to the brotherly discourse preceding the murder (Gen. 4:8) was spiritual and admonitory, causing Cain's rage. The Richardsons also report, "it has been thought that Cain beat...the breath out of his Brother's Body with a great stone," but give no sources. Cowley thought it probable that Cain "knockt [Abel] on the head with some great stone, which was one of the first ordinary and most natural weapons of Anger" (*Davideis* 270n16); this monumental stone is derived from Aeneas lifting a stone that six normal men could not lift (*Aeneid* 12.896–901), derived in turn from Homer's two-man stone (*Iliad* 20.286–87); Cowley also mentions Ovid's centaur Phaeocomes heaving a log that two yoke of oxen could not move (*Metamorphoses* 12.432–33). Himes (*Paradise Lost: A Poem*) thinks that Cain's murder was caused by a blow to the midriff because of Joab's similarly treacherous murders of Abner and Amasa (2 Sam. 3:27, 20:9–10). McColley (*"Paradise Lost"* 183–84, 230) also cites Georgius Cedrenus, *Compendium Historiam;* Georgius Syncellus, *Geographia;* and Andrew Willet, *Hexapla in Genesin.*

446–47. *and deadly pale / Groand out his Soul with gushing bloud effus'd:* cf. similar moments in the *Aeneid,* where Rhoetius "vomits forth his life with wine and blood mixed" (9.349) and Mezentius pours his life out in streams (10.908). In whatever way Abel was killed, however, his blood is properly mentioned, as Scripture particularly mentions it (Newton); cf. Gen. 4:10–11; Matt. 23:35; Luke 11:51; Heb. 11:4, 12:24. Champion argues that in the episodes of the last two books, earlier metaphors are transferred to reality; here, Death's appearance in book 2 is even more monstrous in human form (392).

    groaning: "to breathe (one's life, soul) away or out in groaning" (so *OED* 1c).

    effused: "to pour forth or out (a liquid); to shed (blood)" (*OED* 1). Wesley glosses as "poured out."

449–53. *cri'd…repli'd:* Purcell (172) notes that these lines rhyme with three intervening lines, a category mentioned by Diekhoff, though not for these lines ("Rhyme" 542).

449. *th'Angel:* Darbishire (*Poetical Works*) cites this spelling as an exception to the general principle that Milton elided with *th'* before an unstressed syllable; he consistently spells *the Angel* to this point, after which he repeats the elided spelling five times (*PL* 11.635, 759, 762; 12.485, 574).

450–52. *O Teacher:* Mörs finds the relationship between Adam and the angel similar to that between Dante and his teacher Virgil in *Divine Comedy* (151). Bundy's seminal exploration of Michael as teacher in books 11–12 begins with this passage (147).

    some great mischief: Adam questions divine justice, as the sinner does not appear to be punished (Summers, *Muse's Method* 198).

452–60. Burden contends that Michael's corrective provides Adam's first lesson in divine and hence poetical justice (190).

Pietie has only two syllables. Sprott cites this line as an example of "elision by the synaloepha of vowels" (78–79).

453. *T'whom Michael thus, hee also mov'd:* Wordsworth remarks on Michael's notable sympathy here, since in 11.249–50 the angel "kingly from his state / Inclined not" (Wittreich 108). Milton "makes the first sight of death affect the heavenly nature also" (Keightley). Shumaker finds that this mention of Michael's emotion is exceptional; the affective focus is quite properly on Adam, whose sin has initiated the long history of suffering (*Unpremeditated Verse* 214). Fowler cites the idea that tragedy should move the spectator, as noted, for instance, in Sidney's *Apology*. On the mannerist presentation of Michael, see **11.298–300**.

Bridges cites the elision *T'whom* of this line along with the emphatic *To whom* of line 466 as proof that Milton's rules of elision are "permissive" or arbitrary rather than fixed (34); see also **11.508–09**. On *hee* as non-emphatic, see **11.444**.

455–57. Fox, who traces the Seven Deadly Sins in books 11–12, points out that Cain's motivation for murdering Abel is envy (160). Mollenkott compares the sin of Cain with that of Satan; they are both motivated by envy and both sins are executed violently (34). Cf. *DocCh* 2.11, which includes Cain as an example of envy (Maurice Kelley 190; Patterson, *Works* 17:267).

457. *Fact:* i.e., "deed," from Latin *factum,* "a thing done or performed"; cf. "feat" (*OED* 1). In Milton's time, most commonly "An evil deed, a crime" (*OED* 1c).

458. *th'others Faith approv'd:* Milton's phrase echoes Heb. 11:4 ("By faith Abel offered unto God a more excellent sacrifice than Cain, by which he obtained witness that he was righteous").

459–60. MacCallum stresses how the various "men of faith" (Abel, Enoch, Noah, Abraham) prefigure Christ by their qualities or actions ("Milton and Sacred History" 158); see *PL* 11.701, 808–18, and 12.113.

Rowling in dust and gore: George Coffin Taylor (*Milton's Use* 113) thinks this description may reflect Du Bartas's "The murdered face lies printed in the mud" (1:389.329).

461. *Alas, both for the deed and for the cause:* Adam must first wrestle with the full knowledge of the death he so easily chose, though his compassionate tears are first from self-pity alone (Lawry, *Shadow* 278).

462–65. *But have I now seen Death:* critical comment on this passage has been diverse. Addison praises this passage for how it appropriately combines both Adam's curiosity and natural horror (*Spectator* 3 [Apr. 26, 1712]: 362). Newton thinks, rather, that Milton has forgotten Eve's knowledge of death in *PL* 10.1001–06. Erskine traces a generic shift in the scene: Adam's first sight of death is cast in the epic manner—ostensibly Michael is showing him the future—but the effect is dramatic; we are not concerned with the prophecy but rather with how Adam will adjust his character to the world before him (578–79). B. A. Wright argues from Eve's earlier comment that the pair are ignorant of what form death will take, or who will be its agent; he takes exception to Darbishire's distinction between personified, uppercase *Death* and the lowercase *temporal death* in 12.431–34 (*Milton's "Paradise Lost"* 142). Thompson cites the death of Abel as one example of experience Adam will need in the world; until the ravages of the bird and the beast of prey and the slaying of Abel, Adam has no conception of death ("For *Paradise Lost*" 378). Adam has drawn the wrong conclusion, that he has seen the particular death occasioned by the Fall (Burden 190–91). Michael might also have added that incorporeal beings are only imperfectly known through their physical manifestations—a small point, but the same way of thinking might be dangerously extended to moral decision (Fish 278). Gilbert claims that this passage is one of the few in which Milton presents Adam as inexperienced; usually, he represents the human race and can learn by example as well as experience (*On the Composition* 144–45). Wesley notes this passage as among those particularly excellent.

466. *To whom thus Michael. Death thou hast seen:* Bentley wants to make this "thou *now* has seen," since—he claims—*Michael* is always pronounced as two syllables. Fowler says the word is trisyllabic "in accordance with the slow gravity of the passage." See also Bridges's comment on elision in **11.453**.

467–69. *Death . . . many are the wayes that lead / To his grim Cave, all dismal:* many early commentators have cited a similar phrase from Seneca: "Ubique mors est . . . mille hanc aditus patent" (Death is everywhere . . . there are a thousand ways to it) (*Phoenician Women* 151, 153). Bush also identifies a parallel sentiment in Ovid's *Metamorphoses* (4.439–40), where Hades is described as a city with a thousand wide roads leading to its gates, which stand open on all sides. Several critics cite the Latin phrase "Pompa mortis magis terret, quam mors ipsa" (Death's pomp and display is more terrifying than death itself), quoted by Bacon in his essay "Of Death," though as noted by Bacon's editor (Spedding 6:379), the actual quotation from Seneca's *Epistle* 24.14 is, "Tolle istam pompam sub qua lates et stultos territas" ([Death,] take away all this pomp under which you lurk and terrify fools). Keightley wonders if *all dismal* might not be intended to modify *cave*, rather than *wayes*. Himes (*Paradise Lost: A Poem*) finds it significant that in ancient times caves were used as burial places and that the entrance to Hades is the mouth of a cave (*Aeneid* 6.237); Fowler also records its terrors at the entrance (6.273), death by disease—as here, the result of concupiscence—across from War and Strife, the irascible passions that led to Abel's murder. Fletcher (*Complete Poetical Works*) similarly points out that the cave of death has been a poetic commonplace since the Middle Ages. Erskine (575) reminds readers of the four kinds of death in *DocCh* 1.12–13 (guiltiness, spiritual death, death of the body, and eternal death or damnation [Patterson, *Works* 15:203, 205, 215, 251]), but whereas *DocCh* applies the first two to humankind, in *PL* "their effects are traced more relentlessly in Satan"; see also the information on death **11.57–62** and **11.705–07**. Hughes (*Paradise Lost*) refers to Milton's belief that the body and spirit will both suffer death until the general resurrection; cf. *DocCh* 1.13, when the spirits of the elect will be as easily gathered together as the smallest particles of their bodies (Patterson, *Works* 15:239). Bundy, examining the pedagogical aspects of books 11–12, remarks that Michael the teacher is "far from mild in his methods" (147). As McColley (*"Paradise Lost": An Account* 190) points out, Du Bartas (1:364.259) had spoken of "that feareful Cave" of death and catalogued more diseases than Milton, both mental and physical (1:366–73). Michael here is concerned that Adam's knowledge of death "be more carefully discriminated: Death is less grim than dying" (Burden 191). Fish argues that even in the profusion of detail in book 11, the actual figure of death still eludes the reader, as it did in book 2 (309–10). Hughes (*Complete Poems*) claims that the *Cave* resembles an underworld such as the Sheol of the Hebrews or—as Loane ("Milton and Chapman" 457) suggests—Chapman's paraphrase of Homer's Hades at the very beginning of his *Iliad;* cf. Chapman, "that invisible cave / That no light comforts" (3–4).

471–72. *by violent stroke shall die … by Intemperance more:* cf. *ComBk* 13: "Tertullian fitly calls 'gluttony a man-slayer,' and says that 'it must be punished by … the penalties of fasting, even if God had commanded no fasting,' because our first parents sank into it" (Patterson, *Works* 18:131–32). Hume cites "Plus gula, quam gladius" (More by the throat than by the sword), apparently a version of the proverbial "Plures occidit gula quam gladius" (The throat—i.e., appetite—kills more than the sword)." See also Juvenal's description of the glutton taken by sudden death in *Satire* 1.140–44. Fox identifies gluttony as the second of the Seven Deadly Sins in books 11–12 (163). The potential pessimism of the last two books is "grounded upon man's irrational disregard for the rules of temperance," not only in diet but in the lures of society that "attachd the heart / Of Adam" (Hughes, "Beyond Disobedience" 193); cf. *PL* 11.595–96.

472–77. Book 11 includes four of the sins enumerated as results of the Fall in *DocCh;* this one is gluttony (Maurice Kelley 149); see also **11.445–474**.

473. *Drinks.:* 1667 *Drinks, shall.* 1667 *shal.*

474. *a monstrous crew:* cf. Virgil's account of the evils dwelling at the entrance to Hades (*Aeneid* 6.273–89).

476. *inabstinence:* Milton's usage is the earliest one attested by *OED*. Maurice Kelley (145) notes both here and in 11.514–16 that gluttony is included by Milton (*DocCh* 1.11) among the many sins involved in the Fall (Patterson, *Works* 15:183).

477–93. The lazar-house is the second of six visions in book 11; see **11.429–65**. Newton thinks this passage alludes to Spenser's description of Pain, Strife, Revenge, and others encountered on the way to Pluto's grisly domain, while over them sad Horror is soaring with grim hue and beating his iron wings (*Faerie Queene* 2.7.21–24). Todd cites a similar scene from *Lacrymæ Adami* (10.733–37), but this title does not appear to be listed in any library. Cf. also Sackville's Induction to *Mirror for Magistrates* for allegorical figures "within the porch and jawes of hell" (218), including Death himself, who "His dart anon out of the corps he tooke, / And in his hand (a dreadful sight to see) / With great triumph eftsoones the same he shooke" (379–81), also cited by Todd. Masson recalls the "mask of all the evils" in Milton's projected tragedy; see **11.113–17**. Baumgarten sees a connection with the suffering of the damned in Dante's Malebolge (*Inferno* 29.40–51). Verity infers the influence of "these gloomy abstractions" on the last stanzas of Thomas Gray's Eton *Ode,* especially in the similar images and wording of Gray's lines 61–70 and 81–90, and also Gray's *The Progress of Poesy,* lines 42–45. Champion (392) compares the maladies listed to Sin's hell-hounds in *PL* 2.653–59; cf. **11.446–47**. Godwin records a catalog of diseases from *Piers Plowman* 20.80–101, a scene also mentioned by Todd, which he and "preceding commentators" think "probably furnished Milton with the first hint of his description of a lazar-house" (Godwin 3:361). Hughes (*Paradise Lost, A Poem*), however, finds the spirit of the scene more in keeping with the long account of human disease in Du Bartas (1:366–73). In Du Bartas's text, four "regiments" of various diseases attack, successively, the head, the vital organs, and the "natural powers," while the last regiment causes tumors. These ailments are joined by diseases peculiar to certain countries, to childhood, to age, and to seasons, and by contagious diseases, hereditary diseases, and symptoms without known causes (Weidner). Dick Taylor Jr. remarks that "Milton's little list of diseases...seems puny in comparison with Du Bartas's," and even though Sylvester's translation is fairly literal, it still expands the original 745 lines to 804 ("Milton's Treatment" 62–63). Cf. the brief mention of disease in Avitus, "Then grim disease and various pain crept in; / Corrupted with dread rankness," and the description of the "long, livid Legions of Disease" in Grotius (Kirkconnell 17, 193). Martz cites the lazar-house episode to illustrate his complaint that Milton fails adequately to present an image of grace to counter that of sin, and "instead allows a fissure to develop between the concrete representations of sin and the abstract assertions of Adam's 'Teacher'" (150–51). Mollenkott (35) argues that the second, lazar-house vision is an elaboration of the sin of Eve and specifically identified as such in *PL* 11.475–77. Nelson reports that in 1799 the painter Henry Fuseli exhibited a series of paintings from Miltonic subjects, including a version of this scene, entitled "The Vision of the Madhouse" (46). Svendsen claims that Milton's description of disease sustains the conservative attitude that it is a punishment for sin (*Milton and Science* 203). Cf. Milton's reference in *RCG* to "Pleurisies, Palsies, Lethargies, etc." (Patterson, *Works* 3:189). The poet Shelley cites this passage in his *A Vindication of Natural Diet* of 1812 (Wittreich 528).

477–78. *Immediately a place / Before his eyes appeard, sad, noysom, dark:* responding to some comment from Francis Wrangham in 1807, Wordsworth queried, "Is your objection to the word 'immediately' or to its connection with the others?

The word itself seems to have sufficient poetical authority, even the highest" (Wittreich 115).

479. *A Lazar-house:* "a house for lazars or diseased persons, esp. lepers; a leper-house, lazaretto" (so *OED*), derived from the name of the afflicted beggar in Luke 16:19–31 (*OED*, s.v. *lazar*). The traveler Hentzner, visiting England during Elizabeth I's reign, noted that the English suffered much from leprosy, and that there were many "lazar-houses" (Verity). Wesley glosses the word merely as "an Hospital."

481–88. Oras claims that this passage uses pyrrhic endings "with consider-able force but without any lyrical quality" ("Milton's Blank Verse" 187); cf. **11.660–73.**

481. *racking:* "torturing; causing intense pain, physical or mental" (so *OED* 2).
    Spasm: "sudden and violent muscular contraction of a convulsive or painful character" (so *OED* 1). Wesley glosses as "cramp."

481–82. *qualmes:* "sudden sinking or faintness of heart" (*OED*, now rare).
    heart-sick: "pertaining to or characterized by [being] sick at heart…depressed and despondent, esp. through 'hope deferred' or continued trouble" (so *OED* 1, 2).

482. *all feavourous kinds:* cf. the similar "*febrium…cohors*" ("cohort…of fevers") in Horace, *Odes* 1.3.30–31.

483. *Convulsions, Epilepsies, fierce Catarrhs:* the modern use of *convulsions* as "involuntary contractions or spasms of the muscles, alternating with relaxation" has been attested since 1650 (*OED* 2b), and the modern sense of *epilepsy* (English "falling sickness") since 1578 (*OED* a). *Catarrh* as rheumy inflammation of the upper respiratory system has been attested since 1588 (*OED* 3), but the term once also referred to "cerebral effusion or hæmorrhage, apoplexy," a definition better suited to this context.

484. *Intestin Stone and Ulcer, Colic pangs:* all ailments of the middle body.

Colic: "a name given to severe paroxysmal griping pains in the belly...affecting the colon" (so *OED* A1, B2).

485–87. These three lines were added in the second edition of 1674, and their reception has been mixed. Bentley rejects the addition as spurious, saying that eleven kinds of death were already enough, and that the editor must have consulted a medical book for the additional six, of which the three psychological "shapes of death" can nevertheless be suffered during a long life. A semi-anonymous "A. Z.," writing the same year, counters that 17 diseases are not too many "when we are prepar'd to expect a *monstrous crew,* and *numbers of* all diseas'd," though A. Z. does wonder why Milton did not include the plague in 1667, unless *PL* was finished before its outbreak; he adds that melancholy is often accompanied by other disease (Shawcross, *Milton* 59). Pearce points out that the tenor of the passage is pain and misery, not mortality; in any case, Milton hints at delayed death (491–92). Newton reports that Alexander Pope thought the three added lines "admirable." The three psychic ailments are the conditions most frequent and most voluminously described in the psychiatric sections of Renaissance medical works (Babb 37). Summers finds the original list incomplete without this introduction of the forms of madness and general plague (*Muse's Method* 199). Robert M. Adams cites this list against the current critical theory of the 1950s as proof that Milton the poet is not always concerned with the creation of tensions and contrast but often writes lists or catalogs, going out of his way here, for instance, to add three lines and six diseases (185). Sasek thinks Milton possibly extended the catalog to make the list of human ills more representative, thus to provide a stronger motivation for Adam's violent reaction (190). Shumaker asserts that the word *all* commits Milton to a catalog, which cannot be exhaustive but must adequately represent its contents (*Unpremeditated Verse* 209). Empson, in the course of discussing the history of humankind as "monotonously horrible," comments, "For the second edition Milton divided the last book into two, perhaps to make it less heavy, but added very little except three lines about madness; he had forgotten that Adam ought to have his nose rubbed in having caused all that horrible madness too" (*Milton's God* 190); see **11.518–19.**

485. *Dæmonic Phrenzie:* the later use of *phrenzy* chiefly referred to "uncontrollable rage or excitement...of mania" (*OED*). Hughes (*Paradise Lost*) reports that "the now obsolescent spelling *phrenzy* prevailed in the seventeenth century in consequence of a mistaken Greek etymology. Wesley changes *Dæmonic* to *Demoniac*, adding, "Those term'd Lunatics by one Evangelist, are frequently term'd *Demoniacs*, or Possest of the Devil by another."

   Moaping: "dull, dejected, spiritless; bewildered, confused; wandering aim-lessly" (*OED*, obsolete). Hume glosses the term as "dull, sullen, stupid, because the vital spirits are choked and oppressed by black clouds of choler."

486–88. Wordsworth, according to Henry Crabb Robinson's diary, thought that these lines were an example of Milton's genius finding out "some of the artifices of versification," since the power of the final *rheums* is heightened by *atrophy* and *pestilence* (Wittreich 138).

   pining Atrophie / Marasmus, and wide-wasting Pestilence: the terms are related. *Atrophy* is "wasting away of the body, or any part of it" (so *OED* 1). *Marasmus* once referred to any wasting disorder (*OED* 1). The Richardsons, Hume, and Wesley all cite atrophy and marasmus as types of general consumption, the first by lack of proper digestion of food, the second by fever. *Pestilence* generalizes wasting to large populations.

   Dropsies: "morbid…accumulation of watery fluid" (so *OED* 1).

   Rheums: "mucous discharge caused by taking cold" (so *OED* 2).

486. *Moon-struck madness:* "lunacy" was thought to be caused by the moon.

   pining: see **12.77**.

489–92. Cf. Spenser's personifications of mental torments at the gate of hell (*Faerie Queene* 2.7.21–24), and also Andreini's figures of famine, thirst, lassitude and despair (*L'Adamo* 4.6). Addison finds the personifications of despair and death particularly effective here; he praises the "apt and Judicious use of such Imaginary Beings" (*Spectator* 3 [Apr. 26, 1712]: 362). Benson (46) admires Milton's artful inversion that moves part of the verbal construction to the next phrase, as here ("Death his Dart / Shook") and also in *PL* 7.548–49. Newton is pleased as well with the breaks and pauses in the lines, especially since each clause begins with the *d-* sound; the caesura after *shook* particularly imitates the delayed action of Death. Newton also claims that Latin is almost incapable of this "fire and spirit," comparing this passage to Arruns shaking his lance at Camilla (*Aeneid* 11.767). James Harris cites these lines as his conclusive example of the power of the masculine substantive; "'Death her dart,'" he argues, would weaken "the nerves and strength of the whole Sentiment" (53). Tennyson (in Verity) praises the effect of the monosyllable *shook* and the pause after it: "I hate inversions, but this line is strong."

490. *busiest:* Addison has *busie* (*Spectator* 3 [Apr. 26, 1712]: 362).

491–93. Cf. the description of Death's dart in *PL* 2.672, 786; the Death that "comes not at call" of *PL* 10.858; the "oft-invocated death" of *SA* 575–76, his "cure" in line 630 or "balm" in 651; and also the summoned death that will not come in Sophocles' *Philoctetes* 797–98. Bush adds Horace, *Odes* 2.18.38–40, where Death hears whether summoned or not. Trapp reports a beautiful and elaborate medieval missal illustration of the Fall, made before 1481 for the archbishop of Salzburg, in which Death stands over those who receive the fruit of death and damnation (259). Hughes (*Paradise Lost, A Poem*) thinks Milton may have remembered the classical references echoed in Spenser's *Faerie Queene* 2.1.59, where death is identified as "an equall doome / To good and bad." Ironically, Eve worries before she eats the fruit that she will die the same day, whereas the lazar-house inhabitants wish in vain to die (Mollenkott 35); see the additional comment on irony in **11.515–16**.
   final hope: cf. 2.142.

493. *chief good:* Emma lists this phrase among the earliest uses of "chief" to translate *summum bonum* (43); so *OED* 9, which also lists an earlier usage by Cowley in 1663.

494–97. Wesley notes this passage as among those particularly excellent.

494–95. *Sight so deform what heart of Rock could long / Drie-ey'd behold:* Addison finds that Adam's emotions here are quite natural (*Spectator* 3 [Apr. 26, 1712]: 362). Bentley doubts that deformity would move tears, and emends the passage to, "*Such woful sight* what heart of Rock could long / *Unmov'd* behold?" But Pearce points out that Adam is weeping for his own children, and the Richardsons, in their note to *PL* 5.711, include this passage among examples of appropriate synecdoches. Some commentators cite Horace's *Ode* 1.3.18, which refers to Odysseus looking with dry eyes (*siccus oculis*) on various nautical disasters. Dunster (in Todd) thinks the combination of *heart of Rock* and *Drie-ey'd* evokes Tibullus, *Elegies* 1.63–64, "flebis: non tua sunt duro praecordia ferro / vincta, neque in tenero stat tibi corde silex" (You will weep; your breast is not hard iron, nor is your heart flint). Toole (32) draws parallels between Satan's three episodes of weeping in book 1 and Adam's three episodes here and in 11.674–75 and 754–61; Adam, however, elects to submit to God's justice and finds happiness.

   Deform: Latin, "hideous, unsightly" (Verity); "deformed, misshapen, shapeless, distorted; ugly" (so *OED*).

   Rock: cf. the *stonie…hearts* of 11.4.

496–97. *Though not of Woman born; compassion quell'd / His best of Man, and gave him up to tears:* as various editors have noted, several passages from Shakespeare appear to be merged here: *Macbeth* 5.8.17–18 ("better part of man") and 30–32 ("of no woman born"), and *Henry V* 4.6.28–32 ("gave me up to tears"). Fowler claims that the Shakespearean echo is more extensive, since one theme of *Macbeth* is the drying up of the "milk of human kindness," i.e., the hardening of one's heart against compassion; Fowler also links this compassion to *pity*, the second response to tragedy, of which *terror*—as in 11.465—is the first, and claims that Adam makes the wrong, Stoic response to tragedy. Burden asserts that Adam's response to the tragic scene is pity rather than horror (191). Himes (*Paradise Lost: A Poem*) cites the goddess-born Aeneas weeping over the mutilated Deiphobus in Hades (*Aeneid* 6.495–539). Broadbent finds the language of the last two books "drab," citing this passage and 11.535 as tropes that are "dry, abstract and harsh as in Jacobean drama" (*Some Graver Subject* 271).

499. And scarce recovering words his plaint renew'd: Bentley, "for the construction's sake," substitutes "*When* scarce *recov'ring he* his plaint renew'd," a reading Pearce argues is unnecessary, since the phrase "Compassion…excess" (496–98) is essentially parenthetic.

500–14. Wesley notes this passage as among those particularly excellent.

500. *miserable:* on the pronunciation, see **11.5–7**.

502–07. Cf. the lament in Job 3.

502–04. *Why is life…Obtruded on us thus:* cf. *Aeneid* 6.721. Bundy, analyzing Michael as teacher, explains that although the lazar-house vision led Adam to have compassion, it also leads him to question God's ways, a moral state that stands in need of the immediate discipline of 11.515–17 and, following that, "the precepts of temperance" (147). "Whatever the mind may make of it, the sensitive body continues to feel the threat of unimmortality as an outrage" (Kermode 119). The passage raises again "the thorny question" of just how fully the humans may have accepted the 'propos'd' terms of their creation (Peter 155). Adam is still blaming God's abundance and justice, not man (Lawry, *Shadow* 278). Sasek sees Adam's shift from grief to questions of God's ways as consistent with Milton's development of Adam's psychology (190).

    wrested…Obtruded: Summers finds in these words "Milton's individual, muscular imprint" (*Muse's Method* 200).

    Obtruded: "to proffer forcibly, unduly, or without invitation; to press, impose, or force on or upon a person" (*OED* 1a). Wesley glosses *Obtruded* as "forced upon us."

502. *Better end heer unborn. Why is life giv'n:* R. C. Browne (1877) claims the first line demonstrates a "Sophoclean sentiment" from *Oedipus at Colonus* 1225–26 ("Not to be born at all / Is best, far best that can befall").

504–06. Cf. Sir Thomas Browne, "When the Stoick [i.e., Seneca] said that life would not be accepted, if it were offered unto such as knew it, he spoke too meanly of that state of being which placeth us in the form of Men" (*Christian Morals* 3.25, in *Works* 1:287), citing Seneca's *De Consolatione ad Marciam* 22.3, "Nihil est tam fallax quam vita humana, nihil tam insidiosum: non me hercules quisquam illam accepisset, nisi daretur inscientibus" (Nothing is so deceptive as human life, nothing so underhanded: no, by Hercules, no one would knowingly receive it) (*Moral Essays* 2:78). Bush cites Donne's *Devotions upon Emergent Occasions,* Meditation 11: "oh who, if before hee had a beeing, he could have sense of this miserie, would buy a being here upon these conditions" (Donne 58). Fowler adds Drummond's question from *A Cypress Grove* (2:80) as to whether anyone who knew beforehand of the manifold miseries of life would "enter this woefull Hospitall of the World, and accept of life upon such hard conditiones?"

506. *Thir doctrine and thir story written left:* Keightley claims Milton means "more especially the Gospels of Matthew and John, and the Epistles of Paul."

507–14. Edmundson, who argues that Milton found important material in Vondel's *Adam in Ballingschap,* compares this passage to Lucifer's prophecy that his followers would be worshiped as deities and that most of humankind would perpetuate abominations (83). In *DocCh* 1.12, Milton lists degradation of mind as one consequence of man's sin (Maurice Kelley 152; Patterson, *Works* 15:205). Adam has already heard from Raphael (7.519) that God made man in his own image (Hughes, *Paradise Lost, A Poem*); Milton's angel adds the Platonic argument for human nobility from man's upright stature (Hughes, *Paradise Lost*).

508–09. *Th'Image of God in man created once / So goodly and erect:* Gen. 1:26 and also *PL* 7.506–10, 519. Bridges cites the elision *Th'image* of this line along with the emphatic *The image* of 1.371 as proof that Milton's rules of elision are "permissive" or arbitrary rather than fixed (34); see also **11.453**.

511–13. *Man, / Retaining still Divine similitude / In part:* cf. *PL* 3.384 and also *Tetr* 2.33 ("there are left som remains of Gods image in man" [Patterson, *Works* 4:80]) and *DocCh* 1.4 ("there are some remnants of the divine image left in man" [Patterson, *Works* 14:129]), also noted by Maurice Kelley (84). Fish finds Michael's implication questionable because "obedience is an affirmation of loyalty despite appearances, and not a decision between visible alternatives" (155). Fowler compares Catholic and Protestant understandings of the *imago dei* (God's image in humans) and *similitudo dei* (God's likeness), noting that whereas Catholic theologians judged that the *imago dei* was obscured but not lost in the Fall, with only the *similitudo dei* being lost, Protestant theologians emphasized more strongly the disfiguring of the *imago dei;* Fowler thinks that by "God's image" in *DocCh* Milton meant the *similitudo dei* and not the *imago dei*.

514–16. On gluttony, see **11.476**.

515–25. "By intemperance man has misused that which in nature was essentially good" (Eastland 50). Martz complains that the "cold, defensive tone" of Michael's response to the "appalling effectiveness" of the lazar-house scene recalls only the answer of Job's comforters (151–52). Douady hears in this passage a reference to the perennial "arrière-pensées des anges et leur vieille rancune" (afterthoughts of angels and their ancient bitterness) (198). Radzinowicz claims that Michael expounds the deformity of illness as man's self-defilement (42); see Radzinowicz's further remarks in **11.429–65**.

515–16. *Thir Makers Image... Forsook them, when themselves they villifi'd:* cf. the progressive degradation traced in Rom. 1:22–32. Brooks notes parallel sequences in which Adam, Eve, Satan, Sin, and Death all turn away from their "image," their immediate creator ("Eve's Awakening" 282–90). Samuel cites a similar passage from *Paradiso* 7.85–87: human nature was severed from both dignities and paradise at the first sin (*Dante* 248). Mollenkott identifies the irony of Eve wishing to be godlike by eating the fruit with the result that the intemperate inhabitants of the lazar-house are deformed (35–36); see the comment on additional irony in **11.491–93**. For both this passage and 12.83–90, Patrides cites an Elizabethan homily that identified the effect of the Fall as a shift from the image of God to that of the devil (*Milton* 113). Howard, analyzing *PL* in terms of *Log*, relates this passage to Milton's formal cause; described through its effects, the "form" of man's first disobedience was the accompanying change in human nature; some critics think that Adam's sin must be more than mere disobedience, but they overlook the cause that corrupts acts that are otherwise innocent (163). Even though "it sounds a brutal diagnosis," Michael must here strongly reject Adam's erroneous question in 11.511–14, since it is rooted in feelings and in erroneous deductions (Burden 191–92).

villifi'ed: Fowler, citing *OED* 1, glosses as "reduced to a lower standing."

517–18. *ungovern'd appetite, and took / His Image whom they serv'd:* cf. God's image in *PL* 4.291–92. Bentley objects to *His* here, claiming the referent could be only Satan, but Pearce claims that Gluttony was also personified in *Mask*. Todd notes that appetite is personified in 9.1129, though he acknowledges Dunster's interpretation that this passage refers to *serving* the appetite in terms of both Titus 3:3 ("serving divers lusts and pleasures") and Sallust's *ventri obedientia* ("subservient to the stomach" [*Bellum Catilinarium* 1.1]), making the appetite finally a demon. Hughes (*Paradise Lost*) glosses *His* as "appetite's." Northrop Frye (*Paradise Lost*) cites Phil. 3:19 ("whose god is their belly"), where appetite is personified as a false god.

ungovern'd: "not brought under government or control; uncontrolled" (so *OED* a).

518–19. *a brutish vice, / Inductive mainly to the sin of Eve:* this passage has provoked various interpretations. Stebbing insists that Milton is wrong to refer to Eve's "low sensual feeling" when Gen. 3:5–6 focuses so much on her desire for knowledge. Bush argues, "Gluttony was only part of Eve's intemperance." Muldrow (84–85) compares this vice with that of the third vision, "Mans effeminate slackness" (11.634). Empson reads the lazar-house vision as suggesting that Adam is responsible for causing madness and Eve's overeating for all diseases (*Milton's God* 190); see **11.485–87.** B. A. Wright challenges the common editorial reading of *mainly* as *OED* 3 ("chiefly, principally," etc.), since that gloss crudely oversimplifies the temptation narrative; it should be *OED* 2 ("In a great degree; greatly, considerably, very much, a great deal"), especially since that was its common meaning in Milton's time ("'Mainly'" 143).

inductive: "leading on to some action" (so *OED* 1).

519. Wesley omits this line.

521. *Disfiguring:* "disfigure," "to mar the figure or appearance of, destroy the beauty of; to deform, deface" (so *OED* 1a).

523. Hall cites Paul Thomas Gibbs's idea that, as she says, "Nature develops steadily from initial chaos into perfect order, in full obedience to eternal, nature law" (158).

524–25. *since they / Gods Image did not reverence in themselves:* echoes a similar sentiment in Rom. 1:21, 24.

526. *I yield it just, said Adam, and submit:* the need for patience and submission is a constant theme in book 11 (Fowler). Since Adam is no longer actor, as was Eve in book 9, but rather spectator and critic, he can see that "the tragic scene poses no mysterious and unanswerable question but shows justly the punishment of the wicked" (Burden 192). Adam's words justify the doctrine of original sin (Sasek 190). Martz, who finds a disturbing imbalance in the last two books

between images of woe and abstract statements of grace, complains, "It is all too pat: the problem of sin is no longer being explored: it is being subjected to the easy solutions of the doctrinaire" (151–52). See Toole's comments in **11.314**, s.v. *I submit.*
   yield: 1667 *yeild.*

528. *passages:* i.e., deaths (*OED* 3b, now rare).

529. *mix with our connatural dust:* cf. 11.199–200 and 463.
   connatural: "congenital, innate, natural (to living beings)" (*OED* 1). See also the "connatural force" of 10.246.

530–46. Wesley notes this passage as among those particularly excellent.

531. *The rule of not too much, by temperance taught:* Greek, Μηδὲν ἄγαν, and in Latin, *Ne quid nimis,* which Milton cites as proverbial in *Log* 1.33 (Patterson, *Works* 11:286–87). "The rule of nothing too much goes back in Latin literature to Terence's *Andria* (1.1.34), and in Greek it is much older" (Hughes, *Paradise Lost*). The Greek maxim was said to have been written in the temple of Delphi by Cleobulus, and Plato quotes it in *Protagoras* 343B (Fowler). See also Aristotle, *Nicomachean Ethics* 2.2 (1104a) and Jerome, *Epistula* 60.7.3. Milton praises temperance in *El* 6 59–60, *IlPen* 46, *Mask* 762–79, and *SA* 553–57. The Lady in Milton's *Mask* differentiates between temperance and abstinence (Patrides, *Milton* 117). Cf. *DocCh* 2.9, which includes moderation in food as part of sobriety (Maurice Kelley 190; Patterson, *Works* 17:213).
   Critics have challenged the ancient commonplace. Broadbent, taking a modernist stance, rejects Michael's counsel as naïve in light of the psychological progress of the intervening centuries (*Some Graver Subject* 275–78). Lawry thinks that Michael is urging "neither mortal life nor death...but only...the eternal quality of his living" (*Shadow* 279). In Kogan's reading, in which seventeenth century English history represents the bourgeoisie's struggle to eliminate feudal elements that hinder the growth of capitalism, Adam and Eve's intemperance threatens this growth, leading Michael to expound the bourgeois code of behavior (34); see also **12.561–73**, **12.575–87**, and **12.646–49**. Grierson adds a comma at the end of the line.

532. *In what thou eatst and drinkst, seeking from thence:* Keightley would like to render *drinkst* as *drinkest,* and to strike *from,* finding the line more grammatical and "more Miltonic" without it. Montgomery's comment is milder: "*from thence* is not according to our present notions of grammar."

533. *Due nourishment, not gluttonous delight:* in contrast to Eve's greedy consumption of the fruit (9.791).

534. *return:* the sense can be applied to such immaterial things as time (so *OED* v^{1}1c).

535–40. Martz, who complains that the last two books are less poetic, praises this passage for a brief return to "the promised balance and poise" (152).

535–37. *like ripe Fruit:* see Broadbent's remarks in **11.496–97.** Keightley and others cite Job 5:26 ("Thou shalt come to thy grave in a full age, like as a shock of corn…in his season"), but Newton and others cite Cicero's image of old age as a ripe apple ready to fall (*De Senectute* 19.71). Todd references Spenser's *Faerie Queene* 2.10.32 ("made ripe for death by eld"), as does Hughes (*Paradise Lost*), who claims the commonplace need be sought no further back; Hughes (*Paradise Lost: A Poem* 4), however, traces the simile from Cicero through Dante's *Convivio* and then Spenser. R. C. Browne (1877) cites Antonio in *Merchant of Venice* 4.1.115–16: "The weakest kind of fruit / Drops earliest to the ground." Whaler claims that Milton's passage is one of the rare cases where he uses an individual simile to illustrate a generalization; see also 7.126–28, 8.605–06, and 11.311–13 ("Compounding" 313n2). Whaler also claims that the phrase "contains a whole allegory compressed into three lines" ("Miltonic Simile" 1045–46).

    Into thy Mothers lap: cf. Adam's similar phrasing in 10.775–78, where he wishes to be insensible in death. Bush refers this idea to Milton's mortalism, in which the soul dies with the body until the resurrection; cf. *DocCh* 1.13 (Patterson, *Works* 15:214–51). Milton claimed in *DocCh* 1.8 that although God ultimately determines one's lifespan, it is possible to shorten it by intemperance (Maurice Kelley 134; Patterson, *Works* 15:93).

538–46. *but then thou must outlive / Thy youth:* Thyer (cited by Marchant) thinks that the catalog of diseases must at least in part reflect the infirmities Milton himself was experiencing in old age. Himes (*Paradise Lost: A Poem*) judges that Milton may have had in mind the biblical description of old age in Eccles.

12:1–7. Kermode (119) cites Shakespeare's Duke Vincentio, who treats the same topic; see especially *Measure for Measure* 3.1.28–39. Despite the momentary comfort of dropping into nature's lap, "a potential identification with what is soon to be the 'normal' cycle of nature," Milton does not present temperance as a means to increase longevity (Summers, *Muse's Method* 200–01). Fowler cites the theory of "humours," in which *melancholia* belonged to the fourth age of man, old age, and was especially characteristic of life after the Fall, while the much preferred *sanguine* humour belonging to youth was the humour supposedly prevailing before the Fall; according to one authority, melancholy was born from the breath of the serpent, perhaps influencing Milton's decision to have Satan enter the serpent as a "midnight vapour" (9.159), which would foreshadow Adam's "melancholly damp" in 544, since *damp* can mean not only "depression of spirits" (*OED* 5) but also "vapour" in the physiological sense (*OED* 1); cf. Klibansky et al. 79–80, 122, 149, and 243.

540. *witherd weak and gray:* the Aristotelian qualities of life are heat and moisture (Babb 38); cf. Aristotle, *Parva Naturalia* 466a, 469b.
 weak and gray: 1667 *weak & gray.*

541–42. *all taste of pleasure must forgoe, / To what thou hast:* Bentley wants *hast* changed to *eat'st* as the obvious emendation; Pearce objects that "taste" refers to all the senses in general. Cf. Eccles. 12:1.

541. *Obtuse:* "annoyingly unperceptive or slow to understand; stupid; insensitive" (so *OED* 2a), though Wesley glosses as "blunted, dull."

542. *aire:* B. A. Wright defines this noun as the obsolete and rare "disposition, mood" of *OED* 14b ("Note" 146); see **11.46**.

544. *A melancholly damp of cold and dry:* Todd cites Burton's *Anatomy of Melancholy* that old age is the chief source of melancholy (1.2.1.5), yet Burton himself lists it as one cause, along with God, devils, witches and magicians, and parentage (1.2.1–5, 6). Burton's dictum that since old age is "cold and dry, and of the same quality as melancholy is, must needes cause it, by diminution of spirits and substance" (1:203) is repeated by many later editors, but the idea of melancholy being cold and dry dates from about 400 BCE and was a commonplace for 2,000 years (Klibansky et al. 9–10). "Hopefulness was the normal effect of the blood of 'sanguine' humor" (Northrop Frye, *Paradise Lost*). Cf. *Mask* 809–10 and also Death's "cold and dry" mace in *PL* 10.294.

545. *weigh:* 1667 *waigh* or *waight.*
   Spirits: 1667 *spirits.*

546. *our Ancestor:* Ryken (183) cites epithets for Adam and Eve as one of Milton's means of distancing them from the reader, as he does for "Mother of Mankind" in *PL* 11.158.

547–52. Wesley notes this passage as among those particularly excellent.

547. Regarding similarities between this passage and a seventeenth century consolatory text, see George Coffin Taylor's comments in **12.587**.

549. *combrous:* "causing trouble, distress, or annoyance; full of trouble or care; troublesome; harassing; wearisome, oppressive" (so *OED*).

550. *my appointed day:* Gillies cites Job 14:14, "All the days of my appointed time will I wait, till my change come," which if intended makes a good case for the two half lines added at *PL* 11.551–52, as also noted by Hughes (*Paradise Lost, A Poem*). Sims (*Bible* 270) additionally cites Heb. 9:27: "It is appointed unto men once to die."

551–52. *and patiently attend / My dissolution:* these two half-lines were added in 1674, with *Michael repli'd,* replacing the original *Michael to him repli'd.* The critical response to this addition has been mixed. Bentley claims this passage is the fourth and last of the editor's alternations in the 1674 text, since Adam's impatience in the preceding verses is at odds with these words. The semi-anonymous "A. Z." argues, however, that Bentley's main objection is three syllables for *Michael* instead of two, and Milton varies the syllabic count in numerous proper names (Shawcross, *Milton* 60–61). Pearce argues that Adam does not necessarily express impatience, and that, besides, he is here expressing only his duty, not his inclination. Newton supposes that Milton thought Michael's original speech ended too abruptly, but Grierson insists that the 1667 reading is one that every editor accepts or should accept (Preface, *Poems* 2:xl–xli); see also **11.379–80**. Hughes (*Paradise Lost*) thinks the 1667 phrasing seems "rhetorically complete." Summers claims that although many of Milton's predecessors, classical or Christian, would have thought this sentiment the sum of human wisdom, Milton does not present it as such within the poem (*Muse's Method* 201); cf. **12.575–76**. Fowler claims that the insertion emphasizes the thematic idea of patient resignation in book 11.

Attend: "to wait," from the French *attendre.*

553–54. *Nor love thy Life, nor hate:* this passage has provoked much comment. Newton and many others cite Martial, *Epigrams* 10.47.13 ("Wish not for the day [of death] nor fear it"), and Himes (*Paradise Lost: A Poem*) and others cite the similar advice of Horace, *Odes* 1.9.9, while Allan H. Gilbert cites similar words from Seneca (*Epistle* 24.24 and 65.18) and finds that Milton's discussion of old age in this section is reminiscent of Seneca and similar authors ("Parallel" 121). Thompson, who claims that this sentiment was Milton's own life motto, judges that Adam finally accepts this advice in *PL* 12.561–73; Thompson also claims that the text of *PR* illustrates that "to obey is best" ("Theme" 117–18, 120). Erskine finds the comment to be "but a more sententious phrasing" of the resignation that Adam has already worked out (579), though Stoll counters that rather than being an afterthought, this passage represents a healthy accommodation of religion to life that "every healthy spirit, however illogically, strives to attain," and one that Milton "being more of a man and poet than a Puritan," had already attained ("Was Paradise" 434). Stoll also cites this passage as one of the continual preparations for the final human condition ("From the Superhuman" 14); see **11.138–39**. Tillyard argues that the Stoic passage is one indicator of an underlying but unacknowledged pessimism in the last four or five books that produces a less energetic epic; "it is in the last books that Milton most speaks of reason contending with passion" (*Milton* 291).

Not all commentators refer to the classics. Gillies finds a parallel in Rom. 14:8 ("Whether we live therefore, or die, we are the Lord's"). Greenlaw (214n29), arguing that Milton's central theme is temperance and that Eve is less like Spenser's Una than his Despair, claims that this passage reflects Redcrosse's reply to Despair in *Faerie Queene* 1.9.41. Milton's most serious ideas are put into the mouths of visiting angels (Patterson, *Student's Milton*). Fish argues that Adam conceives of his options too narrowly because he conceives them as merely terrestrial, and in any case he is focused on death rather than the possibility of living for God (278). Michael's correction helps Adam recover something like his unfallen confidence in Providence; his subsequent reactions are less concerned with his own fate and more with his descendants' fate (Summers, *Muse's Method* 201–02). Miner claims that the scarcely consoled Adam has become passive before the vision of disease and death, and thus Michael urges "ethical activity or fortitude and trust in heaven" (47). Wesley notes this passage as among those particularly excellent.

554. *how long or short permit to Heav'n:* Newton and Verity cite Horace, *Odes* 1.9.9: "permitte divis caetera" (leave the rest [i.e., the length of your life] to the gods).

    Permit: "commit, submit, hand over, leave, resign, or yield (frequently *to* or *unto* a person, authority, etc.)" (so *OED* 1, archaic and rare). Fowler argues that since *permit* in this form can take an indirect object, *permit to Heav'n* is not a departure from idiomatic English syntax.

556–627. In the third vision, the *sons of God* marry with the "daughters of men" (Gen. 6:2). Some interpreters claim that the *sons of God* are angels (cf. Satan's reference in *PR* 2.178–81), but Allen ("Milton and the Sons" 73–79) argues that the orthodox interpretation among both the later church fathers and the reformers was that these *sons of God* were righteous men, not angels or demons, and that Milton puts the orthodox reading into Michael's mouth, the unorthodox into Satan's. Nevertheless, Thomas Heywood's *Hierarchies of the Blessed Angels* (1635) argues from Tertullian and Origen that the *sons* had to be angels (Kirkconnell 288). According to Hughes, the crucial words are *sons of God*, which are so rendered in the Vulgate (*filii Dei*) and in the 1611 English version, although the original Hebrew means 'sons of the gods'; the Septuagint made it ἄγγελοι τοῦ θεοῦ; 'angels of God,' and by following the Septuagint in *Antiquities of the Jews* 1.3.1, Josephus encouraged an interpretation which was followed by Justin Martyr, Irenaeus, Cyprian, Athenagoras, and Lactantius; independently of the Fathers, the book of Enoch represented the devil Azazel not only as the inventor of several arts that he is in Milton's reference to him in 1.234, but also as a leader among many apostate angels who conspire in the first seduction of mortal women ("Variorum"). The standard rabbinical commentators all explain *sons of God* in human terms, although some medieval exegetes depart from the standard interpretation and hold that the *sons of God* were outstanding for physical or mental endowment rather than merely for noble rank (Bamberger 149); see also Fisch 39–40. Edward Chauncey Baldwin claims that earlier rabbinical commentary identified the *sons of God* as angels but that later rabbis preferred to think of them as men; he also cites *PR* 2.178–81, where the Son identifies the "false-titled sons of God" as fallen angels ("Some Extra-Biblical Semitic Influences" 393–94). West insists that Milton's fallen angels may be "false-titled" but nevertheless lust after beautiful women ("Milton's Sons" 187–91), even though in *PL* Milton rejects the ancient view that good angels were corrupted by them (*Milton and the Angels* 129); see also **11.621–22**. Himes cites Keightley's judgment that Milton mentions all three possibilities—angels, demons, men—in *PL* 5.447, 11.622, and *PR* 2.179 (see also their mention in *PL* 3.461–65)—but Himes counters that Milton's reference to these possibilities is not his adoption of them: "Raphael, the Angel of Love, and the guardians of paradise were incapable of lust in the very presence of the all conquering beauty of Eve [5.447–50]" (Himes, *A Study* 241, and *Paradise Lost: A Poem*).

Scholarly commentary on this passage also attempts to explain Milton's contrast of hills and plains as the respective origins of the sons of God and men. Allen rejects the suggestion that Milton's hill/plain dichotomy is from the book of Enoch, since the text was not discovered until 1773, but argues that Milton could have known about it from derivative writers, and particularly from the ninth century *Nathm-el Gauher* of Eutychius, a full Latin translation of which was published at Oxford in 1658, and a selection with full critical apparatus by John Selden in 1642 ("Milton and the Sons" 76–79). Fowler reports that Eutychius has Seth's descendants living in the mountains neighboring paradise itself, and therefore on the *hither* side of the plain, whereas according to Gen. 4:16, Cain dwelt "on the east of Eden." According to Hume, "The Master of Scholastick History [i.e., Aquinas], says, Cain dwelt in the Fields where he slew his Brother, but Seth in Cordan [Cirdan?], a Mountain near paradise. Hist. Lib. Gen. c. 32, whom our author has follow'd. Gris[d?] Bo. I. v. 563." Lauder claims that Milton took his treatment of the sons of God from Du Bartas, but Lauder is not to be trusted; see **11.388–411**.

Critics have also linked this passage to apocryphal literature. Saurat, who claims that Milton is heavily influenced by the book of Enoch, maintains that although Milton follows Augustine and orthodox tradition, he does so "with a bad conscience," since he does not become "too precise on the point" in *DocCh* and since his different glosses in *PL* 3 and *PR* indicate that "when off his guard he contradicts himself very beautifully" (212). The Apocalypse of Moses traces human depravity not to the Fall but to "the seduction of the daughters of men by the angels who had been sent down to instruct men" (Kirkconnell 286). McColley (*Paradise Lost: An Account*) thinks that a number of extrabiblical elements were available in such works as the *Chronographia* of Syncellus. Hughes further supplies: "Clement of Alexandria lamented the ruins of these mountaineers who had 'lived the life of angels,' but had been corrupted by the women of the plain (*Recognitiones* [Migne, *Patrologiae... Graeca* 1:1223–24]). Several Greek Fathers followed Clement, and Augustine took the final step in [*City of God*] 15.23 by insisting on the literal meaning of the Hebrew text in Gen. 6:2–4, by arguing that giants had been born without demon fathers, and that angels and men cannot breed together, and by positively identifying the sons of God as Sethites. Their interpretation as fallen angels he treated as the work of heretics." Similar positions were taken by Aquinas (*Summa Theologica* 51.3.6), Luther (2:9–12), and Calvin (1:237–39). Hughes also judges that despite Milton's denial that Belial's "lusty crew" produced offspring (*PR* 2.178–91), "Satan was stating accepted facts. The countless divine seductions of mortal women in the ancient myths had been explained by various Church Fathers as crimes of the fallen angels. The crimes were a part of recorded history no less factual than Raphael's innocent delight in Eve's beauty [*PL* 5.446–48] should seem to us" ("Variorum").

Addison judges that this episode appropriately follows the lazar-house: "As there is nothing more delightful in Poetry than a Contrast and Opposition of Incidents, the Author, after this melancholy Prospect of Death and Sickness, raises up a Scene of Mirth, Love and Jollity. The secret Pleasure that steals into Adam's Heart, as he is intent upon this Vision, is imagined with great Delicacy" (*Spectator* 3 [Apr. 26, 1712]: 363). Burden argues that while the death from intemperance pictured in the preceding spectacle properly belongs to Eve's fall, Adam's own fall, linked to sensual pleasure and the bond of nature, is pictured here (193). Sasek claims that this section begins a new sequence of visions designed to teach Adam to recognize evil in various forms (190). "The sober race of religious men surrender their virtue in imitation of Adam who now compounds his original sin by condoning theirs. More abstractly, the marriage represents an unholy union of complementary idolatries, the worship of sensual pleasure ('lustful appetance') and the worship of art; both are symbolized in the scene by the element of fire" (Fish 299–300). Mollenkott, arguing that book 11 presents a "cycle of sins," identifies this vision as an elaboration of the uxorious sin of Adam (36). Fowler suggests that the more fortunate condition of men in the third vision is appropriate because in number symbolism, three is fortunate; it also supports the nuptial emphasis of the third vision, being a marriage number formed from the union of odd and even. Fowler contrasts Milton's ambivalent treatment of the invention of arts with Du Bartas's far more positive one. Douady complains that angels would have had better knowledge than human metaphysicians, so that heaven should not transfer the dishonor for intercourse onto mere humans; Douady judges that God is growing "more and more sour" (aigri de plus on plus) because he has no more infernal revolt or new worlds to create, which is why he concentrates so obstinately on this little, sometimes turbulent, industrial colony (199–200).

556–73. Milton has expanded on Gen. 4:20–22, which identifies as Cain's descendants Jabal, "the father of such as dwell in tents, and of such as have cattle"; Jubal, who was "the father of all such that handle the harp and organ"; and Tubal-cain, "an instructor of every artificer in brass and iron." For organ, cf. *PL* 1.708–09. Cann suggests that Jubal, "styled Apollo by the heathens," is the source for the mythical god of music (248). According to Allen's reading, Jubal discovers only a substitute for the lost music of heaven, and the ascent toward divine harmony will now be far more difficult (*Harmonious Vision* xv). For references to Jubal after Milton, see also Dryden's "Song for St. Cecilia's Day" 16–24, and especially Marvell's short poem, "Music's Empire," which Verity thinks alludes partly to Milton. Fish (296–98) compares the blurred similarity between these lines and the description of the building of Pandaemonium in 1.700–13; words and images move back and forth between the two contexts until "the scenes merge in the reader's consciousness," appropriately, since many thought that Tubal-Cain was the Hebrew name for Mulciber.

556. *He lookd and saw:* Lewalski traces Adam's purged and exercised physical sight throughout book 11 (26); see **11.368**.

558–63. Cf. the diabolical parallel in the similes used to describe Pandaemonium in *PL* 1.708–13 (Fox 167). Although Milton's descriptions in books 11–12 are usually "rapid and spare," he sometimes lingers over an appealing detail (Shumaker, *Unpremeditated Verse* 206).

559. *melodious chime:* cf. "silver chime...melodious time" in *Nat* 128–29.

560–63. *volant touch / Instinct:* Todd and others cite the lute master's "flying touch" in line 21 of Crashaw's "Musick's Duell" (*The Poems* 149). Cf. similar phrasing in Dryden (Timotheus "With flying fingers touch'd the lyre" ["Alexander's Feast" 22]; Opheus's "flying fingers" can strike seven notes at once [*Aeneid* 6.879–80]; and also in Collins ("flying fingers kiss'd the strings" [*The Passions* 89]). For a re-creation of John Milton Sr.'s musical education at Christ Church, Oxford, and his resulting musical facility, see Brennecke 3–24, 32–33, 39–41, 53–58. Hughes (*Paradise Lost*) finds in *Instinct* ("by instinct or native talent") a possible allusion to Du Bartas's Jubal, who learned his musical art before birth from the music of the "Pole," i.e., spheres (1:395.529–32).

Volant: "moving rapidly or lightly; active, nimble" (so *OED* 5a).

Fled and pursu'd transverse the resonant fugue: the Richardsons gloss *fugue* as "a correspondency of parts in music answering in the same notes [= *all proportions*] above and below [= *low and high*, i.e., treble and bass clefs], and therefore here said to be *resonant*," but cf. Stainer and Barrett's definition: "a polyphonic composition constructed on one or more short subjects or themes, which are harmonized according to the laws of counterpoint, and introduced from time to time with various contrapuntal devices" (also cited in *OED* 1).

Resonant: "re-echoing, resounding; continuing to sound or ring" (so *OED* 1a). R. C. Browne (1877) cites a Professor Taylor's opinion that the pregnant meaning of this entire passage on music can be fully appreciated only by a musician, and quotes him as saying, "All other poets but Milton and Shakespeare make blunders about music; they never." Himes (*Paradise Lost: A Poem*) adds that this citation is in "*Clar. Press.*" The reference may be to Edward Taylor (1784–1863), professor of music at Gresham College, London. Verity claims that Milton revised some passages to be less musically technical: *SolMus* 19–20 originally read "by leaving out those harsh chromatick Jarres / of sin that all our musick marres," and in *Mask* 243 Milton substituted "And give resounding grace" to "hold a counterpoint."

Instinct: Shumaker has "'impelled,' as it were, by a divine afflatus (*instinctus*, 'impelled,' as if by divine inspiration, *instinctu divino*)" (*Unpremeditated Verse* 206). Fowler glosses as "impelled," as in 2.937; cf. *OED* a2. Fowler further suggests that Milton may be alluding to Macrobius's account of Pythagoras discovering the art of music from hearing blacksmiths beating a hot iron

(*Commentary* 2.1.9–12); in addition, *fled* echoes *fugue* (Italian *fuga*, "flight"), "no doubt to remind us that Jubal's race is the fugitive race of Cain." "Jubal's art is inborn (*instinct*) because he has, as 'some think,' absorbed it before birth from 'the warbling Pole' (the heavens)" (Hughes, *Paradise Lost: A Poem*). Whaler uses the phrase *Instinct through all proportions* as the title of chapter 5 of his book, *Counterpoint and Symbol,* which argues that Milton's epic is informed by a complex mathematical system of signification (95–129); Whaler asserts that Milton surely means to apply the "unsurpassable" definition of fugue here to the rhythmic method of his epic style as well as to polyphonic music" (74). Wesley omits these four lines.

561. *chords:* cf. "chord," which refers poetically to "a string of a musical instrument, such as a harp" (so *OED* 2a).

565–73. As Hughes (*Paradise Lost, A Poem*) explains, the lines reflect Lucretius's account of the discovery of metals: they were first laid bare by lightning-kindled forest fires and accidentally fused in natural pits (*De rerum natura* 5.1241–68). Several critics cite Du Bartas's picture of the metal workers over whom "sweating Tubal stands / Hastning the hot work in their sounding hands" (1:395.527–28). McColley traces Milton's emphasis on Tubal-Cain to various medieval and contemporary Bible commentaries ("*Paradise Lost*" 230). Fox observes that Milton's expansion of the bare Genesis narrative lays great stress on mining and refining of ore; Tubal-Cain and his followers in this respect closely resemble Mammon's diabolical followers, and because like Mammon they are unable to create objects of material beauty but refuse to acknowledge the giver of their talents, they are types of avarice (168–70). Svendsen, however, points out that Milton unusually does not comment here on either of the conflicting Renaissance attitudes toward mining, either that God's intention for humans to dig included gold and other metals or that humans should not dislodge nature; here, Tubal-Cain simply finds the ore (*Milton and Science* 117–19). Shumaker claims that an account of origins—to include the beginnings of arts and crafts, as both Lucretius and Du Bartas had done—and the offering of alternatives—*whether...or whether*—was also solidly in the epic tradition (*Unpremeditated Verse* 207).

    clods: cf. "clod," "a coherent mass or lump of any solid matter" (so *OED* 2).

566–70. Wesley revises this passage to a single line, "Had melted; [next] the liquid Ore he dreind."

566. *casual:* "subject to, depending on, or produced by chance; accidental, fortuitous" (*OED* 1a). "Accidental" (Ricks, *"Paradise Lost"*).

568–72. *hot...wrought:* Purcell (172) notes that these lines rhyme with three intervening lines, a rhyme category also mentioned by Diekhoff but not for these lines ("Rhyme" 542).

569. Wesley changes *last* to *lost.*

570–71. *the liquid Ore he dreind / Into fit moulds prepar'd:* this passage recalls the building of Pandaemonium, one example of the "pervasive presence of hell before and soon after the Flood" (Broadbent, *Some Graver Subject* 274).

572–73. *First his own Tooles; then, what might else be wrought / Fusil or grav'n in mettle:* Himes (*Paradise Lost: A Poem*) sees here a fusion of biblical and classical, since the first object of his art is *Use,* the second *Ornament,* just as Vulcan marries the most beautiful of women, Charis, i.e., "Grace" (*Iliad* 18.382), or even Venus, the goddess of beauty; Milton's poetical mind thus saw a larger meaning in the biblical statement that "the sister of Tubal-Cain was Naamah (The Beautiful)." Naamah figures in Hebrew myth as a dangerous seductress from whom, with the more notorious Lilith, "sprang Asmodeus and innumerable demons that still plague mankind" (Graves and Patai 65). Fox reports one rabbinical legend in which Naamah's sensual charms led angels astray, and she bore the lustful Asmodeus from a union with Shamdon the devil (173).

Fusil or grav'n in mettle: "formed by melting or casting" (so *OED* 3); "cast or wrought" (Richardsons).

Fusil: "melted, cast" (Wesley); "cast in moulds" (Stebbing); "formed by casting or melting" (Hughes, *Paradise Lost*). George Coffin Taylor (*Milton's Use* 115), arguing that Milton found some of his material in Du Bartas, finds it significant that the earlier poet (Du Bartas 1:397–98) returned at this point to Adam, who falls into a trance and sees a vision of the future.

573–74. *After these, / But on the hether side:* cf. the "hither side" of 3.722. Cf. the genealogies of the patriarchs in Gen. 5. Keightley claims that the *hether side* is nearer to paradise, for Cain had been sent away to the east, whereas Hughes (*Paradise Lost*) puts it to the west of Eden, where tradition placed the descendants of Seth. See the longer comment on Cain's and Seth's descendants in **11.556–627**.

575. *neighbouring Hills:* cf. 5.547.

576–78. *Just men...bent / To worship God aright:* Fox cites three seventeenth century commentators (Thomas Wilson, Henry More, and John Denham) to argue that Milton and his contemporaries followed traditional thinking that justice was linked to obligations to God as well as to one's neighbors (122–23).

578–79. *and know his works / Not hid:* many commentators cite Josephus's report that the descendants of Seth "were the inventors of that peculiar sort of wisdom which is concerned with the heavenly bodies, and their order" (*Antiquities* 1.2.3). Montgomery adds that they were also concerned "to know those things which might preserve freedom and peace to men," which he presumably draws from the same passage ("as [Seth] was himself of an excellent character, so did he leave children behind him who imitated his virtues"), which Montgomery believes Milton drew "chiefly from oriental writers, and particularly from the annals of Eutychius." Cf. Deut. 29:29: "The secret things belong unto the LORD our God: but those things which are revealed belong unto us and to our children for ever."

579. *nor those things last:* 1667 has *lost,* corrected to *last* in the errata. Bentley emends to *least.* Wesley has *Lost,* and explains *nor those things Lost* [*sic*] as "in their Thoughts." Keightley glosses this phrase as "they did not assign the last or lowest degree to moral and religious knowledge."

582–97. Cf. *PR* 2.153–71, 362–65. Fox, who traces the Seven Deadly Sins in books 11–12, identifies this episode as lust (170–71).

582. *A Beavie of fair Women: fair* is the term in Gen. 6:2 for the "daughters of men," and *bevy* is "the proper term for a company of maidens or ladies, of roes, of quails, or of larks" (so *OED* 1), for which numerous instances have been remarked by critics. The Richardsons note that Spenser has bevies of fair ladies in *Faerie Queene* 2.9.34 and in the *Shepheardes Calendar* ("Aprill," line 118), and Newton adds *Faerie Queene* 5.9.31 and *Henry VIII* 1.4.3–5 ("None here he hopes / In all this noble bevy, has brought with her / One care abroad"). Keightley reports that *bevy* is used for quails, which are "very amorous birds." R. C. Browne (1877) cites Hensleigh Wedgwood ("Fr. *bevée*, a brood, flock, of quails, larks, roebucks, then applied to a company, of ladies especially") and also cites "the old commentator on Spenser" who said the word was used properly of larks. Wesley glosses the word as "a Company."

The etymology is obscure. Hume gives the derivation from the Italian *beva*, a covey of partridges, but *OED* traces it to *buv*–(drinking). Cf. Milton's sardonic rejection in *Apol* of Hall's "nimble dryads": "Delicious! he had that whole bevie at command" (Patterson, *Works* 3:344). "A Bevy of Fair Women" is one of five illustrations for book 11 in Tilt's 1843 illustrated edition of Milton's *Poetical Works* (C. H. C. Baker 116); see further lists of Tilt's illustrations in **11.187** and **12.1–5**.

583–86. *to the Harp they sung / Soft amorous Ditties...till in the amorous Net:* cf. the "amorous dittyes" of 1.449, the "Amorous Nets" of the temptresses in *PR* 2.162, the "Aurea quæ fallax retia tendit Amor" (false golden nets held out by Cupid) of *El 1* 60, and also the *amorose reti* ("amorous nets") of Ariosto, *Orlando Furioso* 1.12. Verity thinks that Tennyson's "all my bounding heart entanglest / In a golden netted smile" ("Madeline" 40–41) may refer to this passage.

Montgomery finds 583–84 a "beautiful copy" of *Iliad* 18.491 and also cites Hesiod's scene of marriage festivities in *Shield of Heracles* (272–85) and the bridal chant in Apollonius Rhodius's *Argonautica* (4.1196). Shumaker claims that a metaphor in a vision ("the amorous net," as well as "all in heat / They light the Nuptial Torch") is comparatively rare in *PL;* the net cannot appear, only the insinuating graces it represents (*Unpremeditated Verse* 208–09).

the Harp: typically elided as a single syllable. Despite the scansion, Bridges denies that there can be a true glide through a consonantal *h* (26). Bentley thinks Milton could not want *amorous* twice in three lines, and wants to render 584–85 as "To th'Harp they sung / Soft *Odes and Ditties.*"

583. *In Gems and wanton dress:* Milton may mean to reference the biblical injunction in 1 Pet. 3:1–6 for holy women to be adorned with meekness rather than "plaiting the hair, and of wearing of gold, or of putting on of apparel." Sims (*Bible* 270) also cites similar counsel in 1 Tim. 2:9: women should "adorn themselves in modest apparel, with shamefacedness and sobriety; not with broided hair, or gold, or pearls, or costly array."

584. *ditties:* "a composition intended to be set to music and sung; a song, lay; now, a short simple song; often used of the songs of birds, or applied depreciatively" (so *OED* 2).

586–87. *Rove without rein:* in Milton's use, always pejorative; of *rove,* he links exploration with sensuality as does Ovid's "forbidden" love stories; cf. "Rove idle unemployed" in 4.617 with "rove / Uncheckt" in 8.188–89 (Grandsen 285). According to Fish, the net is woven by the unreined roving eyes of the grave men themselves, since "the eye is traditionally the entry place for the arrow of lust" (cf. "the lust of the eyes" of 1 John 2:16), and Ps. 141:10 tells us that "the wicked fall into their own nets" (294).

    rein: in the figurative sense, "any means of guiding, controlling, or governing; a curb, check, or restraint of any kind" (so *OED* 2a).

    Fast caught: Bentley emended what he thought was *first* to *fast,* but that is already the reading in both 1667 and 1674. The Richardsons note, as does Hawkey, the later *first* as a corruption. Both Thomas Tickell and Fenton (in Todd) follow *first.*

587. *liking:* "an object liked, (one's) beloved" (so *OED* 5, obsolete).

588. *treat:* "to handle or discuss (an affair) with a view to settlement; to negotiate, arrange, plan" (*OED* 1b, obsolete). "Deal or discuss" (Fowler).

588–89. *th'Eevning Star / Loves Harbinger:* cf. 4.605–06, 8.519–20, and similar references to Hesperus in Virgil, *Eclogue* 8.30, and Dante, *Purgatorio* 1.19, and also the more general description of an evening wedding procession in the *Iliad* 18.491–93. Osgood (42) cites classical references to Hesperus as the bringer of Hymen in Catullus 62, in Claudian 14.1–2 (*Fescennine Verses* 14.1–2), and to some extent in Claudian's *De Raptu Prosperpina* 2.361. Hesperus is also named as *nuntius noctis* ("announcer" or "bringer of night") in Seneca's *Hippolytus* 749–751. The evening star itself lights the "bridal lamp" for Adam and Eve in 8.519, but as Fowler notes, the pagan Hymen is not there invoked.

590–92. Hymen, the son of Bacchus and Venus, presided over marriages. Cf. a similar reference to Hymen, invoking, and the torch at *EpWin* 18–20 and also the wedding description from Achilles' shield in Homer's *Iliad* 18.491–93. Todd cites Apollonius Rhodius, *Argonautica* 4.1196–97, and particularly—as does Stillingfleet—Hesiod, *The Shield of Herakles* 275–76. Masson remarks that Milton uses the phrase in *DDD* ("while they hast too eagerly to light the nuptiall torch" [Patterson, *Works* 3:394–95]). Verity cites Ben Jonson's claim in *Hymenaei* (*Masque of Hymen*) that the nuptial torch was pinewood; Jonson (7:211) cites the *pinea taeda* of Ovid's *Fasti* 2:558, the *Pineam…taedam* from Catullus, *Carmina* 61.15; and the *Pinus amores* from 439 of *Ciri* or *Ciris,* a poem attributed to Virgil. All the Latin terms refer to wedding torches made of pine.

Hume finds that the invocation forsakes the true God in favor of abominable idols. Himes (*Paradise Lost: A Poem*) sees a reference to Gen. 4:26: "Then began men to call upon the name of the LORD," i.e., in idolatry, an interpretation he claims is also rabbinical. Hughes (*Paradise Lost*) references the classical invocation of Hymen in Spenser's *Epithalamion:* "'Hymen, Iö Hymen, Hymen,' they do shout" (140).

marriage Rites: Cf. 8.487.

591. *Hymen:* italicized in 1672 but not 1667.

594. *love and youth not lost:* Fowler suggests that Adam would find this theme particularly attractive, since Michael has just told him that he would lose his own youth (11.536–46). Wesley omits this line.

and youth: 1667 *& youth.*

595–606. Nicolson cites this passage as best contrasting with Thomas Hobbes's view that by nature humans are egocentric, instinctual, and above all motivated by self-preservation; Milton's temperance did not negate pleasure but recognized reason as the highest good ("Milton and Hobbes" 415–17).

595–97. *charming Symphonies attach'd the heart / Of Adam:* cf. the "dulcet symphonies" of 1.712 and the "charming symphony" of 3.368. Burden identifies *charming* as the key word in the passage, denoting marriage based not upon a reasonable institution but rather upon *heat, delight,* and the *bent of Nature* only; the invocation of Hymen further denotes an un-Christian basis (194).

See **11.471–72**. Fish identifies the complexity of the passage, which until the ambiguous word *charming* (either attractive or spellbinding) "could surely be a catalogue of 'unreproved pleasures free,'" and *bent of Nature* as also potentially sinister; here the reader is able to stand outside of the temptation and draw the moral long before Michael speaks (293).

attach'd: Bentley emends to *attack'd,* but Pearce argues that the more forceful *attach* (seize and take possession) better describes the effect of the music on Adam. Wesley glosses *attach'd* as "seised, got possession of."

Symphonies: "harmony of sound, esp. of musical sounds; concord, consonance. Also occas[ionally] of speech-sounds, as in verse" (*OED* 2, rare or obsolete). Verity cites Cotgrave and Bullokar's similar idea that *symphony* in Milton's time referred merely to harmonious sounds or concord in music.

Admit: "to allow to enter, let in, receive" (so *OED* 1).

597–98. *express'd . . . blest:* one of Milton's 17 rhyming couplets identified by Diekhoff ("Rhyme" 539–40); the line numbers are corrected by Purcell (171).

598. *prime Angel blest:* on the fluidity of Milton's names for angels, see West and Gage's comment in **11.101**.

599–602. *Here Nature seems fulfill'd:* critics have focused on the deceptive vision. Williamson finds that "Adam's response suggests the original Adam," i.e., swayed by female charm (107). Sasek compares the scene to that of Achilles' shield showing the occupations of men at peace but put to far different ends by Milton to show the signs of vanity and lust (191). According to Burden, the passage both demonstrates that Adam's hold on the good and true is still tenuous and presents an important lesson about vigilance (194). Fowler underscores the point that these marriages are based on "heat" (11.589) and "delight" (11.596) rather than rational choice, and that Adam is here "transported" as he was in 8.529–30. Lewalski also observes the ironic temporary reversal of Adam to his old blindness, followed in 11.632–33 by a repetition of his earlier attempt to blame woman for man's woes (27).

603–17. Fox points out that the inventors of "Arts that polish life" produce "Goddesses . . . empty of all good" (avarice and lust), just as on a diabolical level

Mammon creates objects of material beauty, and Sin is a fair woman (174). Madsen links these creative activities to those of the fallen angels, so that "the vision of angel without God in the first two books...is paralleled by the vision of man without God in the last two" ("Idea" 260).

603–09. In his discussion of the *felix culpa,* Kermode ties this passage to what he sees as the greater redemptive paradox of the poem; the senses will not recognize that their own destruction will produce eternal bliss and joy (121). Milton's comments here about the misuse of appetite are necessarily simpler than his prelapsarian discussion of angelic appetite (Burden 195). Bundy, analyzing Michael as teacher, has him here attack Epicureanism and then demonstrate the universal war and discord resulting from that philosophy (148). Fish paraphrases Michael's correction: "Not so...the ends of nature have nothing to do with what you see here, since nature begins and ends in the divine" (278–79). Patrides sees this passage as a "poetic affirmation of the fundamental Christian claim that fallen man errs constantly and constantly needs grace to repair mere nature," and also as "another instance of the marriage between poetry and theology" in the epic ("*Paradise Lost*" 109–10).

605–06. *Created, as thou art, to nobler end...conformitie divine:* Himes (*Paradise Lost: A Poem*) here and in line 595 notes the "seductions of pleasure" away from man's true end of holiness, citing 1 Pet. 1:14–16. Cf. the promise of predestined conformity to God's image in Rom. 8:29. Lawry says that Adam must learn a "corrosive truth": he has chosen the passions of the Fall that fill the tents of Cain rather than his *nobler end* (*Shadow* 279). Fowler compares the delight at purely natural ends with the transcendent goal of the Westminster Catechism, in which the chief end of man is to glorify God and to enjoy him forever.

607–23. *the Tents / Of wickedness:* cf. the "tents of wickedness" in Ps. 84:10. Fish argues that although Michael's *moralitas* is " 'bad poetry,' dull, overlong, and unnecessary," it nevertheless frees us from the necessity of drawing the moral and allows us instead to concentrate on the poem's pattern of associations (295–96).

607. *sawst:* a past tense of "see" (so *OED* β).

610–12. *Of Arts that polish Life…his Spirit / Taught them:* cf. Bezaleel's divinely given artistic gifts (Exod. 35:30, 31). "Adam's earlier Robinson Crusoe-like hope that God would provide shelter and fire did not extend to such refinements as metal work, but [those arts] emerge very naturally" (MacCallum, "Milton and Sacred History" 163). Maurice Kelley (109) thinks that *Spirit* cannot refer to the third person of the Trinity, but rather "the virtue and power of God the Father," since according to Milton the Holy Spirit was not sent until "Gospel times" (Patterson, *Works* 14:363). Fowler claims that many commentators on Genesis have used this passage to comment on the existence of secular culture; Calvin applied his doctrine of general grace to account for the inspiration of the heathen.

612. *acknowledg'd:* "to own with gratitude, or as an obligation (a gift, or service rendered)" (so *OED* 4).

613. *beauteous ofspring:* In Hughes's final note for *PL* 11, he points out the odd rendering of *nephilim,* a crucial word in Gen. 6.4, translated as "giants" in KJV but which can also mean either "gods" or "abusers of power" (Geneva Bible). Hughes adds that Milton may have known of Philo's allegorical interpretation of *nephilim.* In *Def 1,* Milton calls Philo a "solid authority studious in the law of Moses" (Patterson, *Works* 7:78). Philo interprets *giants* as "the sons of earth [who] have turned the steps of the mind out of the path of reason," beginning with Nimrod, whose name means "desertion," for he deserted the path of reason and began to be a giant of the earth ("Variorum"); cf. *Philo* 2:477–79.

614–27. Martz complains that Michael is losing the "regard benigne" noted in 11.334 and instead is adopting "the rasping voice so often found among the sermons of Milton's day" (153).

614–20. Whiting cites the Geneva Bible gloss on the "sonnes of God" (Gen. 6:2) as "the children of the godly which began to degenerate" and the fair women as those who "came of wicked parents, as of Kain" (*Milton* 138); the Geneva Bible glosses "fair" as "Having more respect for their beauty and worldly considerations than for their manners and godliness."

614. *For that fair femal Troop:* cf. 11.582. Bentley sees no purpose for *For* and wants to emend it to *Ev'n;* Pearce argues that *For* introduces proof that the women were "Unmindful of thir Maker" (611). Stebbing glosses *For that* as *As for that*. Keightley thinks it not impossible that the printer may have in fact printed *For* for *Ev'n*, but in any case he reads the line as an anacoluthon, or stylistic loss of grammar. Montgomery is surprised that the lines cause any confusion but prefers the reading of Newton, Todd, and "Major": "for thou saw'st that fair female troop, that seem'd of goddesses." Himes (*Paradise Lost: A Poem*) cites the senators' comparison of Helen of Troy to deathless goddesses in *Iliad* 3.158.

614–15. Wesley omits ten syllables, "that seemd / Of Goddesses, so blithe, so smooth."

616–17. *empty of all good:* "Milton could never write coldly about the power of coquettish triviality to seduce unwary wisdom" (Shumaker, *Unpremeditated Verse* 209).

618–25. Whiting contends that Milton's comment is drawn from the Geneva Bible comment on Gen. 6, where the men had "more respect to the beautie, and worldly considerations, then their maners and godliness" ("Before the Flood" 75), though other contemporary sources might have furnished this idea.

618. *completed:* Fowler argues that since the meanings "accomplished" or "equipped" were rare before *PL*, Milton might have intended an academic metaphor in the sense of "graduated." The earliest such meaning of "finished" or "made complete" reported by *OED* is 1665.

619–20. *to sing, to dance:* Walter A. Raleigh cites this passage as one example of Milton's indignation against women (144–45).

619. *appetence:* appetite or desire.

620. *troule the Tongue, and roule the Eye:* Wesley omits this line.
    troule: the term is unclear. *OED* supposes "move (the tongue) volubly," citing only this line and one in the 1747 *New Canto Spencer's F.Q. xviii* (II.4.b). Keightley cites "Troll the catch" (i.e., make it roll off the tongue) from *Tempest*

3.2.117, and also Neal's complaint about the Anglican practice of "trowling of Psalms from one side of the choir to another" (181); he concludes that unless Milton intends *troule* as a contraction for *to roll*, he misuses the word, since the words, not the tongue, are rolled. R. C. Browne (1877) also cites Wedgwood, "To *troll* a song may be to roll it out with rise and fall of voice, but it is more properly the equivalent of Germ. *trallen, trallern,* Swiss *tralallen,* to sing a tune — notes without words — from a representation of the notes by the syllable tra-la-la." The term is glossed as "wag" by Bush, Northrop Frye (*Paradise Lost*), Le Comte, Hughes (*Paradise Lost, A Poem*), and Fowler. Cf. the "warbling charms" of *SA* 934.

roule the eye: some critics see a possible reference to the "wanton eyes" of Isa. 3:16.

621–22. *whose lives / Religious titl'd them the Sons of God:* as opposed to the "false titled" sons of God, the fallen angels (*PR* 2.179). Michael's explanation conforms to Augustine's reading of this passage (West, *Milton and the Angels* 129) that the sons of God are not angels but sons of Seth who lived west of Eden ("on the hither side"), for which Bush cites *City of God* 15.22–23; see **11.556–627.** Fowler links Milton's explanation here to the "down-to-earth demythologizing" of book 11. Cf. *DocCh* 1.23 (Patterson, *Works* 16:51), which identifies the relation of these "sons of God" as adoptive (Maurice Kelley 172).

623–24. *Shall yield up all thir vertue, all thir fame / Ignobly:* cf. Gen. 6:5: "God saw that the wickedness of man was great in the earth, and that every imagination of the thoughts of his heart was only evil continually."

623. *yield:* 1667 *yeild.*

624. *to the traines and to the smiles:* Hughes (*Paradise Lost*) glosses *traines* as "tricks, deceits," Le Comte has "snares," and Fowler has "snares, enticements"; cf. *OED* n.² 1, "treachery, guile, deceit, trickery" (obsolete). Keightley cites Fairfax, *Godfrey of Bulloigne* 4.26.2: "Frame snares, of lookes; traines, of alluring speach."

625–27. *swim in joy:* cf. 9.1009 ("swim in mirth"), Spenser's *Faerie Queene* 1.12.41 ("swimming in that sea of blisfull joy") and 3.1.39 ("swimming deepe in sensuall desyres"). Todd claims that *swim* for "revel" was not uncommon, also citing Phineas Fletcher ("Swimming in waves of joyes" [*Purple Island* 12.76]) and Crashaw ("swim / In riper joyes" ["Out of the Greek: Cupid's Cryer," lines 14–15, in *Delights of the Muses,* in *The Poems* 159]). Fowler identifies the phrase as idiomatic; the phrasing *swim in joy...The world...must weep* is repeated in Adam's reaction in 11.757. Keightley cites this construction in Corneille's *Le Cid* 3.5 ("Je nage dans la joie"; "I swim in joy"). Cf. *OED* 7b: "immersed or sunk in grief."

(Erelong to swim at large)...The world erelong a world of tears must weepe: Bentley finds "at large" unsatisfactory for "the wide Deluge" and the next line a "Jingle," apparently because of the repetition of *world;* he suggests, "Erelong to swim *in flood: Now* laugh, for which / The world a *bitterer flood* of tears must weep." Pearce recalls a similar repetition in 9.11, "That brought into this world a world of woe," and suggests different punctuation, which Newton retains. Verity points out that Shakespeare used *world of* for *much of* in *Richard III* 3.7.223 and *Henry VIII* 3.2.211; cf. *OED* 7f: "used hyperbolically for 'a great quantity.'" Verity also claims that for both Milton and Shakespeare, plays on words often express grim irony. Cf. *Breath / Bread* in 12.78.

Burden argues that the Sons of God passage is "part of the poem's thesis about marriage," that "the corruption of the world...had its origin in a perversion of the marriage relationship" (196).

626–27. Wesley reduces this passage to a single line: "And laugh, for which the world ere long must weep."

626. *large:* 1667 *larg.*

628. Wesley notes this line as beginning a passage of particular excellence but does not mark its end.

629–31. *O pittie and shame...to tread / Paths indirect:* Giamatti identifies these lines as an example of Milton's "satanic" style, "a way of approaching, and controlling, reality appropriate to both the poet recounting subversion and the Subverter himself," though he denies that Milton was thereby of the devil's party without knowing it — "no one was more aware of what he knew, or what he was doing, than John Milton" (298). As Lawry remarks, Adam does not immediately recognize this sin as his own ("'Euphrasy and Rue'" 7).

indirect: "crooked,...devious" (so *OED* 1). "At the time a strong word, synonymous with 'wrong, unfair'" (Verity). Cf. Shakespeare's "by-paths and indirect crook'd ways" (*2 Henry IV* 4.5.184).

630–32. Maurice Kelley claims that book 11 contains four of the sins enumerated as results of the Fall in *DocCh;* this one is uxoriousness (149); see **11.445–74.**

631. *Paths indirect, or in the mid way faint:* Fowler identifies this line as the numeric *mid way* of the *Paths indirect* of the first, destroyed world, as the midpoint between the first line of the first vision (11.423), and the last line of the fifth, the Flood (11.839).

632–33. *the tenor of Mans woe...from Woman:* the *woe-man/woman* pun, remarked by several commentators, is scarcely original with Milton but was an obsolete, pseudo-etymological association used frequently in the sixteenth and seventeenth centuries (*OED* 1k). Todd cites the couplet, "How ill did hee his Grammar skan, / That call'd a Woman *woe to man,*" which appears in William Austin's 1637 defense of women, *Haec homo* (164), giving some sense of the pun's currency at the time, and Hughes (*Paradise Lost, A Poem*) quotes John Heywood's *Proverbs* 2.7: "A woman. As who say, woe to the man." Fowler argues that although Milton indeed often emphasizes marital issues, here he is commenting on the relation of intellect and emotions. Giamatti sees an element of the traditional "garden theme": "a man's self-corruption and lapse into degrading circumstances" (326–27).

633–36. Gilbert, who hears occasional echoes of medieval mystery plays in *PL,* claims that Milton has here reworked the conventional antifeminism of the Chester play, since he believed that man's gifts made him properly the head of the house but did not tolerate the vilification of women ("Milton and the Mysteries" 155–56). According to contemporary psychology and ethics, a woman not properly under the rule of reason becomes the principle source of evil, but since man is responsible for woman, he is also responsible if she becomes the instrument of evil (Saurat 137–38). Patrides finds Michael's correction of Adam to be "cold," here and elsewhere, though only in the light of Raphael's earlier courteous attitude (*Paradise Lost* 109).

633. *Holds on the same:* Bentley emends to *Hold on.*

634. *effeminate:* "unmanly, with suggestion of 'dominated by women'" (Ricks, *Paradise Lost*). Adam must acknowledge his role in men's sins even as Satan had to acknowledge his son, Death (Lawry, *Shadow* 280). For Milton, the purest expression of "effeminate slackness" is the courtly love convention of unquestioning obedience to a mistress (Northrop Frye, "Revelation" 28); cf. *the starv'd lover* of 4.769 and *injur'd Lover's Hell* of 5.450.

   slackness: "lack of diligence or energy; tendency to idleness or sluggishness; remissness" (so *OED* 1a).

635. On the elision, see **11.449**.

636. *receav'd:* 1667 *receavd.*

637–39. *Scene...between:* a case of rhyme after an intervening line, missed by Diekhoff ("Rhyme"), but noted by Purcell (171).

637. *Scene:* Coleridge claims that neither Shakespeare nor Milton ever uses this word without some clear reference to the theatre (Wittreich 224–25).

638–73. In the fourth vision, the secular marriages of the third produce contentious offspring and scenes of war, culminating in Enoch's translation. Addison, having already noted that Milton contrasted the lazar-house with a scene of mirth (see **11.556–627**), here reports that "the next Vision is of a quite contrary Nature, and filled with the horrors of War" (*Spectator* 3 [26 Apr. 1712]: 363). Mollenkott claims that this vision elaborates the violence of both Cain and Satan (37). Fowler compares the discord bred by Spenser's Ate in the fourth book of *Faerie Queene* and also draws attention to four vignettes (foraging [11.646–50], tournament [11.651–55], siege [11.656–59], and council [11.660–71]) that parallel representations on Homer's shield of Achilles (*Iliad* 18.497–540); a corresponding shield of Vulcan was given to Aeneas by his mother Venus (*Aeneid* 8.626–728), and both shields included personified representations of Discord or Strife. Himes assumes that Milton, while not condemning war entirely, nevertheless disdained reasonable beings appealing to physical force (*A Study* 243). Champion (392) connects this passage with

Moloch's speech in 2.51–105; cf. **11.446–47**. Fox argues not only from the details of the episode but also from the larger context of Achilles' shield and the theme of Achilles' anger running throughout the *Iliad* that the marauding in this section represents the deadly sin of wrath, as does Moloch in books 1–2; like him these are rash and impetuous warriors whose primary aim is to plunder and destroy (175–77). Fish (303–04) identifies allusions to at least four earlier scenes in *PL:* the war games in hell (2.528–531) now played in earnest, and in similar phrasing (11.643); the carnage and confusion of war described in 6.386–91 and repeated in 11.651–55; the metaphoric "Herd / Of Goats or timorous flock" (6.855–56) changed to actual "bleating lambs" herded "over the plain" (11.646–49); and the "deeds of eternal fame...infinite" (6.240–41) now echoed in "slaughter and gigantic deeds" (11.659). In addition, in place of the long and dignified (if specious) council of war in hell (book 2), the earthly council is dispatched in a few lines (11.661–64). Steadman (*Milton's Epic Characters* 179–80), claiming that the Sons of God episode provides a point of departure for Michael to condemn both a conventional but vicious conception of "Valour and Heroic Vertu" (11.690) and a false opinion of fame, also argues at length that Milton depended heavily on conventional interpretations of Gen. 6:4 for the subsequent episode, e.g., Castellion and Calvin for the appellation *Heroes,* Calvin also for the viciousness of their exploits, Magius for the equation of giant with "warlike," and the Junius-Tremellius Bible for its gloss on *giants* as an epithet emphasizing their impiety and apostasy. Shumaker claims that the picture of war is general, "freed of limiting circumstances and presented as an archetype" (*Unpremeditated Verse* 210).

638. *He lookd and saw:* Lewalski traces Adam's purged and exercised physical sight throughout book 11 (26); see **11.368**.

640. *Cities of Men with lofty Gates and Towrs:* Low claims that Milton usually links the earthly tower, a symbol of man's glory and transience, with royal ambition and—nearly always—with "that other symbol of man's striving, the city" (177–78).

641–47. Maurice Kelley identifies in book 11 four sins resulting from the Fall and enumerated in *DocCh;* this one is theft and invasion of the rights of others (149); see **11.445–74**.

641. *concours:* "hostile encounter or onset" (so *OED*, obsolete).

642. *Giants of mightie Bone, and bould emprise:* cf. the giants of Gen. 6:4 and also *PL* 11.688. Steadman reports that the Midrash also stressed the massive bone structure of the giants, claiming that the "marrow of each one's thigh bone was eighteen cubits long" (*Milton's Epic Characters* 180–81).

Emprise: "chivalric enterprise, martial prowess" (so *OED* 2, archaic). *Mask* 610 also has "bold emprise." Todd cites Ariosto's "audace emprise" (Italian: *audaci imprese*) of *Orlando Furioso* 1.1; cf. *Faerie Queene* 1.12.18. Bush cites "l'alta impresa" ("high emprise") of Tasso, *Gerusalemme liberata* 1.6.2.

643–44. *part courb the foaming Steed, / Single or in Array of Battel rang'd:* cf. Milton's similar phrasing in *PL* 2.531–32 and 6.391. Bentley thinks line 644 should read, "Battel *stand,*" meaning wield or curb. Milton may have conflated several classical images here. Keightley cites *Aeneid* 7.162–64, which concerns boys' training in horsemanship, not actual battle, while Verity's references (*Iliad* 2.773 and *Aeneid* 6.642) concern adult athletics. Hughes (*Paradise Lost*) claims that Milton uses this epic phrase deliberately to imitate the classics.

645. *nor idely mustring stood:* Newton cites Warburton: "One can't perceive the pertinence of this without supposing that it hinted at the circumstances of the land-army at that time."

646–51. Cf. the capture of sheep and oxen on the shield of Achilles in *Iliad* 18.527–33.

646. *a Band select:* "a band of picked men" (Hughes, *Paradise Lost*).

647. *A herd of Beeves, faire oxen and faire Kine:* Broadbent finds the "real Old Testament pastoral" of the Hebrew history recounted (*Some Graver Subject* 272).

Beeves: "plural of *beef*…now usually poetic for 'oxen, cattle'" (*OED*).

Kine: "plural of *cow*" (*OED* 1, archaic).

650–55. Wesley omits most of this passage to read "Their booty: others to a city strong."

651. *But call in aide, which makes a bloody Fray: call in* was corrected from 1674 *callin* to original 1667.

> *makes.* 1667 *tacks.*

> Robert M. Adams claims (99)—as do the Richardsons, who cite an apparent translation of *Iliad* 18.531—that *tacks* is an idiomatic expression meaning "to join battle"; *OED* lists no such usage. Fowler is willing to concede that *tacks* might be idiomatic, but nevertheless observes that *tacks* as a form of *attacks* would be syntactically difficult, and that *tacks* as "joins" would be unidiomatic with "fray." Northrop Frye (*Paradise Lost*) glosses the word as "equalizes." Grierson insists that the 1674 reading (*makes*) is one that every editor accepts or should accept (*Poems* 2:xl–xli); see also **11.379–80**. Fletcher complains (*Complete Poetical Works*) that no editor has understood *tacks;* he thinks it should be retained, citing *OED*, "to hold one's own with, hold one's ground with, keep up with; to be even with" and especially "to carry on without winning or losing" (10, 11, obsolete; in *OED*'s first edition only). Shawcross judges that the compositor of 1674 may have made the change because he did not understand the line or know the meaning of *tacks* ("Orthography" 149).

652–55. Peck, attempting to attribute two Cromwell panegyrics to Milton, makes the dubious claim that this general description refers to the Battle of Edgehill (*Memoirs* 86–87); see also 11.671–73 and 689–99. Cf. Avitus's picture of warfare: "What shall I say of lofty cities, famed / For their inhabitants, now turned to deserts?" (Kirkconnell 18).

654. *th'ensanguined Field:* "bloodstained, bloody" (so *OED* 1, as first recorded instance). Todd cites *Iliad* 17.360–61 ("the earth with blood dark gleaming grew wet").

655–58. Newton finds Milton's description of the besieged city superior to that from Homer's shield of Achilles in *Iliad* 18.509–40.

656. *Batterie:* "a succession of heavy blows inflicted upon the walls of a city or fortress by means of artillery; bombardment" (so *OED* 3a).

> *Scale:* "escalade,...the action of scaling the walls of a fortified place by the use of ladders" (so *OED* 1, obsolete).

658. *Jav'lin:* "a light spear thrown with the hand with or without the help of a thong; a dart" (so *OED* 1a).

659. gigantic: "giant-like" (Ricks, *Paradise Lost*). Todd, after Dunster, cites "the destructive work of the giants" in Apollonius Rhodius, *Argonautica* 17, though the biblical conflation of *giant* with "men of renown" (Gen. 6:4) is the more obvious allusion.

660–73. Oras compares the pyrrhic endings used to create this "grave, objective narrative" with their contrastingly lyric use in 6.749–59 ("Milton's Blank Verse" 186–87); see **11.481–88**.

660–63. Newton claims that the council Milton describes seems more important than its predecessor from Homer's shield of Achilles in *Iliad* 18.503–06. Himes (*Paradise Lost: A Poem*) cites some additional context (*Iliad* 18.497–508), noting that the city gates were the meeting place for Hebrews, answerable to the Greek agora and the Latin forum.

660. *the scepter'd Haralds:* among the ancients, the scepter was chief mark of the herald's office. Cf. 1.752–55.

661–71. The just man in this passage, Enoch, the seventh from Adam (Gen. 5:21–24), is only finally identified by his translation (11.670; cf. Gen. 5:24) and position in Adam's genealogy (11.700). Arnold Williams reports that Noah was the only Sethite patriarch more interesting to Renaissance commentators than Enoch (*Common Expositor* 149). Enoch and Noah are the true contrasts to the chaos produced by both peace and war; Enoch rebukes the oppressive warlords, and Noah rebukes their licentious progeny (Muldrow 86); see also *PL* 11.719–20. MacKellar suggests that the portrait of Enoch may also be a portrait of Milton's contemporary Hugo Grotius (963). Saurat thought that Milton had amplified the verses in Gen. 5:21–24 into 100 lines with material from the apocryphal *Book of Enoch* (211–12). Fox rejects this suggestion at length, arguing that Milton's depiction differs greatly from the Enoch fragments, where 200 angelic Watchers descend from the heavens to have intercourse with the daughters of men, producing a race of giants who plunder the world until the

Lord threatens the Watchers and they beg for Enoch's intercession. Enoch has no contact with their giant offspring. Fox adds, "the fantastic tone of the *Book of Enoch* is completely foreign to the realism of Milton's world at war....[in which he] followed Homer" (178–80).

661. *To Council in the Citie Gates:* the city gates were the biblical locus of official business. See, e.g., Gen. 34:20; Deut. 16:18, 21:19; Ruth 4:1; Ps. 127:5; and Zech. 8:16. Wesley glosses as "the ancient place of judicature."

anon: B. A. Wright defines this obsolete adverb as "straightway, at once, instantly" ("Note" 147); see **11.46.**

665. *Of middle Age one rising:* Enoch was translated when 365 years old (Gen. 5:23), or at middle age in terms of the long lifetimes reported in Gen. 5 (Richardsons). Keightley refers some of this episode to the apocryphal *Book of Enoch,* as quoted in the New Testament epistle of Jude. Fox (180–82) contends that Milton has violated the biblical chronology by placing Enoch in the same scene as the giants who were apparently contemporaries of Noah and carried on their activities in the period just before the Deluge — Enoch lived some 500 years before "those days" of Gen. 6:4; Milton's violation of the chronology allows him to employ Enoch as a representative of fortitude, in contrast to the giants' excess of rashness and also to the deficiency of cowardice; moreover, Enoch's middle age avoids the rashness of youth and the timidity of old age.

668. *And Judgment from above:* see Enoch's speech of judgment reported in Jude 14–15, probably the "odious truth" referenced in *PL* 11.704 (Newton).

Judgment: 1667 *Judgement.*

669. *Exploded:* Wesley glosses as "rejected, hissed at"; Keightley as "hissed"; Masson has "execrated, hissed at, drove off the stage by hissing — the literal meaning of the Latin *explodo,* from *ex* and *plaudo,*" a definition similar to *OED* 1a. Cf. 10.546. Himes (*Paradise Lost: A Poem*) compares the scene with the Sodomites' treatment of Lot (Gen. 19:9–10).

Exploded: 1667 *Exploded,*

670–71. *a Cloud descending snatch'd him thence / Unseen amid the throng: so violence:* cf. Gen. 5:24 and Heb. 11:5, neither of which specifies details of Enoch's translation beyond that he was "not found" because God "took" or "translated" him. Fowler compares the translation into a cloud with Enoch 14:8–9: "Clouds invited me and a mist summoned me . . . and the winds . . . lifted me upward, and bore me into heaven" (citing Charles 2:197). Though those verses would not have been directly available to Milton, Fowler argues that the book would have been of interest to him, since Enoch like Michael also sees the future, and the book is largely concerned with the origin of evil. Keightley cites Hesiod's *Works and Days* 188–90, which portrays part of a similarly violent society, but not a translation of an Enoch figure; Milton may be referring to the departure from earth of Aidos and Nemesis, which immediately follows in Hesiod (199–201); cf. "Truth shall retire" (*PL* 12.535).

These two lines are one of Milton's 17 rhyming couplets identified by Diekhoff ("Rhyme" 539–40), with line numbers corrected by Purcell (171).

671–73. Francis Peck, attempting to attribute two Cromwell panegyrics to Milton, makes the dubious claim that this general description refers to the Battle of Dunbar (*Memoirs* 95); see also *PL* 11.652–55 and 689–99, as well as Knott's comment on the "subjected Plaine" in **12.640**.

672. *Oppression, and Sword-Law:* Todd hears a refutation of Hobbesian might-makes-right principles; he cites, as does R. C. Browne (1877), *Richard III* 5.3.311 ("Our strong arms be our conscience, swords our law!"). Ricks traces the gradual semantic shift for *Oppression,* from its neutral sense in 8.288 to the negative postlapsarian effect on Adam and Eve in 9.1045, to a prophecy here of what is in store for the world: "what happens in the narrative is reflected in what happens to the words" (*Milton's Grand Style* 115).

674–75. *Adam was all in tears:* Darbishire (*Milton's "Paradise Lost"*) cites this passage as an example of one of the many places "where the simplest things are told in simple English idiom. . . . Milton's decorum was no rigid limiting thing: it was vitally conceived; to him poetic language was simply the most potent language he could find for his purpose" (14–15); she also cites 12.537b. See Toole's comment on Adam's weeping in **11.494–95**.

675–80. *Deaths Ministers, not Men:* Himes (*Paradise Lost: A Poem*) finds a parallel with *Iliad* 18.535–40. As Roland Mushat Frye points out, "Death, the 'vast unhidebound corpse' (10.601), sprung in distortion from the incestuous union of Satan with his own nightmare, now rules in ravin over all the earth" (64). Samuel observes that Dante has no similar description of war-makers, since he cherishes the hope that one will restore monarchy to right function (*Dante* 263). Gardner links these lines to Milton's experience of great political events and disappointed hopes, judging that his delay in composing "was to our infinite gain," since his own experiences give the epic much of its dramatic reality and depth (*Reading* 96–97).

676–99. Summers includes this judgment against earthly heroism in his examination of the many features of *PL* that embarrass a modern reader ("Embarrassments" 69–70).

677. *Inhumanly:* "barbarously, cruelly" (so *OED*).

678. *Ten thousandfould:* 1667 *thousand fould.* Fowler cites the speech attributed to Enoch in Jude 14: "Behold, the Lord cometh with ten thousands of his saints." Cf. the "hunder'd-fold" of *Sonn 18*, 13.

679. *such massacher:* Hume sees a polemical pun on the Roman Catholic Mass and its propagation, which has caused "the most abominable Massacres of Mankind."

681–82. Masson finds the syntax of these lines very peculiar, as *whom* must be resolved not into "and him" but into "who, had not Heaven rescued him."

681. *that Just Man:* Mohl, arguing that Milton's belief in human perfectibility is close to Quaker thought, argues that the term *greater man* (1.4) was by no means limited to Christ, citing this passage and also *PL* 11.876; 12.113, 154, 240, and 587 (*Studies* 83–87).

683–97. Milton goes far beyond what Gen. 6 says about the "sons of God" because here he is rejecting not only the satanic hero who lives for personal glory, but also the more civilized types of heroism that Virgil and others had created (Bowra 197, 229–30). Whiting suggests that Milton made use of the marginal comment on Gen. 6:4–5 in the Geneva Bible: "All were given to the contempt of God, & oppression of their neighbors" ("Before the Flood" 75).

683–88. Fowler reports that the giant offspring of the sons of God and the daughters of Cain are treated at length in Enoch 6–7, a passage paraphrased by many patristic authors. Because of the monstrous births, Huntley links this passage to the Paradise of Fools in book 3 ("Justification" 112). *Product* will be stressed either on the first or second syllables depending on whether *Michael* is made di- or trisyllabic (Newton).

683. *Michael:* 1667 *Michael* has a semicolon; 1674 a period.

684. *ill mated.* 1667 *ill-mated.* Wesley glosses as "ill pair'd, misjoin'd."

685. *Where good with bad were matcht:* cf. Du Bartas's description of the Giants (1:401.735–38).

687. *Produce:* "to give birth to or bear (offspring); to yield (seed, fruit, etc.); to generate by a natural process" (so *OED* 3b).
    prodigious Births: cf. the giants reported in Gen. 6:4. The temperate sons of Seth were larger and more robust than the enervated sons of Cain, and the union of the two lines produced a race even more robust (Hume).

688–97. This passage and the Babel one (12.38–47) are linked to the Limbo of Vanity in book 3, thematically related by history and not merely by allegory (Hughes, "Milton's Limbo" 10–11). Milton rejects military heroism even as he uses much of traditional Western literature, translating the vision instead into one of human freedom (Summers, "Milton" 525). Steadman argues that Milton is like other Renaissance poets and critics in stressing "the destructive character of military valor, its frequent dissociation from reason and virtue, and the transitory nature of its own rewards"; his double-edged condemnation of the biblical "men of renown" (Gen. 6:4) applies both to the antediluvian giants and to most of the celebrated heroes of Greece and Rome, whose great feats are void of true virtue (*Milton* 25). "In secular terms Satan is the 'heroic,' if defeated, military figure, but such a figure is to be admired only in evil days" (Summers,

"Grateful Vicissitude" 252). These remarks are exactly applicable to the code of the Homeric heroes, particularly its destructive pride and its death-defying valor (Harding, *Club of Hercules* 43).

688–90. Bentley argues that since Michael is speaking in the present tense, Milton must have dictated, "Such *are* these giants," as in *PL* 5.683: "These are the product." Montgomery claims that Milton includes both usual interpretations of the "men of renown": either men of great stature, or tyrants and robbers. As Steadman explains, Milton and Calvin alike excoriated the giants' tyranny, their pride in their own strength, and their contempt of God and man, recognizing in these men of renown an unworthy conception of fame: "For Milton, as for Calvin, these pretensions to fame through conquest are merely 'inanes titulorum fumos' [silly smoke of titles]. The men of renown possess no valid claim to their 'high titles.'...the same Might-Heroism equation underlies Satan's characterization as one who 'hard'ning in his strength Glories'" (*Milton's Epic Characters* 181–82; see *PL* 1.572–73). Both the Miltonic hierarchies of heroic virtues identified by Steadman, the Christian one based on goodness and the satanic one based on might, are strongly supported by this passage (Fowler).

689–99. Peck, attempting to attribute two Cromwell panegyrics to Milton, links this passage to Cromwell's campaign in the north of England in August 1651 (*Memoirs* 99); see also 11.652–55 and 671–73. Radzinowicz, who argues that the lessons of time are both ethical and political, claims that here Michael's interpretation moves from the ethical issue of true versus apparent good to the allied political issue of what is honest and heroic in nations (43).

689–90. *Might...Valour and Heroic Vertu call'd:* "*virtue* means primarily 'valour,' from the Lat. *virtus*" (Verity). A *heroic virtue,* defined in ethical and religious terms, would have been available to Milton from many sources, including Torquato Tasso's *Discourse of Heroic Virtue and of Charity* (Hughes, *Paradise Lost*).

Valour: "the quality of mind which enables a person to face danger with boldness or firmness; courage or bravery, esp. as shown in warfare or conflict; valiancy, prowess" (so *OED* 1c).

Fish sees this passage on the "obvious absurdity of might" as a "reproach to our own slowness in abandoning a position the angel does not even bother to refute" (306).

691–97. Wesley omits this passage, which has attracted various comments. Newton cites Warburton's claim that the parallel passage in *PR* beginning in *PL* 3.71 is more masterfully drawn. Himes (*Paradise Lost: A Poem*) refers to the fourth, heroic age, in which Jupiter "made the divine brood of heroes, better and braver than the third or brazen race" (Hesiod, *Works and Days* 157). Patrides notes a similar attitude toward pagan heroism among the early northern humanists, and indeed, in Virgil's criticism of the heroic ideal he inherited (*Milton* 149–52). Whiting suggests that Milton takes this idea and others from the commentary in the Geneva Bible (*Milton* 138–39).

691. *Battle:* 1667 *Battel.*

694–95. *for Glorie done / Of triumph, to be styl'd great Conquerours:* this passage has been variously interpreted. Bentley thinks the line may have been "And for Glory *won* / *Or* Triumph." Pearce approves the first change, but not the second, since he interprets the larger context as saying "it shall be held the highest pitch of glory, to subdue nations and bring home their spoils." Newton, dissatisfied with both Bentley's conjecture and Pearce's, glosses the passage as "To overcome, to subdue, to spoil, shall be held the highest pitch of glory, and shall be done for glory of triumph, shall be achieved for end and purpose, to be stiled great conquerors." Montgomery approves the explanation of Todd and Stillingfleet, that "to overcome in battle, etc. shall be held *the highest pitch of human glory, and of triumph, for that glory achieved*," according to which Milton's passage could be printed with *for Glorie done* in parentheses and *styl'd* changed to *held*. Verity finds Newton's ellipsis *shall be* awkward, and proposes the reading "and to be styled great conquerors shall be held the highest pitch of triumph for glorious deeds accomplished." Grierson, who agrees with Verity, paraphrases as "To overcome in battle, and subdue nations, and bring home spoil with infinite manslaughter shall be held the highest pitch of human glory, and (the highest pitch) of triumph for glory won (shall be held) to be styl'd great conquerors, etc." (*Poems* 2:xlviii–ix); Grierson adds a comma at the end of the first line (xlviii). Barrett (*Poems* 656) reads this phrase as "done for [the] glory of triumph," since Milton tends to invert terminal words before a line beginning with "Of," and because the construction is similar in sense and syntax to that of *PL* 3.100.

696. *Patrons of Mankind, Gods, and Sons of Gods:* Keightley surmises that Milton has in view such titles taken by kings of Syria and Egypt as Soter, Euergetes, and Theos. Banks claims that this is one passage where *gods* must refer to pagan gods ("Meaning" 452). Cf. *PR* 3.81–83.

697. *Destroyers rightlier call'd and Plagues of men:* according to MacCaffrey, this line is Milton's "final opinion of warfare" (129). George Coffin Taylor finds very similar language in Du Bartas: "Plagues of the world, and scourges of Mankind" (*Milton's Use* 119; cf. Du Bartas 1:401.738). Whiting cites similar language in the Geneva Bible commentary, which claimed that the giants of Gen. 6:4 "usurped autoritie over others, and degenerated from that simplicitie wherein their father's lived," and also in the Geneva translation, which advises that "the earth was filled with crueltie" (Gen. 6:11, 13), with the further gloss, "meaning that all were given to the contempt of God, and oppression of their neighbours" (*Milton* 138–39).

698–99. *Fame shall be atchiev'd...hid:* cf. *Lyc* 70–84. Milton's idea has much in common with Plato's τιμή (fame), which by derivation means "worth," but in *PL,* "the esteem won from the ignorant many becomes despicable" and will lead to the desire for a mere name, as Nimrod's in 12.45–47 (Samuel, *Plato* 87–88); Samuel also sees a parallel in Dante's counsel in *Purgatorio* 6.112–17 that the desire for honor and fame compromises actions of true Love (*Dante* 250–51).

698. *atchiev'd:* 1667 *achiev'd.*

700. *the seventh from thee:* Enoch was the seventh from Adam in biblical genealogy (Gen. 5:3–18; Luke 3:37–38; and Jude 14). Hughes (*Paradise Lost, A Poem*) supplies a Geneva gloss: God took him away "to shew that there was a better life prepared, and to be a testimonie of the immortalitie of soules and bodies."

701. *The onely righteous in a World perverse:* much of the comment on this passage stresses the "onely." MacCallum emphasizes how the various "men of faith" (Abel, Enoch, Noah, Abraham) prefigure Christ by their qualities or actions ("Milton and Sacred History" 158); see 11.459–60, 808–18, and 12.113. Cf. Marco's statement in *Purgatorio* 16.121–23 that only three just men are still alive in Lombardy, which Samuel adds could be true "for virtually every city-state that Dante reviews in the *Commedia*—and for virtually every period of history that Michael reveals to Adam" (*Dante* 255); Samuel also cites *Paradiso* 17.67–69: "Of their brutishness their progeny shall make / proof, so that it shall be for thy fair fame to / have made a party for thyself" (256). Martz complains about how far Milton has departed from his allegory of the war in heaven: although Abdiel was indeed the only righteous in Satan's perverse band, he returned to join the greater host of the unfallen angels, but Milton's one just man on earth has no just men to join (153). Summers argues that it is the desire for military fame that has brutally corrupted man in this vision; like Abdiel, Enoch is unsuccessful in his attempt to convert his fellows, but, like Abdiel, he also represents the continuous possibility of true heroism (*Muse's Method* 203).

705–07. Cf. 3.522. As Keightley and others note, Milton applies to Enoch the manner of Elijah's being taken to heaven; cf. 2 Kings 2:11 and also *ProdBom* 7–8 and *PR* 2.16–17. Enoch and Elijah were often associated (Fowler). In *DocCh* 1.12–13, Milton distinguishes four kinds of death: guiltiness, spiritual death, death of the body, and eternal death or damnation (Patterson, *Works* 15:203, 205, 215, 251); Babb concludes that Enoch—and later, Elijah—will undergo spiritualization before translation to heaven (51); see also the comments on death in **11.57–62** and **11.467–69**. Fowler cites Willet's summary (70–72) in *Hexapla* (1608) of Renaissance controversies over Enoch's translation: whether Enoch escaped death, whether he was preserved in some earthly paradise, and whether he would come again to be slain by the Antichrist, as suggested in Rev. 11:3–12. Fowler also cites the Geneva Bible gloss in Gen. 5:24 to claim that Enoch's translation was generally regarded as a type of resurrection: "To show that there was a better life prepared and to be a testimony of the immortality of souls and bodies." The rest of the gloss—"To inquire where he went is mere curiosity"—supports Fowler's report that the translation was controversial. Milton also invokes the popular theory that Enoch and Elijah typified perfect glorification, the former before the Law, the latter under it (*DocCh* 1.33 [Patterson, *Works* 16:337]). The phrase *to walk with God* is used in Gen. 5:24 for Enoch's behavior.

MacCallum notes the persistence of cloud imagery in the last two books, from the cloud of steam from Abel's consumed sacrifice to the cloud from which Christ descends to purge the world by fire ("Milton and Sacred History" 157).

Rapt: both literal and metaphoric senses may be blended (Warton 74).

winged: Oras reports that syllabized *–ed* endings are rare in the later books of *PL* ("Milton's Blank Verse" 173–76); cf. *PL* 11.746–47, 831.

Dennis cites this passage as an example of Milton's "inversion of the phrase" (41).

707.   *Did, as thou sawst, receave:* cf. Gen. 5:24, Heb. 11:5. Bentley thinks it should be "*Will,* as thou saw'st, receive." Pearce rejects this reading because it is not consonant with *sawst,* and also because Adam was having a vision of deeds done in the future. Newton argues that, *pace* Alexander Pope ("While expletives their feeble aid *do* join" [*Essay on Criticism* 346]), not all auxiliary verbs are mere expletives; *Did* strengthens the expression here.

708.   *climes of Bliss:* cf. the "happy climes" of *Mask* 978–79.
        Clime: "region, realm" (so *OED* 2b).

709.   *to shew thee what reward:* cf. 11.357.

710.   *Awaits the good, the rest what punishment:* the 1667 edition has a question mark after *punishment.* Patrides sees in this passage an Augustinian contrast between the *civitas terrena* ("worldly city") of such as Pharaoh and Nimrod and the *civitas Dei* ("city of God") of the servants of God from Enoch to Christ (*Phoenix* 62).

711–62.   The fifth vision begins with civil and domestic sensuality that leads to the Flood. Mollenkott (38), arguing that book 11 presents a "cycle of sins," identifies this vision as an elaboration of the sin of Eve and her inabstinence leading to the lazar-house; it is cut short because Adam cries for a halt to the visions in 11.763, and there is no further vision of sin but rather of redemption, whereas Douady asks whether God has turned murderous because God has too long and too obstinately studied the crimes of men (201).

At least two critics have found systems in the passage. Fowler, tracing numerological categories in the visions, claims that five is both a marriage number (being the sum of two and three, the first female and the first male number in the Pythagorean system) and the number of senses and sensuality; it is therefore appropriate that this vision begin with the corruption of sexual manners. The sensual corruption of the fifth vision is emphasized in the five pairs of actions in 11.714–17. Grandsen (293–94) cites this passage as an example of the Virgilian syntactic pattern he sees throughout the epic: a "sense-break" after the first foot or foot and a half of the line, not to be confused with the metrical caesura between the fourth and fifth foot of the Latin hexameter line; the pattern can be traced in Milton's *Allurd them* (718), *But all in vain* (726), *Contending* (727), *Contriv'd* (732), *For Man and Beast* (733), *Thir order* (736), *With thir four Wives* (737), *Wide hovering* (739), *From under Heav'n* (740), *Impetuous* (744), *No more was seen* (745), *Uplifted* (746), *And stabl'd* (752).

711. *Which now direct thine eyes and soon behold:* "the construction is remarkable; *which* is not governed by the next verb, but by the last" (Montgomery).

712–19. "Milton, to keep up an agreeable variety in his Visions, after having raised in the Mind of his Reader the several Ideas of Terror which are conformable to the Description of War, passes on to those softer Images of Triumphs and Festivals, in that Vision of Lewdness and Luxury, which ushers in the Flood" (Addison, *Spectator* 3 [26 Apr. 1712]: 363). Although this outwardly pleasant scene appears redundant, it shows the divine judgment on pervasive evil; Adam has progressed from dismay at the disguises of evil to joy at the endurance of the faithful just and in God's protection of them (Sasek 191). Fox (183) links this description of decadent luxury with that of Belial's sons in 1.497–505. Fowler prefers a semicolon at the end of line 712.

712. *and saw:* Lewalski traces Adam's purged and exercised physical sight throughout book 11 (26); see **11.368**. 1667 *& saw*.

713. *The brazen Throat of Warr:* cf. *Vac* 86, and also Crashaw's "brazen voyce of warr's Hoarce bird" ("Musick's Duell," line 101).

714–18. Cf. Christ's description (Matt. 24:38) of the days before the Flood (Himes, *Paradise Lost: A Poem*). Champion (392) links this passage to Belial's counsel of ignoble ease and sloth in *PL* 2.108–228; cf. **11.446–47**.

715–18. Sims (*Bible* 270) cites Luke 17:26–27, with its parallel picture of antediluvian decadence: "And as it was in the days of Noe, so shall it be also in the days of the Son of man. They did eat, they drank, they married wives, they were given in marriage, until the day that Noe entered into the ark, and the flood came, and destroyed them all."

715. *luxurie:* "the habitual use of, or indulgence in what is choice or costly, whether food, dress, furniture, or appliances of any kind" (so *OED* 3), but Verity glosses *luxurie* as "lust, lasciviousness," the same obsolete sense as *OED* 1, and also notes this usage in Shakespeare as well as in *Inferno* 5.55 ("*vizio di lussuria,*" or vice of lust); Hughes (*Paradise Lost, A Poem*) supplies *Merry Wives of Windsor* 5.5.94: "Fie on lust and luxury!" Cf. Milton's own usage in *Ref* ("the luxurious, and ribald feasts of Baal-peor" [Patterson, *Works* 3:54]) and also *luxurious* in *PL* 11.788. Ryken contrasts the negative connotation of *luxury* after the Fall with its unfallen meaning of perfect fertility (65–66).

    riot: "wanton, loose, or wasteful living; debauchery, dissipation, extravagance" (so *OED* 1a). Ricks (*Paradise Lost*) briefly glosses the two terms as "lust" and "riotousness."

716. *Marrying or prostituting, as befell:* Shumaker claims that although this hint could be expanded by a movie director for an entire series of dramas, Milton's summary "allows only blurred glimpses of moral corruption" (*Unpremeditated Verse* 210).

717. *faire:* a substantive for "beautiful woman," as noted by Hughes (*Paradise Lost*) and others.

    passing may indicate both senses of "exceedingly" and "passing by."

719–26. Hughes (*Paradise Lost*) thinks Milton is here struck with Josephus's picture of Noah pleading with the giants to change their lifestyle (*Antiquities* 1.3.1), as does Dunster (in Todd). See **11.661–71**. Fox, who traces the Seven Deadly Sins in books 11–12, contends that here the emphasis shifts from the sins of drunkenness, lust, and violence to the sin of sloth: "despite the gravity of these other sins, the state of apathy and indifference is more serious and more fundamental" (185); cf. "pleasure, ease, and sloth" (11.794), Belial's "ignoble ease, and peaceful sloth" (2.227). Hughes (*Paradise Lost, A Poem*) believes that Milton's account is influenced by "countless Renaissance pictures"; Allen's *Legend* reproduces 24 examples of this artwork. Fowler agrees that the Flood is "one of the great subjects of visual art," because it effectively focuses the apocalyptic fears of the time, and in *PL* it particularly provides a complete analogue of the Fall in its loss of a world through sin; Fowler also claims that Noah's preaching to the dissolute is suggested by Luke 17:26–27 (cited in **11.715–18**).

719. *A Reverend Sire among them came:* i.e., Noah. Cf. the "reverend Sire" of *Lyc* 103. According to Gen. 7:6, Noah was 600 years old at the time of the Flood.

Sire: "a person of some note or importance; an aged or elderly man" (so *OED* 5).

721. *And testifi'd against thir wayes:* here and for 11.812–13, Sims (*Bible* 270) cites Heb. 11:7, in which Noah, by building the ark, "condemned the world."

722. *whereso:* "wherever" (so *OED* 3).

723–25. *preachd...to Souls / In Prison:* cf. 1 Pet. 3:19–20, where Christ is said to have preached to spirits of those who had not listened to Noah's preaching. Noah is also called a "preacher of righteousness" in 2 Pet. 2:5.

723. *triumphs:* "a public festivity or joyful celebration; a spectacle or pageant; esp. a tournament" (*OED* 4, obsolete). Keightley quotes a number of early modern examples. Hughes (*Paradise Lost, A Poem*) glosses as "processions, entertainments," citing *L'All* 120.

724. *Conversion:* "the turning of sinners to God; a spiritual change from sinfulness, ungodliness, or worldliness to love of God and pursuit of holiness" (so *OED* 9).

725. *Prison:* 1667 *prison.*

726–27. *he ceas'd / Contending, and remov'd his Tents farr off:* this extrabiblical comment is from Josephus (Newton); cf. *Antiquities* 1.3.1. Cf. also God's pre-Flood decision in Gen. 6:3, "My spirit shall not always strive with man" and also "Lot...pitched his tent toward Sodom" (Gen. 13:12). Stebbing judges that

Milton might have also been thinking of Christ's directions to the disciples to flee from the cities that refused to hear them (Matt. 10:23).

728–32. Shumaker judges that the imagery (*remov'd, hewing, build, Measur'd, Smeard, Contriv'd, laid in*) is primarily motor and the tension therefore minimal, although one can note the tallness of the timber, the gradually shaping hull, and the magnitude of Noah's task (*Unpremeditated Verse* 212). Daniells, citing also 11.745–47, sees Milton's emphasis differently: "the evoked image of a Greek war vessel or armoured knight instantly gives power and purpose to the great act of rescue" (*Milton* 82).

728–30. Johnson rejects the idea that Milton can here, by enumeration alone, replicate the sense of bulk, since there can be no "analogy…between modulations of sound, and corporeal dimensions" (*Rambler* 4 [9 Feb. 1751]: 142).

729. Le Comte claims that *huge bulk* is "always a floating reference," as in 1.196 and 7.410.

730. *Measur'd by Cubit:* Gen. 6:15 lists the ark's measurements as 300 cubits long, 50 cubits broad, and 30 cubits high. A cubit was generally considered to be the length from elbow to end of the third finger.
    and breadth: 1667 *& breadth.*

731. *Smeard round with Pitch, and in the side a dore:* Gen. 6:14, 16.

732. *provisions laid in large:* Montgomery claims that *large* here means "largely," and explains the adjective used adverbially as one of Milton's frequent imitations of Latin writers.

733–36. *when loe a wonder strange!…as taught Thir order:* Loane holds up the lack of detail in this passage as proof that Milton is emotionally distant ("Milton and the Brute Creation" 291).

734. *Insect small:* Fowler, noting that insects are not mentioned in the Genesis account, concludes that Milton agrees with the more modern among contemporary commentators on Genesis rather than with someone like Athanasius Kircher, whose elaborate *Arca Noe* (1675) reasoned that insects arose from putrefaction or spontaneous generation and did not need to be included (quoting Allen, *Legend* 185).

　　every: 1667 *everie.*

735. *Came seavens, and pairs:* the pairs were male with female, but Noah was commanded to bring seven pair of "clean" beasts and only one pair of "unclean" (Gen. 7:2). "Clean" beasts were in this context fit for sacrifice (Gen. 8:20), though later also specified as being appropriate for food (Lev. 11). Northrop Frye (*Paradise Lost*), who understands Gen. 6:19 ("two of every sort") and 7:2 ("by sevens") to come from different sources, judges the different accounts here to be reconciled "by brute strength."

736–37. *the Sire…three Sons…four Wives:* Gen. 6:18. Cf. the "eight souls…saved by water" of 1 Pet. 3:20.

736. *order:* 1667 *order;*

737. *God made fast the dore:* "and the LORD shut him in" (Gen. 7:16). Shumaker wrongly assumes that Milton supplies the detail, but he may well be right that the detail increases the "muscular energy" of 11.728–32, since a greater than human energy is required (*Unpremeditated Verse* 212). As Hughes (*Paradise Lost*) reports, Milton turns from this biblical detail to Ovid's description of Deucalion's flood, a description that also influenced Du Bartas's chapter (1:403–20) on the Deluge. Hughes (*Paradise Lost, A Poem*), asserting that Milton believed that Ovid's story was both foil and corroboration for the biblical account, cites Harding's *Milton and the Renaissance Ovid,* which compares the two accounts (82–84), and Allen's *Legend,* which traces their Renaissance reception (176–77). Reesing finds this "sharply *staccato*" line to be the climax of the small, anticipatory action beginning at 11.712 (93); see **11.1–21.**

738–39. *the Southwind rose, and with black wings / Wide hovering:* Milton's description is similar to Ovid's (*Metamorphoses* 1.264–66). Since contemporary meteorologists thought that rain was caused by the action of the south wind on thick clouds, Milton's inclusion of this detail is "bookish" (Svendsen, *Milton and*

Science 97). Cf. the disastrous thunderstorms, immense and murky, in Virgil's *Georgics* (1.322–26). Todd cites the description of great waves by "Homer, who is supposed by Eustathius to allude to the Mosaic account" in *Iliad* 16.381–83. Broadbent observes that the Flood itself comes like Sin and Death (*Some Graver Subject* 274). Du Bartas also mentions the south wind (personified as "Auster") in his destruction of the Flood, as well as "thick clouds" (G. C. Taylor, *Milton's Use* 117); cf. Du Bartas 1:169.1204, 1209.

738. *and* with: 1667 *& with.*

740–42. *supplie…Skie:* one of 45 instances found by Diekhoff in the epic where two lines rhyme with one intervening nonrhyming line ("Rhyme" 540). See Purcell for additional instances (171). Wesley reduces this passage to a single line: "From under Heav'n; and now the thicken'd sky."

740. *the Hills to their supplie:* so Milton spells his plural possessive (otherwise "thir") when it is rhetorically or metrically stressed (Grierson, *Poems* 2:xl–xli); see also *PL* 12.400.

   supplie: "the act of supplying something needed; the filling up of a place or position; the provision of a person or thing in the place of another" (so *OED* 3a). Fowler glosses as "assistance."

741. *Vapour:* "matter in the form of a steamy or imperceptible exhalation; especially [as] converted by…heat" (so *OED* 1).

   dusk: "dark from absence of light; dim, gloomy, shadowy; dark-coloured, blackish; dusky.…Now usually in reference to twilight" (so *OED* A1).

   Exhalation: "the action or process of exhaling, breathing forth or throwing off in the form of vapour; evaporation" (so *OED* 1).

742–48. The energy of these seven lines is increased by their consistent enjambment (Shumaker, *Unpremeditated Verse* 212–13).

743. *Ceeling:* earlier commentators have insisted that the word is not trivial and therefore not indecorous. The Richardsons refer to Latin *coelum* and Italian *cielo,* "heaven." Todd cites like usage from Giles Fletcher's "Christ's Triumph" ("ceiling gay" [stanza 26]) and Drummond's "Shadow of the Judgment" (*Poems* [1711]). Hulme also cites Sylvester's Du Bartas: "we see Aurora, passing gay, / With Opalls paint the Seeling of Cathay" (95–96); cf. Du Bartas 1:143.295–96. *OED* 6a cites earlier uses for heaven from Drayton (1596) and Adams (1614). R. C. Browne (1877) cites at length Wedgwood's refutation of an "erroneous" derivation from Latinate terms meaning "tilt, canopy, tester." The range of concerns about the word is demonstrated by Henry Bradley's revised note (R. C. Browne 1894): "The etymology of this word is extremely difficult. It originally had, and still has in some dialects, the sense of wainscoting, covering, whether of the walls or the roof of an apartment; it also denoted hangings of tapestry. Dialectically, it is applied to a wooden partition inside a room. The early English word *celure*, a screen or canopy, is identical with the Med. Lat. *celatorium*, a screen or canopy covering the Host, which is apparently from *celare*, to conceal; it is possible that the verb to *ceil* is a back formation from *celure*. But the Fr. *ciel* (Lat. *coelum*), literally sky, had the sense of *canopy*, tester of a bed, and this word has certainly influenced the development of sense in the English words, if it be not their actual source."

down rush'd the Rain: "Milton appears to have followed Ovid in superimposing one detail upon another until a definite climax" (Harding, *Milton* 82–83).

745–46. *the floating Vessel swum / Uplifted:* cf. Gen 7:17, "the waters increased, and bare up the ark, and it was lift up above the earth." On the powerful and purposeful ship imagery, see **11.728–32**.

746–47. *with beaked prow / Rode tilting o're the Waves:* the Genesis account says merely "The ark went upon the face of the waters." The Richardsons explain that the prows of ancient ships projected like a bird's beak and the ark would be properly tilting up and down because it was in a strong gale (11.738).

tilting: "to move unsteadily up and down; especially of waves or a ship at sea, to pitch" (so *OED* 1). Dunster (in Todd) claims that Renaissance poets often described tossing waves as "tilting" with each other, as Drayton in *Polyolbion* 1 ("From the land the tilting waves do break") and Sylvester's Du Bartas ("ever-Tilting Tide" [2:492.112]). Anselm Bayly (300, 302) cites part of this passage—"the floating Vessel / Rode tilting [o're] the waves"—as an example of Milton's use of "hasty syllables without stops, or with very short *caesuras*" in order to express "speed, alacrity and joy," but the omissions suggest that he may be quoting from memory. He also references Ovid's *fluctibus ignotis insultavere carinae* ("the keels contemptuously jumped over unknown waves") in *Metamorphoses* 1.134.

    beaked: Oras reports that syllabized *–ed* endings are rare in the later books of *PL* ("Milton's Blank Verse" 173–76); cf. *PL* 11.705–07, 831, and also the "beaked Promontory" of *Lyc* 94.

747–52. MacCaffrey, reading *PL* in terms of myth, asserts that these lines stir deep fears, because in myths of the hero, the night journey is usually followed by a sea journey or descent into the earth to encounter the monster (167). Ricks uses the words *grandeur* and *terror* to refer to this description (*Milton's Grand Style* 126).

747. *all dwellings else:* cf. *Metamorphoses* 1.289–90, where roofs and towers are covered by the flood.

748. *pomp:* Ryken (70) contrasts the word's negative, postlapsarian connotation with its innocent prelapsarian use for Eve's "pomp of winning Graces" in *PL* 8.61.

749–50. *Sea cover'd Sea, / Sea without shoar:* cf. 2.912, 939–40 and 9.117. Most commentators link Milton's phrase to Ovid, *Metamorphoses* 1.292: "Omnia pontus erant, derant quoque littora ponto" (All was sea; there was also no shore to the sea). Numerous early commentators find Milton's description superior to Ovid's. Addison praises Milton's avoidance of "every thing that is redundant or puerile in the Latin Poet. . . . The latter part of that Verse [about sea without shore] in Ovid is idle and superfluous; but just and beautiful in Milton. . . . In Milton the former part of the Description does not forestall the latter" (*Spectator* 3 [26 Apr. 1712]: 364). The Richardsons cite Seneca's comment that Ovid did not know when to stop (*Controversiae* 7.27), whereas Milton finishes the image with his repetition. Todd notes that Francis Goldsmith uses the phrase "a sea without a shoar" in his 1634 translation of Grotius's *Sophompaneas* 10; in that passage, Ramses is describing Noah's Flood. Cf. Du Bartas, "now th'Ocean hath no shore" (1:169.1223) and "Rivers and seas have all one common shoare" (1.401.764).

750–52. *and in thir Palaces…Sea monsters whelp'd / And stabl'd:* Addison judges this image to be far superior to Ovid's image (*Metamorphoses* 1.299–300) of ugly sea-calves resting in the places where goats had browsed (*Spectator* 3 [26 Apr. 1712]: 364). Todd cites, for a similar picture of land and sea becoming confused, Lycophron, *Cassandra* (also known as *Alexandra*) 82–84. Both George Coffin Taylor (*Milton's Use* 117–18) and Hughes (*Paradise Lost, A Poem*) note the quaint picture in Sylvester's Du Bartas: "The Sturgeon, coasting over Castles, muses / (Under the Sea) to see so many houses" (1:169.1231–32). Fletcher (*Complete Poetical Works*) claims that this passage is "the watery counterpart" of Isa. 13:19–22 and 34:11–15, with their scenes of (dry) desolation. Fowler claims that this picture of an inverted world was very popular in Milton's time, citing not only Du Bartas but also Drayton, *Noahs Flood* 729–34, and Cowley, *Davideis* 263.

stabl'd: "to live as in a stable" (so *OED* v^2 2b). But the better sense in context is "had their lairs," as the "stabled wolves" of *Mask* 534; cf. *stabulum*, "lair," as in Virgil's "stabula alta ferarum" (deep lairs of beasts) (*Aeneid* 6.179). Fowler also reports that in Milton's day, *to stable* could mean "to stick fast in the mud" (*OED* v^3).

752–53. Newton cites Thyer's reference to Vida's *Christiad* 50.1 [*sic*], "Omnibus hic pauci extinctis mortalibus ibant / Inclusi ligno summas impune per undas" (1.718–19) (A chosen few, the race of mortals drown'd; / Here sail'd in safety o'er the vast profound) (47).

753. *All left, in one small bottom:* cf. "Noah only remained alive, and they that were with him in the ark" (Gen. 7:23).

bottom: "ship" (*OED* 7a); R. C. Browne (1877) cites several similar uses of the term in Shakespeare. MacCallum points out that Milton is endorsing traditional typology, based on 1 Pet. 3:20–21, in which the flood is taken as a type of baptism ("Milton and Sacred History" 156); cf. *DocCh* 1.28 (Patterson, *Works* 16:191), and also a similar statement in *PL* 12.442. Shumaker asserts that although Milton cannot, in his quick summary of biblical history, exploit all the visual possibilities of the Genesis passage ("All flesh died…fowl…cattle…beast, etc."), yet this passage "is by no means sensorially blank"; Milton does, however, offer a panoramic view, since the "huge bulk" of the ark (11.729) has become a *small bottom* (*Unpremeditated Verse* 212–13).

754–61. Addison judges this transition from the vision of the Deluge to Adam's concern to be copied from Virgil, despite its Ovidian spirit (*Spectator* 3 [26 Apr. 1712]: 365). Wesley notes this passage as among those particularly excellent. Dunster (in Todd) reports John Callander's note that Achilles' grief is compared to a father's in *Iliad* 23.222, but also cites the parental sorrow of Rachel weeping for her children (Jer. 31:15–17). See Toole's comment on Adam's weeping in **11.494–95**. Radzinowicz asserts that the voice here is Milton's own, interrupting the narrative with a foregrounded scene in which the audience sees Adam and identifies with him (43).

754–56. Assman finds this outburst typical of Milton's personal sympathy with his characters, also citing as examples *PL* 1.75; 4.1, 774; and 9.403 (68).

756–57. Lawry interprets Adam's tears as his own baptism (*Shadow* 280). Cf. the contrast to weeping in **11.625–27**.

756. *Depopulation:* "reduction of population; depriving of inhabitants; unpeopling" and, particularly in the seventeenth century, "the clearance of the peasantry from their estates by the land-owners" (*OED* 2). Broadbent approves of Milton's word choice, typical of his tendency to "control and categorise experience"; the word comprehends the experience telescopically ("Milton's Mortal Voice" 116–17). Reesing describes the word as "Latinate, polysyllabic, emphatically placed in the midst of all those simpler words" (94).

758–59. *till gently reard / By th'Angel:* cf. the discussion of angelic raising in **11.421–22**. On the fluidity of Milton's names for angels, see West's and Gage's comments in **11.101**. On the elision, see **11.449**.
   reard: "to lift (a person or animal) to or towards an erect or standing posture; usually, to set (one) on one's feet, assist to rise" (so *OED* 2a, now mostly dialectical).

760. *comfortless:* "unconsoled, inconsolable," now rarely applied to persons (so *OED* 3).

761. *Children:* 1667 *childern* or *Childern;* see also *PL* 11.772 and Shawcross: "*childern* occurs in 11.772, and in the first edition in 10.194, 330, and 11.761, but these latter three cases in the second edition and that at 1.395, in all three texts, read *children*. Thus, generally Milton's spelling was followed" ("Orthography" 132–33).

762. On the elision, see **11.449**.

763–86. Reesing finds "slow, listless monotones" in this speech, caused by Adam's hopelessness in the face of what he thinks is humankind's final and total annihilation (94); see **11.1**. Muldrow points out that Adam's lament here is the longest in the book and the most contrite; Adam's full realization of the terrible consequences of the Fall coincides in the narrative with the Flood, God's rejection of sinful humankind (87).

763. *O Visions ill foreseen! better had I:* cf. *Mask* 359–65, cited by Verity, who claims that avoiding knowledge of future disaster is a "common sentiment" in poetry. R. C. Browne (1877) cites Sophocles, *Oedipus the King* 316 ("Alas, alas, what misery to be wise / When wisdom profits nothing!"). "Adam must accept the hard truth that in history either war or human peace produces almost identical corruption" (Lawry, *Shadow* 281). Du Bartas's Adam is similarly distraught (1:401–02.767–74), especially in 1.401.761, "ô children whither flie-you?" (G. C. Taylor, *Milton's Use* 119).

765–66. *each dayes lot / Anough to beare:* cf. Matt. 6:34: "Sufficient unto the day is the evil thereof."

766–67. *dispenst / The burd'n of many Ages:* the Richardsons note the classical propriety of *dispenst*, having a sense of due distribution, from Latin *penso* (to weigh) with its derivative *pensum* (the daily quantity of wool weighed out to spinners), and thence to *task* in general. Wesley glosses *dispenst* as "distributed, dealt out in parcels." Himes (*Paradise Lost: A Poem*) finds Adam's burden similar to the one in Dan. 8:1–27.

Darbishire (*Poetical Works* 1:xxvii) claims that this *burd'n* is the only monosyllable for the usually disyllabic *burden*. "Milton, in the case of syllabic *n* followed by a vowel, reserves the apostrophe spelling to show elision" (B. A. Wright, *Milton's Poems* xx).

766. Wesley changes *those now* to *not those*.
   beare. 1667 *bear*.

767–70. Wesley reduces this passage to a single line: "The burd'n of many Ages. Let none seek."

770–76. Newton cites Warburton's reminder that in Milton's time horoscopes were still being cast. Fowler judges that Adam has fallen into the error of despair because of a false deterministic doctrine of predestination.

772. *Childern*: See **11.761**.
   evil he: the scansion requires the last two syllables to be elided into a single one. Sprott cites this line as an example of elision of a semivowel before the aspirate *h* (87).

773–74. *Which neither his foreknowing ... And*: since there is no sequel to *neither*, Bentley thinks this line should read, "Which *never* his foreknowing can prevent." The Richardsons claim that the construction is the Latin *neque ... et*, citing Terence *Eunuchus* 5.5.23, "Quid Agas? Ne neque illis profis et tu pereas" (What are you doing? You will neither do them good, and you will die) and referring to such constructions in Cicero and Boethius; the construction is also found in Greek. Todd cites the preface to *DDD:* "the Jews, who were neither won with the austerity of John the Baptist, and thought" (Patterson, *Works* 3:387). Hughes (*Paradise Lost*) explains that the two conjunctions of the Latinism are parallel, as in "both ... and." Bush also glosses the phrase as "a Latinism." Fowler, who doubts that Adam would be so elegant in his despair as to employ the *neque ... et* idiom, asserts rather that it is good, albeit ungrammatical, English. *OED* lists *neither ... and* as obsolete (1e), furnishing an example from Marvell's *Rehearsal Transpros'd* (1673).
   foreknowing: "to have previous knowledge of" (so *OED* b).

777–78. *those few escap't / Famin and anguish will at last consume*: cf. Ovid, *Metamorphoses* 1.311–12, where Ovid describes the Flood's survivors later slowly dying of starvation.

777. *Man is not whom to warne:* the Richardsons find this phrase "exceeding tender." N. O. (82) finds it "a remarkable instance of what the Messieurs de Port Royal call 'the preceding and following cases both understood'" (82), citing Horace *Odes* 1.3 ("Sunt quos curriculo" [There are who in the race]) and 1.19, 21 ("Est qui nec veteris pocula Massici...spernit" [There is who scorns not a cup of old Massicum]).

779–83. *I had hope:* Adam lists himself among the hopeless because he assumes there can be no world for so few; he is deceived not by hope but by carnal reasoning (Fish 279). Adam laments not only the future event but also his knowledge of it, dramatizing "the burden of foreknowledge more movingly than any other [speech] in the poem" (Summers, *Muse's Method* 203).

779. *Wandring that watrie Desert:* cf. similar phrasing in 2.973. *Wand'ring* is also a transitive verb in *PR* 2.246, similar to the transitive use of *roam'd* in *PL* 1.521 and *roving* in *Mask* 60. See **11.281**; cf. *long wanderd man* (*PL* 12.313).

MacCallum, tracing the development of typological significance in books 11 and 12, claims that the line also connotes the chosen people on their way to Canaan and also Adam's later expression of concern in 12.480–83 for the church after the death of Christ ("Milton and Sacred History" 156). Fish argues that *wandring* is transformed in book 12; see **11.281**.

watrie: "of natural features, as the sea and rivers" (so *OED* 5, chiefly poetic and rhetorical).

781–84. Wesley reduces this passage to a single line: "All would have then gon well, but now I see."

782. *dayes:* 1667 *days.*

785–86. Burke judges that Adam is motivated here by "a sudden intuition that life is good" (215).

785. *Celestial Guide:* Milton uses *celestial* most frequently in his descriptions of apocalyptic reality (Ryken 56–57).

786–809. Ross (*Milton's Royalism* 89–90) notes the same sentiments about "Causes of misery and thraldom" here and at the end of *HistBr* (Patterson, *Works* 10:316): "Both the conquerors and the conquered, the rulers and the ruled are corrupt and incapable of practicing or understanding true liberty."

786. *the Race of man:* cf. 2.382–83; 3.161, 280, 679; 7.155; and 11.13, 782.

787–829. B. A. Wright cites this section as an example of Milton's being a little too wordy, "no doubt under Ovid's influence," with Adam moralizing the Flood and describing it all over again. "Milton fell into this fault because there is no press of action, nothing to restrain him from the superfluity and iteration of the preacher" (*Milton's "Paradise Lost"* 199). Fletcher (*Complete Poetical Works*) identifies "the repetition in Michael's words of what Adam has already seen in vision." Summers observes that Milton refuses to glorify not only the conquerors but also the conquered (*Muse's Method* 204).

787–807. "These ideas recur often in Milton and seem to include his own age as well as earlier history" (Bush).

787. Wesley indents this line.

788. *luxurious wealth:* in *Paradiso* 15.97–129, Cacciaguida traces the degeneration of Florence to the growth of luxury; cf. the gradual decline to degenerate wealth in *PL* 12.350–52 (Samuel, *Dante* 263–64). Ryken contrasts the negative connotation of *luxurious* after the Fall with its unfallen meaning, where it describes perfect fertility (65–66). See also **11.715.**
    Triumph: 1667 *triumph.*

789. *prowess:* "an act of bravery; a valiant deed; a daring feat or exploit" (so *OED* 1a, now historical or literary).

793–807. Greenlaw cites this passage to illustrate his contention that Milton's central theme is Temperance; according to him, the events of book 11 represent the Seven Deadly Sins — "Cain represents Wrath; the coming of diseases is attributed to Gluttony; the sons of Seth are betrayed by Lechery; the coming of war brings Pride, Avarice, Envy, and is followed by an epoch in which Idleness is mingled with the other Seven Deadly Sins" (215).

793. *Fame in the World, high titles, and rich prey:* on titles, see **11.158–59**.

795. *wantonness:* Ryken contrasts the word's negative, postlapsarian connotation with its innocent prelapsarian uses, a shift constituting another of "Milton's etymological arguments"; the pejorative shift mirrors "a parallel movement in human experience from innocence to evil" (70).

796. *hostil deeds:* Wesley glosses as "acts of enmity."

797–808. Fox, who argues that the episode with Noah represents the sin of sloth, claims that the emphasis here is on the political consequences of that sin: "when men lose the moral virtue of zeal, they easily succumb to political enslavement" (186–87); cf. Milton's characterization of episcopacy in *Ref* as a "seething pot set to coole" that renders a "skinny congealment of ease and sloth at the top" (Patterson, *Works* 3:11). Fowler judges this passage to be one of the direct topical allusions in the epic.

798–99. Cf. the connection between moral corruption and loss of liberty in *SA* 268–70 and Milton's prose works. As pointed out by Verity in a note at 2.255–57, Milton's favorite Roman historian, Sallust, has Lepidus say, "I looked upon freedom united with danger as preferable to peace with slavery" (Accipite otium cum servitio...mihi potior visa est periculosa libertas quieto servitio) (*Speech of Lepidus to the Roman People,* 25–26); cf. *Epistol* 23 for Milton's preference for Sallust, a preference mostly based on concise style (Patterson, *Works* 12:93). Verity also refers to John Aubrey's note that Milton's intense zeal for liberty and his republicanism came largely from his admiration of Roman writers and the Roman commonwealth, and similarly that Hobbes (6:192–93) complained that young men reading the classics at university learned to despise monarchy. Dunster (in Todd) finds the comment "unquestionably political," since Milton was "well aware of the 'feign'd piety' of many of his own party, whom he had once considered as saints; and whose temporizing at the Restoration completed in his mind the hypocrisy of their character."

798. *loose:* Fowler asserts that this spelling in both 1667 and 1674 could indicate either "lose" or "loose" (relax), but this double meaning is not attested in *OED.*

799. *fear:* 1667 *feare.*

800. *In sharp contest of Battel:* Verity and others read the accent as *contést,* as in 4.872 and *SA* 461, 865.

801–05. *therefore coold in zeale:* many editors (e.g., Masson) suspect a political reference.

804–05. Milton regarded wealth itself as potentially a source of social corruption (Good 228). Michael's lesson here concerns personal moderation (Radzino-wicz 44).

805. *that temperance may be tri'd:* intemperance "was the special sin of the Ante-diluvians" (Himes, *Paradise Lost: A Poem*). Cf. Milton's statement in *DocCh:* "God tempts even the righteous for the purpose of proving them...for the purpose of exercising or manifesting their faith or patience...or of lessening their self-confidence, and reproving their weakness, that both they themselves may become wiser by experience, and others may profit by their example" (Pat-terson, *Works* 15:87–89). Cf. James 1:2–4 on the value of temptation.

806–09. Cf. the description of universal corruption in Gen. 6:12–13. Martz judges that life on earth is here "explicitly and flatly equated with the life of Satan's host" (153–54). Hughes (*Paradise Lost, A Poem*) thinks the passage might well record Milton's disillusionment with his earlier picture of England in *Areop* as a "noble and puissant Nation" destined to be great by its "Truth and prosperous vertue" (Patterson, *Works* 4:344).

806. *deprav'd:* "rendered morally bad; corrupt, wicked" (so *OED* 2).

807–08. *Truth and Faith forgot; / One Man except:* Bentley rejects this line as a "flat solecism," supplying instead "Truth and Faith *forgetting*," claiming that

Milton often closes his verses with a disyllable. Pearce rejects this emendation, as he reads *forgot* as a form of *forgotten;* as usual, Pearce makes part of the phrase into a parenthesis. Cf. 9.545.

807. Wesley omits this line.

808–18. Verity reads these lines as a self-portrait of Milton "in the lonely last years of his life"; the "dark Age" was the Restoration, the "wicked ways" were demonstrated by Charles II's courtiers, and the "wrath to come" was a second revolution predicted more clearly in *SA*. Williamson draws angelic parallels between the corrupt world and Belial and between Noah and Abdiel (107). "Noah and Enoch are earthly counterparts of Abdiel" (Bush). MacCallum stresses how the various "men of faith" (Abel, Enoch, Noah, Abraham) prefigure Christ by their qualities or actions ("Milton and Sacred History" 158); see *PL* 11.458–60, 701, and 12.113.

812–13. *admonish:* see **11.721**.

814–15. Wesley reduces this passage to a single line: "The paths of righteousness, denouncing wrauth."

815. *And full of peace:* cf. 9.1126.
     denouncing: "to give formal, authoritative, or official information of; to proclaim, announce, declare; to publish, promulgate" (*OED* 1). See **11.106–08**, s.v. *denounce*.

816. *impenitence:* "hardness of heart; obduracy" (so *OED*).

817–18. *Of them derided, but . . . The one just Man alive:* Todd finds a possible reference to the apocryphal Old Testament book of Wisdom, "This was he whom we had sometimes in derision. . . . How is he numbered among . . . the saints!" (5:3, 5). Shawcross argues that although references to Ps. 2:4 ("He that sitteth in the heavens shall laugh") are generally appropriated by the satanic crew in the second half of *PL,* Michael makes it clear in this passage that their laughter is specious and misdirected ("Son" 399); see also **12.59–61**.

of God observd: Sims (*Bible* 270) cites Gen. 6:8: "Noah found grace in the eyes of the LORD."

819–21. Cf. Gen. 6:13–17. The ark as Milton describes it connotes traditional typology, prefiguring both Christ and his church (MacCallum, "Milton and Sacred History" 155).

821. *A World devote to universal rack:* see similar language in Du Bartas: "ô universall wracke!" (G. C. Taylor, *Milton's Use* 118–19); cf. Du Bartas 1:402.770.
    Some spellings and meanings in this passage are contested. Stebbing has *denote,* in the sense of *denoted,* but Hughes (*Paradise Lost*) understands *devote* as "dedicated to destruction." Ricks (*Paradise Lost*) glosses it "doomed." Cf. "to devote," "to give over or consign to the powers of evil or to destruction; to doom, to invoke or pronounce a curse upon" (*OED* 3); cf. *PL* 3.208: "But to destruction sacred and devote." Hume claims "rack" should be spelled "wrack," as in "shipwrack"; cf. *PL* 6.669–70: "all Heav'n Had gone to wrack." Newton has *wrack.* Dobson (186) judges that Milton did not distinguish pronunciation between *wr-* and *r-,* as he spells *wrack* as *rack* in *PR* 4.452. As *wrack,* the word means "destruction" (so *OED* v5 1a).

823. *Select:* "chosen out of a larger number, on account of excellence or fitness" (so *OED* A1). Wesley glosses as "whom God had set apart, to preserve them." Verity has "set aside."

824–35. Mahood praises Milton's "power to convey the force of water"; in this passage, "both rhythm and sound are handled...to suggest the vigorous fluid strength which water has in a restricted space spending itself over a wider area and at last wasted to calm in the sea's expanse" (199). The Flood has already been described in *PL* 11.738–53; Milton may have incorporated different drafts represented by the Trinity Manuscript entries on "The flood" and "The Deluge" (Gilbert, *On the Composition* 34–35).
    Cataracts: "the 'flood-gates' of heaven, viewed as keeping back the rain" (so *OED* 1a). Cf. "the windows of heaven" of Gen. 7:11, and also of 2 Kings 7:2 and Mal. 3:10. *Cataracts* is the expression in the Septuagint and Vulgate versions; cf. Vulgate Gen. 7:11, "et cataractae caeli apertae sunt" (the windows of heaven were open); 2 Kings 7:2, "si Dominus fecerit etiam cataractas in caelo"

(if the LORD would make windows in heaven); Mal. 3:10, "si non aperuero vobis cataractas caeli" (if I will not open to you windows in heaven), and Newton says this usage occurs in the Syriac and Arabic as well. The Vulgate additionally has the expression in Isa. 24:18 ("cataractae de excelsis apertae sunt" [the windows from on high are open]). In the English section of *Justa Edovardo King Naufrago* (1638), the collection of elegies that includes *Lyc*, Samson Briggs has in his poem the lines "For when because of sinne God opened all / Heavens cataracts, to let his vengeance fall" (14).

826. *all fountains of the Deep:* cf. Gen. 7:11: "the same day were all the fountains of the great deep broken up." Hume reports Renaissance concerns over the source of so much water, explained by some as "chambers of waters under the earth," although some early church fathers thought the reference was miraculously to "the waters above the heavens"; Hume supposes that there was far more water vapor in those days, in huge dark clouds; cf. Ps. 148:4.

   fountains: 1667 *fountaines.*

828–29. *Above the highest Hills:* cf. Gen. 7:19, "All the high hills, that were under the whole heaven, were covered."

829–43. Cf. Luther's opinion that "The first paradise was ruined and laid waste by the Flood" (1:310; see also 2:52 and 2:204). This opinion became the popular one (Himes, *Paradise Lost: A Poem*), which Fletcher (*Complete Poetical Works*) locates in Persian literature, though Verity claims that Milton's particular explanation of Eden's destruction is his own. Genesis commentators had various theories on the fate of paradise (Allen, *Legend* 153–54). Fowler links this passage to the otherwise puzzling reference to the Tigris in *PL* 9.69–73; Milton's identification of the *great river* as "the ordinary, mundane, present-day Tigris or Euphrates" makes a simple homiletic Protestant point: "After all the splendid exotic geographical suggestions...after all the esoteric theories about the locations of the terrene paradise, the matter is settled for us and we come down to this: a bare island in the Persian Gulf....The lesson in the concluding lines is...that the existence of paradise is inward and spiritual, and not to be superstitiously localized."

   Tillyard identifies embedded contrasts in this passage: 11.829–35 raise "primitive feelings," while 836–38 abruptly voice stern Protestant sentiments, and

840–43 present a description "coming from a very different place in his mind" (*Miltonic Setting* 55–58). "When paradise is destroyed the rhythm is grand, but the words are nearly all monosyllabic; 'Verdure' alone represents the classical, epic splendour of paradise as it was once" (Broadbent, *Some Graver Subject* 273). This "highly didactic piece of Protestantism" is an example of Milton's under-estimated and colossal sense of humor (Tillyard, *Studies in Milton* 80–81).

829–35. Wesley notes this passage as among those particularly excellent.

831. *pushd by the horned floud:* several classical references to rivers as horned bulls have been noted, such as Horace's *Carmina* 4.14.25 ("Sic tauriformis…Aufidus" [Aufidus, with bull-like horn]), Virgil's *Georgics* 4.371 ("gemina auratus taurino cornua vultu" [Bull-browed / 'Twixt either gilded horn] [trans. Greenough]); and *Aeneid* 8.77 ("Corniger Hesperidum Fluvius Regnator aquarum" [Hesperian Streams, / O river god that holdst the plenteous horn]). As Wesley explains, "a River oppos'd in its Course by an Island or Mountain, divides, and seems to push as with Horns." Cf. Homer's powerful flood that destroys the remains of Troy in *Iliad* 12.24–25. Todd observes that the expression *horned Floud* is used by Ben Jonson in *Volpone* 3.7.153 and by William Browne in *Britannia's Pastorals* 2.5.270. Ricks (*Paradise Lost*) glosses *horned* as "branching." Oras reports that syllabized *–ed* endings are rare in the later books of *PL* ("Milton's Blank Verse" 173–76); cf. *PL* 11.705–07, 831, and also the "horned Moon" of *Ps 136, 32*.

832. *verdure:* "green vegetation; plants or trees, or parts of these, in a green and flourishing state" (so *OED* 2a).

833. *Down the great River to the op'ning Gulf:* Milton's editors have wanted to positively identify the river as either the Tigris or the Euphrates, but both of them empty into the Persian Gulf. Hume cites the Tigris River, Newton and others point out that it is the Euphrates that is called "the great River" in Gen. 15:18 (and elsewhere), and Todd claims more equitably that it was one or the other. Bush says, "presumably the Euphrates," and Hughes (*Paradise Lost, A Poem*) "probably." Both are rivers of Eden (Gen. 2:11–14), where Hiddekel is the same as Tigris. Keightley thinks Milton invented the fiction of Eden's being washed into the gulf because he had to account for there being no mountain of paradise on the Mesopotamian plain.

Gulf: "a portion of the sea partially enclosed by a more or less extensive sweep of the coast; often taking its name from the adjoining land," distinguished from a bay in that "in general a *bay* is wider in proportion to its amount of recession than a *gulf;* the latter term is applied to long land-locked portions of sea opening through a strait, which are never called *bays*" (so *OED* 1). Though *op'ning Gulf* is fairly redundant, Wesley glosses it for his lay audience, "The Sea opening wider and wider."

834–38. *Iland salt and bare:* possibly the future site of Ormus, a barren but strategic and fabulously wealthy island in the Persian Gulf, held by the Portuguese until it was sacked and left desolate in 1622 by a temporary alliance of English and Persian forces. See John W. Draper (323–27) and also *PL* 2.2. Hume cites Sir Walter Raleigh's opinion in *History of the World* that the Flood might spoil the beauty of paradise but not move it from its original site (2:78–82). Whereas medieval commentators tended to claim that paradise could not be attained because of the abrupt mountain or its ferocious beasts, Renaissance commentators mostly asserted that the identifying beauty of paradise had been destroyed by the Flood (A. Williams, *Common Expositor* 99). Weidner cites similar language in Du Bartas, whose "wreakfull nature-drowning floud / Spard not this beauteous place"; cf. Du Bartas 1:321.186–87). Gardner calls the dislodging of the mount of paradise "one of Milton's grand inventions" (*Reading* 80–81). Broadbent references several elements from contemporary travel literature, such as details of huge logs floating down the flooding Euphrates, islands and whales (orcs) and seals, and deserted, bird-covered islands ("Milton's Paradise" 163). Camoëns refers to Ormus/Eden being now a barren mountain of salt (*do sal os montes*) in *Lusiads* 10.41.1–2 (Sims, "Camoëns' *Lusiads*" 38). See **11.336**.

This passage indicates "a Puritan who will find holiness in nothing...but the soul of man regenerated by the Grace of God" (Grierson, *Milton and Wordsworth* 46). Bush identifies 11.834–35 as "one of Milton's most 'romantic' evocations, with a quite unromantic reason," and cites Spenser's desolate "Rock of vile Reproch," populated by "yelling Meawes, with Seagulles hoars and bace, / And Cormoyraunts, with birds of rauenous race" (*Faerie Queene* 2.12.8) as well as the personified fear of the island of Delos that it would be wasted by the ocean and populated by sea creatures and black seals (*Homeric Hymn to Apollo* 3.74–78). Whereas Dante allowed his ideal of Italy to shape his earthly paradise, Milton differentiated his new paradise as not only better but utterly unlike the old, dismissing Eden as a vain and useless remnant (Herford 232–33); cf. *Purgatorio* 28–33. Ricks judges that "Nowhere else in the poem, not even at the magnificent moments when Milton lavishes his full luxuriance on the garden, do we so yearn for paradise" (*Milton's Grand Style* 149). "Place...is well on the way to coming full circle, with the outside of paradise, our first view with Satan of the savage wilderness, preparing us for our last view of the inside" (Stein, *Answerable Style* 72).

835. *The haunt of Seales and Orcs, and Sea-mews clang:* cf. Ovid's sea monsters in *Metamorphoses* 1.300 and also *Lyc* 157–58.

    Orcs: "by earlier authors applied, after the mediæval Latin writers, to more than one vaguely identified ferocious sea-monster" (so *OED* 1). Keightley points out that Ariosto uses *orc* to denote a huge voracious fish, similar to the Greek *kêtos;* Todd has recorded their appearance in Drayton's *Polyolbion* and Sylvester's translation of Du Bartas. For *orc,* Wesley has "a large kind of sea-fish," and Marchant, "a great fish. Enemy to the whale." Broadbent finds frequent descriptions of "islands of whales (orcs)" by voyagers in eastern seas ("Milton's Paradise" 163). Since orcs are also by definition "leviathans" or devouring monsters, Satan as leviathan in 1.200–08 is properly an orc (Fowler). The "wild beasts of the islands" parallel the amphibious seals in the desolation described in Isa. 13:22 (Himes, *Paradise Lost: A Poem*).

    Clang: "the loud harsh resonant cry or scream of certain birds, as in Latin and Greek" (*OED* 2). Thyer claims that "the *clangor* of the Latins...is a Word that they almost constantly use to express the Noise made by the Flight of large Flocks of Birds" (cited by Marchant). Cf. "with Clang despis'd the ground" (7.422).

836–39. Pecheux links this passage to the long Abraham narrative in 12.111–54, since Abraham is the example par excellence of the detachment of faith, for which he was praised by the church fathers ("Abraham" 368). Berkeley sees a thematic connection in books 11–12 to the Paradise of Fools, and here specifically to pilgrims "grasping to heaven without the benefit of right reason" (6). This passage, "abstractly worded, fairly slow, firm and moderately loud, extremely austere and demanding," is the climax of the passage rather than the much-admired 11.834–35 (Reesing 94). Knott identifies this moment not only as an essential part of Adam's education—he must not look back nostalgically to Eden if he is to create a new order for himself—but also as "almost unendurable...paradise itself, by a kind of brutal realism that denies the validity of myth, is transformed from an ideal world into an actual place" ("Symbolic Landscape" 53). Cf. *DocCh* 2.4: "With regard to the place of prayer, all are equally suitable" (Maurice Kelley 188; Patterson, *Works* 17:93). Sims (*Bible* 270) also cites Lam. 2:7 ("The Lord…hath abhorred his sanctuary"), Ezek. 24:21 ("I will profane my sanctuary"), and 2 Macc. 5:19 ("God did not choose the people for the place's sake, but the place for the people's sake").

836. *attributes:* "to ascribe to as belonging or proper; to consider or view as belonging or appropriate to" (so *OED* 3).

837. *No sanctitie, if none be thither brought:* Michael's speech reflects the human condition. Adam himself must cooperate with and persevere in grace, humbly seeking the will of God (Burke 216).

840–69. This image is appropriate for Adam's sixth vision, since six is the number of days in the Creation referenced in *PL* 11.852–54 and also the number of ages from the first coming of Christ to the last day (Fowler).

840. *He lookd, and saw:* Lewalski traces Adam's purged and exercised physical sight throughout book 11 (26); see **11.368**.

   hull: said of a ship, "to float or be driven by the force of the wind or current on the hull alone; to drift to the wind with sails furled" (*OED* v² 1).

841. *abated:* "to decrease in size or bulk" (*OED*). B. A. Wright includes this *a-* word among his survey of those that have been unreported, unglossed, or incorrectly glossed by Milton's editors ("Note" 145).

842–44. *Drivn by a keen North-winde:* cf. the mere *wind* of Gen. 8:1. Though Milton probably took the wind direction from Ovid, *Metamorphoses* 1.328, Himes (*Paradise Lost: A Poem*) suggests that winter came on after the 150 days during which the biblical "waters prevailed" (Gen. 7:18), that the days grew warmer after the tenth month (Gen. 8:5–6), aiding evaporation, and that the *watrie glass* may thus have been ice. Verity also cites Prov. 25:23, "The north wind driveth away rain," and points out that the northeast wind typically clears the sky in poetry, as in Dante's *Paradiso* 28.79–84.

North-winde: Fowler claims that this term was often hyphenated in the seventeenth century.

Wrinkl'd the face of Deluge: the word *wrinkl'd* suggests that the Flood is, as it were, growing old (Hume). Thyer finds this allusion boyish but the rest of the description of the waters abating admirably concise (Newton). As Todd reports, Habington's *Castara* (1635) also has "wrinkled brow" for the sea—and in a passage describing a gradually calming ocean (81). R. C. Browne (1877) is the first to cite Tennyson's later line, "The wrinkled sea beneath him crawls." Tillyard surmises that Milton is paying unconscious tribute to a passage in Sidney's revised *Arcadia* (1593) that includes both the rare verb *hull* and the metaphoric image of "wrinkles" on the sea's "face" ("Milton and Sidney's *Arcadia*" 153); cf. Sidney 66. Milton knew the *Arcadia* well enough to recognize Pamela's prayer when it appeared in *Eikon Basilike;* see his discussion in *Eikon* (Patterson, *Works* 5:86–89). Cf. also Cowley's description of the Flood, in which "The face of shipwrackt Nature naked lay" (*Davideis* 1.263).

844–54. Peter complains about the "semi-personifications" in this passage, "the sun staring into a mirror and then sucking up the waters, the ebb 'tripping'...the deep like a farmer engaged in some mysterious form of irrigation, and heaven a householder shutting out the rain," though he thinks the verse finally succeeds when it "shakes off this integument of half-formed and jumbled images" (139–40). Fowler, on the other hand, identifies the wordplay as a "half-pun" wherein *face* and *Gaz'd* "lead us to take *glass* = mirror, until *fresh...thirst* shows this to be wrong"; Fowler finds deep meaning in the shift, since the world as a vain reflection is indeed wrinkled and old, but as an instrument of God it again becomes *fresh.*

tripping: "running swiftly along" (Wesley).

cleer: originally "expressing the vividness or intensity of light: Brightly shining, bright, brilliant" (so *OED* 1a).

844. *glass:* "applied to water as a mirror" (so *OED* 13c).

845–46. *Gaz'd hot, and of the fresh Wave largely drew...thir flowing:* cf. how the sun "sups with the ocean" in 5.426. Newton claims that *Wave* in the preceding line must be a "noun of multitude" and therefore plural. Verity surmises that Milton either dictated a plural or meant *wave* as a collective noun. Robert M.

Adams claims that *Wave* was unanimously chosen by the eighteenth and nineteenth century editors he discusses (82); he also points out the grammatical problem of *Wave*-singular / *drew*-plural / *thir*-plural, for which eighteenth century emendations have been rejected by modern critics; "neatness is obviously not the supreme value of Milton's grammar" (92). N. O. claims the passage is taken from Shakespeare (*Comedy of Errors* 1.1.88–89): "At length the sun gazing upon the earth / Dispers'd those vapors that offended us" (82). Warton, though less insistent, finds that the passage expresses almost the same thought (145).

847–49. *tripping ebbe, that stole / With soft foot:* the Richardsons cite Horace, *Epodes* 16.47–48, "Montibus altis / Levis crepante lympha defilit pede" (the water comes leaping lightly down from the high hills with splashing feet). The Richardsons also reference the "Vulgate reading" of 1 Kings 18:41, *sound of the foot of the rain,* for what is *sound of abundance of rain* in the KJV, though what they mean by "Vulgate" is not clear. The Latin Vulgate of Jerome has "sonus multae pluviae est" (there is the sound of many waters) and the Douay-Rheims wording is the same as KJV.

    tripping: a favorite term for Drayton's personified rivers (Todd). Johnson complains that Milton here "describes the gentle glide of ebbing waters in a line remarkably rough and halting" (*Rambler* 4 [9 Feb. 1751]: 141).

848–49. Gen. 8:2. According to Hughes (*Paradise Lost*), the shutting of the windows of heaven is harmonized with Milton's understanding of the "waters which were above the firmament" (Gen. 1:7); cf. *PL* 7.261–71. George Coffin Taylor reports very similar phrasing in Du Bartas: "Now stopping close the vaines of all the fountaines, / Shutting heav'ns sluces" (*Milton's Use* 118); cf. Du Bartas 1:412.330–31.

850–55. For the details of the ark's settling and the waters' receding, see Gen. 8:4–5, which also specifies the gradual appearance of *mountains;* Milton's *Hills* parallel those of Ovid (*Metamorphoses* 1.344).

850. *flotes:* Newton defends Milton's spelling as coming from the (Old) French *floter.*

851. *som high mountain:* Gen. 8:4 identifies the resting place of the ark as "the mountains of Ararat." Milton deliberately avoids such localization (Fowler).

852. *the tops of Hills as Rocks appeer:* Hume has "tops of Trees," saying Milton's line is better than Ovid's "Postque diem longam nudata cacumina silvae / Ostendunt" (After a long time the bare tops of trees showed), but cf. Gen. 8:5: "And the waters decreased continually…in the tenth month, on the first day of the month, were the tops of the mountains seen."

853–54. *rapid Currents…furious tyde:* cf. 4.227. Despite the slow retreat of waters reported in Gen. 8:1–14, Milton conceived of the waters as retreating swiftly, as did Du Bartas (McColley, *Paradise Lost: An Account* 193); cf. Du Bartas 1:413.345–50. Fowler compares the swiftly receding waters to those at Creation (7.285–95), the connection implying that "one whole world" (11.874) has been destroyed, and that God is creating a new creation.
 retreating: "that retreats; retiring" (so *OED* 1).

855–67. Milton's text closely follows Gen. 8:6–22.

855–60. Wesley omits this passage. The dove returning to the ark is one of five illustrations for book 11 in Tilt's 1843 edition of Milton's *Poetical Works:* the dove illustration is the "tail-piece" at the end of the book (C. H. C. Baker 116); see further lists of Tilt's illustrations in **11.187** and **12.1–5**.

858. *whereon his foot may light:* a discrepancy with the female dove in Gen. 8:9 (Keightley).

860. *An olive leafe he brings, pacific signe:* Gen. 8:11. Cf. *Aeneid* 8.116. The olive symbolized peace in classical mythology; as the symbol of plenty, it was sacred to Pallas Athena; cf. *Georgics* 2.425 ("Placitam Paci nutritor olivam" [The olive's fatness well-beloved of Peace]) and *Aeneid* 7.154, where peace-seeking envoys are wrapped in olive leaves. A late-nineteenth-century commentator cites this passage as one proof that a primary source for Milton was Avitus ("Precursor" 50), though it is more likely that Milton and Avitus were both drawing from earlier sources; see also **12.197**.

861–62. *from his Arke / The ancient Sire descends with all his Train:* the biblical account lists the "train": "sons…wife…sons' wives…every beast…creeping thing…fowl…whatsoever…after their kinds" (Gen. 8:18–19). Cann includes a detail from supposed Bible chronology: Noah left the ark on Sunday, November 27 (253).

861. *Anon:* see **11.433**.

863–64. *Then with uplifted hands, and eyes devout, / Grateful to Heav'n:* Milton's narrative omits Noah's altar and sacrifice (Gen. 8:20–21). Cf. also Odysseus's thanksgiving prayer with upstretched hands (χεῖρας ἀνασχών) when he is returned safe to Ithaca (*Odyssey* 13.355).

    Grateful: cf. 11.323. "Through the fluidity of the syntax, [Noah's] gratitude to heaven is itself pleasing to heaven" (Ricks, *Milton's Grand Style* 114); cf. *PL* 11.323 and 442.

865–67. *in the Cloud a Bow…Betok'ning peace from God:* Gen. 9:12–17. Sims (*Bible* 271) cites Rev. 4:3, with its rainbow around the throne of heaven. Even pagans knew the rainbow as a sign; in *Iliad* 11.27–28, Zeus puts rainbows in the clouds as a portent for mortals (Himes, *Paradise Lost: A Poem*). "The early history of man, mainly of evil, ends on a note of partial reassurance" (Bush). Svendsen judges that Milton's description is typical of "his persistent attention to natural causes" in *PL* (*Milton and Science* 98).

866. *three listed colours gay:* Todd points out that both Sylvester, in his translation of Du Bartas, and Drummond allow only three colors to the rainbow; cf. Du Bartas, "an even-bent bowe / Contriv'd of three" (1:416.478–79). Todd also cites Stillingfleet that the three colors accord with peripatetic philosophy. Montgomery claims that three was typically the number of colors believed to be in the rainbow, though Boyer reports some disagreement even among the ancients (48–49). Cf. 11.897.

    listed: "bordered, edged; striped. Also (of colours), arranged in bands or stripes" (so *OED* a¹2). Some early commentators refer to the *list*, or edge of a cloth, but Keightley glosses it as *striped*, from the Italian *listato*. Dunster (in Todd) cites Ariosto's "E di nero et d'azur listato un panno" (And bordered with black and azure cloth) (*Orlando Furioso* 10.82). Wesley glosses *listed* as "bordering on each other."

867–68. *Cov'nant new:* i.e., the new agreement that God would never again destroy the world by water, an agreement signaled by the rainbow (Gen. 9:11–17). Cf. God's command that Michael "intermix" information about God's covenant (11.115–16).

    Whereat: Adam refers to the rainbow, since he knows nothing yet of covenants (Fish 281).

    erst: "sooner, earlier" (*OED* 4). "Previously" (Fowler).

867. *Betok'ning:* "to be a type or emblem of; to typify, symbolize" (so *OED* 2).

870–78. Adam is becoming reconciled to the new order of things; his thinking will change from now on until in the next book he arrives at his final conclusion about the Fall (Patterson, *Student's Milton*). For the first time, Adam truly responds to the situation (Fish 280). Adam's mixed emotions anticipate the poem's final vision of history (Summer, *Muse's Method* 205).

870. *O thou who:* 1667 *O thou that.*

871. *instructer:* cited by Shawcross as an example of Milton's tendency to use vowels phonetically ("Orthography" 139).

874–78. Cf. 2 Pet. 2:5, which contrasts the ungodliness of the destroyed with Noah, "a preacher of righteousness." Renaissance commentators, who celebrated Noah's faith, constancy, and perseverance, did rejoice more over him than they lamented the lost world (A. Williams, *Common Expositor* 237). Martz (154) finds that this "unfatherly utterance of a rigorous doctrinaire" owes more to Milton's remnant theology than to poetic decorum, whereas Mollenkott (40) thinks that the passage "parallels Adam's ecstatic comment on the fortunate fall (12.469–78)." Miner notes the modulated tone with which book 11 ends, as Adam "assesses the mingled cause for lament and rejoicing" (47).

876–78. The description of Noah clearly prefigures Christ (MacCallum, "Milton and Sacred History" 155).

876. *so perfet and so just:* on human perfectibility, see **11.681**. Cf. *DocCh* 1.21 (Patterson, *Works* 16:23), which explains that the appellation *perfect* is given in Scripture to those who, though really imperfect, are so called because "although sin resides within them, it does not reign over them"; Noah is the first example (Maurice Kelley 170). Sims (*Bible* 271) also cites Gen. 6:9: "Noah was a just man and perfect in his generations."

877. *another World:* cf. 2.347, 1004; 5.569; 7.155.

879–83. Even as Adam is asking Michael for the rainbow's meaning, he is careful to supply the meteorological data (Svendsen, *Milton and Science* 98). Fish insists that Adam "*chooses*—there is no other word for it—to see in [the cloud] the signification a merciful God must have intended"; the rainbow might have meant any number of things, including further threat (281). Wesley notes this passage as among those particularly excellent.

880–81. *Distended as the Brow of God appeas'd:* Todd rejects Fenton's emendation to *Bow of God;* Milton's sublime expression requires no alteration. For reasons unspecified, Keightley has *Distended? as the Brow of God appeased?,* though Verity explains that the question mark could supply a direct alternative to *Or serve* (881); Verity himself thinks the line sounds more natural as a statement by Adam, not a question, with the second alternative as an afterthought. Fowler claims that in modern usage, *Or* might be preceded by a dash to indicate the introduction of a sudden afterthought.

   distended: "to stretch asunder, stretch out, extend; to spread out at full length or breadth" (*OED* 1, obsolete). Ricks (*Paradise Lost*) glosses as "extended" and Fowler as "expanded (i.e., not contracted in anger)." For smoothing a rugged (wrinkled) brow, cf. *IlPen* 58 and *PR* 2.164.

884. *th'Archangel:* on the fluidity of Milton's names for angels, see West's and Gage's comments in **11.101**.

   Dextrously thou aim'st: Michael "approves Adam's new way of seeing, as one approves an archer who, suddenly, after long trial and many misses, finds the mark" (Fish 282).

885. *So willingly doth God remit his Ire:* Peter thinks this line represents "indecision or volatility" on God's behalf (146).

886–90. Milton's text closely follows Gen. 6:5–8.

Though late repenting him: "and it repented the LORD that he had made man on the earth" (Gen. 6:6). Bentley's rejection of Fenton's emendation, which puts a comma after *late,* is one with which all subsequent editors have apparently agreed. Le Comte glosses *late* as "lately."

886–89. Wesley omits this passage.

889. *Corrupting each thir way:* e.g., "each in its own way" (Hughes, *Paradise Lost*). Cf. the positive creative analog of "each in their kind" in 7.453, itself a reference to similar language in Gen. 1, and also the mention in Gen. 6:11 of the "corrupt" earth prior to the Flood.

thir way: 1667 *thirway.*

890–901. Milton draws the final speech of book 11 into "more and more predominantly iambic cadence, the great C Major of the poem," concluding in "a firm and stately tempo that rounds out the visions with a glowing sense of finality" (Reesing 94); see **11.1–21.**

890. *Such grace shall one just Man find in his sight:* "But Noah found grace in the eyes of the LORD" (Gen. 6:8). Prince identifies this conception as "characteristically Miltonic" (44).

892–97. Cf. the details of the covenant in Gen. 9:9–16, which Milton follows closely, except for *nor let the sea / Surpass his bounds.* Fowler thinks that Milton omits the curse on the ground (Gen. 8:21) because he has already dealt with the macrocosmic changes in the earth occasioned by the Fall (*PL* 10.649–706).

Covenant: pronounced as two syllables.

894. *Surpass:* "to pass over, go beyond, overstep (a limit)" (so *OED* 1, archaic).

895. *With Man therein or Beast:* citing Gen. 9:9–10, Bentley claims that the birds would properly have been included here as part of the covenant and therefore that Milton must have dictated, "With Man or Beast, *or Fowl.*" Pearce counters that in Scripture (Ps. 36:6, Jer. 21:6, and 32:43), "Man and Beast" includes birds and that Milton has already twice spoken of the inhabitants of the ark as "Man and Beast" (11.733 and 822).

897. *triple-:* the adjective in combination (so *OED*).

898–901. *call to mind his Cov'nant:* i.e., the promise that God would never again flood the entire earth (Gen. 9:12–17). Hume agrees with "the learned Dr. Gregory" and others that it had in fact rained on earth before the Flood. Milton's phrasing avoids the reading of some commentators on Genesis that the Flood has removed God's curse on the ground (Burden 184–85).

898–900. Cf. the details of God's promise in Gen. 8:22, which Milton follows closely, except for his expansion of *cold* to *hoary frost* and his addition of the eschatological fire. "All the cyclic patterns of order broken with the Fall of Eden are restored with the rainbow arc at the end of the Deluge" (Carnes 538). Yet "this is not the seasonless round of unfallen nature which Adam and Eve knew," but rather one marked by heat, frost, and labors, though with secular rewards of seed time and harvest while the world lasts (Ferry, *Milton's Epic Voice* 176–77).

899–901. The new covenant means that "history shall go forward for the sake of the one just man it may bear" (Radzinowicz 44).

900–01. *till fire purge all things new:* Christian eschatology expects new heavens and a new earth after the "elements shall melt with fervent heat" (2 Pet. 3:10). See also Milton's statement on the final conflagration in *DocCh* 1.33 (Patterson, *Works* 16:369–71, 375) and **11.66**. "As a theme for poetry, the final conflagration of the world had found striking expression in Vida's *Hymn to the Son of God,* and as a scientific dogma it held its place until after the publication in 1696 of William Whiston's *A New Theory of the Earth, from Its Original to the Consummation of All Things, . . . the General Conflagration*" (Hughes, *Paradise Lost*). Patrides, who surveys the range of eschatological opinions in Milton's time, finds it significant that Milton divided books 11 and 12 at this point for the 1674 edition: "Milton, indeed, leaves no doubt about his literal belief in the termination of universal history by fire," and Michael returns to the topic of the purified world in 12.462–65 and 12.547–51 ("Renaissance and Modern Thought" 182; *Milton* 277–78). Fowler finds it fitting that "an apocalypse should end the visions of the first 'world.'"

901. *Both Heav'n and Earth, wherein the just shall dwell:* cf. the promise in 2 Pet. 3:13 of "new heavens and a new earth, wherein dwelleth righteousness," also cited by Milton in *DocCh* 1.33 (Patterson, *Works* 16:381). Bentley, assuming that Milton must have intended another formula expressed in both 10.647 and 12.549, emends this line to "Both *Heavn's,* and Earth *whereon* the Just shall live," but Pearce argues that "heaven and Earth" refers to the world, and therefore is here correct. This moment finishes the active phase of Adam's education, which was to discover order and meaning in the world as God works through history; further revelations can only extend the implications of this insight (Fish 319–20). Lewalski (31) links Adam's faith to that of Noah, who in Hebrews 11:7 "condemned the world"; Adam verbally condemns it as far inferior to the new world to come, a sentiment anticipating Adam's later *felix culpa* speech in 12.469–78; see also **11.368**.

Paradise Lost, Book 12

The Argument. The original Argument from book 10 was divided between the two new books 11 and 12, and the 1668 *phrase…Flood; thence from the Flood relates, and by degrees explains, who,* becomes 1672 [book 11]*…Flood.* [book 12] *The Angel* Michael *continues from the Flood to relate what shall succeed; then, in the mention of* Abraham, *comes by degrees to explain, who.*

1669 has a comma after *Ascention,* and 1672 a semicolon; 1669 *relations* is 1672 *Relations;* 1669 has a comma after *Promises* and 1672 does not. 1668 is the same as 1672 except where noted otherwise.

1–5. These lines were added in 1674, when the original book 10 of 1667 was divided into books 11 and 12. Reesing (72–73) sees structural similarities between book 6 and 12; here, the beginning of book 12 is similar to that of book 6 (a journey and an angel); it is significant, however, that the Father treats Satan's rebellion differently from Adam's. Whaler argues through a complicated mathematical analysis that "it was Milton's early and steadfast plan to divide *PL* into twelve books" (*Counterpoint* 144–49). Summers claims that the division of books emphasizes the poem's basic pattern of destruction followed by a new and greater creation (*Muse's Method* 206). In 1667, Milton did not even start a new verse paragraph to mark the pause in the archangel's journey (Fowler). "Michael Foretells the Future" is one of four illustrations for book 12 in Tilt's 1843 edition of Milton's *Poetical Works* (C. H. C. Baker 116), though as Baker reports *passim,* this scene is typically used for book 11; see also **12.211–13, 12.365,** and **12.637,** as well as **11.187** for a list of Tilt's illustrations for book 11.

1–2. *bates at Noone:* commentators differ on what is meant. Verity glosses the term as " 'slackens,' i.e., *abates,* his course." Fletcher (*Complete Poetical Works*) cites the definition in *New World of Words* by Milton's nephew Edward Phillips, "to stop to eat, drink, or take some refreshment on a journey" and judges that the word is derived from *abate.* Northrop Frye (*Paradise Lost*) similarly glosses *bates* as "stops to eat." The Richardsons deny that Milton is referring to refreshment here; it rather refers merely to pausing. A falcon is said to *bate* when it beats its wings impatiently and flutters away from the fist or perch (*OED* 2); it also may mean to flutter downwards, as in *Ref:* "till the Soule by this meanes of over-bodying her selfe . . . bated her wing apace downeward" (Patterson, *Works* 3:2).

Noone: Fowler claims that noon, the "sixth" hour of the biblical day, marks the transition between one world and another, referencing "a great deal of mystical speculation" based on the tradition that the Fall, the Expulsion, and the death of Christ all took place at the sixth hour.

Though bent on speed: Stapleton maintains that change in pace here is strengthened by Michael's announcement that he will relate, rather than present visually, further scenes from human history (746); see **11.134–35**. Samuel compares the sense of urgency here with that in *Purgatorio* 12.84–86 (*Dante* 221).

2. *the Archangel:* on the fluidity of Milton's names for angels, see West's and Gage's comments in **11.101**.

3. *Betwixt the world destroy'd and world restor'd:* Carnes links this passage to the epic's relation to time; after the Fall, paradise "takes on its characteristically Janus-faced thrust of retrospect and anticipation and acquires both a past to recall in sacred metaphor and a future to anticipate in sacred typology" (519–20). Lieb, who traces the "concept of generation" in the poem, claims that since Noah is the "second stock" from whom man will "proceed" (*PL* 12.7), he stands as a type of Christ, from whom man will receive new life, as does Abraham (*Dialectics* 215); see **12.120–26**. Broadbent claims that the promise of "paradise nearly regained" is frustrated in book 12 (*Some Graver Subject* 274).

4. *If Adam aught perhaps might interpose:* Brisman argues that "revelation is essentially an experience of the arrested moment" and that poetry must bridge the gaps between such moments. She compares the "consciousness of fictive interposition" here with *Sonn 20* (213, 215, 217).

5. *Then with transition sweet new Speech resumes:* Dunster (in Todd) and others note that *transition* here refers to a part of an oration that summarizes what has been said and proposes what is coming. Cf. [Cicero], *Rhetorica ad Herennium* 4.26; the text is no longer thought to be Cicero's.

    sweet: Shumaker applauds the adjective; book 11 lacks sweetness, but the angel's manner is sweet, as partly demonstrated by his courteous pause for Adam's comment (*Unpremeditated Verse* 217). Fowler finds the speech "sweet" because "honey of doctrine can be extracted from it"; Michael's pause has marked the transition not only from vision to narration but also to a second section of the last two books analogous to the second of the three drops put in Adam's eyes; see also **11.416** and **12.467**.

6–32. Michael's words typify the Exodus as a people's moving from bondage to freedom (Shawcross, "*Paradise Lost*" 18).

6–7. *one World begin and end:* this division into ages reflects traditional schemes; Milton normally thought of biblical history as rhythmic phases of fall and reformation, as exampled in the anti-episcopal tracts (MacCallum, "Milton and Sacred History" 152n8).

6. *Thus:* not indented in 1667.

7. *second stock:* the promise of a new beginning is a governing motif in book 12 (Lawry, *Shadow* 282).

    stock: in the figurative sense, "the source of a line of descent; the progenitor of a family or race. In law, the first purchaser of an estate of inheritance" (so *OED* 3a). Fowler points out the ambiguity of *stock,* which can refer both to "human line of descent" and to the "olive tree" of Christ onto which the Gentiles are grafted in St. Paul's allegory of redemption (Rom. 11:17).

8–11. Addison famously says, "Milton, after having represented in Vision from the History of Mankind to the First great Period of Nature, dispatches the remaining Part of it in Narration.... If Milton's Poem flags any where, it is in this Narration, where in some Places the Author has been so attentive to his Divinity, that he has neglected his Poetry" (*Spectator* 3 [3 May 1712]: 386). The Richardsons claim that Milton's varying of the narration judiciously avoids tediousness and also that the following events are better told than shown. Stebbing approves of the switch to narration for two reasons: it would have been unnatural to keep Adam in a trance any longer, and the action of the poem would have been interrupted for too long had the vision continued. Dunster (in Todd) answers that rendering the material of book 12 in vision form would have made the narration disproportionately long (377). Himes (*Paradise Lost: A Poem*) finds a similar movement from vision to narration in Dan. 10:21, where the angel promises to relate Scripture for the exhausted human. Miner judges that the alteration from vision to narration makes the last book more theological than narrative and brings "a kind of plain-speaking that allows Adam less scope for human comment on human history" (47).

Although Adam's visions have been produced on the visual organs rather than in the mind, they have not been bright enough to cause visual failure; the real issue is avoiding the length of further narrative (Keightley). Adam could not physically sustain the presence of God for very long even before the Fall (Reesing 84; cf. *PL* 8.452–59, 11.315–27). Radzinowicz claims that Adam is actually put to sleep here, "and hears what follows as in a dream," albeit a shallow one that does not prevent him from responding (44). Martz complains that Milton devotes his last book primarily to a rational account of remnant theology, attempting as it were to "set together, within the borders of one poem, both the optimistic view of Augustine's *Confessions,* and the less inclusive, darker view of the later Augustine, as found in *City of God* 22.22," thus inevitably moving away from the poise and tempering of attitudes promised by Michael and God at the outset of book 11 (156–57).

human sense: cf. 4.206; 5.565, 572; 9.554, 871.

objects divine: Ryken cites this phrase as an example of Milton's "modified empiricism," by which an empirical noun is modified by an "apocalyptic" adjective (56).

12. *Thou therefore give due audience, and attend:* an example of repetition very common in the *Aeneid,* the structure, language, and syntax of which is omnipresent in *PL* (Grandsen 281, 288).

attend: B. A. Wright defines this archaic use of the verb as "to turn one's ear to; to listen, heed" ("Note" 149); see **11.46**.

13–24. The Richardsons relate the sentiment to the classical idea of the Silver Age, with the Golden Age being paradisal, and the Iron beginning in line 24. Masson adds that Noah's descendants (the "second source") lived under patriarchal or family government in a state of peace and religion inferior indeed to the paradisal age, but superior to what was to follow. Whiting rejects Verity's claim that this description is similar to Hesiod's Silver Age, "when men could not keep from sinning and wronging one another and would not serve the immortals" (*Milton* 173–74). Fowler likewise objects that the correspondence with the Ovidian Silver Age is not very close. Himes (*Paradise Lost: A Poem*) cites the temporary faithfulness of the Israelites after the Exodus (Judg. 2:7).

13. *few:* 1667 *few,* or *few;* Fowler asserts that the comma is probably correct.

16. Wesley omits this line.

18. *Labouring:* "to spend labour upon (the ground, vegetable growths, etc.); to till, cultivate" (so *OED* 1). Cf. Virgil, *Georgics* 1:118–19 ("Hominumque boumque labores / Versando terram" [the labors of men and cattle, accustomed to turning the soil]) and also *SA* 1298, where *Laboring* has the active sense of "causing to labor" (Verity).

19. *Corn wine and oyle:* Fowler, though acknowledging more distant echoes with the Old Testament expositions of the law of tithes (e.g., Deut. 14:23, Neh. 10:38), thinks this line specifically echoes the version of Ps. 4:7 found in the Book of Common Prayer for the office of Compline, "Thou hast put gladness in my heart: since the time that their corn and wine and oil increased."

21. Wesley omits this line.
   Feast: 1667 *Feast.*

23. *Tribes:* "a particular race of recognized ancestry; a family" (so *OED* 1b).

24–70. Lewis cites this passage as one example of his argument that for Milton, one can rebel only against a natural superior, so that Milton's assertion of divine monarchy is compatible with his republicanism; Adam's fatherly displeasure (*PL* 12.63) asserts the true hierarchical principle (*Preface* 75–77).

24–66. This passage exemplifies how Milton synthesizes information derived from various sources, including probably contemporary dictionaries (Starnes and Talbert 264).

24–44. Cf. Gen. 10:10, which identifies Babel as the beginning of Nimrod's kingdom. Milton follows common opinion in making Nimrod the builder of Babel and also the first monarch, an opinion reported at least as early as Josephus (*Antiquities* 1.4.2), who claimed that Nimrod gradually changed the government into tyranny. In *Purgatorio* 12.34–36, Dante links Nimrod with Satan as a type of pride; Dante also describes Nimrod's language as confused (*Inferno* 31.77–78, *Paradiso* 26.124–29). Hume cites the influential note of Jerome on Gen. 10:10 for the conflated traditions that Nimrod was the first tyrant, that he ruled in Babylon, and that Babylon gave its name to the Tower of Babel where languages were confused (Migne, *Patrologiae . . . Latina* 23:953B). Hughes (*Paradise Lost*) cites Sir Thomas Browne for an example of the prevalent seventeenth century view that "the secret designe of Nimrod, was to settle unto himselfe a place of dominion, and rule over his brethren," even while Nimrod publicly agreed with the building of Babel (*Pseudodoxia epidemica* 7.6), and Hughes (*Paradise Lost, A Poem*) adds Gregory's picture of Nimrod as the foiled empire-builder in *On the Trinity and Its Works*. As Keightley points out, the assumption that human government was patriarchal until Nimrod established monarchy is extrabiblical. Whiting reports that in its marginal note for Gen. 10:8–9, the Geneva Bible proclaims Nimrod a "cruel oppressor and tyrant" whose tyranny was proverbial, "for he passed not to commit crueltie even in Gods presence" (*Milton* 134). The Nimrod episode is central because books 11–12 transfer earlier metaphors to reality; Nimrod is the human embodiment of Satan the rebel building Pandaemonium (Champion 393). Schultz asserts that in the details extraneous to both Scripture and Josephus, Milton draws Nimrod "very like a type of Antichrist. . . . Thus the lesson directed at tyrants may have been to brand them as antichristian" (126); see also **12.506–40.** Reesing sees structural similarities between book 6 and 12; Nimrod's tyranny reflects Satan's archetypal tyranny in heaven (73). Verity's comment on this passage is extensive; he claims that Nimrod's name persisted in a Babylonian temple tower *Birs-Nimrud*, some ruins of which remained at least to Verity's day; he also cites references to Nimrod as early tyrant in Dryden (*The Hind and the Panther* 1.282–83) and Pope (*Windsor Forest* 61–62). Although Verity also cites a passage from the Camden Society revised edition of *ComBk* ("199…Monarchia…The Lordly Monarchy first among men.—In Assyria under the power of Nimrod called a great Hunter, an Hebraisme for a Great Theife.—Before his time was no sovereign" [41–42]), this page is not Milton's but rather among those blank pages later filled by Sir Richard Graham, Viscount Preston (1648–95), as noted by Mohl (Preface 1:344, 345n6). Newton makes an extended attempt to defend Nimrod—and monarchy—though he admits that Milton and "the greatest number of interpreters" condemn him. Thompson, arguing for the value and necessity of the last two books, thinks that the shift from vision to less graphic narration may be necessitated in part by more complex social and political problems that call for explanation, as here ("For *Paradise Lost*" 380). George Coffin Taylor identifies many similarities between the beginning of book 12 and the beginning of Du Bartas's "Babilon," including implied or explicit references to tyranny in the poets' home countries; Taylor finds the rest of the episode is too similar to Du Bartas to be explained by an undiscovered common source (*Milton's Use* 121–23); cf. Du Bartas 1:422–26.

24. *one:* i.e., Nimrod (Gen. 10:8–10).

25. *proud ambitious heart:* Fox, who traces the Seven Deadly Sins in books 11–12, identifies the major sin here as pride as described by various medieval authors, and particularly Satan's own sin of "exclusive pride," or the desire to be the exclusive possessor of a good, which in this case is political authority and takes the form of monarchy or tyranny; as symbolized by the tower, this pride is motivated by a desire to preserve reputation and be set apart from humankind (190); see Fox's comments at **12.33–35**, s.v. *from Heav'n claiming second Sovrantie,* and **12.43–57**, s.v. *get themselves a name.* Numerous commentators have remarked on the parallel between the Tower of Babel and Pandaemonium (see especially Cope 145 and Low 171).

27. *arrogate:* an example of the word used "with simple object only" (so *OED* 2b).

28. *dispossess:* "to drive out (from a possession); to expel, banish" (so *OED* 1c, obsolete). Keightley claims the word is used in its legal sense. Verity points out the frequency in Milton of the negative prefix *dis-*.

29. *the law of Nature from the Earth:* cf. the biblical parable of Jotham (Judg. 9), in which productive members of society (symbolized by the olive, fig, and vine) refuse human monarchy, which is claimed instead by the ignoble bramble; an ardent republican like Milton would favor the parable (Himes, *Paradise Lost: A Poem*) See **12.64–71**.

30. *Hunting…Men:* in Xenophon's *Kuropaedeia,* hunting is preliminary to warfare (Hume). St. Maur reports, "Nimrod…first took up Arms against the wild Beasts, which were then very numerous, powerful, and mischievous; then he made himself the Head of his Companions; then the King over all the rest" (411). As Keightley remarks, the idea that Nimrod hunted men was the extrabiblical interpretation of some Jewish and Christian expositors. Hughes (*Paradise Lost*) cites Du Bartas's epigram: "Leaves hunting Beasts, and hunteth Men to trap"; see Du Bartas 1:423.80. Cf. the prediction that Fulcieri da Calboli would become a hunter of "wolves" (i.e., Guelfs) in *Purgatorio* 14.58–63 (Samuel, *Dante* 257–58). Dryden refers to Nimrod as "the mighty hunter of his Race" in *Hind and Panther* 1.283.

33–35. *A mightie Hunter…Before the Lord, as in despite of Heav'n:* Gen. 10:9. Augustine translates *before* as "against," while Vatablus and others interpret it as "under," i.e., usurping all authority under God, and claiming it by divine right. Sims (*Bible* 271) cites Gen. 13:13, where "the men of Sodom were wicked and sinners before the LORD," and also Gen. 38:7, where "Er, Judah's firstborn, was wicked in the sight of the LORD." Newton claims that Milton follows both opinions here, while Fowler thinks that he follows the constitutional sense of Vatablus (and also Mercerus), citing *TKM:* "to say Kings are accountable to none but God, is the overturning of all Law and government" (Patterson, *Works* 5:11–12). Among modern editors, Northrop Frye (*Paradise Lost*) reads *before* as "against." Keightley claims that "before the LORD" is merely a superlative, like *trees of God.* According to Verity, the Hebrew word translated "hunter" would appear, from other passages, to indicate a warrior making raids on his enemies, so that Milton viewed Nimrod as a tyrant extending his enemy by force; cf. *Eikon* 11: "the bishops could have told [Parliament] that Nimrod, the first that hunted after Faction, is reputed by ancient Tradition, the first that founded Monarchy" (Patterson, *Works,* 5:185). Hughes (*Paradise Lost, A Poem*) cites the opinion of the fifteenth century lawyer Sir John Fortescue (1.7) that Nimrod was "an oppressor and destroyer of men; even as hunters are destroyers, and not rulers, of wild beasts"; Milton quotes Fortescue on English kings in *Def* 1.9: "the king of England, says he, can neither alter the laws, nor lay taxes without the people's consent" (Patterson, *Works* 7:477).

from Heav'n claming second Sovrantie: Milton interprets Nimrod's usurpation of authority and tower-building as an attempt to go beyond the legitimate power already given to the fallen state; Nimrod is implicitly linked with Satan's rebellion, because he invests his state with spiritual sanctions and aspires to be thought of as god-like (Fixler 231). Fox identifies the species of pride here as "meritorious and originative" (192); see **12.25** and **12.43–47**. Steadman judges that "in their 'despite of Heav'n,' both Satan and Nimrod exhibit the same overweening hubris, and the rewards of their pretentious exploits are virtually the same" (*Milton* 91). Summers also finds that Nimrod is the "human type of Satan" for whom it is impossible to have any sympathy (*Muse's Method* 209). On titles, see **11.158–59**.

35–39. Wesley omits these lines.

36–37. *from Rebellion shall derive his name / Though of Rebellion others he accuse:* Newton thinks Milton's inclusion of these lines was influenced by his own situation.

Most commentators through Stebbing make the problematic claim that "Nimrod" is derived from the Hebrew root *mârad,* "to rebel." Keightley may be the first to doubt the derivation, thinking the name is probably Assyrian, while Masson lists the etymology as one of many and implies that Milton's ironic use of it (kings and tyrants always accuse their subjects of rebellion, yet the first king was a rebel par excellence) is intentional. Northrop Frye is still proposing *rebel* as a possible gloss in 1951 (*Paradise Lost*), and Hughes in 1962 (*Paradise Lost, A Poem*) has "Nimrod, whose name means 'rebel.'" According to Starnes and Talbert, much of Milton's information on Babel appears to come from Charles Stephanus's *Dictionarium,* including the comment, "Nemrod, filius Chus. Gen. 10. Lat. *rebellis,* vel dormitio descensionis, aut dormiens dominans" (Nimrod, the son of Cush, Gen. 10. From the Latin *a rebel,* or "ease of descent," or else "resting while dominating") (264–68). Lejosne explains that Milton made use of a false but accepted etymology (97). Although the derivation of Nimrod is still uncertain, some biblical scholars have linked it with Ninurta, the Assyrian god of hunting and warfare, or with the Assyrian King Tukulti-Ninurta, 1235–1198 BCE (Koehler and Baumgartner 2:701). Fox (188–89) cites

Ginzberg's *Legends of the Jews* concerning rabbinical legends that "Nimrod was the first ruler to hold universal sway; that he induced men to place all trust in their own abilities rather than in God; that he was the instigator of idolatry, eventually setting himself up as a god; and that he and his followers climaxed their iniquity by building the tower of Babel"; cf. Ginzberg 1:177–81.

   Rebellion: "organized armed resistance to the ruler or government of one's country; insurrection, revolt" (so *OED* 1).

38–62. On the building of Babel, Milton closely follows Gen. 11:2–9. Hughes links this passage to the Limbo of Vanity (see **11.688–97**). Berkeley likewise links Babel with Milton's Paradise of Fools because both depend on "outward rites and specious forms" to deem "Religion satisfied" and because Milton "declines rigorously schematic treatment of sinners in *Paradise Lost*" (7). Steadman identifies similarities between the builders of Babylon and Pandaemonium: both are motivated by ambition, both seek to "dispossess Concord and law of nature from the Earth" (*PL* 12.28–29), the founding of both empires represents rebellion against God and imitates divine majesty, both pursue glory and fame by evil means, and both find their aims frustrated by divine judgment (*Milton* 91). For Nimrod as the founder of Babylon, see Augustine, *City of God* 16.4. Milton links Babel with Babylon in *PL* 12.343.

38. *crew:* "any organized or associated force, band, or body of armed men" (so *OED* 2).

40–41. *from Eden towards the West…The Plain…a black bituminous gurge:* cf. Gen. 11:2 for this movement, though according to Gilbert, Milton is apparently alone in his opinion, no other source having been found; Gilbert cites Bochart as having thought the people came from Armenia. Gilbert also lists Servius, Hayklut, and Marlowe as possible sources for Milton's lake of asphalt (*Geographical Dictionary* 42–43). See also Gen. 11:3 for "slime had they for mortar" (Newton: Hebrew *chemar*, Greek *asphaltus*, Latin *bitumen*) found at Shinar, as well as *PL* 10.562 for a *bituminous Lake* similar to the one near Sodom. Fowler claims that *slime* for *bitumen* was a common synonym at the time; *OED* 1 includes a reference to Blount's *Glossographia* (1656), which defines *bitumen* as "a kind of clay or slime naturally clammy, like pitch, growing in some Countries of Asia." The Richardsons describe the local asphalt as like brimstone but also initially slimy. Cf. the *asphaltic slime* of the bridge from hell in 10.298 and the *bituminous lake* near Sodom in 10.562, also reminiscent of the *Lago d'Averno* in Campania, called *Alta Ostia Ditis* (high gates of Dis [god of the underworld]) in Virgil, *Georgics* 4.467. Vitruvius describes a large bituminous lake near Babylon called *limne asphaltitis* (asphalt lake) (8.3.8). Sandys (in Todd) observes that the subterranean fires near Puteoli had a similar reputation. Himes (*Paradise Lost: A Poem*) finds the connection likely between Avernus and Babylon, as Babylon was often used for Rome in Reformation thinking, and Lake Avernus was near Rome; cf. the mouth of hell in Spenser's *Faerie Queene* 1.5.31. Josephus had claimed that bitumen was used in the mortar of Babel to keep out water (*Antiquities* 1.4.3). Milton refers to the *Plain of Shinar* as "Sennaar" in 3.467, which Starnes and Talbert link to Charles Stephanus's *Dictionarium* (265–68); see **12.24–66**.

gurge: "a whirlpool (so *OED* 1). Fowler calls *gurge* "almost certainly a Latinism," since *gurges* is Latin for "abyss" or "whirlpool." Fletcher (*Complete Poetical Works*) has "swirl, eddy." Wesley glosses *gurge* as "bubbling spring," adding that since bitumen is "a kind of pitchy substance," "this spring was black, like the mouth of hell."

42. *the mouth of Hell:* cf. 10.288, 636. Since Bentley cannot believe that Milton would place hell underground where the heathen did, he wants this phrase to read, "*th'Image* of Hell," also citing "Type of Hell" (1.405), though Moody wants to explain this passage as Milton momentarily losing sight of his cosmology and reverting to the classical conception of a subterranean hell. Empson, who sometimes finds Bentley's readings reasonable, complains here as well as in 5.140, 11.14, and 12.50 that Milton's process of substituting concrete for abstract is "caught half-way"; he also thinks it is irritating to have "hell…replanted inside the earth" (*Some Versions* 154–55). Broadbent claims that this passage is one among many linking the earlier picture of hell to its figuring forth in the last two books; the linkages work to "focus ethic in aesthetic" (*Some Graver Subject* 274). Roland Mushat Frye points out that the material for the tower that should reach to heaven is taken from hell (65–66). In Du Bartas, the workers of Babylon "digg to hell" (1:425.155).

43–47. *whose top may reach to Heav'n:* the language here follows Gen. 11:4.
cast: Fowler glosses as the obsolete, reflexive sense of *OED* 34, "set themselves with resolution," though *OED* 30, "to form by throwing up, to raise (a mound, bank, earthwork, or the like)," likewise obsolete, is also possible.

get themselves a name: on the debased wish for notoriety, see **11.788**. Fox identifies the species of pride here as "boastful" (191); see **12.25** and **12.33–35**.

44. *Towre:* "a building lofty in proportion to the size of its base, either isolated, or forming part of a castle, church, or other edifice, or of the walls of a town" (so *OED* 1). R. C. Browne (1877) refers to Thomas Browne's *Pseudodoxia epidemica* 7.6 ("That the Tower of Babel was erected against a second deluge"), which argues among other things that despite the stated memorial goal for the tower (to make a name when people were scattered), "the secret designe of Nimrod, was to settle unto himselfe a place of dominion, and rule over his brethren, as it after succeeded."
    and Towre: 1667 *& Towre.*

46. *lost:* 1667 *lost,*

47. Wesley omits this line.

48–62. "Nothing could be further from the promised sympathy and consolation.... In presenting the close of this new cycle of degeneration, Milton seems to have forgotten Michael's benign and all-inclusive promise that the presence of God would never be lost to man" (Martz 158). Saurat cites this passage as an example of divine irony, which is the one personality trait of God that is richly developed in the epic (192–93); see also Saurat's comment in **11.84–98**.

48–49. *oft descends to visit:* cf. 3.532, 661; 7.570.
    visit: "to come to (persons) in order to observe or examine conduct or disposition; to make trial of; to subject to test or scrutiny" (so *OED* 2, obsolete).
    visit... Unseen: Ryken includes this phrase in his discussion of how Milton's epithets for heavenly realities deny empirical qualities (97–98).

49–50. Wesley omits these lines.

50. *To mark thir doings:* Empson complains that here as well as in 5.140, 11.14, and 12.41, Milton's process of substituting concrete for abstract is "caught half-way"; he finds it irritating to have "heaven placed in reach of Babel" (*Some Versions* 154–55). Fowler insists, *pace* Empson, that the passage is ironic.

51–52. *ere the Tower / Obstruct Heav'n Towrs:* Hume judges this speech derisive. See also Newton's comment in **12.73**. Peter thinks it represents "feeble credulity" on God's behalf (146).

51. *Comes down to see thir Citie:* cf. similar language at Gen. 11:5, but Milton may also intend a parallel with God's promise in Gen. 18:21: "I will go down now, and see" Sodom. Newton points out a similar movement of classical gods coming down to observe human actions, as in the stories of Lycaon and of Baucis and Philemon. Wesley notes this line as beginning a passage of particular excellence, but does not mark its end.

52–53. *in derision sets / Upon thir Tongues a various Spirit:* echoes Ps. 2:4: "the Lord shall have them in derision." Bentley emends *a various Spirit* to "a various *Speech*," but Pearce argues that by a "various spirit" is meant one of contention, since God intended in Gen. 11:6 to divide the unified people. Wesley glosses the phrase as "a Spirit varying the Sounds, by which they would express their Thoughts." Hughes (*Paradise Lost*) provides "a spirit of variance or contradiction," and in *Paradise Lost: A Poem* "a spirit of contradiction, a quarrelsome spirit."

　　various: "calculated to cause difference or dissimilarity" (so *OED* 5b, obsolete). Bush has "a spirit of diversity, discord." Cf. 2 Chron. 18:22, "the LORD hath put a lying spirit in the mouth of these [Ahab's] prophets." Milton's contemporaries generally believed that the separation of language into distinct individual languages occurred at Babel, and because of the strong contemporary interest in synthetic universal languages, the Babel story was particularly fascinating (Fowler); see Knowlson 9–15. Milton declares in *Log* 1.2 that the languages of Babel were divinely given (Patterson, *Works* 11:221); Allen argues that Milton's description of Babel is therefore brief, since he would have thought a scientific study of philology was "an unwarranted intrusion on the mysteries of theology" ("Some Theories" 5–7). Northrop Frye (*Paradise Lost*) notes the contrast with the linguistic concord of Pentecost (Acts 2).

52. *Heav'n:* "simple attributive…in sense 'of heaven'" (so *OED* 10a).

55. *a jangling noise:* Sylvester translates as "a jangling noyse" Du Bartas's description of the confusion of tongues (Du Bartas 1:426.191).

56. *gabble:* "voluble, noisy, confused, unintelligible talk" (so *OED* 1).

58. *Not understood:* cf. Gen. 11:7, "Go to, let us go down, and there confound their language, that they may not understand one another's speech."

59–61. Cf. Ps. 2:4, 37:13, 59:8, Prov. 1:26, and *PL* 2.191 and 8.78. Bentley objects to the past tense, and also the syntax of "and looking down," and wants it emended to "Great laughter *is* in Heav'n; / *All* looking down," and in 61, "Thus *is* the Building left." Newton cites Thyer's opinion that it is rather too comic for the grave character of Milton's God to be laughing at mere mortals. Wordsworth (in Wittreich 108–09) considers the reaction wrong for superior beings, preferring instead the heavenly sorrow of Shakespeare's "Man, proud man…plays such fantastic tricks before high heaven / As make the angels *weep*" (*Measure for Measure* 2.2.117, 121–22; emphasis added). Montgomery, however, argues that there are analogous passages both in Homer (*Iliad* 1.599) and the Psalms. Walter A. Raleigh cites these verses as one proof of Milton's "wilful [and] persistent accumulation" of God's harsh traits (132–33). Ryken claims that while laughter is one emotion that celestial agents share with humans, "heavenly laughter is scornful rather than joyous," citing also 2.731; 4.834, 903; 5.735–37; heavenly anger, prompted by righteousness, is not selfishly vindictive but rather results from a general moral order set in motion by the evildoer (136–37). Although the pride of Babel is comically humbled, the human passions that go into its building are tragic since tyranny, oppression, and homicide remain (Low 172–73). See **11.817–18**. Wesley reduces these three lines to "As mockt they storm; thus was the building left."

60. *hubbub:* cf. Milton's "universal hubbub wild" in *PL* 2.951 and Spenser's "shrieking Hububs" (*Faerie Queene* 3.10.43). Cf. *OED* 2: "Noisy turmoil; confusion, disturbance; an instance of this; a tumultuous assembly or demonstration; a riot, 'row.'"

61. *thus was the building left:* cf. Gen. 11:8: "So…they left off to build the city."

62. *Ridiculous:* Sprott thinks that the final two syllables are probably meant to be elided into one around the *l*, but how completely depends on the length of the first vowel and how easily it may be absorbed into the particular vocalic sound of the *l*; the *u* almost certainly has less value in seventeenth century speech than in modern (89–90).

    the work Confusion nam'd: cf. Gen. 11:9: "Therefore is the name of it called Babel; because the LORD did there confound the language of all the earth." Josephus (*Antiquities* 1.4.3) glosses *Babel* as Hebrew for "confusion," a gloss repeated by the KJV and other translations, though the gloss has been contested; Fowler calls the etymology "popular but false." Keightley reports the conjecture that Babel is *Bâb-Bêl,* or Gate or Court of Belus, and judges the most probable etymon to be *Bêth-Bêl,* House of Belus. Verity, citing Smith's *Bible Dictionary,* claims that "native" etymology renders the word *Bab-il,* or "gate of the God Il," or "perhaps more simply 'the gate of God,'" an etymology also cited by Hughes (*Paradise Lost*). Starnes and Talbert suggest the influence of the *Dictionarium* (1553) of Charles Stephanus, who renders Babel as *Confusio* (267). *Bilbul* is one word in Hebrew that can be translated as "confusion" (Ben Abba, s.v. *confusion*). Newton finds the normally nonpoetic phrases *jangling noise* (55), *hideous gabble* (56), and *hubbub strange* (60) to be appropriate in this passage.

64–71. Himes (*Paradise Lost: A Poem*) sees the same dissension played out in Judges 9 among the followers of Abimilech, who slew his brothers, and in Nimrod's confused followers at Babel; see **12.29.** Adam's response is correct only for prelapsarian man, since degenerate men are not worthy to govern; this passage should be balanced with 12.92–96, where Milton is able to make tyrants of divine-right kings (Lejosne 97–98). Arnold Williams claims that among Renaissance commentators of Genesis, the domination of man over beasts led naturally to political issues, such as whether an unfallen man would have ruled also over other men (*Common Expositor* 220–21). Rajan identifies as the "pivot of the argument of the last two books" the assertion that outer servitude is the consequence of inner depravity (*"Paradise Lost" and the Seventeenth Century* 86).

64–66. Lawry sees this outburst as proof that Adam has "fully exorcised the Cain from himself" in his growth in self-knowledge and repentance ("'Euphrasy and Rue'" 9). Muldrow argues that Adam's speech represents his real rejection of evil, the first that goes beyond "mere lament"; the Nimrod section of the epic is a necessary part of Adam's spiritual growth (88–91).

64. *execrable:* "of persons and things: Deserving to be execrated or cursed; abominable, detestable" (so *OED* 2).

Son: a key word in book 12; cf. 80, 101, 145, 153, 155, 160, 161, 268, 327, 332, 357, 381, 388, 447, 448 (Reesing 73).

67–68. *over Beast, Fish, Fowl / Dominion absolute:* cf. the similar statement in Gen. 9:2.

69–70. *Man over men / He made not Lord:* Patterson (*Student's Milton*) cites *DocCh* 1.29: since Christ is the head of the mystical church, only he has the right or power to preside over the visible church (Patterson, *Works* 16:227). Milton's presentation of Nimrod is tinged with republicanism, both in its appeal to natural law and its ideal of a *fraternal state;* the presentation has been prepared by the preceding Senecan idyll of virtuous primitive governors (Fowler).

69. *donation:* "the action or faculty of giving or presenting; presentation, bestowal; grant" (so *OED* 1).

70–71. *such title to himself / Reserving:* cf. God's reaction to Israel's demand for a king in 1 Sam. 8:7.

71–78. Wesley omits these lines.

71. *human left from human free:* cf. Augustine, *City of God* 19.15: "For [God] did not wish a rational creature, made in his own image, to have dominion save over irrational creatures: not man over man, but man over beasts." Fletcher (*Complete Poetical Works*) sums up this line in the single word *toleration*.

72. *encroachment:* wrongful acquisition.

73. *to God his Tower intends:* Newton approves of Adam speaking only conjecturally, since Nimrod's intention is not clear in Scripture, and he wishes Milton had taken the same care in 12.51–52. Cf. 1.589–91 ("[Satan] above the rest...Stood like a Tower"), which Watson includes in his list of specific passages in book 12 that are symmetrically linked with cognate passages in the early books (148–50), the other passages of which are 12.185–88, 210, 211, and 342–43. Josephus identifies Nimrod's motives as escaping another deluge and taking vengeance on God for the Flood's destruction of their forefathers (*Antiquities* 1.4.2); see **12.24–44**.

75–76. *up thither to sustain / Himself and his rash Armie:* Himes (*Paradise Lost: A Poem*) remarks, "The fate of aspiring leaders who fight against God seems to be desertion. The thin air of the upper regions accurately symbolizes the ever-decreasing number of adherents as tyranny becomes more exacting."

76–78. *thin Aire / Above the Clouds…famish him of Breath:* Keightley finds this statement "a degree of knowledge to which Adam could hardly have attained," but Babb cites this natural fact, as well as the subterranean generation of gems (*PL* 3.608–12) and the dryness of old age (*PL* 11.542–46) as something Milton would have considered knowledge rather than opinion, significant because natural philosophy leads one to perceive God's nature; Adam is appalled not only by Nimrod's impiety but also by his foolishness (27, 29). Fowler compares this passage with other references to atmosphere in *PL*, such as the "purer air" of paradise (4.153) and the "thinner air" that fish are unable to breathe (8.348), and concludes that in the epic, atmosphere is a symbol of degree or station, both moral and natural.

famish: "to deprive (a person) of anything necessary to life" (so *OED* 2b, obsolete).

77. *pine:* the obsolete transitive verb (*OED* 1) may also be intended in 11.486 and in Shakespeare, *Richard II* 5.1.77.

78. *of Breath, if not of Bread:* for the play on words, see **11.625–27**.

79–101. Cf. the "unjust" thralldom to self in 6.174–82. Hughes (*Paradise Lost*) finds this passage the epitome of Milton's conviction that reason must control the passions, a principle with which, like Plato in the *Republic* (4, 8, and 9), he correlates political freedom. Cf. Bush's note that "the linking of order in the soul with order in the state is in the vein of Plato's *Republic*." Hughes also notes the Platonic ideal in Castiglione's *Book of the Courtier*, that true liberty is not living "as a man will," but rather as living "according to good lawes" (*Paradise*

Lost: A Poem 275) and asserts that this creed is equally biblical and humanistic, as demonstrated by Sir John Eliot's conclusion to *Monarchie of Man* (ca. 1631), that the "perfection of our government" is man's "intire rule and dominion of himselfe" (2.227). Ross links this admonition to the earlier *HistBr*, where Milton warned against the unseasonable quest for mere political and economic liberty; here, though he retains the ideal, he removes it from history (*Milton's Royalism* 88, 90–91); cf. Patterson, *Works* 10:316. Tillyard identifies Milton's idea of the Fall as primarily a fall from true liberty to mental anarchy due to a lack of self-knowledge, allowing man's passions to deceive and overrule his judgment and leading to chaos, anguish, and loss of liberty (*Milton* 266–67). Cf. the Son's comment on dissolute Rome "thus degenerate, by themselves enslav'd" (*PR* 4.144) and Samson's rebuke of his countrymen, who "by thir vices brought to servitude...love bondage more then Liberty" (*SA* 269–70) and whose "servile minds" would not receive him as their deliverer (1213–14). See also *PL* 6.41–43 and 9.1127–31. "Poor Adam...each time [he] affects horror with his future sons and their generations, he finds the horror original with himself, the type of human prodigal son who relinquishes his birthright of liberty and reason" (Lawry, *Shadow* 283). Rajan sees this passage, as well as 9.1121–31 and 11.358–60, as adumbrating Michael's announcement of "the paradise within" in 12.587 ("*Paradise Lost:* The Hill" 44–45). Dick Taylor Jr. compares this passage to Abdiel's rebuke of Satan in 6.174–82, since Satan does not understand that true liberty involves certain kinds of submission; Taylor also identifies a "complex and closely woven pattern" of obedience, free will, and Christian liberty in the epic ("Battle" 76–77). "In one of Milton's most famous passages on liberty and the problem of God's permission of evil tyrannies, Michael approves Adam's 'abhorrence,' but reminds him that man is no longer unfallen and that the Nimrod-Satan figure is inevitable in a world corrupted by sin and death"; Milton links virtue with reason rather than with Machiavellian cleverness or intellectual agility, which is the corruption of reason (Summers, *Muse's Method* 209–10). Fowler judges that this passage closely follows Augustine's thought in *City of God* 19.15: "For [God] did not wish a rational creature, made in his own image, to have dominion save over irrational creatures....Wherefore we do not read of a slave anywhere in the Scriptures until the just man Noah branded his son's sin with this word [Gen. 9:25]; so he earned this name by his fault, not by nature."

79. *To whom thus Michael:* this speech is Michael's longest, at 191 lines (12.79–269); Reesing finds that Milton is successful in keeping up "the impression of life in a single voice" because of his "wonderfully alert sense for variation in tempo" (95); see **11.1**.

Justly thou abhorr'st: Fish cites this passage and 12.372–76 as proof that Adam's "progress is regular and measurable, marked by the experiencing of insights which do not desert him under pressure" (290). The topical interest of Michael's speech for Milton's contemporaries is less important than the growth of Adam's conscience; the passage could be topical in any age (Sasek 193).

thus: "an ellipsis for *thus says, said* (referring either to a preceding or subsequent speech)" (so *OED* 1d).

81. *Such trouble brought, affecting to subdue:* because the action is future, Bentley wants "Such trouble *brings*"; Pearce objects that Michael is not recalling anything here but rather reflecting on what he had been telling Adam. Verity glosses the second clause as "aiming at subduing," linking the construction to the Latin *affectare* with the aim in the accusative, as in *PL* 3.206. The verb *affect* once included the meaning "to aim at, aspire to, or make for" (*OED* 1).

83–101. Most commentary on this passage refers to Milton's association of freedom with reason; cf. *PL* 3.108–10 and 9.351–52, *PR* 4.143–45. Maurice Kelley cites *DocCh* 1.12, where the first result of spiritual death is the obscuring of right reason to discern the chief good and the second the loss of righteousness and liberty to perform it, along with " that slavish subjection to sin and the devil, which constitutes, as it were, the death of the will" (Patterson, *Works* 15:207). Kelley (73–74, 153) also cites *DocCh* 1.2, where, he notes, the existence of God is further proved by the existence of "conscience" or "right reason" (Patterson, *Works* 14:29). Cf. also *HistBr:* "But when God hath decreed servitude on a sinful Nation, fitted by thir own vices for no condition but servile, all Estates of Government are alike unable to avoid it" (Patterson, *Works* 10:198). Patterson, who claims that "no one has ever surpassed, or perhaps equaled Milton, in his sound definitions of liberty," supplies further Miltonic references in his note at *PL* 12.79 (*Student's Milton*): in *Def 2*, that liberty is the fruit of piety, justice, and temperance (Patterson, *Works* 8:241); in *Ref*, that liberty consists of "manly and honest labours, in sobriety and rigorous honour to the Marriage Bed" (Patterson, *Works* 3:53); in *DDD*, that "honest libertie is the greatest foe to dishonest license"; that a knowledge of liberty's extent is necessary for restraining the reasonable soul of man within due bounds; and that liberty is a natural vent to prevent "some wide rupture of open vice, and frantick heresie" (Patterson, *Works* 3:370, 373, 510). In *TKM,* Milton insists that only good men can heartily love freedom, since "the rest love not freedom but licence," and argues that men should be governed by reason instead of the "double tyrannie, of Custome from without, and blind affections within"; such self-rule would help men to discern political tyranny (Patterson, *Works* 5:1). In *Eikon*, he proclaims man's title to his freedom greater than any king's to his crown (Patterson, *Works* 5:255). At the end of *Def 2*, he concludes that the nation that cannot rule itself but "has delivered itself up to the slavery of its own lusts, is itself delivered over, against its will, to other masters—and whether it will or no, is compelled to serve" (Patterson, *Works* 8:251), and in *REW*, Milton insists that "liberty of conscience...ought to be to all men dearest and most precious" (Patterson, *Works* 6:142). Diekhoff (*Milton's "Paradise Lost"* 147–48) denies that Milton was talking directly about England in this passage, but acknowledges that he did make that application in the *HistBr*, where Milton references those who "did not onely weak'n and unfitt themselves to be dispencers of what libertie they pretended, but unfitted also the people, now growne worse & more disordinate, to receave or to digest any libertie at all" (Patterson, *Works* 10:323–24). Rajan compares the clarity of Michael's answer here with the Son's answers to Satan in *PR*, that "clarity of certain kinds must skirt the edge of cruelty" ("Jerusalem" 65). Saurat identifies the "passion triumphant over reason" in this passage with the "evil concupiscence" of 9.1121–31; he concludes that the epic is "largely a political poem," albeit in the Augustinian sense (125, 164, 229); cf. *City of God* 19.15, where the prime cause of slavery and servitude is identified as man's sin and God's judgment on it. Green (562–63) claims that the word *reason* has a double sense both here and in Adam's lecture to Eve in 9.343–56, since in 12.84 it means "the moral law of the universe," whereas in 12.92 in means "rational faculty"; these two meanings helped Milton reconcile his humanistic interest in patristic intellectualism with his theological commitment to patristic voluntarism. Agar compares the process detailed here–loss of inner, psychic freedom causing loss of outer, political freedom—to a similar process described in Plato's *Republic* (15–16, 31, 51–53). Samuel disagrees with Agar, however, that these ideas were particular to Milton or foreign to the spirit of Renaissance Platonism (*Plato* 41). Fowler compares *right reason* with the "rectifi'd reason" of *OAP* (Patterson, *Works* 5:268). Hoopes explains that according to Milton's thinking, appetite cannot lead to action; it can only be led, so that when "appetite is indulged, the will has surrendered to claims from without, and action cannot rightly be called voluntary" (191); see also **12.575–76**. In a review of Hoopes, Woodhouse (103) reports that in *DocCh*, the term *reason* "ranges all the way from an intuitive apprehension of the law of nature...to a rigorous application of the canons of logic," and also that Milton recognized Plato's two operations of reason, the discursive and the intuitive. Like Satan, a bad ruler interferes with other men's use of right reason to adjust their lives to the wishes of their maker; cf. *Eikon:* "Did he not forbidd and hinder all effectual searches of Truth, nay like a beseiging Enemy stopd all her passages both by Word and Writing?" (Patterson, *Works* 5:204). For Milton, full education includes the activity of both intellect and conscience; reason supplies, for him, man's best and only law. Disregarded, it is soon choked out by "upstart passions" that reduce man to subjection (Hall 192). According to Bowra, the central sin in *PL*—disobedience—is wrong because by it man denies his rational nature and so cuts himself off from God, who is known through reason; true liberty is found in doing what God demands (206, 217). Joseph cites this passage as one proof that a central thesis of *PL* is free will's dependence on reason (268). To right reason and liberty, Roland Mushat Frye adds love; he claims that "the three are indissolubly linked, and Satan fell from all three" (34). This passage is one of the few in the last two books where Milton's historical survey can go into an issue at any length, because Milton must not obscure his main theme—the election of the Jewish people and the promise of Messiah (Burden 179–80); see *PL* 12.507–39. "Milton seems to be blaming the failure of the Commonwealth on original sin.... They had failed through their own weakness, their own lack of faith, their own passions and greed, their own sin. God was not to blame" (Muir 128–29). Steadman compares human loss of rational liberty with Satan's own: "Like fallen man, the fallen angel is enslaved to his own passions.... Colonizing the earth and air, [devils] can gain only the accidents of liberty, not the substance or the reality" (*Milton* 96–97). Good asserts the importance to Milton of combining liberty with righteousness, equally the basis of individual and social happiness (223). Nicolson contrasts Milton's ideal state of nature ruled by reason with the egocentric state of universal warfare proposed by his contemporary philosophical opponent Thomas Hobbes, for whom choice lay in the perception of the individual will; for Milton, reason is choice because things are good and bad in themselves ("Milton and Hobbes" 418–19). Radzinowicz, who claims that Milton breaks a pattern of continued reliance on the roll call of the faithful in Heb. 11 to revert to the discussion of Nimrod and monarchy in Gen. 10 and 11, argues that Adam needs no explanation for this scene; Michael needs only to explain "the inner logic of tyranny" and make explicit the connection between the soul's and the state's condition (45). Bailey, surveying similarities between Milton's thought and Jakob Boehme's, points out that Boehme made rulers responsible for looking after their people; prideful, neglectful rulers set up a kingdom of Antichrist (164).

83–90. Rajan praises Milton's typically significant musicality in this passage: "The accentuation of the sense by the sound, the use of words like 'dividual,' 'twinned,' and 'catch,' the internal assonance which binds and strengthens the paragraph, all these add to the lucidity of the best expository writing a fervour and persistence of conviction which expository prose could never hope to attain" (*"Paradise Lost" and the Seventeenth Century* 115–16). For both this passage and 11.515–16, Patrides cites an Elizabethan homily that identified the Fall's shift from the image of God to the image of the devil (*Milton* 113).

83–84. *Since thy original lapse:* Hawkey reports that several editions have it corruptly as *Since by.* Newton complains that *by* "hardly makes sense or syntax."

    lapse: Ryken contrasts the word's negative, postlapsarian meaning with the "liquid Lapse" of water in 8.263, where the word simply means "fall" (70).

85. Newton glosses the line as "twinned at birth with right reason." Dunster (in Todd) thinks Milton is alluding to Shakespeare's *Timon of Athens* 4.3.3–5: "twinn'd brothers of one womb, / Whose procreation, residence, and birth / Scarce is dividant." Fowler argues that *Twinn'd* implies a reflexive relation in which free will is a true image of reason, since in such Neoplatonic systems as Pico's the mind (*intellectus*) was supposed to have a reflexive relationship with the faculty of choice (*ratio*); the passage obviously bears on Adam and Eve's separation immediately before the Fall, since without Adam's *reason*, Eve's *liberty* led only to *upstart passions.*

    dividual: "that is or may be divided or separated from something else; separate, distinct, particular" (so *OED* 1). Wesley has, "Liberty is the twin sister of reason, and cannot exist divided from her."

86–89. *Reason in man obscur'd, or not obey'd:* Himes (*Paradise Lost: A Poem*) cites the first sentence of *TKM*, where Milton wishes men would be governed by reason rather than abandoned to tyranny (Patterson, *Works* 5:1). Broadbent claims that whenever Milton talks authoritatively about ethics or psychology, the language is Greek, and he complains that here the critical tone separates the soul's elements beyond hope of integration, a move fatal to Milton's Hebraic integration of body and soul (*Some Graver Subject* 212). Lewis (*Preface* 68), however, includes this passage in his discussion of Augustinianism (*City of God* 14.15): since man was disobedient to his superior, he has lost his authority over his inferiors, which were chiefly his passions and his physical organism; "Man has called for Anarchy; God lets him have it." Empson judges that Milton "protests overmuch that there was no danger of sensuality at all among the pleasures of Eden" (*Some Versions* 180).

90–101. "The idea that national corruption invites conquest is recurrent in Milton's prose and verse" (Bush). Cf. 11.797–801, *PR* 3.414–40, 4.131–45, *SA* 268–71.

90–95. Renaissance commentators Peter Martyr and Pareus urge that tyranny is imposed as punishment on sin; they are substantially in agreement with Milton's sentiment here (A. Williams, *Common Expositor* 223).

92–96. See Lejosne's comments in **12.64–71**.

93. *Subjects him:* in the archaic reflexive, "to make (persons, a nation or country) subject to a conquering or sovereign power; to bring into subjection to a superior; to subjugate" (so *OED* 1). William Aldis Wright notes that 1719 has *it* for *him*.

95–96. The "joy of battle and the exultation in the ordeal are muted in the last books of *Paradise Lost*" (Rajan, "*Paradise Lost:* The Hill" 61). Summers cautions the reader against thinking that evil is exonerated because Providence is miraculously larger, since "neither sexually nor politically did Milton make a simple identification between the inevitable and the good" (*Muse's Method* 89). Cf. the tension in Matt. 18:7, "it must needs be that offences come; but woe to that man by whom the offence cometh," and Milton's similar rejection of necessity in *PL* 4.393–94.

95. *Tyrannie:* "the action or government of a tyrannical ruler; oppressive or unjustly severe government" (so *OED* 2).

97–104. Wesley omits these lines.

97–101. *Yet somtimes Nations will decline so low:* this passage is the counterpart of the warning words that Milton addressed to the English people in *REW* (Hutchinson 122–23); cf. Patterson, *Works* 6:111–49.

98. *From vertue, which is reason:* one of Milton's "most connotative ellipses" (Burke 219). Cf. Cicero, "For virtue is reason completely developed" (*De Legibus* 1.16.45) and also *DocCh* 1.2, where Milton equates conscience with "right reason" (Patterson, *Works* 14:29), an equation that Babb, citing Willey, relates to general seventeenth century thinking that reason (understanding plus will) is "the godlike principle in man...the principle of moral control rather than of intellectual enlightenment" (46); see Willey 239. Todd quotes from *HistBr:* "But when God hath decreed servitude on a sinful Nation, fitted by thir own vices for no condition but servile, all Estates of Government are alike unable to avoid it" (Patterson, *Works* 10:198).

99. *annext:* "added, attached, or appended as subordinate or supplementary; subjoined; rendered subject" (so *OED* 2).

101–04. This passage recounts Noah's cursing of Ham, the father of Canaan, after Ham had willfully seen Noah's nakedness (Gen. 9:25). Bentley wants to change the past tense to present in 102 (*builds*) and 103 (*hears*); Pearce counters that Adam had seen the ark built in the preceding book, and that the cursing of Ham was antecedent to the present subject. Peck (*New Memoirs* 197) cites book 3 of the spurious *Antiquities* of "Berosus," published by Giovanni Nanni (1432?–1502), that Ham hated Noah and rendered him sterile by a magic spell while he slept; cf. "Berosus," *Antiquities* 80 and also **12.640**. Thyer (in Newton) points out that Adam is told, impossibly, as though he knew the story. Douady claims that God carefully preserves some "leaven"—i.e., the Old Testament metaphor for sin—by including a denatured son among those saved from the Flood (202). Cf. Milton's note in *DocCh* 1.11 that even just men have not thought it evil to curse the offspring of offenses against themselves (Maurice Kelley 147; Patterson, *Works* 15:191).

As Shumaker notes, here and in *PL* 12.158–59 ("See where it flows") and 342–43 ("whose high Walls thou sawst"), Adam cannot in fact now see; his eyes were preternaturally open in book 11 but failed at the beginning of book 12, and it may be that the visions are produced directly by God or the Son and that Michael himself learns the future only as he sees it (*Unpremeditated Verse* 218–19).

103. *heard this heavie curse:* Gen. 9:25. Tonson (in Todd) first had *his heavie curse,* and was followed by Tickell, Fenton, and Bentley. William Aldis Wright also has *his* instead of *this.*

heavie: "hard to bear, endure, or withstand; oppressive, grievous, sore; distressful" (so *OED* 23).

104. *vitious Race:* probably a reference to Horace's *progenium vitiosiorem* (Le Comte; see Horace, *Carmina* 3.6.48).

105–16. "The banal denunciation is unworthy of Michael and of the poem" (Martz 158–59).

105–06. *this latter…World…from bad to worse:* as demonstrated by Nimrod and Babel, "this new world rapidly loses its pastoral simplicity" (MacCallum, "Milton and Sacred History" 152). Reesing identifies the "summary" rhythms of these two lines as "disgusted, perhaps even bored," a tone caused by the disheartening story of Nimrod and its implications (95); see **11.1**.

from bad to worse: proverbial (so *OED* B3c).

106–09. Nearly a literal translation from Euripides' *Hippolytus* 938–42 (Todd). Cf. Horace, *Odes* 3.6.46–48, which claims that each succeeding generation is more vitiated. Hughes (*Paradise Lost*) finds the Horatian reference "vague at best," but does assert that Milton was undoubtedly influenced by the classical tradition of the world's degeneration as well as by the Bible's in his "pessimistic" view of history. Patrick links this passage to the offspring of Spenser's Errour (*Faerie Queene* 1.1.15): "in both Spenser's and Milton's allegories, the progeny of Sin feed upon Sin—that is, the fruits of sin lead simply to more extensive and greater sin, as Michael affirms in his brief explanation of man's future history" (39–40).

107.   *Wearied with their iniquities, withdraw:* very possibly a composite of Isa. 43:24 ("thou hast wearied me with thine iniquities") and Hosea 5:6 ("he hath withdrawn himself from them"). See also Acts 14:16 ("Who in times past suffered all nations to walk in their own ways"). Douady sees a link with God's abandoning the wicked to the Flood, which God will not repeat, possibly because he is afraid of not being able to master it (203).

    Wearied: "to tire the patience of; to affect with tedium or ennui; to satiate" (so *OED* II 5).

108.   *avert / His holy Eyes:* Dunster (in Todd) cites Hab. 1:13 ("Thou art of purer eyes than to behold evil") and Ps. 5:5 ("The foolish shall not stand in thy sight: thou hatest all workers of iniquity").

111–13.   *one peculiar Nation to select:* cf. Exod. 19:5, Deut. 14:2, 26:18, and Ps. 135:4 for the references to Israel being God's special or "peculiar" people. For the distinction between the ancient election of a whole people versus the later eternal predestination of an individual, cf. *DocCh* 1.4: "I do not understand by the term election that general or national election, by which God chose the whole nation of Israel for his own people" (Maurice Kelley 83; Patterson, *Works* 14:97–99); cf. also 12.214–15. Hughes (*Paradise Lost, A Poem*) claims that Milton thus rejects the doctrine of election, but Fowler argues that what Milton rejects is the doctrine of reprobation, or the predetermined damnation of an individual. The Messiah was to descend from Abraham; both Milton and his Old Testament source text focus from this point on Abraham's family and the eventual nation produced from the offspring of Abraham's grandson Jacob. From the calling of Abraham, subsequent figures are selected for the historical or prophetic roles they will play in preparing the way for the Redeemer, who will release humankind from the thralldom of the Seven Deadly Sins (Fox 193). Reesing (85) argues that despite the outward dullness of passages about the merely human, book 12 is full of passages about supernal grace, beginning here; see also 120–26, 147–48, 170–72, 200–05, 208–10, 227–28, 245–48, 307–14, 324–30, 345–47, 358–71, 419–35, 450, 458–65, 485–502, 539–51.

113. *A Nation from one faithful man:* i.e., Abraham. Cf. Gen. 12:2, where he is still Abram. The various "men of faith" (Abel, Enoch, Noah, Abraham) prefigure Christ by their qualities or actions (MacCallum, "Milton and Sacred History" 158); see *PL* 11.459–60, 701, 808–18. Muldrow identifies Abraham's call as the first episode important to the recovery of true liberty (93). See the comment on human perfectibility in **11.681**.

114. *on this side Euphrates yet residing:* see **12.129–31**. Bentley wants "*then* residing," but Pearce argues that the "yet" was when God elected Abraham's descendants. "The word *'ibrī*, whence *Hebrew*, which was first used of Abraham (Gen. 14:13), signifies 'living across,' i.e. across, or east of, the Euphrates" (Verity). *Hebrew* was the term applied by Canaanites to Jewish immigrants into Canaan. Weidner claims that since Adam is being told this in Eden, which is "eastward," "this side" means "east side." The "clear Euphrates" is one of the venues cited by William Mason in a 1747 poem commending Milton (Good 71). Cf. Josh. 24:3: "I took your father Abraham from the other side of the flood."

115–20. The unreliable Lauder accuses Milton of taking this passage from Du Bartas's more diffuse outburst on the corruption of Seth's line (1:400–01.725–34); see **11.388–411**. Hartwell (122–23) finds similarities between this passage and Lactantius's *Divinae Institutiones* 1.5, which includes the complaint that men prefer the dead to the true and living God. Reesing identifies this passionate outburst as *allegro* (96); see **11.1–21**.

115. *Bred up in Idol-worship:* cf. Josh. 24:2 on the idol worship of Abraham's father, and in the Apocrypha also Jth. 5:6–8, which traces the Israelites back to Chaldeans who were expelled from Mesopotamia because they would not worship idols. St. Maur claims that the Chaldeans of Ur (Hebrew, "light") worshiped the sun or fire, and that this worship was the earliest form of idolatry, "worshiping the hosts of heaven," which preceded worshiping demons, heroes, images, and other false objects of veneration (414). Cf. *DocCh* 1.17, specifying that Abraham was an idolater when called by God (Maurice Kelley 166–67; Patterson, *Works* 15:351). McColley traces Milton's emphasis on idol worship to various contemporary Bible commentaries ("*Paradise Lost*" 231) and also claims (*Paradise Lost* 197) that Du Bartas made idolatry a form of tyranny "in keeping with Protestant tradition."

116–19. *grown…Stone:* one of the 52 instances of rhyming lines with two intervening non-rhyming lines (Diekhoff, "Rhyme" 541–42); see Purcell for additional instances (172).

117. *While yet the Patriark liv'd who scap'd the Flood:* Bentley emends to "While yet the Patriarch *lives,* who *scapes* the Flood." According to Gen. 9:28, Noah lived 350 years after the Flood, and Abram, according to the genealogy in Gen. 11:10–26, was born only 292 years after, though Pearce claims that at the time being discussed, Noah was dead and his actions were in the past. Newton cites Jewish legend that Terah, his father Nachor, and his grandfather Serug made statues of idols as a profession.
    scap'd the Flood: cf. 1.239.

118–20. Cf. the attack on idol worship in Isa. 37:19 and also the more general biblical criticism of idolatry as illogical, since its adherents worship unresponsive natural materials (e.g., Deut. 4:28; 2 Kings 19:18; Isa. 40:18–20, 44:9–20, 46:6–7; Jer. 2:27, 10:14, 51:17; Hab. 2:18–19; Acts 17:29; 1 Cor. 8:4), like the "Stocks and Stones" of *Sonn 18*, 4. Cf. Mammon's suggestion in *PL* 2.229–83 that human skill with gems and gold from the soil can raise men's own magnificence (Champion 392); cf. **11.446–47.**

118. *the living God:* a common biblical phrase, occurring in KJV 30 times from Deut. to Rev. (e.g., 1 Sam. 17:26, Isa. 37:4, Matt. 16:16, 1 Tim. 4:10, Heb. 3:12), and also *SA* 1140.

120–26. One of the passages about supernal grace identified by Reesing; see **12.111–13.** Lieb (*Dialectics* 215), who traces the "concept of generation" in the poem, argues that since Abraham turns away from an alien world and leaves his *Fathers house* to a land where God *from him will raise / A mightie Nation* in whom *All Nations shall be blest,* he stands as a type of Christ, a role also played by Noah; see **12.3.**

120. *most High:* the name of God used by the priest-king Melchizedek when he blesses Abraham (Gen. 14:19). It is also used by Milton when God translates Enoch (*PL* 11.705) and to describe the Father of the prophesied redeemer (12.369, 382).

121. *To call by Vision:* cf. Acts 7:2 ("The God of glory appeared unto our father Abraham"); God's message is recorded in Gen. 12:1–3. Verity asserts that visions were thought to be the highest form of revelation.

123–26. *raise . . . obeys:* one of the 52 instances of rhyming lines with two intervening non-rhyming lines (Diekhoff, "Rhyme" 541–42); see Purcell for additional instances (172).

   raise: "to bring into existence, to produce, beget (offspring)" (so *OED* 9a, now rare).

125–26. *in his Seed / All Nations shall be blest:* Milton conflates Abraham's promised seed with the promised seed of the woman. Cf. Gen. 3:15 and 12:3, and also *PL* 12.148–50, 273, and 450.

126–34. *he straight obeys, / Not knowing to what Land, yet firm believes:* a restatement of Heb. 11:8: "By faith Abraham, when he was called to go out into a place which he should after receive for an inheritance, obeyed; and he went out, not knowing whither he went." Abraham displays the very faith that Adam must also display (Pecheux, "Abraham" 367). Fish demonstrates how Milton's restatement of Heb. 11:8 emphasizes both definiteness and provisionality, the curious blend of which Milton sees as heroic (200–01). Reesing claims *he straight obeys* regains a fast tempo after the climax and grandeur of 124–26 (96); see **11.1–21**.

126. *he:* 1667 *hee.*

128–51. Milton's insistence on detail here implies Adam's strong curiosity and Michael's own interest, and "the lack of urgency in sound, metrics, and diction is partly compensated by syntactical stress" (Shumaker, *Unpremeditated Verse* 220–21).

128–43. Martz cites this passage as an example of his disappointment with books 11–12: "the writing has become, at its worse, the biblical paraphrase of an almost ordinary versifier" (142).

128. *I see him, but thou canst not:* Milton may be alluding to the biblical definition of faith as the "evidence of things not seen" (Heb. 11:1). This part of the narration is particularly lively, because "The Angel is described as seeing the Patriarch actually traveling towards the Land of Promise" (Addison, *Spectator* 3 [3 May 1712]: 387). This phrase varies and enlivens the narration, and also appropriately honors Abraham by bringing him as it were before our eyes (Richardsons). Thyer (in Marchant) points out additionally that Michael's seeing the vision is yet a third method of narrative. Dunster (in Todd) first calls attention to Oberon's similar wording: "I saw, (but thou couldst not)" (*Midsummer Night's Dream* 2.1.155). Here and in 11.377, Sister Margaret Teresa Kelley sees a suggestion of the intuitive, angelic mode of reasoning with which Dante invested Cacciaguida and Beatrice in *Paradiso* (116). Lewalski (31–32) finds Michael intimating that Adam must now rely entirely on faith rather than sight; he cannot see Abraham because the covenant of grace goes beyond the partial restoration of the Law of Nature, a point also suggested by Augustine's declaration that with Abraham the divine promises fulfilled in Christ are more fully revealed; cf. Augustine, *City of God* 16.12 and also **11.368**.

129–31. Cf. Gen. 11:31. Keightley complains that Milton has Abram called in Ur, when it was apparently in Haran, and thinks that Milton may have been fooled by the pluperfect tense instead of the perfect in Gen. 12:1, though various commentators have thought that Terah responded to Abram's call by traveling at least as far as Haran. Gilbert (*Geographical Dictionary* 306) reports that Ur of the Chaldees, both now and in Milton's time, though usually placed on the west bank of the Euphrates below Babylon, has also been identified with the Greek city of Edessa in Mesopotamia. Such a location would agree with Acts 7:2, where Abraham is said to have dwelt beyond the river before he dwelled in Haran, and seems to be accepted above in 12.114 ("on this side Euphrates"), i.e., on the eastern side near the garden. But in this passage, Abraham passes the ford to Haran, which would not have been possible were Ur on the east bank of the Euphrates, where Haran is. Were Ur on the west bank, Abraham would have crossed the Euphrates on his way north, as is represented by Ortelius on his map of Abraham's journeys. Milton may have written first with one site in mind, then the other. Dunster (in Todd) believes that Milton followed the *Geographia Sacra* of Bochart (1651), in which Haran lies directly in the route from Ur of the Chaldees, on the west side of the river Chebar. Milton implies that Abraham's journey was continuous, only stopping in Haran, whereas the Bible indicates he lived there for some time (Verity); see Gen. 11:31, Acts 7:4. McColley notes that the place where God called Abraham was also a matter of controversy in Milton's time ("*Paradise Lost*" 231n245).

132–36. The migration in Gen. 12:5–6 is traced below Ortelius's large map of Canaan in a diagram called *Abrahami Patriarchae Peregrinatio et Vita* (i.e., The Wanderings and Life of Abraham the Patriarch) showing *Sechem,* where Abraham first camped in Canaan, lying between Mts. Ebal and Gerizim, and also showing the plain of *Moreh* (Hughes, *Paradise Lost, A Poem*).

132. *numerous servitude:* i.e., many servants. "Slaves or servants collectively" (so *OED* 1e, obsolete). Several early commentators note this figure of speech as the abstract for the concrete. Peter cites it as an example of Milton's marked tendency toward personification (139).

133. *Not wandring poor:* cf. the possessions described in Gen. 12:5. Abraham is not wandering precisely because he has faith in God, even though he is going into the unknown, as Adam must also do (Pecheux, "Abraham" 367). See Fish's comments in **11.281**.

134. *With God, who call'd him, in a land unknown:* as usual, Bentley wants *calls* to remove the past tense of a future vision, and he also substitutes "*to* a land." Pearce finds neither change justified, since Abraham trusted God *after* being called, and trusted him in an unknown land.

135–51. Fowler, arguing for a numerological underpinning to *PL,* remarks that nine places are named in this passage, nine being the "uncorruptible number of heavenly things"; he asserts that the Jordan is in the eighth position because eight is the number of baptism and regeneration and reasons that *Hermon* (12.142) occupies "the central position of sovereignty" because of its connection with King Solomon, as in Song of Sol. 4:8.

135–37. *his Tents / Pitcht about Sechem, and the neighbouring Plaine / Of Moreh:* cf. Gen. 12:6, "Abram passed through the land unto the place of Sichem, unto the plain of Moreh." Sichem (Sechem in the Vulgate) is modern Nablus, located on the central plain 30 miles north of Jerusalem.

138. *Gift to his Progenie of all that Land:* Gen. 12:7.

139–46. Milton also surveys Canaan in *PL* 3.536–38, but this survey is the more elaborate, seeming to conflate such various scriptures as Num. 34:1–15,

Deut. 34:1–4, Josh. 13:1–33, 1 Kings 8:65, and Ezek. 47:13–21 (Gilbert, *Geographical Dictionary* 71). "A more exact account of the boundaries of the promised land we shall hardly find in any prose author, than our poet has given us here in verse" (Newton). Wesley omits this passage.

139. *Hamath:* a city of Syria on the River Orontes, frequently identifying the northern boundary of the land of Israel, as in 1 Kings 8:65, mistakenly identified by Thomas Fuller and Samuel Bochart (in Gilbert, *Geographical Dictionary*) as Antioch. See also Josh. 13:5, where God promises to drive out all the inhabitants "under Mount Hermon unto the entering into Hamath" (Hughes, *Paradise Lost: A Poem*). Verity identifies Milton's *Desert South* as the "wilderness of Zin" of Num. 34:3, part of the southern border of Israel.

140. *(Things by thir names I call, though yet unnam'd):* Addison guesses that Virgil's vision in *Aeneid* 6 probably suggested this entire episode to Milton (*Spectator* 3 [3 May 1712]: 387); cf. *Aeneid* 6.776: "Haec tum nomina erat, nunc sunt sine nomine terrae" (These were then their names, when lands [were] without name). Newton (61–62) reports—in advance of Lauder and with none of Lauder's horror—that the same passage shows up in Grotius's *Adamus Exul:* "Innominata quaeque nominibus suis, / Libet vocare propriis vocabulis" (It is permitted to call unnamed things by their names, properly designated). On Lauder's impostures, see **11.388–411.** In contrast to the multiplicity of names after the Fall, the names in the garden were genus or species designated according to their natures; we can now know the world only in fragments and experience its details rather than its wholeness (Ferry, *Milton's Epic Voice* 76).

141–59. Just as Abraham lived "in a strange country" (Heb. 11:9), viewing God's promises "afar off" (Heb. 11:13), so Adam is here allowed to see afar off the great symbolic Old Testament places (Lewalski 32); see also **11.368.**

141–42. *Hermon:* i.e., Mt. Hermon, also known as Senir or Shenir (Deut. 3:9); the multiple names may explain why the maps of Milton's time show it as a long chain rather than a single peak (Gilbert, *Geographical Dictionary* 142), though Hughes (*Paradise Lost*) still claims it to be "really a ridge of mountains." It was the highest mountain in ancient Israel, now on the Lebanon-Syria border. As a boundary line of the Israelites, cf. Josh. 13:5–6.

Hermon East: i.e., Hermon located in the east.

141. *the great Western Sea:* i.e., the Mediterranean. Cf. the "great sea" of Num. 34:6.

143–44. *on the shoare / Mount Carmel:* a hilly promontory breaking the northeast coast of Israel. The *shoare* may refer to "Carmel by the sea" of Jer. 46:18 (Gilbert, *Geographical Dictionary* 74). Since the Jeremiah context is the swearing of an oath ("Surely as...Carmel [is] by the sea, so shall he come"), the "very landscape is prophetic of deliverance" (Fowler).

143. *as I point them:* "in all his panoramic views, Milton is most careful to establish a clear perspective: the places are not only visualized, but visualized from one particular standpoint" (Fowler).

144–45. *the double-founted stream / Jordan:* Newton and others report the common misunderstanding that the River Jordan rose from two sources, called Jor and Dan, at the foot of Mt. Libanus, also noting more accurately that the Bible made clear distinctions between the promised land of Canaan and those additional lands east of the Jordan. Sandys's *Travels*, cited by R. C. Browne (1877), includes this mistaken geography at the beginning of book 3, where the holy land is described as being "watered by many Springs and Torrents, but not many Rivers: Jordan the prince of the rest; seeming to arise from Jor and Dan, two not far distant Fountains. But he fetcheth his birth from Phiala, a round deepe well an hundred and twenty furlongs off; and passing under the earth ascendeth at the places aforesaid" (141). Purchas also includes the error (1:1630), as does Du Bartas, who refers to the Jordan in terms of "the Cristall of his double source" (1:174.67). Keightley identifies the streams or fountains as "the one named that of Hasbany near Hasbeiya, about twenty miles north of Baneas or Caesarea Philippi; the other the fountain of Tell-il-Kadi, sixteen or eighteen miles south of that of Hasbany, by the site of the ancient city of Dan," for which his source is surely the long topographical description of "The River Jordan" and "Lake Huleh" in Kitto's *Scripture Lands* (108–12), also cited by Montgomery. Verity's long note is instructive:

double-founted; probably an allusion to the old belief that the Jordan, in its upper course, was formed by the union of two streams thought to give the river its name; these were the *Dan* and the *Jor,* and their supposed place of confluence lay near Caesarea Philippi. In reality, *Jordan* is from a Heb. root "to flow down, descend," and the sources of the river must be looked for in the water-shed of Libanus on the one hand, and of Mt. Hermon on the other. Sylvester, however, had mentioned its "double source." . . .

Probably Sandys was Milton's main authority for the topography of Palestine. His *Travels,* first published in 1615, were very popular, often reprinted, and often quoted. They contain a vivid and detailed account of the holy land. Milton mentions Sandys in *Of Reformation in England* (Patterson, *Works* 3:22), and borrowed from him (almost certainly) the account of the rites of Moloch in the Nativity Ode 204–10, and *Paradise Lost* 1.392–96; and there is reason for thinking that in *Samson Agonistes* the description of the amphitheatre in which the catastrophe of the play occurs was inspired by a passage of the same writer. It is quite likely therefore that Sandys was responsible for *double-founted* here.

For Sandys in *Ref,* see Patterson, *Works* 3:22.

Hughes (*Paradise Lost*) traces the Jor/Dan confusion to Jerome's commentary on Gen. 14:14, that is, in *Liber Hebraicarum quaestionum in Genesim:* "*Dan* autem unus e fontibus est Jordanis. Nam et alter vocatur *Jor,* quod interpretatur ῥεῖθρον: id est, *rivus.* Duobus ergo fontibus, qui haud procul a se distant, in unum rivulum foederatis, *Jordanis* deinceps appellatur" (Dan is also one of the fountains from which is the Jordan, and the other is called Jor, which is translated *rheithron,* that is, *stream.* Thus, these two fountains, located not far from each other, are called by the name *Jordan* after they flow together) (Migne, *Patrologiae . . . Latina* 23:960–61). Starnes and Talbert claim that Milton's source for the phrase *double-founted* is the *duobus fontibus* in Renaissance dictionaries by Calepine and by Charles Stephanus (323).

145. *true limit Eastward:* although by special arrangement the tribes of Reuben and Gad along with the half-tribe of Manasseh settled east of the Jordan (Num. 32:1–32), the north-south flowing Jordan is listed as the eastern boundary of the holy land in Num. 34:12 and elsewhere.

146. *Senir, that long ridge of Hills:* cf. 1 Chron. 5:23. Maps of Milton's time identified Senir as a long mountainous ridge on the south side of the Dead Sea, about 46 miles from Jerusalem (cf. St. Maur 417), but *Senir* is the Amorite name for Mt. Hermon, the highest mountain of Palestine (Gilbert, *Geographical Dictionary* 142), and identified as such in Deut. 3:9, although the phrasing of the larger context, "the land that was on this side Jordan, from the river of Arnon unto mount Hermon: (Which Hermon the Sidonians call Sirion; and the Amorites call it Shenir)" (3.8–9), may have indicated that the name was attached to the region as well. Cf. 1 Chron. 5:23.

147–51. *This ponder:* in keeping with Michael's shift from vision to narration, the importance issue is the spiritual significance of the relation rather than its geographical details (Summers, *Muse's Method* 211). "The promise to Abraham (Gen. 12:1–3) renews the promise implicit in the curse on the serpent" (Fowler).

147–48. One of the passages about supernal grace identified by Reesing; see **12.111–13**.

148–50. *Shall in his Seed be blessed … Plainlier shall be reveald:* cf. not only Gen. 12:3 but also Gal. 3:16, which insists upon the singular number of "seed." Milton links Abraham's seed with the woman's "seed" promised in Gen. 3:15, which is frequently repeated in Michael's narration; see **11.115–16**. Abraham's seed is also mentioned in 12.125–26, 273, and 450.

   Plainlier: without Michael's help Adam has already discovered that a deliverer shall be born (Parish, "Milton" 245). Cf. *DocCh* 1:27: "The Gospel [was] announced first obscurely, by Moses and the prophets, afterwards in the clearest terms by Christ himself" (Maurice Kelley 175; Patterson, *Works* 16:113).

149. *deliverer:* "one who sets free or releases; a liberator, rescuer, saviour" (so *OED* 1).

150. *anon:* see **11.433**.

152. *faithful Abraham due time shall call:* cf. Gal. 3:9: "They which be of faith are blessed with faithful Abraham." His original name, *Abram*, means "high or exalted father" (Strong), while *Abraham* means "father of a multitude," as also noted in the KJV gloss. Since Bentley assumes that "Abraham" would always be pronounced as two syllables, as in 12.260, 268, 273, 328, and 449, he emends this line to "Whom faithful Abraham *future* time shall call," but Pearce believes that Milton here intended to stress the additional syllable God had added to Abraham's name.

153. *A Son, and of his Son a Grand-childe:* i.e., Isaac (Gen. 21:3) and Jacob (Gen. 25:26), later Israel (Gen. 32:28), the father of Jacob and Jacob's elder brother Esau (Gen. 25:20–26). Hughes (*Paradise Lost*) points out that Milton begins summarizing the Bible record here.

154. *Like him in faith, in wisdome, and renown:* on human perfectibility, see **11.681**.

155–63. *with twelve Sons increast:* the Richardsons claim this phrase is a Latinism similar to Plautus, *Truculentus* 2.6.35, "Cumque es Aucta liberis" (since you are blessed [*aucta,* increased] with offspring), and also refer to Tacitus, *Life of Agricola* 6.3, "auctus est...filia" (a daughter...added). The births of Jacob's 12 sons (Reuben, Simeon, Levi, Judah, Dan, Naphtali, Gad, Asher, Issachar, Zebulon, Joseph, and Benjamin) and his daughter Dinah are related in Gen. 29:31–30:24, and 35:16–18. Martz complains that "the principle of God's goodness has now become an abstract test of faith; for the chosen few, it seems, no demonstration of that goodness is needed" (160).

155–57. *departs / From Canaan, to...Egypt:* this move is recounted in Gen. 46:5–7.

157–59. *Egypt, divided by the River Nile:* Milton's numerous references to Egypt are almost all dependent on the Bible and mostly celebrate the Hebrews' miraculous delivery from slavery (Gilbert, *Geographical Dictionary* 111). In *PL* see also 1.399, 421, 480, 488, 721; 3.537; 4.171; 5.274; 9.443; 12.182, 190, 219. Broadbent complains that this line of verse is one of the worst in English, and that in book 12 Milton is striving "to assert by dogma truths that need subtler substantiation" (*Some Graver Subject* 279–80).

disgorging at seaven mouthes / Into the Sea: see **12.191**. The seven mouths were famous even in antiquity, as in *Aeneid* 6.800 and *Metamorphoses* 1.422–23 and 2.256; Milton refers to them in the second draft of *LetFr* (Patterson, *Works* 12:325). Milton's contemporary Fuller called the Nile the "septemfluous river." Milton puts its headwaters in Ethiopia, at Mt. Amara (Gilbert, *Geographical Dictionary* 208). Fowler, arguing for a numerological underpinning to *PL*, asserts that seven is the number of mortality and mutability, in contrast to the nine places of the promised land; a frequent opposition between seven and nine parallels the traditional contrast between Egypt (fleshly, sinful) and the promised land (spiritual, regenerate).

disgorging: in the absolute sense, "to discharge as if from a mouth; to empty forth" (so *OED* 1b, c).

158–59. *See where it flows:* on Adam's vision, see **12.101–04**.

159–216. The reader's response to the Exodus is conditioned by Milton's earlier description, with its cluster of similes, of Satan's rallying his defeated legions in book 1 (Fish 313–15).

160. *invited by a yonger Son:* i.e., Joseph (Gen. 45:9).

162–63. *second in that Realme / Of Pharao:* cf. Gen. 41:40, "Only in the throne will I be greater than thou" and 41:43, where Pharaoh "made him to ride in the second chariot."

163–64. *his Race / Growing into a Nation:* as St. Maur (418) notes, the "seventy souls" who went into Egypt increased to a nation whose adult males alone numbered 603, 550. See Gen. 46:27, Exod. 1:5, and Deut. 20:22.

163. *there he dies:* Gen. 50:26.

165–74. Cf. Exod. 1:8–22. *King* = Pharaoh, ruler of Egypt. The new Pharaoh, like Nimrod, is a tyrant, who ignores God's institution of human freedom

(Muldrow 94). Both Pharaoh and Nimrod are types of Satan, to whom Adam and Eve were in bondage through their sin (Shawcross, "*Paradise Lost*" 11, 25n13; cf. Whaler, "Miltonic Simile" 1047). The only affective words from 165 to 172 are *Inhospitably* and *With glory and spoile;* the latter praise of conquest is "careless"; Milton's condemnation of the tyrant may be an attempt to "retrace his steps" (Shumaker, *Unpremeditated Verse* 221).

165. *Suspected to:* "mistrusted by" (so *OED* 1b, obsolete). The phrase is a Latinism (Montgomery).

sequent: "that succeeds or is subsequent in time or serial order" (so *OED* 1b, now rare). Wesley glosses as "following."

166. *inmate:* "dwelling in the same house with, or in the house of, another" (so *OED* 2b, obsolete).

168. *Inhospitably, and:* Johnson lists this vowel elision among those "vicious" because the vowel is strongly sounded and thus makes "a full and audible syllable" (*Rambler* 4 [19 Jan. 1751]: 103).

169–70. (*those two brethren call / Moses and Aaron*): cf. the birth narrative (Exod. 2:1–10) and genealogy (Exod. 6:20). The present-tense immediacy of this parenthesis "gives the sense of calling history into being" (Brisman 278).

170–72. One of the passages about supernal grace identified by Reesing; see **12.111–13**.

Muldrow, stressing the recovery of true liberty in book 12, underscores the two episodes Milton chooses from Moses' life—leading the Jewish people out of captivity and receiving the "schoolmaster" law on Sinai (94).

171–72. *they return / With glory and spoile:* cf. Gen. 15:14 and Exod. 12:36. Hughes (*Paradise Lost; Paradise Lost: A Poem*) complains that the Israelites' spoiling of the Egyptians was a "rather dubious trick," and Fowler similarly complains that they were "extorted as a 'loan'" when the Egyptians were anxious to see the Israelites leave as soon as possible. One might remember, however, that the Israelites were subjected by the Egyptians to both slavery and genocide (Exod. 1:8–16). MacCallum asserts that the basic pattern in *PL* 12 is that "we are first shown a moment of triumph, and then led back in time to a survey of the trials which preceded it," demonstrating this pattern with the Exodus narrative ("Milton and Sacred History" 166–67). Shawcross, identifying Michael as a Christianized form of Hermes, the conductor of the dead, argues that Michael likewise leads people out on their journey toward God at the expulsion (*"Paradise Lost"* 14).

173–74. *denies / To know:* a Latinism for "refuses to acknowledge" (Montgomery); cf. *OED* 5 for *deny,* "to refuse or withhold (anything asked for, claimed, or desired)." Cf. e.g., Exod. 5:2: "And Pharaoh said, Who is the LORD, that I should obey his voice to let Israel go? I know not the LORD, neither will I let Israel go."

176–90. Milton names in summary all the ten plagues directed by Moses onto Egypt (Exod. 7:19–12:30). Hume claims that the first miracle (blood) refers to the earlier drowning of Hebrew babies in the Nile. Reesing (97) identifies these lines as a "superb *bravura* passage," since all ten plagues are included in "one single overwhelming sentence" that moreover steadily picks up speed and volume through 188 and then pauses emphatically on the final plague; see **11.1–21.** "God sends signs and judgments to Pharaoh...just as Satan is shown a sign in the sky after he is found at the ear of Eve" (Shawcross, *"Paradise Lost"* 11; cf. 4.995–1004). Martz, who complains of a decrease in poetic power and decorum in the last two books, nevertheless finds Milton's descriptions of sin to be potent, as here (160).

177. *must all his Palace fill:* Bentley, assuming Milton would not have *fill* two lines in a row, changes this one to *foul.* Cf. Exod. 8:3, which specifies that the frogs will come into Pharaoh's house, bedchamber, bed, ovens, and even kneading troughs.

178. *loath'd:* "that is an object of loathing or disgust; utterly disliked, abhorred, detested" (so *OED*).
     intrusion: Wesley glosses as "thrusting in."

179–82. *die...Skie:* one of the 52 instances of rhyming lines with two intervening nonrhyming lines (Diekhoff, "Rhyme" 541–42); see Purcell for additional instances (172).

179. *Rot:* "a virulent disease affecting the liver of sheep which are fed on moist pasture-lands; inflammation of the liver caused by the fluke-worm, liver-rot" (so *OED* 2a).

Murren: cf. Exod. 9:3–6, and also *HistBr* 6.245: "The next year was calamitous, bringing strange fluxes upon men, and murren upon Cattel" (Patterson, *Works* 10:252–53).

180. *Botches and blaines must all his flesh imboss:* cf. the plague of boils in Exod. 9:8–12 and also perhaps the boils of Job 2:7–8.

Botches: "a boil, ulcer, or pimple" (so *OED* 2).

blaines: "an inflammatory swelling or sore on the surface of the body, often accompanied by ulceration; a blister, botch, pustule; applied also to the eruptions in some pestilential diseases" (so *OED* 1).

imboss: "to cause to bulge or swell out, make convex or protuberant; to cover with protuberances" (so *OED* 1). Masson glosses *imboss* as "cover with lumps or swellings (Fr. *bosse*, a lump, or swelling)," and repeats Todd's citation of Shakespeare's *King Lear* 2.4.224: "an embossed carbuncle." R. C. Browne (1894) renders *boss* as another form of *botch;* this edition also cites the "embossed sores" of *As You Like It* 2.7.67 but rejects "the poor cur is embossed" from *Taming of the Shrew*'s induction (1.17), saying the verb differs etymologically and refers rather to so driving a creature as to cause it to foam at the mouth; cf. *OED* v.² 3.

181–82. *Thunder mixt with Haile, / Haile mixt with fire:* cf. Exod. 9:22–26. Svendsen finds in this description a doubly ironic metaphor of demonic concord (*Milton and Science* 98–99).

must rend th'Egyptian Skie: cf. *Hamlet* 2.2.486–87, "the dreadful thunder / Doth rend the region [i.e., air]," and also the "Whirlwind and dire Hail" of *PL* 2.589.

rend: "used to denote the effect of sounds, esp. loud noises, on the air" (so *OED* 4b).

181. *And all his people:* Bentley emends to *people's.*

183. *wheel:* "to roll along like a wheel" (so *OED* 7, rare).

rouls: "to move or sweep along or up with a wave-like motion; to advance with undulating movement; to ascend or descend in rolls or curls" (so *OED* 17b).

185–88. *darksom Cloud of Locusts…three dayes:* cf. Exod. 10:12–15, 21–23. Cf. Du Bartas, "Then, the Thrice–Sacred with a sable Clowde / Of horned Locusts dooth the Sunne be-clowde" (2:560.533–34) and George Coffin Taylor, *Milton's Use* 120. See also the "pitchy cloud / Of Locusts" in *PL* 1.340–41 as well as **12.73** on other symmetries.

   darksom: "somewhat dark in shade or colour; sombre" (so *OED* 2).

   Locusts: "especially…the Migratory Locust, well known for its ravages in Asia and Africa, where, migrating in countless numbers, it frequently eats up the vegetation of whole districts" (so *OED* 1).

187–90. *bounds…wounds:* one of the 52 instances of rhyming lines with two intervening nonrhyming lines (Diekhoff, "Rhyme" 541–42); see Purcell for additional instances (172).

188–92. The death of Egypt's firstborn, the attendant institution of the Passover, and Israel's expulsion from Egypt are described at length in Exod. 11–12.

188. *Palpable darkness:* a paraphrase of Exod. 10:21, "darkness which may be felt"; Milton's phrasing may reflects the Vulgate's *tam densae ut palpari queant,* cited by Newton. Cf. *PL* 1.63 and 2.406. Todd also cites Drayton's line, "Darkenesse is now so palpable and much, / That as 't is seene, as easily is felt" (2.495–96) and Henry More's "palpable thick night" (3.32), as well as the "thick and palpable clouds of darkness" mentioned by the KJV translators in their dedicatory preface to King James.

191. *The River-dragon:* i.e., crocodile. Cf. Ezek. 29:3: "Pharaoh king of Egypt, the great dragon that lieth in the midst of his rivers." Himes (*Paradise Lost: A Poem*) sees a parallel with the seven-headed dragon of the Apocalypse, who casts out a flood of water from its mouth, since the Nile has "seaven mouthes" in 12.158. Verity notes that *dragon* (Vulgate *draco,* Septuagint δράκων) is the translation in several places of the Hebrew word *tannín,* applied to any monster, as in Job 7:12 (translated "whale") and Ps. 91:13 (translated "dragon"). This passage prefigures signs and judgments from the book of Revelation, since in *RCG* Milton connects "that huge dragon of Egypt" with the dragon of Revelation (MacCallum, "Milton and Sacred History" 157; Patterson, *Works* 3:275). The plagues of Egypt symbolize the judgment and ultimate destruction of Satan's "perverted world" (Summers, *Muse's Method* 211). Fish (36) sees the river-dragon metaphor as ultimately linked to the leviathan and falling leaves similes of 1.84–126 and 301–03. The crocodile "abounds in Egypt" (Wesley).

The: 1667 *This,* retained by Bentley. Grierson insists that the 1674 *The* is the version that every editor accepts or should accept (*Poems* 2:xl–xli); see **11.379–80**.

submits: "to yield so far as to do [something], consent to; occasionally, to condescend to" (so *OED* 2b, obsolete).

193–94. *as Ice / More hard'nd after thaw:* as predicted in Exod. 4:21, 7:3, and 14:4, Pharaoh's heart is repeatedly "hardened" (7:13, 14, 22; 8:15, 19, 32; 9:7, 12, 34, 35; 10:1, 20, 27; 11:10; 14:8). Cf. the hardness of the impenitent heart in Rom. 2:5, cited by Origen (Peck, *New Memoirs* 197–98). For the natural history metaphor, cf. Virgil's description of stiff, clinging ice (*Georgics* 3.366). Newton explains that "ice warmed gently into a thaw, is made more receptive of those saline and nitrous particles, which fill the freezing air, and insinuating themselves into the water already weakened, are the cause of a harder concretion." Keightley denies that this opinion of Milton's time is actually fact, whereas Whaler claims that Milton's simile is "uncannily prescient of twentieth-century research," but does not elaborate ("Miltonic Simile" 1069n28). Svendsen attributes an erroneous claim to both Fulke's *Meteors* and in Swan's *Speculum Mundi* (1635) that snow "melting on the high hilles, and after frozen againe, becommeth so hard, that it is a stone, and is called Christall" (*Milton and Science* 99). William Fulke (1538–89) first made the claim in *A Goodly Gallerye* (fol. 53v), a text that went through further editions and titles into the later seventeenth century, and Swan prefixed its repetition with "as some affirm" (*Speculum Mundi* 162), suggesting that the claim was already suspect. See also Broadbent's comments in **11.311–13**. Milton uses Pharaoh in *DocCh* 1.8 as an example of one whose heart was hardened (cf. Patterson, *Works* 15:71), as he does with Charles I in *Eikon:* "But whom God hard'ns, them also he blinds" (Patterson, *Works* 5:231).

196–98. A birth metaphor, since the sea is a female archetype (Shawcross, "*Paradise Lost*" 22).

196. *Swallows him with his host, but them lets pass:* cf. Exod. 14:23–31. Bentley objects that since the sea does not swallow the host until 213, this line should read, "*Receives* him with his Host." Pearce objects that the first mention is general, while the second supplies specific details; Bentley's reading also implies that Pharaoh hardened his heart only until he was in the sea bed.

197. *As on drie land between two christal walls:* the "waters" on either side are described as walls in Exod. 14:22, 29. Many commentators, including George Coffin Taylor (*Milton's Use* 123–24) have noted the influence of Sylvester's Du Bartas, where the same sea is referred to as "walls of cristall" (2:564.690); cf. the "Walls of Glass" in *Ps 136.* Fowler insists that the most important reference is the division of waters in Milton's account of creation, "Part rise in crystal wall" (7.293). See similar language in 1.227 and 6.860. A late nineteenth century commentator cites this passage as one proof that a primary source for Milton was Avitus ("Precursor" 50), though it is more likely that Milton and Avitus were both drawing from earlier sources; see also **11.860.** MacCallum, suggesting that the Egypt sequence prefigures the signs and judgments of the book of Revelation, compares the walls of crystal to the "sea of glass" of Rev. 4:6 and the river "clear as crystal" of Rev. 22:1 ("Milton and Sacred History" 156–57).

198–201. Wesley omits the first three lines, and modifies the last to read, "[God] present in his Angel, ~~who~~ [then] shall go."

198–99. *Aw'd by the rod of Moses so to stand / Divided:* cf. Exod. 14:16. Shawcross argues that Moses' rod is akin to Hermes' caduceus here and in *PL* 12.211–12 ("*Paradise Lost*" 12); see also **12.235–44.** This passage symbolizes justice and creative power; as the Nile "divided" Egypt in 12.157, so Moses' rod *Divided* the water (Fowler).

200–20. Shawcross compares Moses' leading the chosen people forth under God's guidance to the expulsion scene in 12.628–40 ("*Paradise Lost*" 15). Moses in the Red Sea, the Son in Creation, and Noah in the Flood all confront and conquer chaos to give new life, whereas when Satan in book 2 confronts Chaos to deliver his people from bondage, the result is finally illusory (Lieb, *Dialectics* 215).

200–05. One of the passages about supernal grace identified by Reesing; see **12.111–13.**

200. *Saint:* cf. 5.247. Verity points out Milton's fondness for this term. In St. Paul's epistles, the word identifies any believer, as in Phil. 4:21. Some Puritans in the sixteenth and seventeenth centuries so described themselves (*OED* 3a).

201–03. *Cloud…Pillar of Fire:* Exod. 13:21. Broadbent identifies this passage as Milton's most elaborate example of *antistrophe* (i.e., ending different lines with the same word or phrase); his anaphoristic phrases (i.e., those beginning with the same word or words) are always short ("Milton's Rhetoric" 242). On God lending his name to an angel rather than personally leading the Israelites, see *DocCh* 1.5, also noted by Maurice Kelley (88; Patterson, *Works* 14:289); cf. *PL* 12.259. B. A. Wright cites *Pillar of Fire* as an example of Milton's elision of unaccented vowels separated by *l, n,* or *r* (*Milton's Poems* xiv); Bridges identifies such elision as "the rule of R," and cites this instance as one example (29); see **12.332–34** and also **11.306–07**.

203. *Pillar:* 1667 *pillar.*

204–05. *and remove / Behinde them:* cf. Exod. 14:19: "And the angel of God, which went before the camp of Israel, removed and went behind them."

205. *th'obdurate:* stressed on the second syllable. Darbishire spells without the final *e*, claiming such Miltonic spelling indicated an unstressed final syllable after a stressed one (*Poetical Works* 1:xxix).

206–10. Wesley omits this passage.

207. *Darkness defends between:* Exod. 14:19–20. Newton glosses *defends* as "hinders, forbids," and commentators have cited such examples as Chaucer's lustful Wife of Bath denying that God ever "defended mariage" (*Wife of Bath's Prologue* 60). Fowler glosses the term as either "wards off, averts" (*OED* 1) or the obsolete "hinders" (*OED* 2). The term is prevalent in ancient laws and statutes (Todd). Cf. 11.86 and *PR* 2.370.

208–10. One of the passages about supernal grace identified by Reesing; see **12.111–13**.

209. *God looking forth will trouble all his Host:* a summary of Exod. 14:24–25. *trouble:* "to do harm or hurt to; to injure; to molest, oppress" (so *OED* 4).

210. *And craze thir Chariot wheels:* cf. Exod. 14:25, which has "took off their chariot wheels" and also *SA* 571, "sedentary numbness craze my limbs."

craze: "to break by concussion or violent pressure; to break in pieces or asunder; to shatter" (so *OED* 1). Milton's use, from French *écraser,* to break or bruise, expounds the biblical remark that the Egyptians drove their chariots "heavily" (Richardsons). Bible commentator John Gill reports that the Targum of Jonathan renders the verb in Exod. 14:25 as "cut" or "sawed off": "Milton seems to have a notion of Pharaoh's chariot wheels being broken, when he says, 'and craze' (i.e. break) 'their chariot wheels'; or, as Jarchi suggests, he burnt them, through the force of the fire or lightning." Cf. the "brok'n Chariot Wheels" of *PL* 1.311 and also Chaucer's "the pot was crased" (*Canon's Yeoman's Tale* 934); on other symmetries, see **12.73.**

Milton's extended treatment of the chariot is his own "and should be referred to the central image of the poem, the chariot of cosmic justice," as in *PL* 6.749–59 (Fowler).

211–13. Exod. 14:26–28. Cf. the same "potent Rod" in *PL* 1.338, and see **12.198–99** on other parallels. "Moses…His Potent Rod Extends" is one of four illustrations for book 12 in Tilt's 1843 illustrated edition of Milton's *Poetical Works* (C. H. C. Baker 116); see further lists of Tilt's illustrations in **11.187** and **12.1–5.**

212. *the Sea his rod obeys:* cf. Du Bartas on Moses at the Red Sea: "He smote the Sea with his dead-living Rod: / The sea obay'd" (1:564.682–83) and also Matt. 8:27 ("even the winds and the sea obey him!"), the reaction of Jesus' disciples to his stilling the storm.

213. *imbattelld:* "drawn up in battle array, marshalled for fight" (so *OED a*[1]1).

214–19. This route is explained in Exod. 13:17–18. Apparently Warburton (in Newton) thinks this passage refers to the later wandering of the Israelites, caused by the "poltron mutiny" of the disheartened spies (Num. 13–14); were Michael not comforting Adam, he might have gone into more detail, since "the story of the brazen serpent would have afforded noble imagery." Hughes (*Paradise Lost, A Poem*) points out that "the devious route of Israel during its thirty-eight years in the wilderness on the way to Canaan was clearly traced on contemporary maps," and Fowler cites Milton's comparison, in *Eikon,* of the civil war to the Israelites' wandering in the wilderness (Patterson, *Works* 5:288). On election, see **12.111–13**.

214. *overwhelm thir Warr:* "the apparatus of war is called war by the poets" (Richardsons). Cf. 6.712–13: "bring forth all my Warr, / My Bow and Thunder."

   Warr: "soldiers in fighting array" (so *OED* n¹6b, obsolete). Hughes (*Paradise Lost*) glosses as "army"; Ricks (*Paradise Lost*) has "troops."

215. *Safe towards Canaan from the shoar:* i.e., of the Red Sea. Although Milton's *toward* or *towards* (pronounced *too'-rd[s]* rather than the modern *t'ward[s]*) is usually monosyllabic, the pronunciation here is disyllabic; other exceptions are 8.257, 9.495, 12.296, and *SA* 682 (Bridges 22).

217. *allarmd:* Bush glosses as "roused to arms," and Ricks (*Paradise Lost*) as "armed." Cf. *alarm,* "to call to arms" (*OED* 1a, obsolete).

218. *Warr…inexpert:* Dunster (in Todd) identifies the phrase as classical, comparing the synonymous *bellis inexpertus* of Tacitus, *Historiae* 1.8.

219. *Return:* "to turn back; to force (one) to return to a place" (so *OED* v¹15b, rare).

220–22. Masson glosses as, "For life is more cared for by those who are not trained to military exercises, whether they are constitutionally noble or ignoble, than by those who are so trained—except in those cases where mere rashness may lead untrained men to risk their lives," and Verity as, "Noble men and ignoble alike—if untrained in arms—prefer life to freedom, except in cases where mere rashness transports them from their usual characters." Cf. Aristotle's discussion of courage, fear, and rashness in battle (*Nicomachean Ethics* 3.6–7). Himes (*Paradise Lost: A Poem*) cites the dead Achilles' preference for life even devoid of nobility (*Odyssey* 11.488–91). Cf. 2.255–57, 11.798–801, and *SA* 268–71.

223–26. Wesley omits the details of establishing the Jewish government in the desert.

224–25. *found / Thir government, and thir great Senate choose:* cf. Exod. 18:25–26, 24:1–9, and Num. 11:16–17. In his 1935 *Paradise Lost*, Hughes judges as "tenuous" the claim that the 70 elders were a "senate," but later in *Paradise Lost, A Poem*, Hughes seems to reverse himself: "Milton accepted the Seventy Elders as a divinely constituted Senate." Cf. Harrington 1: "Ancient prudence" (i.e., government by law rather than royal prerogative) was "first discovered to mankind by God himself, in the fabrick of the Commonwealth of Israel." In *REW*, Milton argues that commonwealths, governed by such senates as "the Sanhedrin, founded by Moses," are more stable than monarchies (Patterson, *Works* 6:128). Though talmudic tradition linked the Sanhedrin with Moses' 70 elders, some sources list the membership at 71 or 72. Verity sees a possible glance at Moses' initial delegation of authority at the advice of his father-in-law Jethro (Exod. 18:13–26). In Milton's time, "the Jewish constitution" was proposed fairly often as a model commonwealth, though by no means by all (Fowler). Hobbes "expressly repudiated the view of Moses as the institutor of a conciliar government" (Hughes, "Three Final Issues" 3.89n9; cf. *Leviathan* 3.40). The KJV rendering of Acts 5:21 refers to the Sanhedrin as "all the senate of the children of Israel," though Tyndale and Geneva both translate the original Greek *gerousia* as "elders"; Liddell and Scott supply both options in their initial definition, "Council of Elders, senate"; "elders" (teaching or ruling) also govern the church in Presbyterian ecclesiastical polity.

226. *by Laws ordaind:* cf. Milton's comment in *Educ* about "Law, and legall Justice; deliver'd first, and with best warrant by Moses" (Patterson, *Works* 4:285).

227–28. *Sinai, whose gray top / Shall tremble:* cf. Exod. 19:18, *Nat* 157–59, *PL* 11.73–75. One of the passages about supernal grace identified by Reesing; see **12.111–13**. Milton also mentions God's descent on Sinai in *DocCh* 1.2 (Maurice Kelley 117n84; Patterson, *Works* 14:61). Hume claims that gray (*canus*) is the usual Latin epithet for mountains, as in Virgil: "Gelidus canis cum montibus humor / Liquitur" (when the gray ice covering melts from mountains) (*Georgics* 1.43–44). The epithet was even more proper for Sinai when it was covered in fire and smoke (Newton). Verity thinks that *gray* may be merely an "epithet of adornment."

228. *he descending:* Bentley objects to the grammar and emends to "*him* descending." In his influential grammar, Lowth argues that Bentley's reasoning, based on an ablative case foreign to English, is itself in error (107). Citing Lowth, Todd argues that the "case absolute" in English is the nominative.

229. *loud Trumpets sound:* cf. 1.754. Verity writes the possessive as *trumpet's* in his edition, quoting John Bradshaw as his authority that the passage in Exodus requires the singular. Modern spelling can obscure some double syntax; *Trumpets* without an apostrophe may at first be felt as a verb (Fowler).

230–35. *sacrifice, informing them . . . of that destind Seed:* cf. "the Lamb slain from the foundation of the world" (Rev. 13:8). Jewish sacrificial laws are particularly detailed in Leviticus. Michael first hints here of how the Messiah will redeem humankind, though Adam overlooks the word *sacrifice* (Parish, "Milton" 245). The religious rite of sacrifice foreshadows later symbols of sacrifice by which humankind may be delivered (Stroup 45).

230. *Ordaine them Lawes:* cf. Moses' description of receiving the Ten Commandments in Deut. 5:22. Milton's thinking was limited to what he saw in the small presbyterian systems; "otherwise the true idea of the theocracy would have afforded some noble observations" (Warburton, in Newton). Greenwood (in Todd) infers that Milton did not include the Ten Commandments because they were ideally to be written in the heart of man, though given their solemn delivery on Sinai, he wishes Milton had included them anyway. Because Milton's sole object was to show how events led to Christ's appearance and kingdom, he needed to include from the Old Testament only what typified them; the unchanging moral law belongs to no one time or system (Stebbing). Douady accuses God of multiplying laws for the Machiavellian purpose of having "mille occasions de les prendre en faute" (a thousand occasions of finding fault) (204).

231–32. *informing them, by types / And shadows:* see **12.302–03** and also *DocCh* 1.14, "There was a promise made to all mankind, and an expectation of the Redeemer, more or less distinct, even from the time of the fall" (Maurice Kelley 159; Patterson, *Works* 15:257), and also *PL* 11.113–17. Sims (*Bible* 271) cites Gal. 3:16–22 and Heb. 8:4–7, both asserting typological readings of biblical history. Christians traditionally view Jewish ceremonial law as not literally binding on Christians but rather to be taken as an allegory of spiritual truths revealed in the Gospel (Northrop Frye, *Paradise Lost*).

    Shadows: "an obscure indication; a symbol, type; a prefiguration, foreshadowing" (so *OED* 6c).

    shadows: 1667 *shadowes.*

233–34. *of that destind Seed to bruise:* i.e., of that seed destined to bruise. For the oft-repeated promise of Gen. 3:15, see **11.115–16**.

234. *means:* 1667 *meanes.*

235–44. The people's terror at God's voice is related in Exod. 20:18–19 and extensively in Deut. 5:22–31; see also Heb. 12:18–21. Muldrow (94), who stresses the recovery of true liberty in the last book, points out how the foreshadowing rites represent *Mankinds deliverance;* cf. *DocCh* 1.15: "The name and office of mediator is in a certain sense ascribed to Moses, as a type of Christ" (Patterson, *Works* 15:287). The role of Moses is divided between Raphael (Hebrew, "the medicine of God") and Michael, who bears a rod similar to Hermes' caduceus because it becomes a snake when dashed to the ground (Shawcross, "*Paradise Lost*" 12); see also **12.198–99**. Ryken traces throughout the epic a motif of God as transcendent voice (151–52).

237–38. *That Moses might report…he grants what they besaught:* objecting to the tense, Bentley emends the relevant verbs to "*may* report" and "*beseech.*" Pearce reports that 1667 has "He grants *them thir desire*"; in any case, since the Israelites' request preceded this moment, the past tense is not inappropriate. Grierson insists that the 1674 reading for 238 is one that every editor accepts or should accept (*Poems* 2:xl–xli); see **11.379–80**.

239–40. *Instructed that to God is no access / Without Mediator:* Moses is an even better example than Abraham of the meaning and limitations of election; Moses and the Jews functioned to bring men, via the Law, to the fullness of a promise that they themselves could not enjoy (Fixler 232).

    access: B. A. Wright ("Note" 145) defines this noun as the obsolete "the action of coming to; coming into the presence; approach" (*OED* 10); see **11.46**.

240–42. *Mediator…Moses in figure beares:* "Christian commentators treated Moses as the first of the types of Christ as *Mediator,* mainly because Deut. 18:15 is quoted in Acts 3:22, 'For Moses truly said unto the fathers, A prophet shall the Lord your God raise up unto you of your brethren, like unto me'" (Hughes, *Paradise Lost: A Poem*). Cf. Gal. 3:19 and Heb. 9:19–26 on the mediation of Moses and also *DocCh* 1.15: "The name and office of mediator is in a certain sense also ascribed to Moses, as a type of Christ" (Maurice Kelley 161; Patterson, *Works* 15:287). Milton calls the Son "Mediator" in 10.60. On types, see **12.302–03.** Sprott elides and stresses the middle syllable of *Mediator,* in order to preserve the scansion, as an example of "elision by the synaoepha of vowels" (78, 80–81). Babb relates this passage (as well as 12.291 and 12.303) to the frequent doubling of images in *PL*—the forbidden tree, golden staircase, and bridge to hell are both symbols and physical realities (12). On human perfectibility, see **11.681.**

243. *all the Prophets:* cf. Acts 10:43: "To him give all the prophets witness."

244. *great Messiah:* cf. 5.691.
  Laws and Rites: Fowler cites their enumeration and subsequent typological gloss in Heb. 9:19–23.

245–48. One of the passages about supernal grace identified by Reesing; see **12.111–13.**

246–58. Wesley omits the details of the tabernacle, reducing this passage to a single line, "Obedient to his will. At length they come."

247. *set up his Tabernacle:* described in Exod. 25:8–9; cf. Milton's reference to the "Mercie-seat" in *PL* 11.2. *Tabernacle,* with its unstressed ending an unvoiced consonant after a stressed vowel, is an example of Milton's later style in the last six books (Oras, "Milton's Blank Verse" 166); cf. *PL* 12.255, 408–09, 518–21.

248. *holy One:* "a holy person; used as a title of God or Christ; one dedicated to or consecrated by God" (so *OED* s.v. *holy* 5a).
  mortal Men: Le Comte identifies this as a Homeric expression; cf. 1.51 and 3.268.

249-56. The biblical text in Exod. 25–27 insists on precise dimensions and materials for the sanctuary, which were precisely followed in Exod. 37; the precision is given allegorical meaning in Heb. 8:5. "The Description of the tabernacle in general follows Exod. 25–26, but mindful of his theme, Michael adds from Heb. 9:4 the identification of the *Testimony* as The Records of his Cov'nant" (Fowler).

prescript: "command" (*OED* 1), as in *SA* 308. Verity also cites *Antony and Cleopatra* 3.8.5: "the prescript of this scroll."

250. *Of Cedar:* Keightley argues that since the original tabernacle was constructed with shittim (acacia) wood, not cedar (Exod. 25:1–9), Milton may have been thinking of Solomon's temple, which made use of cedar, fir, and algum (2 Chron. 2:8). Himes (*Paradise Lost: A Poem*) counters that the ark (of acacia wood) was not the sanctuary, and since the temple was built partly of cedar, Milton was probably right. Verity wonders if Milton equated shittim with cedar. Fowler hears a reference to tabernacles compared to cedar trees in Num. 24:5–6.

251. *Ark:* in Jewish history, "the wooden coffer containing the tables of the law, kept in the Holiest Place of the Tabernacle" (so *OED* 2).

255-56. *Seaven Lamps as in a Zodiac representing / The Heav'nly fires:* cf. Philo's allegorical explanation of the Jewish Tabernacle: "the seven lamps are symbols of the planets....And the movement and revolution of these through the zodiacal signs are the causes, for sublunary beings, of all those things which are wont to take place" (78). The Richardsons explain that the lamps appear as the 12 signs of the zodiac as to their form, but in number representing the seven planets (i.e., those then known); the planets were often called "fires" in antiquity. Newton and some later editors attribute the sevens to Josephus (*Antiquities* 3.6.7; *Wars of the Jews* 5.5.5), who glossed the seven lights as the seven (known) planets, and the slope of their position as the obliquity of the zodiac, though Himes (*Paradise Lost: A Poem*) judges the seven candlesticks of Rev. 1:12–20 to be a clearer reference than Josephus. The Josephus passages provide Milton with "a means of unifying the astronomical and historical parts of his poem" (Fowler). Newton also cites Joseph Mede's Discourse 10, "The Number of Seven Arch-angels Asserted from Scripture," from *Diatribae* 120–30, and Cornelius à Lapidus on Exod. 25:31, though Lapidus cites both Philo and Josephus. "The end of learning...as in *Of Education,* is a happiness specifically connected with gaining knowledge of God" (Samuel, "Milton" 718). Michael may intend a prophetic reference to the *wondrous gifts...to speak all tongues* in 12.500–01 (Burke 220). The various spiritual gifts described in Rom. 12:3–8; 1 Cor. 12:1–11, 28–31; 14:1–33; and Eph. 4:7–13 are sometimes linked with the "seven Spirits of God" (Rev. 3:1).

255. *representing:* the word's unstressed ending is an unvoiced consonant after a stressed vowel is an example of Milton's later style in the last six books (Oras, "Milton's Blank Verse" 166); cf. 12.247, 408–09, 518–21.

256–58. Cf. the conclusion of Exod. (40:34–38). The cloud and/or pillar are also referenced in Exod. 13:21–22, 14:19 and 24, 33:9–10; Num. 12:5, 14:14; and Deut. 31:15. Milton cites "the redoubled brightnesse of [God's] descending cloud" in *Animad* 4 (Patterson, *Works* 3:147). The Richardsons find the Exodus passage so sublime that they quote it at length; they find Milton too concise.
Heav'nly fires: "poetic, the stars" (so *OED* 10b, s.v. *fire*).

257. *fiery:* 1667 *fierie.*

258. *Save:* "followed by an adverb or adverbial phrase or clause, expressing the manner, time, etc., in regard to which an exception is to be made" (so *OED* 3).

259–60. *the Land / Promised to Abraham and his Seed:* for the announcement and repetition of this "Abrahamic covenant," see Gen. 12:1–3, 13:14–17, 15:4–5, 17:15–19 and 21, 22:17–18, 24:60, 26:3–4, 28:13–15.
Abraham: must be elided as "Abram" for the scansion. Sprott wonders if the spelling is a misprint (87).

259. *Conducted by his Angel:* cf. Exod. 23:23, with its promise that "mine Angel shall go before thee." See **11.201–03**.

260–62. *Were long to tell:* Milton may intend a pun here by having Michael use this verb before *how many*, since *telling* can also mean "counting"; he also may be referring to "time would fail me to tell" in Heb. 11:32, which announces a more constricted summary of biblical history after a more dilated one. George

Coffin Taylor, arguing that parts of book 12 are heavily influenced by Du Bartas, thinks Michael's comment may refer to the ponderousness of that enormously detailed source (*Milton's Use* 124). *Were long to tell,* coming just before time standing still (12.263–67), indicates precisely the difference between the narrative and the extended history it relates (Brisman 280–81). Milton's hurried summary is underscored by the regular iambs that may nevertheless be read as dactyls (Reesing 97); see **11.1–21**.

263. *in mid Heav'n:* cf. 3.729, 6.889, and 9.468.

265–69. Wesley omits this passage.

265–66. *Sun in Gibeon stand / And thou Moon in the vale of Aialon:* cf. very similar wording in Josh. 10:12, where the location is the "valley of Ajalon." *Aialon* or Ajalon is a broad valley about 14 miles west of Jerusalem (Gilbert, *Geographical Dictionary* 13). McColley (*Paradise Lost: An Account*) identifies close similarities to the phrasing of Sylvester's Du Bartas, since whereas the biblical text has "Joshua said," "upon Gibeon," and "valley," both Milton and Du Bartas substitute "command," "in Gibeon," and "vale," and in fact no translation uses the phrase "in Gibeon" (194); cf. Du Bartas 2:604.537–40. As Verity notes, "Josuah [*sic*] in Gibeon" is one of the possible epic topics listed in the Trinity Manuscript, as is destruction of the cities of the plain ("Sodom") and "Adam in Banishment" (Patterson, *Works* 18:236); see **12.637**. The incident was often treated as an example of faith, as in Spenser's *Faerie Queene* 1.10.20, where it is linked with Moses' parting of the Red Sea (Fowler).

267–69. *Israel…so call the third…Canaan win:* Jacob, Abraham's grandson, was renamed Israel ("prince with God") after he wrestled with an angel (Gen. 32:24–32); his descendants are collectively Israel the nation. Reesing finds the musical tone here appropriately moderate and unemphatic, as Milton must summarize extensive scriptural material (97–98); see **11.1–21**.

270–84. *Here Adam interpos'd…Favour unmerited by me:* the pause here is artful, and the speech indicates the progress of Adam's regeneration (Richardsons). Newton also approves of Adam's interpositions, since they prevent Michael's narration from being too long or tedious. Friedrich Buff claims a similar interruption in *Iliad* 1.292, when Achilles interrupts Agamemnon (30–31), but that context is antagonistic. The blessings described here by Adam are one of three results of Michael's "grace-impregnated tidings," the others being that his heart is eased and his true eyes are opened (Boswell 92–93). Adam's silence—he has not spoken in nearly 200 lines—is part of the "growing impersonality of tone," as Michael and Adam, no longer dramatic characters, assume parts in a ritual dialogue (Fish 322).

270. *interpos'd:* "to interrupt, make a digression" (so *OED* 5b).

271–74. *Enlightner … Mine eyes true op'ning:* as Adam's bodily vision declines his spiritual vision grows paradoxically clearer; his faith reflects that of Moses, who "endured, as seeing him who is invisible" (Lewalski 32), citing Heb. 11:27. Cf. also **11.368.**

    Enlightner: "one who, or that which, enlightens; one who imparts intellectual light, informs or instructs. Rare in physical sense" (so *OED* a).

    Mine eyes true op'ning: cf. the serpent's false promise regarding the fruit, "in the day ye eat thereof, then your eyes shall be opened" (Gen. 3:5), and also 9.705–08, 865–66, 875, 985, 1070–71.

273. *Just Abraham and his Seed:* Milton conflates Abraham's promised seed with the promised seed of the woman. Cf. *PL* 12.125–26, 148–50, and 450.

276–77. *now I see / His day:* i.e., through the "eyes" of faith. Cf. Christ's statement, "Abraham rejoiced to see my day" (John 8:56). Critics differ on the significance of Adam's reaction. According to Summers, Adam is beginning to see, just as his descendant Abraham (*Muse's Method* 212), whereas MacCallum judges that "Like the younger Milton, [Adam] clearly believes that the end of history is imminent" ("Milton and Sacred History" 164). Sasek reads the passage as overly optimistic, as Adam assumes that the successes of the Jews represent the conclusion for his earthly descendants (193–94). Fowler takes the passage to be ironic, that Adam means only that he can imagine the time of Abraham and that he expects the promise to be realized then; he still has to learn that the promise of the seed contains another mystery. Lewalski compares this passage with Simeon's words on beholding the infant Christ (32); cf. Luke 2:25–32 and see also **11.368.**

277. *in whom all Nations shall be blest:* quotes the promise to Abraham's seed in Gen. 12:3.

278–79. *sought / Forbidd'n knowledge by forbidd'n means:* Peter, who judges Milton's picture of God to be distasteful, finds Adam's self-accusation "unnecessarily severe" (150). Cf. this construction with the "golden…golden" repetition of 3.337 (Pironon 124). Cf. 4.515. Wesley omits these lines.

283. *So many Laws argue so many sins:* cf. Tacitus, *Annals* 3.27.5, "Corruptissimae Republicae plurimae leges" (When the state was most corrupt there were the most laws) and also Milton's comment in *Def 2,* "laws are commonly bad, in proportion as they are numerous" (Patterson, *Works* 8:237). Todd finds a further classical reference in Mariana's *De Rege* 1.2: "Legum multitudinem tempus et malicia invexit tantam, ut jam non minus legibus quàm vitiis laboremus" (The time of bad behavior brought in such a great multitude of laws that now we are worried no less by the laws than by the vices) (23–24). Newton cites numerous New Testament discussions of the law as teacher (Rom. 3:20, 4:22–24, 5:1, 7:7–8, 8:15; Gal. 3:11–12, 19, 23, 4:7; Heb. 7:18–19, 9:13–14, 10:1, 4–5) and praises Milton's ability to summarize so much theology so concisely. Adam's studious tone is "far different from his rash questioning of Raphael" (Burke 220). Adam's question is appropriate; he lived under no written laws in paradise and under only one precept (Muldrow 94–95). Le Comte glosses *argue* as "indicate." Adam's first interruption since the Nimrod episode misses the hints about the Law's deficiencies; Michael must explain "the meaning of heroic martyrdom for the redemption of history" (Radzinowicz 46).

285–313. Since Milton's original audience "had heard of sin but had never heard of progress," this passage was a sufficient announcement of various doctrines; in fact, Milton's summary is masterful, and Rajan celebrates "the upsurge of joyousness [by which Milton] celebrates the union of discipline with freedom" (*"Paradise Lost" and the Seventeenth Century* 89–90).

285–306. "This is one of those theological passages into which Milton distils the doctrines of a number of texts (as interpreted by himself)," such as Rom. 3:20, 4:22–25, 5:1, 17, 21; 7:7–8, 8:15, 10:5; Gal. 3–4; and Heb. 7:19, 9:13–14, 10:1, 4–5 (Verity). Bush calls this passage "Milton's grandest statement of the central doctrine of 'Christian liberty,' the individual freedom of the Christian as contrasted with the bondage of the Mosaic law." Cf. *DocCh* 1.26, "Under the gospel both the Redeemer and the truth of his redemption are more explicitly understood" (Patterson, *Works* 16:101); "what neither the law itself nor the observers of the law could attain, faith in God through Christ has attained" (Patterson, *Works* 16:111), and 1.27, where the stated purposes of the Mosaic law are to "to call forth and develop our natural depravity...that it might impress us with a slavish fear...that it might be a schoolmaster to bring us to the righteousness of Christ" (Patterson, *Works* 16:131); Maurice Kelley even claims that the epic passage is a "poetic restatement" of the doctrine found in *DocCh* (174, 175–76, 199).

285–86. Cf. *DocCh* 1.11, which denotes the effects of the Fall on Adam and Eve's progeny (Maurice Kelley 147; Patterson, *Works* 15:183); see also 11.106–08, 423–28; 12.398–400.

287–88. *given:* Darbishire (*Poetical Works* 1:xxvi) deems this spelling "possibly" a disyllable, though she judges the disyllabic spelling to be in error in 5.454 and 9.951; Milton's usual spelling is the monosyllable *giv'n.*

    evince: either "prove by argument or evidence; to establish" (*OED* 4), or (as noted by both Ricks [*Paradise Lost*] and Fowler), "to overcome, subdue, prevail over" (*OED* 1), a meaning that may have been particularly prevalent in Milton's time, since all four *OED* citations for that meaning are taken from the seventeenth century, with *PR* 4.235, "Error by his own arms is best evinc't," furnishing another, whereas Rom. 4:1–5:21 discusses how the law "evinces" or proves the presence of sin. Milton declares in *DocCh* 1.27 that the law was enacted to stimulate our depravity, to inspire us with slavish fear, to be "a schoolmaster to bring us to the righteousness of Christ" (Patterson, *Works* 16:131), a restatement of Gal. 3:24.

    pravitie: "tendency to evil." Although Verity claims that the word is only used here by Milton and by Johnson in "Milton" ("Ariosto's pravity is generally known" [192]), *OED* furnishes quotations from 1550 to 1847. Wesley glosses *pravitie* as "depravity, wickedness." Northrop Frye (*Paradise Lost*) glosses *natural pravitie* as "depraved nature."

288–89. *Sin against Law to fight:* cf. Rom. 7:23: "But I see another law in my members, warring against the law of my mind." Wesley reduces these two lines to one: "Their natural pravity, that when they see."

289–306. Milton's method in *Paradise Lost* is similar to this sequence that begins with an imperfect law as a stimulus to inductive reasoning (Fish 318).

290–314. Kurth finds that this passage weaves together two elements, man's limited efforts and God's providence, to sum up "the whole design of universal history"; man cannot make full restitution for original sin and requires the intervention of divine grace and mercy (124–25).

290. *Law can discover sin, but not remove:* cf. the function and limits of the Law in Rom. 3:19–20. This important shift in emphasis from law to grace, also found in the Geneva Bible commentary, suggests "a way or pattern of Reformation thinking...a fundamentally Protestant interpretation of Scripture" (Whiting, *Milton* 140).

291. *those shadowie expiations weak:* following Heb. 10:1–4, Milton characterizes the sacrifices as shadows or types of Christ's final expiation of sin. See also **12.302–03.** Sprott elides the last five letters of *shadowie* into a single syllable (85).

293–96. On the mechanics of justification, see Patrides (*Milton* 191) and **11.63–64.**

293. *Some bloud more precious:* cf. the comparison of sacrifices in Heb. 9:13–14 and 10:11–12 and also the more precious blood of 1 Pet. 1:18–20. Cf. *DocCh* 1.14: "God would not accept any other sacrifice, inasmuch as any other would have been less worthy" (Maurice Kelley 160; Patterson, *Works* 15:277).

294–99. Wesley omits this passage.

294–96. Cf. *DocCh* 1.22: "justification is the gratuitous purpose of God, whereby those who are regenerate and ingrafted in Christ are absolved from sin and death through his most perfect satisfaction, and accounted just in the sight of God, not by the works of the law, but through faith" (Maurice Kelley 171; Patterson, *Works* 16:25).

294. *Just for unjust:* cf. 1 Pet. 3:18, "Christ also hath once suffered for sins, the just for the unjust, that he might bring us to God." Milton's phrase defines, "in the careful disequilibrium of its language, the only way in which the 'rigid satisfaction' [*PL* 3.212] of justice can be transcended" (Rajan, "*Paradise Lost: The Hill*" 54).

295–306. On tempered justice and mercy, see Huntley's remarks in **11.360–64**.

295. *imputed:* Northrop Frye (*Paradise Lost*) glosses as "transferred." *OED* has "ascribed by vicarious substitution" (*OED* 2). Cf. the "merit / Imputed" of 3.290–91.

296–97. *Justification towards God and peace / Of Conscience:* cf. Rom. 5:1: "Therefore being justified by faith, we have peace with God through our Lord Jesus Christ." Cf. also *DocCh* 1.22: "From a consciousness of justification proceed peace and real tranquillity of mind" (Maurice Kelley 172; Patterson, *Works* 16:49).
    towards: pronounced as two syllables (Bridges 22); see also **12.215**.

297–99. Cf. Gal. 2:16, on righteousness being imputed by faith rather than achieved by works. Verity glosses this passage as "The law cannot appease the conscience, nor can man perform 'the moral part' of the law." Northrop Frye (*Paradise Lost*) explains, "The paradox of the law is that man must be morally perfect to satisfy the law, and no man can be." Cf. *DocCh* 1.27, where both the "ceremonial law" and "entire Mosaic law" are found wanting (Patterson, *Works* 16:135–37), and "there could be but little inducement to observe the conditions of a law which has not the promise" (Maurice Kelley 176; Patterson, *Works* 16:141).

300–14. Shawcross links the Israelites' exodus out of Egypt to the expulsion of Adam and Eve from paradise; each had fallen into bondage to a false god ("*Paradise Lost*" 14).

300–06. As Fowler notes, the thought follows Gal. 3:22–26. Michael's response to Adam's question about the relation between law and sin is "a series of stately and perfectly sculpted progressions"; the passage is not only high poetry but also a conclusive statement that seems to gather and consummate the entire tradition to which it responds (Rajan, "*Paradise Lost:* The Hill" 53–54). Maurice Kelley (175–76) refers this passage to statements in *DocCh* 1.27: "The Gospel [was] announced first obscurely, by Moses and the prophets, afterwards in the clearest terms by Christ himself" (Patterson, *Works* 16:113); "the law [of works] is abolished principally... that it might give place to the law of grace" (Patterson, *Works* 16:133); "Under the law, those who trusted in God were justified by faith indeed, but not without the works of the law.... The gospel, on the contrary, justifies by faith without the works of the law" (Maurice Kelley 175, 176; Patterson, *Works* 16:151). Madsen cites Milton's opposition to the liturgy and hierarchy of the Anglican church in *RCG*, "all corporeal resemblances of inward holinesse and beauty are now past" (Patterson, *Works* 3:246) and in *Hirelings,* where any attempts to fetch them back are superstitious (Patterson, *Works* 6:65); Madsen also claims that Milton effectively telescopes Joachim di Fiore's "Age of the Son," an age of study and wisdom, with di Fiore's "Age of the Spirit," in which all verbal mediations, along with ecclesiastical hierarchy and the sacraments, will be abolished, and *significantia,* i.e., those things signifying, will pass over to *significata,* or that which is signified (*From Shadowy Types* 107–08, 179–80, 191–92; cf. Madsen, "Earth" 524). On types, see **12.302–03**. This passage provides a connection between inward and outward liberty that is "Puritan, rational, and firm" (Radzinowicz 47).

300. *So law appears imperfet:* cf. Heb. 7:19 and other discussions of law versus grace, by which *appears* should have the sense of "is revealed to be."
　　but: Fowler glosses as "only."

302–03. *disciplin'd / From shadowie Types to Truth:* Bush usefully glosses *shadowie Types* as "persons and events in the Old Testament as prophetic or allegorical of their full realization in the New." See, for instance, the picture of the Mosaic Law as a "schoolmaster to bring us unto Christ" (Gal. 3:24), the Jewish priests who serve as an "example and shadow of heavenly things" (Heb. 8:5), and the Law characterized as "having a shadow of good things to come" (Heb. 10:1); cf. also the "shadowie expiations weak" of 12.291. Milton may have had Plato's Ideas in mind (Agar 53). Milton embraces a kind of moral evolution: "the development of higher types of morality out of lower and the (sparingly developed) mystical element in Milton's mentality fitted him to see evidences of this progressive scale in the allegorical interpretation of outstanding events in the past" (Bøgholm 47). Milton was little interested in traditional typological links between Old and New Testaments; "the Protestant bias of his thought consistently caused him to emphasize the inward and spiritual nature of the antitype" (MacCallum, "Milton and Figurative Interpretation" 407) and to locate the type in a person ("Milton and Sacred History" 158); along with Milton's repetition of a pattern (fall, judgment, regeneration, and renewal), there is also progress from implicit to explicit (MacCallum, "Milton and Sacred History" 154). Madsen claims that Milton's rejection of physical matter—usually to metaphorically reject an attitude or mental state—is literally intended here ("Idea" 231); and Madsen (*From Shadowy Types* 48–52) also remarks, in his monograph that takes its title from this passage, that Milton's "theory and practice of biblical interpretation may fairly be described as that of conservative Puritanism," comparing the thorough orthodoxy of this statement with Milton's careful explanation in *DocCh* 1.30 of how Scripture may occasionally have a double sense (Patterson, *Works* 16:263). Most of Milton's references to typology appear when he opposes the carnal law and the spiritual gospel, as in his discussion of Ezekiel's vision of a new temple in *RCG* (Patterson, *Works* 3:191) and his contrast of the priesthood of Aaron and Melchizedek in *Hirelings* (Patterson, *Works* 6:53–57); in *CivP* he rejects contemporary applications of Jewish ceremonial law as "beggarly rudiments" (Patterson, *Works* 6:29, citing similar language in Gal. 4:9) and complains in *Hirelings* that those who wished to perpetuate them had "Judaiz'd the church" (Patterson, *Works* 6:63) and in *Ref* that vestments indicate an attempt to make "God earthly, and fleshly, because they [can]not make themselves heavenly, and Spirituall" (Patterson, *Works* 3:2). Madsen (*From Shadowy Types* 51) takes exception to Ross (*Poetry and Dogma* 99), who complains that typological readings have God "dying for a bundle of metaphors and illustrations." The Jewish observation of the Sabbath is described as a "shadow" in *DocCh* 2.7 (Patterson, *Works* 17:174). Carnes identifies typology as a result of the Fall: "Only when the archetypes of prehistory were shattered could the types of history be revealed" (537). This passage, the clearest allusion in *PL* to the typological method, emphasizes the spiritual nature of the antitype as opposed to the physical nature of the type, a difference not purely temporal but also between the physical and spiritual or between the external and internal (Ryken 28). Milton believed in a dynamic typology that changed progressively with sacred history and in which symbols valid before the law were afterward worthless; God's appearance to Moses established a new form of typology and established Moses as a temporary mediator and master typologist (Allen, "Milton and the Descent" 614–15). On types, see also **11.22–30, 12.231–32, 12.240–42, 12.291, 12.300–06, 12:394–95,** and **12.543–47**.

302. *a better Cov'nant:* this phrase implies the role of Christ in Heb. 8:6, where he is named "the mediator of a better covenant, which was established upon better promises." Although Milton insists in *DocCh* 1.14 that Christ is the only redeemer, as a poet he must still demonstrate in the other characters a reflection of the divinity of Christ's mission (Lieb, "*Paradise Lost*" 38); cf. Patterson, *Works* 15:257.

304–06. *From...Laws, to...Grace:* cf. John 1:17, "the law was given by Moses, but grace and truth came by Jesus Christ," and *DocCh* 1.27, where the Law is externally imposed on unwilling followers but the internal law written on the hearts of willing Christian followers; it also compares the slavery of the Law with the liberty of the Gospel and defines Christian liberty as freedom from sin's bondage and consequently as "adult" service of God in love (Maurice Kelley 176–77; Patterson, *Works* 16:151–55).

304. *strict Laws:* cf. 2.241.

305–06. *from servil fear / To filial:* cf. "the Spirit of adoption, whereby we cry, Abba, Father" (Rom. 8:15) and also the servant-to-son movement in Gal. 4:7. Berger, applying various theories of Hegel, Haeckel, and Eliade, proposes that the movement of Old Law to New affects God as well as humanity's image of him, since the more personal attributes of the Son and the Holy Spirit must be given greater play (50).

servil: "of personal attributes and action: Befitting, or characteristic of a slave or a state of servitude; slavish, ignoble" (so *OED* 3c, which also references *servile fear* as "A mingled feeling of dread and reverence towards God (formerly also, towards any rightful authority)" (*OED* s.v. *fear,* 3d).

filial: "of sentiments, duty, etc.: Due from a child to a parent" (so *OED* 1a).

305. *large Grace:* cf. the "free gift" of Rom. 5:15–16.

306. *works of Law to works of Faith:* cf. the definition of *justification* in *DocCh* 1.22, "those who are regenerate and ingrafted in Christ are...accounted righteous in the sight of God, not by the works of the law but through faith" (Patterson, *Works* 16:25), and also Milton's explanation that faith has its own works that may be different from the works of the law. "We are justified, therefore by faith, but a living, not a dead faith, and that faith alone which acts is counted living" (Patterson, *Works* 16:39); cf. James 2:17, 20, 26.

307–14. One of the passages about supernal grace identified by Reesing; see **12.111–13.** Reesing also claims that the tempo slows here for "extraordinary imaginative expansion.... Both abstract doctrine and the narrative...are caught up for one splendid moment in a total cosmic vision" (99–100); see **11.1.** Cf. *DocCh* 1.26: "The imperfection of the law was manifested in the person of Moses himself...but an entrance was granted to [the children of Israel] under Joshua, [that is], Jesus" (Maurice Kelley 174–75; Patterson, *Works* 16:111). Fowler finds that part of *DocCh* 1.26 is "almost a prose version" of *PL* 12.307–11. For the transfer of power from Moses to Joshua, see Deut. 34 and Josh. 1.

307–09. *shall not Moses...his people into Canaan lead:* because of one act of disobedience, Moses was not allowed to enter Canaan (Num. 20:1–13); the people were led in by Joshua after Moses' death. Christian commentators since Origen have made much of the parallel between Moses as Old Testament law and Joshua ("Jesus," as noted below) as New Testament grace; see Northrop Frye's discussion of Jesus as Joshua ("Typology" 229) and also Fixler's (232–33). Cf. *DocCh* 1.26: "The imperfection of the law was made apparent in the person of Moses himself. For Moses...could not lead the children of Israel into the land of Canaan" (Patterson, *Works* 16:111).

310–11. *But Joshua whom the Gentiles Jesus call / His Name and Office bearing:* Jesus ('Ιησοῦς) is the Greek form of the Hebrew *Joshua*, "savior." The Septuagint always renders Joshua as Jesus, and KJV uses Jesus for the Old Testament Joshua twice (Acts 7:45, Heb. 4:8); in Christian thinking, they both lead God's people after the "death" of the law represented by Moses (Newton). "Only the Saviour can enter and conquer man's promised land" (Northrop Frye, *Paradise Lost*). Starnes and Talbert (260–61) think that Milton's phrasing here may be derived from the Latin of Charles Stephanus's *Dictionarium* (1553): "Iosue, & Iesus, idem est nomen...Josue, Typum Iesu Christ non solum in gestis, verum etiam in nomine gerens" (Joshua, and Jesus...the same is the name Joshua, a type of

Jesus Christ not only in action, truly also in name acting). Whiting notes the important shift in emphasis from law to grace, one he also finds in the Geneva Bible commentary (*Milton* 140).

311–12. *who shall quell / The adversarie Serpent:* The word *quell,* i.e., "crush utterly," was a stronger word in Milton's time (Verity). *OED* records the obsolete sense of "kill, slay, put to death, destroy (a person or animal)" and also the continuing sense of "to crush or overcome (a person or thing); to subdue, vanquish, reduce to subjection or submission; to force down." For the oft-repeated promise of Gen. 3:15, see **11.115–16**.

312–14. The endless biblical pilgrimages "telescope the theme of the life journey," indicated by *bring back* (circular journey), *wilderness* (the forest and maze), *Safe* (danger), *long* (temporal dimension), and especially *wanderd,* a key word that summarizes the theme of "the erring, bewildered human pilgrimage" (MacCaffrey 188, 205–06). Michael here voices "sympathy for frail, erring humanity," though for the most part the accents of Michael's message are necessarily harsh, and the contrasts violent (Madsen, "Idea" 267). The action is telescoped at this point of the narrative, as the need to reach the Incarnation will push swiftly past David to the second Adam (Lawry, *Shadow* 284). Lieb identifies the Messiah as "the final apotheosis of the rebirth pattern," who causes the "final return to the womb" (*Dialectics* 215).

313. *long wanderd man:* see **11.281**; cf. also *Wandring that watrie Desert* in *PL* 11.779.

314. *Safe to eternal Paradise of rest:* Milton here moves through the type of Joshua-as-Jesus, whose "rest" was insufficient (Heb. 4:8), to Christ himself.

315–58. Michael hurries through succeeding eras because he is concerned with the "second Joshua," or Christ; the events related before his birth exemplify dissension, both political and religious, and Michael speaks favorably only of David and Solomon (Muldrow 96).

316. *but:* except for.

318–20. *enemies / From whom … he saves them penitent:* this cyclical history of sin, servitude, repentance, and deliverance is related in Judges and 1 Samuel.

321. *second:* David succeeded Saul, the first king of Israel, the failure of whose dynasty failed is recounted from 1 Sam. 8 to 2 Sam. 5.

323–24. *his Regal Throne / For ever shall endure:* this promise is made in 2 Sam. 7:16 and repeated in Ps. 89:34–36, Jer. 33:20–21, and elsewhere. Montgomery and others also cite Gen. 3:15, 22:18; Isa. 9:7; Matt. 22:42; Luke 1:32, 33; and Rom. 15:12.

324–30. In many Old Testament passages, the royal line of David takes on messianic significance, as recognized in Luke 1:32, where Jesus is promised "the throne of his father David" (Fowler). One of the passages about supernal grace identified by Reesing; see **12.111–13**. The 250 lines of Jewish history up to the Messiah's birth are "remarkably uneven in poetical quality," and the writing quality deteriorates painfully: "instead of the promised consolation, one feels rather a dogged insistence on getting through with the job" (Martz 159).

324–25. *the like shall sing / All Prophecie:* Milton refers to the numerous Old Testament passages interpreted as referring to Christ; cf. *DocCh* 1.14: "The nativity of Christ is predicted by all the prophets" (Patterson, *Works* 15:281). The Richardsons, who also note the elevated and often versified style of ancient prophecy, find it "truly poetical" for Milton to substitute *Prophecie* here for *Prophets,* a gloss also supplied by Wesley.

327. *the Womans Seed to thee foretold:* for the oft-repeated promise of Gen. 3:15, see **11.115–16**.

328–29. *in whom shall trust / All Nations:* cf. Isa. 42:4, Matt. 12:21. *Ha-goyim* is Hebrew for "nations," i.e., the Gentiles.

328. *Foretold to Abraham:* cf. the promise to Abraham that in him "shall all families of the earth be blessed" (Gen. 12:3) and Christ's comment in John 8:56, "Abraham rejoiced to see my day," i.e., prophetically.

329–30. *and to Kings foretold, of Kings / The last:* Bentley emends to "foretold; Of Kings / *He* last." Pearce objects to the punctuation, as well as to the change to *He,* which obscures the meaning that Christ will be the last king. Although Christ's being named at the beginning of the epic but then here seemingly for the first time seems contradictory, Milton "subordinated strict theology to patristic traditions" (Maurice Kelley 104).

330. *of his Reign shall be no end:* cf. the similar angelic promise to Mary in Luke 1:33.

332–34. *his next Son... shall in a glorious Temple enshrine:* David's son Solomon built the first temple in Jerusalem (2 Kings 6–7 and 2 Chron. 3–4). Relics are put in shrines, and the original ark that held other relics—the tablets of the Law, the pot of manna, and Aaron's rod that budded (Heb. 9:4)—has itself become a relic (Richardsons). Lauder claims that a Latin version of the Dutch poet Jacob Catsius supplied the *prima stamina* of books 11–12 of *PL,* since Catsius not only mentions Enoch, Melchizedek, Noah, Abraham, Moses, David, and Solomon, but he particularly stresses Solomon's wisdom, riches, and building of the temple (112–14); on Lauder's impostures, see **11.388–411**. Bridges cites the elision of *Temple enshrine* as an example of what he calls "the rule of L," by which unstressed vowels on either side of an *l* may be elided (30); see **12.201–03** and also **11.306**. Milton identifies Solomon only by symbolic deed, assuming his readers will recognize the true temple of which Solomon's was a type (Summers, *Muse's Method* 214). Because the building of the temple was occasion of "yet another divine Covenant (1 Kings 9:1–9)," its mention is relevant here (Fowler).

333. *clouded:* a cloud covered the tabernacle in the wilderness (Exod. 40:38, Num. 9:16, 14:14). Clouds also filled both the tabernacle and Solomon's temple at their dedications (Ex. 40:34–35, 1 Kings 8:10–11, 2 Chron. 5:13).

334. *Wandring:* Fish (140–41) argues that this action is transformed in book 12; see **11.281**.

335–36. *registerd / Part good, part bad, of bad the longer scrowle:* 1 and 2 Kings chronicle the reigns of kings in Judah and Israel, formulaically listing them as either good or bad. Milton must be referring to both kingdoms, as the "longer scroll" of Judah was good (Keightley). Michael's words to Adam translate the words of Dante's Thomas Aquinas on the nature of kings, "che son molti, e i buon son rari"; (There are many, and the good are rare) (Samuel, *Dante* 256; cf. *Paradiso* 13.108).

    scrowle: i.e., *scroll:* "A list, roll, or schedule (of names)" (so *OED* 2b).

337. *foul Idolatries:* cf. the reference in 1.399–405 and 1.446.

338. *Heapt to the popular summe:* "i.e., added to the aggregate of the sins of the whole people" (Masson). Wesley glosses as "sins of people." Fowler has "added to the sum of the people's faults."

339–43. Milton's contemporaries linked this city to the Babel of Gen. 11 (Gilbert, *Geographical Dictionary* 42–43). Adam did not actually see the walls narrated by Michael; by *saw'st,* Milton may have meant *perceived* (Newton). Stebbing claims *thou saw'st* is poetic, not literal. Cf. the mention of Babylon in 1.717, and see **12.73** on other symmetries and **12.101–04** on Adam's vision.

    proud Citie: cf. 2.533. The fall of apostate Judah and Jerusalem to Babylon is detailed in 2 Chron. 34.

344–47. *in captivitie…The space of seventie years:* the 70-year Babylonian captivity was foretold by Jeremiah (Jer. 25:12) and is described in 2 Kings 25, 2 Chron. 36, Jer. 39 and 52. Modern biblical commentators vary in its chronology, e.g., between the roughly 70 years from the destruction of the temple in Jerusalem (587 BCE) to its rebuilding (516–15 BCE) or in whether the number 70 represents a rounded or symbolic number. Ussher reports the destruction of the temple as 588 BCE and the completion of the rebuilt temple as 515 BCE (*Annals* 91, 113).

345–47. One of the passages about supernal grace identified by Reesing; see **12.111–13**.

346. *Remembring mercie:* cf. the prophet Habakkuk's "in wrath remember mercy" (Hab. 3:2).

347. *stablisht as the dayes of Heav'n:* "Milton followed prophetic tradition in making the exile...end as a fulfillment of God's covenant with David to make 'his throne as the days of heaven' (Ps. 89:29)" (Hughes, *Paradise Lost*). Cf. also Jer. 33:20–21, where God's covenant with David is as certain as day and night. Milton's juxtaposition of *seventie years* and *dayes of Heav'n* might recall Josephus's identification (*Antiquities* 3.7.7) of the 70 parts of the candlestick of the tabernacle as the *Decani,* or 70 divisions of the planets in the zodiac (Fowler).

348. *Returnd from Babylon by leave of Kings:* i.e., Persian kings. For Cyrus the Great's initial role in reestablishing the temple, see 2 Chron. 36:23 and Ezra 1:2; the temple was finished in the sixth year of Darius (Ezra 6:15). For Artaxerxes' assistance, see Ezra 4 and Neh. 2.

350–52. *till...factious:* cf. the change recounted in the *Republic* (2.372–4) from the primitive State with its simple needs to the luxurious 'State at fever-heat,' that requires a military class (Samuel, *Plato* 83); see *PL* 11.788.

351. *moderate:* see Darbishire's comments in **11.5.**

353–58. *at last they seise / The Scepter.../ Then loose it to a stranger:* Michael relates the events of the Maccabean and early Roman periods from Josephus (*Antiquities* 12.4–5) and 2 Macc. 3–4. An initial contest for the high priesthood and collaboration with outsiders led to Antiochus IV Epiphanes' entry into Jerusalem (168 BCE), his hellenization of the country, and his defiling the Jewish temple and dedicating it to Jupiter (167 BCE); the temple was subsequently recaptured by Judas Maccabeus and rededicated (164 BCE). During ensuing struggles with the Greeks, the regal power and high priesthood were united under Aristobulus, oldest son of the high priest John Hyrcanus of the Maccabean family (107 BCE). This founder of the Asmonean dynasty thus "seized the scepter" or, as Josephus states, "first of all put a diadem on his head" (*Antiquities* 13.11.1). A later contest between Aristobulus and Hyrcanus led to the Roman power under Pompey setting Antipater, an Idumaean, over the region (61 BCE). His son, the celebrated Herod the Great, became king of Judea in 40 BCE, and the scepter was thus lost to a "stranger" or non-Jew, though Hughes thinks the "stranger" may be Antiochus the Great; Hughes also reports that the Asmonean family retained the high priesthood from 153 to 35 BCE (*Paradise Lost*). These events meant that Jesus, David's direct descendant, was born in obscurity (Northrop Frye, *Paradise Lost*). Milton would see a strong connection between the civil strife, foreign occupation, and foreign forms of worship in the Maccabean period and the events of his own day (Fowler).

353–55. *springs…brings:* one of 45 instances found by Diekhoff in the epic where two lines rhyme with one intervening nonrhyming line ("Rhyme" 540). See Purcell for additional instances (171).

357–58. *regard not Davids Sons…a stranger:* the last Davidic king was Zerubbabel, under whose leadership the Jews returned from captivity (536 BCE). The word *stranger* "includes the Syrian and Roman conquerors of Palestine as well as Herod" (Northrop Frye, *Paradise Lost*).

358–71. One of the passages about supernal grace identified by Reesing; see **12.111–13**. Parish ("Milton" 246) calls "uninspired" the 14 lines devoted to the Nativity, even though they lead to a high point in the narrative, Adam's response in 12.375–84.

359. *Anointed King:* cf. 5.664, 777, 870 and 6.718.

360–67. Cf. the numerous verbal echoes with *Nat* and *PR* 1.242–54. The biblical nativity accounts are in Matt. 1–2 and Luke 2.

360–63. *a Starr…guides the Eastern Sages:* Matt. 2:1–11.

360. *Barr'd of his right:* Milton purposefully uses a legal term (Verity). As a descendant of David, Christ was born "King of the Jews" (cf. Matt. 2:2). Despite this information, Adam will still expect a literal kingship and a literal contest with Satan in 12.383–85 (MacCallum, "Milton and Sacred History" 164).

362–67. Wesley omits this passage.

362–66. *enquire…Quire:* Purcell notes that these lines rhyme with three intervening lines (172); this rhyme category was also mentioned by Diekhoff but without specific verse numbers ("Rhyme" 542).

364. *His place of birth a solemn Angel tells:* i.e., Bethlehem, "the city of David" (Luke 2:11). "Milton seldom used *solemn* without a clear trace of its Latin signification of something belonging to a religious festival or ceremonial" (Hughes, *Paradise Lost*). Northrop Frye (*Paradise Lost*) glosses the term as "heralding." Fowler glosses it as "holy" (*OED* 1) and "awe-inspiring" (*OED* 7).

365. C. H. Collins Baker (4, 19, 116) reports that the Richters, who in 1794 doubled the usual number of *PL* illustrations, included among new themes one of "To Simple Shepherds Keeping Watch"; "Adoration of the Shepherds" is one of four illustrations for book 12 in Tilt's 1843 edition of Milton's *Poetical Works;* see further lists of Tilt's illustrations in **11.187** and **12.1–5**.
    simple: "of persons, or their origin: Poor or humble in condition; of low rank or position; undistinguished, mean, common" (so *OED* 4a).

366–68. *Quire…Sire:* one of 45 instances found by Diekhoff in the epic where two lines rhyme with one intervening nonrhyming line ("Rhyme" 540). See Purcell for additional instances (171).

366–67. *They gladly thither haste, and…hear his Carol sung:* cf. Luke 2:8–16. The biblical order of events is reversed—the shepherds hear the angels in Bethlehem rather than in the field; Milton may have been thinking of a Nativity painting combining angels and shepherds (Dunster, in Todd).
    Quire: i.e., choir. The sense is transferred from the organized body of singers to "angels, birds, echoes, etc." (so *OED* 3b).
    Carol: "a song or hymn of joy sung at Christmas in celebration of the Nativity. Rarely applied to hymns on certain other festal occasions" (so *OED* 3b). R. C. Browne (1894) links the etymology to the French *carole,* properly a round dance; the term was later applied to the song accompanying the dance, and hence used generally for a joyous song. *OED* reports the Old French etymology as uncertain but does list the round dance as one possibility.

367. *squadrond Angels:* i.e., assembled in troops. Cf. "squadrons bright" of *Nat* 21. Milton uses the Italian participle *squadronato* (Todd).

368–71. Because of the epic description, Adam foresees the Messiah's battle with Satan in epic terms (12.384–85), which Michael corrects in tragic terms (12.404–14), yet "what, on Earth, is the tragic mode turns out, in heaven, to be the epic one" (Burden 197–98). Cf. 12.419–23 and also *DocCh* 1.14, that the efficient cause of Christ's conception is the Holy Spirit, "the power and the spirit of the Father himself" (Maurice Kelley 160; Patterson, *Works* 15:281).

368–69. *A Virgin is his Mother:* neither Michael nor Adam (12.379) questions the Incarnation; both their speeches "reflect Milton's own quiet acceptance of the union of Christ's human and divine natures in one person" (Muldrow 97); cf. *DocCh* 1.14, where despite the fact that Christ, "being God, took upon him the human nature, and was made flesh," he did not cease "to be numerically the same as before" (Patterson, *Works* 15:263). Here and elsewhere, the theology of *PL* is in conformity with the Roman Catholic Church (Joseph 255).

    his Sire / The Power of the most High: cf. Gabriel's words to Mary in Luke 1:35: "the power of the Highest shall overshadow thee: therefore also that holy thing which shall be born of thee shall be called the Son of God." Bentley emends to "*God* most High." In *DocCh* 1.14, however, Milton understands the phrase as "the power and spirit of the Father himself" (Patterson, *Works* 15:281).

369–70. *and bound his Reign / With earths wide bounds, his glory with the Heav'ns:* both classical and biblical references are possible here. Newton and others cite *Aeneid* 1.287–88, "Imperium Oceano, famam qui terminet astris" (he shall bound his empire by the ocean, his fame by the stars), but also see the promises of Christ's worldwide dominion in Ps. 2:8, Isa. 9:7, Dan. 7:13–14, Matt. 28:18, and Luke 1:32. Hughes (*Paradise Lost*) sees a conflation of the messianic promise in Ps. 2:8 ("Ask of me, and I shall give thee…the uttermost parts of the earth for thy possession") with Virgil's prophecy. "By an implied comparison between Christ and Augustus, strategically placed near the end of *PL*, Milton reaffirms the transcendent grandeur of his epic idea" (Harding, *Club of Hercules* 38). Cf. *DocCh* 1.33 on the extent of Christ's glorious reign (Patterson, *Works* 16:359–63), and also *DocCh* 1.15, where Christ "conquers and subdues its enemies" by the power of God (Maurice Kelley 163, 183; Patterson, *Works* 15:297). Milton was referring to Christ's earthly kingdom of glory, which would begin with Christ's second advent, as distinguished from the kingdom of grace, which began with his first advent, though Milton may be combining the two kingdoms here (Fowler). See also the apocalyptic paragraphs closing *Ref.*

bound: "to set bounds to, limit; to confine within bounds; to mark (out) the bounds of" (so *OED* 1, obsolete).

372–76. Fish cites this comment on Adam's joy and understanding as further proof of Adam's sure progress (290); see **12.79.**

373. *Surcharg'd, as had like grief bin dew'd in tears:* that is, "overburdened, overloaded, charged to excess" (*OED*). Cf. the weeping Dalila as a "fair flower surcharg'd with dew" in *SA* 728.

375–85. Adam's speech has been variously interpreted by commentators. Rajan judges that Adam's very confidence in recognizing the Incarnation, despite the "studied vagueness" of Michael's announcement, means that Adam has learned much in the last two or three hundred lines (*"Paradise Lost:* The Hill" 53). Empson reads this interruption as a sign that "History has been adequately covered when we reach the birth of Christ," and glosses the action as "Poor Adam starts crying and says he's sure it's going to be all right after all. . . . Michael snubs him and proceeds to a more exact statement of the doctrine of Atonement" (*Milton's God* 190–91). Lewalski (32–33), who traces the development of Adam's faith to perceive the "things not seen" of Heb. 11:1, finds nevertheless vestiges of spiritual myopia; though Adam claims now to understand "clearly," he is still expecting a physical combat with Satan, just as his Hebrew progeny will expect a military messiah; Adam might well expect physical combat, since the war in heaven related by Raphael was physical (book 6), Michael shows up in military garb (11.241), and Death is pictured as shaking his "Dart" (11.491–92); Adam himself speaks of "arming to overcome" in 11.374. See also **11.368.**

375. *O Prophet of glad tidings:* Sims (*Bible* 272) cites Rom. 10:15 (itself a citation of Isa. 52.7): "How beautiful are the feet of them that preach the gospel of peace, and bring glad tidings of good things!"

finisher: Fowler finds this term ironic, since Adam does not yet understand how Christ himself is the "finisher of our faith" (Heb. 12:2). *Finisher* consciously echoes the Hebrews passage, especially since Heb. 11:1—"Now faith is the substance of things hoped for, the evidence of things not seen"—is the key to Milton's visionary symbolism (Lewalski 29).

376. *utmost hope:* since such hope is but one step from full possession, this line indicates how evangelical virtue is growing in Adam's heart, according to 3.375–76 (Richardsons).

378–79. *call'd / The seed of Woman:* the promise of Gen. 3:15 is frequently repeated in Michael's narration, but only at this point does Adam understand it; see **11.115–16**. Steadman reports Moslem, Hebrew, and Christian parallels to this revelation, though the identity of the revealing angels varies, as does the nature, object, and time of Adam's enlightenment; Milton's particular combination of these features is by no means typical of the tradition ("Adam" 214–25). Michael must correct Adam's expectation of an epic hero by stressing Christ's tragic role (Fowler).

379–82. As Fowler explains, this passage is a chain of phrases from the angel's address to Mary in the Annunciation (Luke 1:31–35). See also *PL* 5.385–87 and **12.368–69**, s.v. *A Virgin is his Mother.* Joseph, arguing that *PL* conforms to Roman Catholic theology, finds that "Milton beautifully celebrates the part the Virgin Mary played in the Redemption (265).

380–82. Sims (*Bible* 272) cites John 1:1, 14, which claims Christ's deity. Cf. various statements in *DocCh* 1.14 on Christ's nature: "His nature is twofold; divine and human" (Patterson, *Works* 15:259), Christ is formed from "a mutual hypostatic union of two natures" (Patterson, *Works* 15:271), and "the Son of God...was made flesh, that he is called both God and Man, and is such in reality" (Maurice Kelley 159; Patterson, *Works* 15:273).
    So God with man unites: cf. the promise of God's incarnation at Matt. 1:21–23. The "nondescript, unemphatic conclusion" keeps Adam expecting more information about the Incarnation, rather than expecting that Canaan itself is the final goal (Reesing 99). Adam, like the early disciples, expects an earthly kingdom and an immediate and final victory over Satan (Summers, *Muse's Method* 215).

381. *proceed:* "to be descended or spring *from* (formerly *of*) a parent, ancestor, or stock" (so *OED* 1c, now rare).

383. *now:* Adam responds to a survey of history without dates or secular events to indicate the passing of time; Milton is indefinite about such details, here and elsewhere, to advantage, since the apparently unlimited future is both impressive and true (Whiting, *Milton* 190).

    capital: in Latin, literally "pertaining to the head," where the serpent is to be bruised (Gen. 3:15), with a play on the derived meaning, "fatal" (Hughes, *Paradise Lost*). Cf. *PL* 2.752–58, where Satan suffers head pain at the birth of Sin (Le Comte). Verity claims that *capital* is always disyllabic in Milton; Bush judges this instance to be a disyllable.

384–85. On the epic-tragic paradox, see **12.368–71**, s.v. Burden.

386–465. The tone of Michael's long speech on Christ's mediation reflects the legalistic way Milton views the atonement; "there is no lyrical outburst as the Crucifixion is reported as we might expect from a more evangelical Christian poet" (Muldrow 97–98); the overall speech thematically links human restoration with the Fall (100). The speech teaches Adam the nature of "Messiah's warfare"—it is inward, and humanity is the battlefield—and also responds, in its falling and rising emotions, to the descents and ascents of the poem, the "vicissitude" that the Messiah's death and resurrection make "grateful" (Summers, *Muse's Method* 215–16); cf. *PL* 6.8.

386–419. Tillyard judges that Milton's comparative lack of energy and passion in this "culminating scene in the great Puritan drama" indicates that he was unable to free himself from the legalism that pervaded Christianity in his time, though for Michael to explain God's redemptive plan seems far more appropriate than for God himself to do so in 3.80–343 (Tillyard, *Studies in Milton* 162–64). Madsen counters that Milton is not trying to write a "culminating scene" but rather to expound a doctrine, that Milton's lines have their own kind of intellectual energy, and that such compression is usually a virtue ("Idea" 258–59). Empson judges the only appropriate response to this passage to be "cold horror at the 'justice' of God" (*Milton's God* 268).

386–95. Here, as elsewhere in books 11–12, Adam's emotional response is dramatically urgent; Michael brushes aside the heroic argument of an apocalyptic war in favor of the struggle of the old and new Adam in each heart (Radzinowicz 48).

386–87. *Dream not of thir fight, / As of a Duel:* cf. *PR* 1.174. Only Satan would believe such a duel possible; the seventeenth century reader would be looking for emphasis and proportion in the presentation (Kurth 122). Tuve refers back to *Nat* as an early version of this conflict that redefines itself; it is not the false gods who are fought with, but how they have been conceived: "of their own motion they flee; are not destroyed, simply lose their own power to impose upon man's credulity" (63). Because Adam has received angelic instruction about the nature of divine language, as do the "naïve chiliastic Apostles" of *PR*, he need not struggle as Satan toward appropriate instruction (Stein, *Heroic Knowledge* 13). Peter asks if Michael's de-emphasis of Satan's physical defeat implies that Milton was less interested in the war in heaven than in Satan's later history (74). Given the structural similarities between books 6 and 12, it is not surprising that Adam expects to hear about another physical combat and victory over Satan (Reesing 74). Fish also links this passage to the inconclusive battle in book 6 (179). Northrop Frye (*Paradise Lost*) acknowledges the "dense mass of biblical echoes in the next hundred lines," though he does not identify them. Fowler claims that among the church fathers and medieval hymnists, the duel was a favorite image for the action of Christ on the cross, but Milton rejects the idea as misleading, because Christ is too transcendent for such an equal contest. Cf. *DocCh* 1.15: "the weapons of those who fight under Christ as their King are exclusively spiritual" (Maurice Kelley 163; Patterson, *Works* 15:299).

387–88. Wesley reduces these two lines to one: "As of a Duel: not therefore joins the Son."

387. *local:* "pertaining to a particular place in a system, series, etc., or to a particular portion of an object" (so *OED* 4).

388–90. Michael explicitly confirms what Adam had implied about the Incarnation in the preceding lines (Rajan, "*Paradise Lost:* The Hill" 53).

390–404. "The wilderness that Adam and Eve face as they leave paradise becomes the theater of continued temptation—with resistance by some and fall by others.... Only reliance... upon God's Providence... will allay such perturbations of the mind and soul" (Shawcross, "*Paradise Lost*" 16–17).

392. *Disabl'd not to give thee thy deaths wound:* Verity glosses, "whose fall did not disable him from giving thee thy death's wound" and Bush as, "did not disable from giving." Todd puts a comma after *Disabl'd*, which considerably changes the meaning.

   deaths wound: cf. *PL* 3.252.

393–419. Milton's forensic terminology here is typical of most Calvinist commentary on the atonement and even of much of the Anglican, including that of Archbishop James Ussher (Patrides, "Milton and the Protestant Theory" 11–12); see also Patrides, *Milton* (140–41).

393. *who comes thy Saviour:* for "who comes" as a Messianic formula, see Matt. 11:3 and Luke 7:19.

   recure: "to cure (a disease, sickness, etc.); to heal, make whole (a wound or sore)" (so *OED* 2). This Spenserian term was obsolete even in Johnson's time (Todd). Masson claims the word was once common. Montgomery notes a similar usage of "recover" for "heal" in 2 Kings 5:7. Verity cites *Venus and Adonis* 465 ("recures") and "unrecuring" in *Titus Andronicus* 3.1.90.

394–465. This long speech is needed for Adam to go into the world as a justified sinner; though the passage is too densely theological to succeed poetically, it does crown Adam's "confirmation course" and also continue the pace of Michael's increasingly summarized narration (Fowler).

394–410. Michael's demonstration of God's providence is here completed, since the Son of God's mercy satisfies the judgment (preserving God's justice) and redeems the race (Diekhoff, *Milton's "Paradise Lost"* 124).

394–95. *destroying...his works / In thee and in thy Seed:* cf. 1 John 3:8, which identifies the Son's task as destroying the devil's works. The new covenant thus reveals "a benediction so long concealed in the malediction spoken against the serpent" (Parish, "Milton" 246). Williamson compares Adam's delayed understanding of the types of Christ to his earlier delayed understanding of sin in the shapes of death (107); cf. **12.302–03**.

395–97. *by fulfilling...Obedience:* *DocCh* 1.16 describes Christ's "fulfilling the law" (Maurice Kelley 166; Patterson, *Works* 15:315–17). Obedience is the central theme of *PR*.

   that which thou didst want: what you lacked.

398–400. *penaltie...due to theirs which out of thine will grow:* an example of Milton's spelling of the plural possessive (otherwise "thir") when it is rhetorically or metrically stressed (Grierson, *Poems* 2.xl–xli); see also *PL* 11.740. Cf. *DocCh* 1.11, which denotes the effects of the Fall on Adam and Eve's progeny (Maurice Kelley 147; Patterson, *Works* 15:183) and *PL* 11.106–08, 423–28; 12.285–86. Sims (*Bible* 272) also cites Ezek. 18:4 ("The soul that sinneth, it shall die"), Rom. 5:14 ("Death reigned...even over them that had not sinned after the similitude of Adam's transgression"), and Rom. 6:23 ("The wages of sin is death").

401–08. Cf. *DocCh* 1.14, "Redemption is that act whereby Christ, being sent in the fulness of time, redeemed all believers at the price of his own blood, by his own voluntary act, conformably to the eternal counsel and grace of God the Father" (Patterson, *Works* 15:253) and *DocCh* 1.16, "The effect and design of the whole ministry of mediation is, the satisfaction of divine justice on behalf of all men" (Maurice Kelley 157, 165; Patterson, *Works* 15:315). Milton apparently considered "settled" his explanation that God was just in punishing infants (Empson, *Milton's God* 200); cf. Patterson, *Works* 15:187.

401. *appaid:* "satisfied" (Wesley). Keightley glosses as "paid, satisfied" from the Italian *appagato* and notes its frequency in Chaucer and Spenser. Verity also cites Shakespeare's "apaid" in *Rape of Lucrece* 914. *OED* 2 reports the obsolete sense as "repaid, requited, rewarded." Cf. "pay / The rigid satisfaction" (3.211–12). The theology of the payment is explained in Rom. 3:24–26.

402–27. Cf. the promise in *PL* 3.236–41, 285–97.

402–04. On filial fear, see **12.561–64.** Patrides identifies this passage as the third and last in which Milton attempts to link obedience and love, the other two being 5.501–03 and its repetition in 8.633–37 (*Milton* 163–64).

    The Law of God exact he shall fulfill: cf. Jesus' concern for keeping the law in Matt. 3:15 and 5:17. Cf. *DocCh* 1.16: "Christ fulfilled the law by perfect love to God and neighbor" (Maurice Kelley 166; Patterson, *Works* 15:317).

403–04. *love / Alone fulfill the Law:* paraphrases Rom. 13:10; cf. Matt. 22:36–40 and also similar sentiments expressed by Milton's contemporary Joseph Glanvill:

"Love . . . is the vital grace of our religion: 'tis the law and gospel in a word, for love is the fulfilling of the Law, and the Gospel is a Law of Love" (*Catholick Charity* 3). Although for Milton love fulfills the law, his experience and temperament stresses the will (Grierson, *Milton and Wordsworth* 179). Shawcross links this passage with the invocation to book 7, which surveys the creation of all things out of chaos and the nature of love ("Balanced Structure" 696, 698).

403. *Both by obedience and by love:* cf. biblical comments on the Passion in John 15:10 ("I have kept my Father's commandments, and abide in his love"), Phil. 2:8 ("He humbled himself, and became obedient unto death, even the death of the cross"), and Heb. 5:8 ("Though he were a Son, yet learned he obedience by the things which he suffered").

404–23. On the epic-tragic paradox, see **12.368–71**.

404–19. Reesing contrasts the Son's humiliation here with his physical splendor and might in book 6 (74).

405–06. "*Paradise Lost*, as an assertion of eternal providence, of God's reversal of evil, is far less concerned with the commission of sin than with the triumph of grace" (R. M. Frye 70).

406. *reproachful life and cursed death:* cf. *DocCh* 1.16 regarding Christ's voluntary submission to humiliation (Maurice Kelley 164; Patterson, *Works* 15:303); cf. *PL* 12.412–13.
   cursed death: i.e., hanging on the "tree" of the cross; it was so defiling that bodies were not allowed to be so hung after sundown (Deut. 21:23, Gal. 3:13). Despite the reproach, the Son will purge evil in a second creation in some ways holier than the first (Lawry, *Shadow* 284).

407–35. God's decision to forgive human trespass, and in fact to let that forgiveness run backward to the original Fall, is a matter of his somehow changing his mind rather than from having a predestined purpose, so that the fear of God is no longer the beginning of wisdom, because the newly proclaimed law of Christ softens the rigors of the ancient law, and servitude to multiplied legal formulas gives place to joyous and confident liberty, which is, however, illusory: the future is still as somber as the past (Douady 205–06).

407–08. *Proclaiming Life to all who shall believe / In his redemption:* cf. the similarly worded corporate or universal promises of John 6:40 and Rom. 5:19. Sims (*Bible* 272) also cites John 5:24, 6:47, and 11:25–26, which include similar promises to the individual believer.

407. *Proclaiming:* 1667 *Proclaming.*

408–10. *Faith… not… works:* the foundational Protestant tenet of *sola fide* ([saved] by faith alone) for which biblical proof-texts include Gal. 2:16, Eph. 2:8–9, and Tit. 3:5. Cf. *DocCh* 1.22, "We are justified therefore by faith, but a living faith…which acts" (Maurice Kelley 171–72; Patterson, *Works* 16:39); cf. *PL* 11.63–64, 12.426–27, and **11.63–64**. Bentley, also citing the Gal. passage, considerably emends 409–10 to, "Imputed *becomes Theirs* by Faith; His Merits / *Do* save them; not their Own *through* legal works." Pearce rejects *Do,* and though he sees the argument for *through,* still argues that the original *though* could be insisting that the works are strictly conformable to the law. The Richardsons refer to *PL* 3.235 and 285. Newton claims that the verb *believe* governs both clauses in 408. Todd reports the suggestion of an "ingenious gentleman" that *merits* is an elision, and that the lines should thus read "his *merit is* / To save them." Mitford wants "So save them" (Keightley). Verity complains that "the verb *believe* has already taken two different constructions." Fowler remarks that "imputation" played a large role in the Protestant doctrine of justification by faith, since it was held that Christ's righteousness and faith were *imputed* to the believer, covering by means of a "legal fiction" one's misdeeds by the righteousness of Christ. Cf. **12.295** and also the discussion of justification in *DocCh* 1.22: "As therefore our sins are imputed to Christ, so the merits or righteousness of Christ are imputed to us through faith" (Maurice Kelley 171; Patterson, *Works* 15:27). "Merit" is a forensic term with implications far beyond book 3; the discussion in book 12 is linked to the exaltation of the Son, the rebellion of Satan, and the nocturnal temptation of Eve (Patrides, "*Paradise Lost*" 111). Wesley omits this passage.

  though legal: "though their works were in accordance with the law (there being no justification by works)" (Fowler).

408–09. *obedience…merits:* the unstressed ending in an unvoiced consonant after a stressed vowel is an example of Milton's later style in the last six books (Oras, "Milton's Blank Verse" 166); cf. *PL* 12.247, 255, 518–21.

408. *redemption:* "deliverance from sin and its consequences by the atonement of Jesus Christ" (so *OED* 1a).

411–35. The phonological and grammatical features of this passage make it immediate: the participles (*hated, blasphem'd, Seis'd,* etc.) strike hammer blows at the body that seems even now being nailed to the cross; the prolonging of the long *a*'s (*Shameful, naild, Nation,* etc.) emphasize the continuance of the event, as does the shift from future perfect to present tense; the reversibility of *nails* and *slain* suggests a shift from referential language to ritual incantation; and the submergence of syntactic structure suggests an eternal present despite the linear presentation (Fish 325–26).

411–19. "It is impossible to disregard the weight of the assertion: the poignancy of the crucified Redeemer's death, the inexhaustible mercy which his sacrifice releases, the charity of God" (Peter 156).

411. *live hated, be blasphem'd:* cf. John 15:18, "The world…hated me before it hated you" and the blasphemies spoken against Christ in Luke 22:65.

412–13. *to death condemnd / A shameful and accurst:* cf. Deut. 21:23 and Gal. 3:13. Bentley emends 413 to "*Death* shameful and accurst." Cf. *DocCh* 1.16, "This death was ignominious in the highest degree" (Maurice Kelley 164–65; Patterson, *Works* 15:305), and also *PL* 12.406. C. H. Collins Baker notes that among Blake's illustrations for *PL* is "Michael Foretells the Crucifixion"; "The Crucifixion" is also a design by John Martin used in an 1844 edition of *PL* (106, 116).

414. *slaine for bringing Life:* cf. the similar paradox in Acts 3:15, where the apostle Peter claims that the religious leaders "killed the Prince of life."

415–16. *But to the Cross he nailes thy Enemies, / The Law that is against thee:* cf. Col. 2:14: "Blotting out the hand-writing of ordinances that was against us...nailing it to his cross." Bentley wants to make *Enemies* single (*Enemy*), but Pearce objects that *Sins* in 216 are also enemies. Newton makes the enemies of Adam both the law against him and the sins of all humanity springing from and therefore chargeable to him. Cf. *DocCh* 1.15, where Christ "overcomes and subdues his enemies...the world...Death, and the law, and sin," and 1.27, "That law which not only cannot justify, but is the source of trouble and subversion to all believers...must necessarily have been abolished" (Maurice Kelley 164, 175; Patterson, *Works* 15:301, 16:137); cf. *PL* 12.430–35.

418. *who rightly trust:* cf. *DocCh* 1.15: "Faith is also called...'trust'" (Maurice Kelley 169; Patterson, *Works* 15:397).

419–35. One of the passages about supernal grace identified by Reesing; see **12.111–13.** This passage completes the pattern formed by the association of light and dark imagery with vertical images of fall and resurrection (Cope 127–28). These lines, like the closing lines of *Lyc,* transmute pastoral images lost by Adam's Fall into the triumphant images of Christianity that finally transcends nature (Ferry, *Milton's Epic Voice* 177). Reesing (100) characterizes this passage as, first, "short summary clauses" (419–21), then "surging, soaring energies" (421–23), then "slower, louder rhythms" for doctrine (424–25), then "slow, loud, emphatic, and triumphant" for revelation (427–29), then "strenuous, even fierce muscularity" (429–33), then "serene *allegretto* cadences" (434–35); see **11.1–21.**

419–22. *dies...rise:* one of the 52 instances of rhyming lines with two intervening nonrhyming lines (Diekhoff, "Rhyme" 541–42); see Purcell for additional instances (172). Cf. Rom. 6:9: "Death hath no more dominion over him." Milton has Rev. 1:18 in mind (Todd).

419. *satisfaction:* "[a] theological term, meaning generally payment of a penalty due to God on account of man's sin. Here Christ's vicarious satisfaction is meant" (Fowler).

421–23. Christ's resurrection is the first image of renewal in Michael's discourse that employs metaphors of returning light; Adam (12.471–73) proclaims it to be more wonderful than the original creation of light (Brockbank 219–20). See **12.271–73**. Knott compares the joy of this daybreak with Adam's much more tentative expectations of the day ("joy, but with fear yet linkt") in *PL* 11.139 ("Pastoral Day" 178–79). Cf. *DocCh* 1.16, which describes three degrees of Christ's exaltation: "his resurrection, his ascension into heaven, and his sitting on the right hand of God" (Maurice Kelley 165; Patterson, *Works* 15:313) and also Christ's Ascension in 12.451–52 and taking his seat in 12.456–58. In Tonson's 1720 edition of *PL*, the "tail-piece" to book 12 (i.e., ornament at its ending) is "Christ Risen" by Chéron and DuBois, a subject also among Francis Hayman's designs of 1749 (C. H. C. Baker 13, 14).

   ere the third dawning light: cf. dawn in Matt. 28:1.

422. *Starres of Morn:* This phrase is complex; Milton primarily uses morning as an image of Christ's Resurrection (the morning star is the evening star that sets to rise again, symbolism going back at least to Rabanus Maurus), but the stars may be angels, in which case they really do *see* (Fowler). Cf. Satan's counterfeiting the morning star in 5.708–10 and the image of the reviving "day-star," i.e., the sun, in *Lyc* 168–71.

424–25. *Thy ransom paid … His death for Man:* cf. 1 Tim. 2:6: "[He] gave himself a ransom for all." Bentley emends to "*The* ransom" and "for *Men*." Pearce objects that *thy* is appropriate, since Adam's offspring are included, as in 12.427; the Richardsons agree, even claiming that *thy* is more beautiful and energetic. Many later texts change *thy* to *the* (Verity). Fowler also retains *thy*, since it "implies that Adam is being addressed as representative of fallen man."

   Patrides traces the "ransom theory" of atonement to Irenaeus, though Origen implied a similar one; that theory was often distasteful, since the Son's ransom was offered to Satan himself, and it died out until the Reformation revived a modified version in which the Father was the recipient ("Milton and the Protestant Theory" 8–10; see also *Milton* 130–42).

425–26. *as many as offerd Life / Neglect not:* cf. John 1:12, where eternal life is offered to all believers, and also *DocCh* 1.4: "God, out of his infinite mercy and grace in Christ, has predestinated to salvation all who should believe" (Patterson, *Works* 14:125). Fowler finds a hint at the doctrine of election. Hope and consolation are offered only to those who accept it; Adam is already repentant and eagerly seeking an escape from sin (Moore 26–27).

426–27. *By Faith not void of workes:* cf. James 2:20, 26, "Faith without works is dead," and also **11.408–10**, as well as "Faith and faithful works" (11.63–64) and "Faith not void of workes" (12.426–27). See also **11.63–64**.

427–35. Cf. the account of Christ's triumph over death in 3.241–53.

427. *this God-like act:* Sims (*Bible* 272) cites Rom. 1:4, where Christ is "declared to be the Son of God…by the resurrection from the dead."

429. *In sin for ever lost from life:* cf. Eph. 2:1, "dead in trespasses and sins." This passage is Milton's clearest statement on the death of the soul, about which he says far less than, say, either Dante or Bunyan, because once Milton had explained how to escape this death he only needed to vindicate the God's providence (Moore 26).

430–35. *Shall bruise the head of Satan…fix farr deeper in his head thir stings:* another announcement of Gen. 3:15. "This theme of triumph transforms the ending" (Di Cesare 24). According to Rev. 20:10, the devil will be tormented forever. See **12.415–16** on *DocCh* 1.15.

431–35. Wesley omits this passage.

431–34. *Death…temporal death:* Milton uses capitalization to distinguish certain uses of a word, including personification (Darbishire, *Poetical Works* 1:xxxi); see B. A. Wright's remarks in **11.462–65**. Cf. Milton's conception of *temporal death* in *PL* 11.469 (Hughes, *Paradise Lost, A Poem*).

434–35. *a death like sleep, / A gentle wafting:* cf. death as sleep in 1 Cor. 15:51 and 1 Thess. 4:13–15, and also the similar deathlike sleep that overtakes Odysseus's Phaiakian oarsmen (*Odyssey* 13.80). Some editions print *a death-like sleep,* which—as Todd argues at length—changes the meaning from a comment on the nature of the death; Verity complains that the hyphen is "a mere tampering with the text." In later rabbinical tradition, Adam was promised resurrection (E. C. Baldwin, "Some Extra-Biblical Semitic Influences" 394). This passage is one of only two in *PL* that refer to Milton's mortalism, the other being 3.329 (Babb 53); cf. *DocCh* 1.13 on the death of the body (Patterson, *Works* 15:215–51). Radzinowicz concludes that end is finally accomplished here, as Adam lays hold of the faith that recognizes death as the gate of life and evil as the means toward good; "to this wisdom is then coupled right acts" (42); see also Radzinowicz's comments in **11.429–65**.

wafting: Verity reads as "passing."

437–38. *to appeer / To his Disciples:* recorded in all four Gospels (Matt. 28:16–17, Mark 16:14, Luke 24:36, John 20:19) and also in the history of the early church (Acts 1:3).

Disciples: "one of the personal followers of Jesus Christ during his life; esp. one of the Twelve" (so *OED* 1a).

438–39. *Men who in his Life / Still follow'd him:* cf. Luke 22:28, Acts 1:21–22.

440–42. *To teach all nations…Baptizing in the profluent stream:* Christ's "great commission" in Matt. 28:19 is similarly worded: "teach all nations, baptizing them." The ministry of Christ and his apostles combines the ideals of savior, martyr, and teacher (Steadman, *Milton* 101–02). Michael's vision of the future alludes only to baptism; the other Protestant sacrament of Eucharist (Lord's Supper) was fiercely debated at the time (Patrides, *Milton* 217).

Milton believed that baptism should take place in running water; cf. *DocCh* 1.28, where the Latin for "in[to] running water" is *in profluentem aquam* (Maurice Kelley 178; Patterson, *Works* 16:168–69). Schultz praises "the irenical intent running through the *Christian Doctrine*": Milton went out of his way to say a kind word for the Seventh-Day Baptists; baptism of adults is also implied here, though not prescribed (119).

stream: 1667 *streame.*

441. Wesley omits this line.

443. *washing them from guilt of sin:* Milton's description of baptism draws on biblical language, such as in Eph. 5:26, where Christ is said to cleanse the church "with the washing of water by the word" or in Tit. 3:5, "the washing of regeneration." Sims (*Bible* 272) also cites the exhortation to be baptized in Acts 22:16.

444–45. *death, like that which the redeemer dy'd:* cf. Christ's assurance to his disciples that they would share his fate (Matt. 20:23, Mark 10:39), referred to as a "cup" in John 18:11. Bentley emends to "*their* redeemer," which Newton finds "not improbable." Todd finds no reason for the emendation, since the original reading is "surely…very emphatical." Stoll exclaims that here "the verse itself is such a sigh" ("From the Superhuman" 14).

446–49. Cf. *DocCh* 1.26: "This wall of partition between the Gentiles and Israelites was at length broken down by the death of Christ" (Maurice Kelley 174; Patterson, *Works* 16:105); the barrier metaphor is from Eph. 2:14.

448–49. *the Sons / Of Abrahams Faith:* cf. similar typological statements in Rom. 4:16, Gal. 3:7–18, 4:22–26. Fixler summarizes traditional Christian understanding: "The Jews were really the children of the bondswoman…under the bondage of the old law, while all others who accepted faith in Christ were the true or spiritual seed of Abraham" (256). Hughes (*Paradise Lost*) may be guilty of some hyperbole when he says, "In the following eighty lines Milton fuses together countless reminiscences from the New Testament, the Psalms, and the Prophets," but the task of tracing the pervasive biblical echoes is indeed a critical problem. According to Sims, even the clear references to Scripture in Milton's epics have been considerably underglossed (*Bible* 2–3).

450. *So in his seed all Nations shall be blest:* one of the passages about supernal grace identified by Reesing; see **12.111–13**. Milton conflates Abraham's promised seed with the promised seed of the woman, as does Gal. 3:7–9. Cf. *PL* 12.125–26, 148–50, and 273.

451–65. "The heroic triumph over Satan [12.451–55] is told in fast and powerful tempos, and these are followed by a gradual retard (with no diminution of volume) for the elaborate vision of judgment and a redeemed creation" (Reesing 101); see also **11.1**.

451–52. *he shall ascend:* cf. *DocCh* 1.16, which describes three degrees of Christ's exaltation: "his resurrection, his ascension into heaven, and his sitting on the right hand of God" (Maurice Kelley 165; Patterson, *Works* 15:313); cf. also Christ's Resurrection in 12.421–23, Ascension in 12.451–52, and taking his seat in 12.456–58. In *DocCh* 1.5, Milton denies that this position indicates equality with God (Maurice Kelley 90; Patterson, *Works* 14:337).

452–56. Wesley reduces this passage to a single line, "With victory, triumphing, and resume."

452. *With victory, triumphing through the aire:* cf. Ps. 68:18, Eph. 4:8–10, and Col. 2:15, often read as expressions of Christ's "harrowing of hell." One need not stress the second syllable of *triumphing,* since substituting a trochee for an iamb in the third foot "breaks and accelerates the movement of the line consonantly with the sense" (Moody). Verity wants the stress on the second syllable, as it is in 1.123. Dunster credits the influence of Du Bartas's line, "Death, ghastly Death, triumpheth every where," with Milton's stressing the second syllable of *triumphing,* and also at 1.123 and 3.338 (*Considerations* 196); cf. Du Bartas 2:561.595.

453–55. *there shall surprise / The Serpent, Prince of aire, and drag in Chaines / Through all his Realme:* cf. Satan's addressing his followers "in mid air" (*PR* 1.39–47) and in the "middle Region of thick Air" (*PR* 2.117) and Satan's title, "Prince of the Air" (*PL* 10.185), cf. also Eph. 2:2, "prince of the power of the air." By using this title, Milton not only joins "a host of pious commentators" but also avoids "the classification of devils, which made Aerial Powers the sixth order, with Meresin as its chief" (West, *Milton and the Angels* 156–57). See also the biblical account of Satan's being chained for 1,000 years (Rev. 20:2–3) and, as Babb (29) points out, the overly thin air of *PL* 12.76–78.

Serpent: "the serpent, 'more subtil than any beast of the field,' that tempted Eve (Gen. 3:1–5); the Tempter, the Devil, Satan. Also, *the Old Serpent* (after Rev. 12:9)" (so *OED* 2).

455. *and there:* 1667 *& there.*

456–58. *and resume / His Seat…exalted high / Above all names in Heav'n:* paraphrases Eph. 1:20–21. Cf. similar statements of exaltation in Luke 24:26,

Acts 2:33, and Phil. 2:5–11, as well as the Son's position at God's right hand in 3.62–63.

458–65. One of the passages about supernal grace identified by Reesing; see **12.111–13**. Cf. the description of the end of time in *PL* 3.323–41. Milton repeats the ending of the world in 12.546–49, but he may have decided that they were both well handled and that combining them would not have improved the epic (Gilbert, *On the Composition* 136–37).

459. *When this worlds disolution shall be ripe:* cf. the harvest metaphor of Rev. 14:18–19. Bentley has "*the* world's," as do some later editions; Pearce prefers the "this" of the first two editions, because it preserves the stress of the line.
   disolution: 1667 *dissolution.*

460. *With glory and power to judge both quick and dead:* cf. Luke 21:27 ("with power and great glory") and 2 Tim. 4:1, "Jesus Christ…shall judge the quick and the dead." "Power," frequently repeated in the epic, denotes a leading characteristic of God (Ryken 203).
   quick: "living persons. (Chiefly in echoes of Acts 10:42 or the Apostles' Creed, in the phrase *quick and dead*)" (so *OED* B1a).
   and dead: 1667 *& dead.*

461–65. *judge th'unfaithful…reward / His faithful:* cf. similar statements in Matt. 25:31–46, John 5:28–29, and Rev. 11:18. The future state, though without evil, will be possessed only by those who struggle faithfully against evil; thus, the greatest happiness is dependent on and conditioned by the evil of the world (Gilbert, "Problem" 188). The images of terrestrial paradise, including the specious beauty of enchanting mythology, are only prefigurations of this interior state (Blondel 82). The days will be happier only for the redeemed; neither the fallen angels nor the majority of humankind will experience a "fortunate fall" (Ogden 17). Martz complains that although the Second Coming should provide the poetic equilibrium promised at the outset of book 11, Milton is "a man of his time" who must have Michael set forth "the final dark cycle of the vicious world's decay" (164).

462. *receave them into bliss:* descriptions of heaven as a place of bliss abound in *PL* (Ryken 209–10).

463–67. See Stapleton note at **11.134–35**.

463–65. Daniells argues against viewing the garden as a transitory springboard to project Adam into the future, since the waiting paradise, though outside human experience, is "the world to which the visions of Dante, of Raphael, of Bach...leads us," and the garden is therefore a durable image of abundant joy and vitality ("A Happy Rural Seat" 16–17). Giamatti finds in this passage the culmination of movement from phenomenon to figure, from object to metaphor; "the greatest of former realities, the garden, is now an image...not only of what we lost, but what we will gain" (349). Empson thinks that this passage suggests that "even the elect will perhaps never be allowed into heaven" (*Milton's God* 191). On conflagration and renewal, see **11.66**. Wesley omits this passage.

463. *Whether in Heav'n or Earth:* Empson thinks this phrase expresses doubt about the Millennium, but Fowler glosses it as something like "both in heaven and on earth," since a backward syntactic link makes the text express the comprehensiveness of the Last Judgment (i.e., angels and well as humans), while a forward syntactic link makes the point that "bliss will be general, so that the distinction between heaven and earth is insignificant"; cf. *Milton's God* 127.

465. *far happier daies:* Empson asserts that "any angel instructed in theology" should realize that God's intent is to spite Satan eternally (*Milton's God* 145–46). Milton constructs the apocalyptic state by contrast, either quantitatively or qualitatively, with ordinary reality (Ryken 50).

466. *So spake th'Archangel Michael, then paus'd:* Bentley, claiming as always that *Michael* is disyllabic, emends to "then *he* paused."

467. *As at the Worlds great period:* OED does not quote this line in its various definitions for *period*, which include "length of time" (1), "duration" (2), "an age; era" (3a), and an end, conclusion" (11a). Ricks (*Paradise Lost*) glosses *period* as "ending," and Le Comte as "end." Verity cites *1 Henry 6*, "The period of thy tyranny approacheth" (4.2.17), and Himes (*"Paradise Lost": A Poem*) refers to Rev. 10:6–7, since "the second Angel that appeared to John in the vision of the trumpets likewise announced the end of the world." Because, Babb says, the beginnings of both time and space correspond logically with the effluence of matter from God, when "things durable" first came into being, the "world's great period" will be the end both of time and of matter as we know it (121). The *as* signals an important simile; Adam must learn the difference between the working out of things in history and the "false surmise" about the vision he is being given (Brisman 263). The epic begins and ends with the exaltation of the Son, and refers to the Platonic year in 5.582–83 and here, the decisive closing of the circle (Rajan, "*Paradise Lost:* The Hill" 46). Fowler, who argues that the three divisions of Michael's instruction are meant to correspond to the "three drops" of the well of life placed in Adam's eyes (11.416), notes that this is Michael's second pause, the first being at noon; it is now 6:00 P.M., or 6,000 years later; see also **11.416** and **12.5**. Michael's pause is appropriate, since the Second Coming is the event he has prophesied (Miner 48).

469–78. This passage has occasioned more comment than any other passage in *PL* 11–12. The most influential comments have been made by Addison and by Lovejoy. Addison, cited in whole or in part by many subsequent critics, judges that these lines brilliantly supply the "natural defect" in *PL,* since a heroic poem should end happily (*Spectator* 3 [3 May 1712]: 388). Lovejoy's watershed article, "Milton and the Paradox of the Fortunate Fall" (1937) sets the parameters of discussion on this passage at least through 1970. Lovejoy links this passage to "O felix culpa quae talem ac tantum meruit habere redemptorem" (O happy crime that deserv'd to have such and so great a redeemer!), a line from the Roman Catholic liturgy of the Easter vigil, i.e., the day before Easter. He cites Ambrose, Gregory the Great, Du Bartas, and Giles Fletcher to suggest that Milton was echoing a church tradition that considered the result of Adam's sin to be so positive as to gladden: "A fall from Eden which made the joys of heaven possible was plainly no mishap" (167). Herbert J. C. Grierson, also writing in 1937, appears to take a similar position: "In the end Adam acknowledges that even his Fall is to be valued as the *occasion* of Christ's goodness" (*Milton and Wordsworth* 104).

"O felix culpa quae talem ac tantum meruit habere redemptorem" was first quoted by the Richardsons, who attribute it to Gregory, a church father. Newton calls the line, "that rant of one of the Fathers," also citing Luke 2:14: "Glory to God in the highest, and on earth peace, good will toward men." Todd thinks that Milton rather had in mind 2 Cor. 4:15: "For all things are for your sakes, that the abundant grace might through the thanksgiving of many redound to the glory of God"; see also Rom. 5:20: "But where sin abounded, grace did much more abound." Wesley (1763) omits most of this passage, retaining only "O goodness infinite, goodness immense! / That all this good of evil shall produce."

Various early twentieth century critics before Lovejoy have commented on the passage. Thompson (1913) does not propose a fortunate Fall but rather interprets Adam's outburst as his recognition that the powers of evil are "chained absolutely by the will of God" ("Theme" 112). Erskine (1917), though he thinks Milton may have been suggesting that the retention of innocence may have been a loss, finds the suggestion unorthodox and is surprised that "Michael, the epic messenger, permits such demoralizing comfort" (574, 578). Stoll (1918) puts the passage in the context a gradual "humanizing" in the last two books, a consciously structured modulation toward the human ("Was Paradise" 431). Moore (1921) recognizes the paradox but does not think that it strains orthodoxy, citing Du Bartas, Giles Fletcher, and Sir Thomas Browne (29–30). Gilbert (1923), dealing with the problem of evil in *PL*, identifies Eve's prelapsarian view with Milton's postlapsarian one that evil is necessary for the development of virtue, as in *Areop* ("Problem" 185–86). Saurat (1925) also sees the passage as indicating God's providential use of evil, answering the epic aim to "justify the ways of God to men"; Saurat even claims that Milton "saw advantages in the Fall" (108, 209). Buxton (1929), however, denies that Milton succeeds in justifying the ways of God to man. In fact, Buxton seems to doubt that Milton himself believed in the Bible any more than he did in Greek and Roman antiquity—it was part of his culture whether or not it was factual (72–74). Ransom (1931) does not comment specifically on this passage, but he does argue against a perception of Edenic stasis that underlies many *felix culpa* readings of the epic: "[Milton] did not leave Adam and Eve stranded without a natural career...[or] intellectual life" (*God* 130–31). Stoll (1933) again claims a pattern of humanizing throughout the epic, a "mingled web, good and ill together, that complex of thoughts and emotions which makes up the situation at the close and represents human experience ever since" ("From the Superhuman" 14); cf. Stoll, "Was Paradise" (1918). Hughes's initial annotation (*Paradise Lost* [1935]) makes this passage the pivot of Milton's justification of the ways of God to men, also citing Du Bartas as well as Rom. 5:20 ("But where sin abounded, grace did much more abound"), but Hughes's revised annotation (*Paradise Lost, A Poem* [1962]) echoes Lovejoy.

Though some critics may have anticipated Lovejoy, nearly all discussion of *PL* 12.469–78 for the next several decades refers to his 1937 article. The following year, Green (1938) agrees with Lovejoy and asserts that the form the paradox takes reconciles Milton's humanistic concern for rationality with his theological commitment to voluntarism: "as a Humanist he had to get Adam out of paradise, where real knowledge and its consequence, ethical evolution, were impossible; and paradoxically, it was as a combined intellectualist and voluntarist that Milton got him out" (570). McColley (1939) relates Adam's outburst to orthodox justifications of God's ways to men: "Because of God's benignity and foreknowledge, and his tempering of Justice with Mercy, good was born out of evil … the Fall became the *felix culpa* which brought the greater glory to God" ("*Paradise Lost*" 204). In 1940, McColley cites Milton's contemporary Andrew Willet that "as God foresaw Man's transgression, so he knew how to turn it to good"; McColley seems to assume that the paradox is inherent in God's foreseeing the good and permitting the evil (*Paradise Lost: An Account* 202, 212).

Though Lovejoy's argument initially received some positive responses, they were followed by assessments that found it insufficient or even erroneous. Arnold Williams (1941) insists that the greater good produced by the Fall is that the individual has the choice of choosing between good and evil and that a static paradise might have been unacceptable to Milton ("Conservative Critics" 97). Lewis (1942) shifts the focus to how the good produced by evil is "the exact reverse" of Satan's program to pervert the end of any good God wanted to do through him; instead Satan "is allowed to do all the evil he wants and finds that he has produced good. Those who will not be God's sons become His tools" (*Preface* 66). In a novel published by Lewis the following year (1943), set in an unfallen world and obviously influenced by his thinking on *PL,* he criticizes the very idea of a fortunate Fall: "The first King and first Mother of our world did the forbidden thing; and He brought good of it in the end. But what they did was not good; and what they lost we have not seen. And there were some to whom no good came nor ever will come" (*Perelandra* 125). Thompson (1943) identifies the passage as one indication that Adam has learned what Michael had intended and is no longer in despair, rather than either Adam or Milton being pessimistic ("For *Paradise Lost*" 381). Diekhoff (*Milton's "Paradise Lost"*) devotes several pages (126–32) to whether Milton believed in the *felix culpa;* he concludes that Milton was unwilling to choose between the horns of the dilemma (131).

Much of the criticism in the next several years considers the degrees of happiness produced by the so-called *felix culpa*. Howard (1946) assumes that man's sin and the introduction of death into the world were necessary for the happier outcome of the paradise within: "In the customary phrase, so popular among the Puritans, the final cause of the Fall was the 'greater glory of God'" (165). Hutchinson (1946) sees the sentiments of Adam's speech as "similar" to the *O felix culpa* hymn and finds an similar emphasis on redemption in the angelic hymn after the temptation in *PR* 4.633–35 (164–65). Rajan (1947) claims that the paradox of good emerging from evil runs throughout the epic and especially in the last two books, in every special dispensation toward the righteous (God's providence) and every punishment of the wicked (his justice) (*"Paradise Lost" and the Seventeenth Century* 47). Arnold Williams (1948) cites two Renaissance commentators who develop the paradox: Pererius includes it among the examples of how God turns evil into good, even citing the liturgical hymn, which he erroneously attributes to Gregory the Great, while Alexander Ross follows Pererius in calling attention to how God turned the evil of man's disobedience into the greater good of the incarnation and redemption (*Common Expositor* 139). Mohl (1949), arguing that Milton and the Quakers shared a belief in human perfectibility, asserts, "Adam's ecstatic vision of such 'goodness infinite, goodness immense' is ample assurance that paradise is not lost, that, by the grace of a living God, mankind is on the way to a new paradise" (*Studies* 129). George Coffin Taylor (1949), who explicitly aligns himself with Lovejoy's argument, finds Adam's outburst as evidence that life outside of paradise will be endurable and in fact for some "even preferable to the life of Adam in the age of innocence" ("Did Milton" 207), but Tillyard (1949) argues that even Adam's happy outburst represents only Milton's constantly professed conscious optimism; in reality very few will be saved from the wreck of the world, a state of affairs for which Milton does not blame God (*Milton* 272–74, 286–877); see **12.524–51**. Mahood (1950) sees as irrelevant the question of whether Milton would have been bored or happy in his own Eden, because as Milton says in *Areop,* he is concerned with the state of humanity as it now is (Patterson, *Works* 4:311); although he believed in a fortunate Fall, that is "something quite different from believing the Fall to be a commendable act" (246–48). Brooks (1951), without explicitly discussing the last two books of *PL,* does discuss Adam's paradoxical inability to know his own prelapsarian happiness; Brooks, moreover, contests the idea that the Fall was just a developmental stage ("Milton" 1045–54). Kirkconnell (1952) reports that in Serafino della Salandra's *Adamo Caduto* of 1647, Mercy rejoices in Adam's "fortunate fault" and is upbraided by Omnipotence for being glad at the pain and ruin of another (334).

Weisinger (1953) devotes a book-length study to the paradox as a "mythic ritual pattern" in Western culture with implications for Hebrew and Christian thought, beginning with this passage and with Lovejoy's reading of Milton (*Tragedy* 19–20), but most responses in the mid- to later 1950s concern how critics can reconcile the passage with the rest of the epic and with Milton's own religious and philosophical positions. Bell (1953) sees Milton as a monist for whom humanity was always already fallen, so that redemption is the only hope that Adam or we ever had of paradise (880–81). Bell's view is soon debated by Shumaker (1955), who finds her position to be the logical conclusion of Tillyard's assumption that Adam and Eve are already fallen in Eden ("Notes" 1185–87). Ogden (1957) argues against the "already fallen" premises of Bell and Tillyard, and also against the assumption that the Fall is the climax of the poem, since after book 9 we are no longer in suspense about the Fall occurring, as well as against the assumption that that the Fall was fortunate; Adam says he is in doubt, and nothing states or implies that man's lot is or will be better than if Adam and Eve had not fallen (17–18).

In the meantime, Brooks (1954) rejects the critical presupposition that the Fall in *PL* was necessary for human happiness ("Eve's Awakening" 297–98). Burke (1954) finds Adam's doubt in the face of the paradox to be "exceptionally human" but entirely orthodox; it provides the "necessary equipoise" to prevent Adam's sense of humility from turning to pride (225). Joseph (1954) stresses the importance of perspective: "To Satan, Adam's fall appears as consummate victory and revenge, whereas it is really a 'happy fault' that makes manifest the great love of the Redeemer" (259). Muir (1955) ties Adam's outburst to the 'better fortitude of patience' and the Christian virtues mentioned by Michael, and especially to how God has used their sin for his own purposes; they and their descendants possess a paradise within them happier far than that from which they are being expelled (162). Svendsen (1956) judges that Lovejoy's reading not only satisfies both Christian dogma and epic decorum but also argues that it reinforces the epic's central theme, "the conflict of good and evil and the suspension of final decision between them" (*Milton and Science* 105–06). Madsen (1958) links the mention of Creation in the final redemptive process to "the great series of contrasts on which the poem is built—creation versus destruction, light versus darkness, order versus disorder" ("Idea" 219–20). MacCaffrey (1959) assumes that the *felix culpa* is a given; she names it in passing (86) but focuses instead on light imagery in *PL* 12.471–73 (175). Madsen ("The Fortunate Fall" 1959) stresses the triumph of the Incarnation enunciated in book 3, and though he does not indicate how that triumph is specifically related to the fortunate Fall, he claims that in Milton's universe humanity in its humiliation can only be exalted in Christ to the throne of God if hell were also possible (103–05). Ransom (1959) suggests that Milton parted company with God over the Expulsion, realizing that "not the dull sheltered garden, but the unknown forbidding world at large, is what we must identify in all piety...as 'the best of all possible worlds'" ("Idea" 137). Dick Taylor Jr. (1959) argues that although Adam's emotional outburst is dramatic, Milton's poetic method shows effects that are quite the contrary of the fortunate Fall ("Milton" 37, 49).

Critical readings of this passage particularly proliferated in the 1960s, which produced an average of over five articles per year, versus the average of two articles per year in the 1950s. Many earlier concerns were voiced in the numerous studies published in 1960, often with a concern for how the paradox itself is worded. In that year, Broadbent cautions the reader that Milton treats the idea of *felix culpa* "less sharply and less joyfully than Du Bartas," and in fact Broadbent complains that in line 470 ("That all this good of evil shall produce"), "the lyric impulse is geared down into mechanics...as though the cosmos were a factory" (*Some Graver Subject* 282–84). Colie calls the idea of the fortunate Fall a "doctrinal paradox" among other "orthodox paradoxes" that are the subject of her study (127). David Daiches says that *Paradise Lost* is not about the fortunate Fall in the sense of it having brought about Christian redemption (which he finds underemphasized) but that it is rather about how it exhibits the paradox of humanity's nature and destiny (59). Kermode finds that Eve's statement, "I who first brought Death on all, am grac't / The source of life" (11.168–69) is "a paradox more central to the mood of the poem than the famous *felix culpa*" (120). Patrick (20) links the passage to Augustine's statement (*Enchiridion* 100) that God, being himself supremely good, permits anything evil among his works only because he can bring good even out of evil; cf. Rozenberg 105–40 (1967). Pecheux assumes that Adam's reaction to the divine plan ("his famous 'felix culpa' speech") "completes the program adumbrated in the opening passage of the epic 'till one greater Man / Restore us, and regain the blissful Seat'" ("Concept" 366). Peter accepts the label of *felix culpa* (which he equates with the atonement) but thinks the moment of climax fails to the extent that the reader does not accept the Father's portrayal in the text; the reader acclaims the Son for his redemption but is not overwhelmingly grateful to God for permitting it (156).

Because so many critics had taken up the issue of the *felix culpa*, critical readings in the 1960s first needed to situate themselves in the growing discussion, although some still proposed systems of their own. Empson (1961), who reads this passage as Adam's emotional recognition that God wanted them to eat the fruit after all, concludes that "the doctrine of the fortunate fall...removes from God the last rag of excuse for his plot to corrupt the whole race" and that humanity therefore worships a devil (*Milton's God* 191–92). Hughes (1961) holds up Blake's illustration of the Expulsion as an expression of possible joy and lyric feeling denied by Broadbent's discussion of the fortunate Fall ("Some Illustrators" 673); cf. Broadbent, *Some Graver Subject* 282. Le Comte, in his edition of *PL* (1961) identifies similar phrasing to *goodness infinite* in *PL* 1.218, 4.414 and 734, and 7.76; for *good of evil*, cf. 1.163 and 7.188; for *evil turn*, cf. 11.373; he also judges line 474 to be "The doctrine of the happy fall—*felix culpa*," with a further reference to 12.587. Marshall (1961) proposes that *PL* is constructed on two systems, a dramatic system in which Eve seeks one kind of knowledge, and an intellectual system in which Adam finds another kind of knowledge, and that the intellectual meaning of the poem is ultimately the paradox of the fortunate Fall (18). Cope (1962), tracing a pattern of light and darkness that is complementary to falling and rising, reads the last two books as an expression of the fortunate Fall (142–48). Ferry (1962) judges that throughout the 1950s, opposing readings of the final lines of the poem were produced by opposing opinions of how important a role the *felix culpa* played in Milton's attitude toward the Fall; Adam apprehends here as a theological truth the paradox that Eve understands intuitively when she accepts her banishment from paradise ("Bird" 184, 198). Sasek (1962) argues that the phrasing that suggests the *felix culpa* is not Adam's final comment on the human predicament, since Michael's response is a pessimistic survey of the history of the Christian era (195). Summers (1962) claims that the passage represents the climax, where another poet would have ended the narrative, but God's providence is infinitely larger than the sinfulness of man here and for neither Adam nor for most of his descendants is the 'final vision' the end of life" (*Muse's Method* 218). Daniells (1963) emphasizes Adam's experience in its artistic context: God's purposes are "richer, more mysterious, more beneficent than we had thought," and Adam experiences "an illumination of such scope and profundity...that it breaks the normal bounds of epic or drama" (*Milton* 108).

Critical readings in the 1960s continued to invoke religious or philosophical issues. Ferry (1963) insists that the Fall was necessary to demonstrate divine love in the redemption to teach good by contrast with evil (*Milton's Epic Voice* 39). Lewalski (1963) links this passage to the end of book 11, where she remarks that Adam, like Noah, "condemns the world" by faith (31). Patrides (1963) cites seventeenth century discussions of the paradox, claiming it was widely maintained and that the notion of the "happy fault" survived the Reformation because "it is in fact a vital aspect of the *total* structure of Christian dogmatics" ("Adam's 'Happy Fault' "241). Williamson (1963) announces the fortunate Fall as a topic in his article, but only briefly notes "Adam's wonder at the paradox of his fall" in the midst of a much longer exposition of moral instruction in the entire epic (96, 108). Martz (1964) does not find that these few lines represent a poetic balance, that 100 lines of hopeful doctrine do not outweigh 600 of visionary woe, especially when Adam immediately asks about future persecutions (163). Patrides (1964) complains that although Dryden includes a version of this passage in *The State of Innocence and Fall of Man* (1677), or his "opera" of *Paradise Lost*, the four-line outburst is out of place because Dryden does not include the Christocentric messages that so naturally introduce the fortunate Fall into the epic (*Phoenix* 67).

Watson (1964) links this passage to 1.162–65, where Satan plans to pervert God's plan for Providence to bring forth good from evil. The two passages identify opposing forces at work in the poem (148–49). Pecheux (1965) thinks the *felix culpa* likely because of the implied parallel between Adam and Abraham, both leaving for a "new destiny rich in promise" ("Abraham" 369). Shawcross (1965) discusses this passage within his argument that *PL* is a comedy rather than a tragedy: "In tragedy evil must be driven out because it is imperfect, the order of the universe insisting on perfection; in *Paradise Lost* evil has been the means of Man's knowing truly what good is" ("Balanced Structure" 716). Bush (1966) glosses this passage, "The traditional paradox of Adam's *felix culpa,* the 'fortunate fall': Adam's sin, with all its evil consequences, provided the motive for Christ's incarnation and sacrifice, the working of divine love and grace, and hence man's reception into heavenly bliss." Champion (1966) assumes that the *felix culpa* is a "controlling pattern" (393). Giamatti (1966) finds less comfort in the passage than he thinks there should be, partly because the outburst is so sudden and pat, and its "doctrinal enthusiasm" somewhat forced, but mostly because what lingers is not joy at the implications of the *felix culpa* but rather a pervasive melancholy (349–50). Mollenkott (1966) finds this passage, which she calls "Adam's ecstatic comment on the fortunate fall," to parallel Adam's statement in 11.874–78 (40). Patrides (1966) calls the passage "the climax of God's constant creation of good out of evil," a theme he sees emphasized in 1.163–65, 217–19; 7.187–91, 613–16; and 12.565–66 (*Milton* 40); he also claims that although most commentators did not question the theory of Adam's "happy sinne," Milton was aware of theological traps inherent in the paradox and thus allowed Adam also to express doubts about its validity (142–43). Samuel (1966) finds echoes from the *Commedia* in Adam's speech: the words *infinite* and *immense* recall Dante on the divine goodness (e.g., *Purgatorio* 3.122; *Paradiso* 7.109), and the closest parallel is the final address to Beatrice in *Paradiso* (31.79–87); in both poems a series of lesser redeemers leads climactically to Christ (*Dante* 229–30). Burden (1967) connects *PL* 12.473 ("full of doubt") with Adam and Eve's "joy...with fear yet linkt" (11.139); because joy and woe are subtly balanced, "the thesis of the fortunate fall cannot be allowed to cancel out the tragic element in the poem or the tragic element still possible [for] Man's life" (199–200). Fish (1967) reads this passage as a statement of "total and self-annihilating union with the Divine," though it is also right that Adam descend from the moment, as he will need to descend to the subjected plain of life (324, 330). Hagenbüchle (1967) sees the idea of *felix culpa* as the result of Milton's attempt to justify God in a teleological proof (100). Lawry (1967) ignores the *felix culpa* passage in favor of a broader argument regarding Adam's tragic/Christian growth of self-knowledge and repentance (" 'Euphrasy and Rue' "). Patrides asserts the presence of "the paradox of the 'fortunate' Fall," but also notes other paradoxes in the poem ("*Paradise Lost*" 112–13). Rajan (1967) remarks that God's command to Michael in *PL* 11.117 ("So send them forth, though sorrowing, yet in peace") "is scarcely to be avoided except by those who seem to think that Adam should leave Eden in a state of blurred elation, inebriated, as it were, by the *felix culpa*" ("*Paradise Lost: The Hill*" 47). Rozenberg (1967) summarizes Augustine's comment in *Enchiridion* 96 and 100: "It was by the will of God that he did that which the Creator forbade, and accomplished that which He wanted" (135–36). Shumaker (1967) sees in the passage an expression of the balance in the epic; its universe responds to moral shocks just as it does to physical ones, but God's reactions "are not meanly punitive but benevolent and gracious," and Adam's final understanding of God's plan provokes his exclamation here (*Unpremeditated Verse* 35). Huntley (1968) ties the fortunate Fall to character development, a means of "a more difficult perfection," but although in Western thought bad things can have good effects, the experience of evil has cost us humans something, and in fact Adam has already forgotten Michael's warning (12.395–404); the final lesson is not that the Fall is fortunate but that obedience is best ("Before and After" 2, 7, 12–13).

Lawry (1968) argues that this passage is not about the *felix culpa*, since man's evil never is in doubt, but rather about Adam's amazement to see the spiritual "creation" (*PL* 12.472) of such good from such evil, an act that seems more wonderful even than the material creation from chaos (*Shadow* 285). Miner (1968) argues that Milton's view has been oversimplified; in context, the Fall is fortunate but only for a few, and in no wise a contradiction of anything else in the poem, nor is Michael's silence after Adam's outburst conclusive, and Adam's enthusiasm is adjusted if not wholly tempered by the eschatological context that stresses a long delay before the Fall can possibly be felt to be fortunate. In any case, the idea of the fortunate Fall is one that does credit rather to God than to man, because it is God alone who can bring good out of evil (44–46, 48). Radzinowicz (1968) also denies that Milton intended to suggest a fortunate Fall, since the most Milton says is that the Fall cannot thwart God's power and glory, and "he does not hint that Adam and Eve receive a better reward for the struggle to repair what they needlessly defaced"; she does, however, see Christian liberty as "the completest expression of what might be called the paradox of the fortunate fall," since the doom of the Law disciplines man to the next stage of freedom (36, 47–48); see also Radzinowicz's comments in **11.429–65**. Reesing (1968) denies that this passage can be Adam's final word, because he will not hear about the Resurrection until *PL* 12.539–46 and has missed Michael's hints that extinction may not after all be the end of his existence (60). Samuel (1968), arguing that the "wound" of Adam and Eve's fall infects the last two books with pathos, insists that "against readers who want to rename the poem 'All for Salvation, or Eden Well Lost' we can only argue that cancer is not a great good because it enables surgeons to show their skill" ("*Paradise Lost*" 29). Toole (1968), tracing behavioral contrasts among the epic's characters, judges that Adam's reaction is tied to having acted in humility rather than arrogant defiance; the fortunate Fall is not the unmixed blessing Satan envisaged (33). Trapp (1968) notes that although the first illustrations of the *felix culpa* are in early medieval manuscripts, the Fall is less important from the thirteenth century onward, when Christ's redemption is stressed (238, 243–44).

Lieb (1969) traces the paradox back to the promise in book 1 that Satan's evil would result only in more good (1.216–19), also linking it to Adam's *fides historica,* or doctrinally correct understanding of history (*"Paradise Lost"* 30–32). Avery (1970) identifies the parallel paradox of creaturely knowledge being an absence, just as abstention from the tree was the single absence that would have paradoxically enriched the experience of paradise (79–84). Carnes (1970) sees the Fall as necessary and therefore fortunate: "There seems little doubt that, for the eye of the poet at least, the color of time was infinitely more pleasing than the relative blankness of the prelapsarian world" (538–39). Lieb (1970) judges the paradox to be generative, informing the entire texture of the poem: re-creation is much more glorious than creation because it triumphs over those forces that would have returned it to chaos (*Dialectics* 216–17). Muldrow (1970) calls these lines the beginning of Adam's conversion to good, the last step of his repentance; Adam also recognizes the pervasive irony Satan's fall is different from man's, and he brings destruction on himself even while he brings good to man (101); cf. *PL* 3.129–32 and also *DocCh* 1.8: "Nor does God make that will evil which was before good, but the will being already in a state of perversion, he influences it in such a manner, that out of its own wickedness it either operates good for others, or punishment for itself, though unknowingly, and with the intent of producing a very different result" (Patterson, *Works* 15:73–75);

Not all post-Lovejoy commentary on this passage considers the *felix culpa.* Maurice Kelley, for instance, glosses Adam's speech with *DocCh* 1.8: "the end which a sinner has in view is generally something evil and unjust, from which God uniformly educes a good and just result, thus as it were creating light out of darkness" (132; Patterson, *Works* 15:75). Prince comments only briefly on the passage: "Adam responds fully in joy at the climax of the Christian revelation, the redemption which Christ brings and promises" (42). Parish says that this passage represents not only the emotional climax of *PL* but also the ultimate solution of the witty riddle of redemption via the seed of the woman ("Milton" 247). Roland Mushat Frye does not identify this passage as being about the *felix culpa* but rather says it is Adam's response to God's redemption; Adam's progress in entering the new life, the paradise within, is most marked here, "when his delight over God's perfect righteousness, goodness, and love raises him entirely above despair over his own sin" (81, 89). Samuel finds that the closest analog for this passage in Dante's *Commedia* is the final address to Beatrice in *Paradiso* 31.79–87, except for the words *infinite* and *immense,* which recall Dante on the divine goodness (*Dante* 229–30); cf., e.g., *Purgatorio* 3.122 and *Paradiso* 7.109. Blondel draws attention to how much the "infinite goodness" of God was earlier expressed in the marvels of paradise (59). Fowler comments on this passage at length, recognizing that some paradox is inherent in the story, though Milton in fact avoids paradox in its expression, and that instead, "Milton's special contribution to the idea is an infusion of hard realism. He never allows us to lose sight of the plain misery brought by the Fall. We may rejoice in God's grace, not that man gave him occasion to exercise it."

Among the more improbable explanations of this passage have been that of E. B. N. Dhabar (1900), who argues that much of *PL* is derived from Zoroastrianism and that this passage parallels sections of the Bundahishn, and of John R. Adams (1941), who performs a reading entirely in the service of "personalistic theism," in which the God of *PL* "is the chief person in a universe of developing persons" but in which reading "O goodness infinite!" is admittedly illogical (177).

The idea of a fortunate Fall generated by this passage has migrated into discussions of other literatures. Moorman (1953) cites 12.469–78 when describing a fortunate Fall in Melville's *Pierre* (29). Moss (1964) makes no mention of Milton or Lovejoy, yet reports "sporadic controversy" about the theme of Hawthorne's novel *The Marble Faun* and Hawthorne's relation to the "doctrine of the fortunate fall" ("Problem" 395); Moss's lack of any attribution whatever suggests that the idea has become a critical commonplace fewer than 30 years after Lovejoy's essay appeared. In 1968, Moss makes a similar suggestion, again without attribution: "I take it to be clearly established in the criticism, if it is not already self-evident in the novel, that the theme of *The Marble Faun* involves a version of the fortunate fall" ("Symbolism" 332). Haworth (1970) does cite Lovejoy and *PL* 12.469–78 to compare the fall of the Titans in Keats's "Hyperion" to a blend of Milton's falls of the rebel angels and that of Adam and Eve (643–44).

469. *immense:* Ricks (*Paradise Lost*) glosses as "immeasurable." Cf. *OED* 1 (obsolete), "Unmeasured; so great that it has not been or cannot be measured; immeasurably larger; of boundless extent; infinite."

470–71. Cf. Satan's words in *PL* 1.162–65, 217–20.

471–73. *more wonderful / Then … / Light out of darkness:* cf. the creation of light in Gen. 1:3–4 and also 2 Cor. 4:6: "For God, who commanded the light to shine out of darkness, hath shined in our hearts, to give the light of the knowledge of the glory of God in the face of Jesus Christ." Adam understands a new sense of cosmic time purposely conveyed to him, as it was earlier in the account of the war in heaven and of the Creation (Stapleton 746); see **11.134–35**. Milton links light association not only with the Creation but also with the Resurrection in *PL* 12.421–23 (MacCaffrey 175).

Lieb sees no reason to think that Milton does not endorse Adam's enthusiasm, since "Adam's celebration completes a round of hallelujahs" and also since God progressively glorifies himself more fully, first by destroying the rebel angels, then by creating the universe, and finally by effecting man's regeneration (*"Paradise Lost"* 31).

473–78. *full of doubt I stand:* Hughes (*Paradise Lost*) cites a portion of a similar sentiment from Du Bartas, which in full reads:

> and but that thou didst erre,
> Christ had not comme, to conquer and to quel
> Upon the Crosse, sinne, Sathan, death, and hel
> Making the[e] blessed more since thine offence,
> Then in thy primer happie innocence.   (1:352.512–16)

Lovejoy also quotes this passage in his seminal article (164). Stoll cites this passage as one of the continual preparations for the final human condition ("From the Superhuman" 14); see **11.138–39**. Wickert judges that the paradox of mercy transforming Adam's *mortificatio* into a *vivificatio* is similar to the double movement of *Adam Unparadiz'd* in the Trinity Manuscript: "[Adam] repents[,] gives god the glory" (202–03); cf. Patterson, *Works* 18:232. Adam's doubt distances him to be both actor and observer and thus establishes his freedom of action (Brisman 265). Reesing reads this passage as a "retardation" that reflects "the questing, probing activity" of Adam's mind as he labors to comprehend the marvels he has been hearing about before he returns to the "brisk tempo" of his eager questions (95); see **11.1–21**. Adam's doubt is consonant with his earlier shifts between joy and despair (Sasek 194). Both here and in *PL* 11.139, joy and woe are subtly balanced, so that "the thesis of the fortunate fall cannot be allowed to cancel out the tragic element in the poem or the tragic element still possible [for] Man's life" (Burden 199).

476. *Much more, that much more good thereof shall spring:* Keightley links this line to "Weep no more, woful shepherds, weep no more" (*Lyc* 165), in a long annotation (1:140–142) in which he catalogs the frequency of "more…more" repetitions in world and English poetry.

477–93. Verity references numerous Bible passages about confidence in God (Ps. 56:11), the promised sending of the Spirit (Luke 24:49; John 14:18, 23, 15:26), the description of coming persecutions (John 16:1–3), the triumph of grace over sin (Rom. 5:20, 2 Cor. 4:15), the work of faith (Gal. 5:6), and the armor of god (Eph. 6:11, 13, and 16).

477. *To God more glory, more good will to Men:* "according to the heavenly hymn, 'Glory to God in the highest, etc.,' Luke 2:14" (Hume).

478. *over wrauth grace shall abound:* cf. Rom. 5:20: "Where sin abounded, grace did much more abound." Roland Mushat Frye claims that the Atonement is divinely symmetrical and aesthetically beautiful (79–80). On Milton's exposition of prevenient grace, see Patrides' comment in **11.22–23**.

479–84. Cf. Adam's fear voiced in 11.777–79 that Noah and his family will perish, as well as to Adam's knowledge that God protected the Israelites in the desert (MacCallum, "Milton and Sacred History" 156, 165). "There is nothing at all in Milton's account of the redemption to evoke this sort of pessimistic query" (Martz 163). Rajan is disappointed with what he calls Adam's "craven query" and with Michael's failure to even attempt to answer the disconcerting question (*"Paradise Lost" and the Seventeenth Century* 84). Fish, however, finds the anticlimax is appropriate: "the world does go on," and our descent from the mount of speculation mirrors Adam's (330). "Adam has seen enough of the history of mankind to guess at what will follow" (Summers, *Muse's Method* 219). Miner, arguing that the Fall is fortunate for only a few, asserts that this passage has rarely received critical attention (51).

480. *what will betide the few:* this question was already answered in John 14:1–4, where Christ promises before his Passion to prepare his followers places in heaven (Himes, *Paradise Lost: A Poem*).

485–502. The *Comforter* in this passage is the Holy Spirit; cf. the similar promise in Luke 24:49 and Acts 1:4–5. In John 14:16–16:14, Christ describes the future activity of the Holy Spirit at length, including its coming to "his own" (13:1); see also Heb. 8:10. "Milton uses the word 'Comforter'...not in the modern flaccid and sentimental sense, but in the root meaning of strengthener, the fulfillment of the promise of the Father" (R. M. Frye 82). Maurice Kelley (169–70) cites various places in *DocCh* 1.21 that identify the believer's comprehension of heavenly things as a result of being "ingrafted" in Christ (Patterson, *Works* 16:7), and that cite Christ's promise to his followers in John 16:13 that the Spirit of truth would guide them into all truth (Patterson, *Works* 16:9), in *DocCh* 1.6, which glosses the Holy Spirit as the Comforter (Maurice Kelley 109; Patterson, *Works* 14:389), in *DocCh* 1.8, which identifies the Holy Spirit as the source of signs and wonders for witnessing (Maurice Kelley 134; Patterson, *Works* 15:95), and in *DocCh* 1.27, which proclaims the Gospel to be written in the hearts of believers by the Holy Spirit (Maurice Kelley 175; Patterson, *Works* 16:113).

Babb, claiming that Milton is uncomfortable with pneumatology (i.e., theology of the Holy Spirit) and also sometimes inconsistent in applying it to his epic (126–27), cites various places in *DocCh* 1.6, e.g., that the Spirit is a minister of God and therefore an inferior creature that is created or produced later than the Son (Patterson, *Works* 14:403); that the Father's promise to "put his Spirit" upon the Son (Patterson, *Works* 14:341) indicates that the Spirit is an emanation from the Father, not a creation of the Son; that the Spirit seems to have been active only since the advent of the Son; and that the Spirit is not a "person" or definitively described (Patterson, *Works* 14:367–69). Because the Spirit is a gift whom one implores of God, he cannot himself be "an object of invocation" (Patterson, *Works* 14:395), even though—as Babb notes—Milton himself invokes the Spirit at the beginning of his epic (127).

Joseph cites this passage as one proof that the theology of *PL* is in conformity with the Roman Catholic Church (255).

Patrick cites myths of snake-limbed giants fighting men, "shadowy, gigantic combatants" that "loom cloud-like and vast in the Miltonic background" (43–45). These lines compose one of the passages about supernal grace identified by Reesing; see **12.111–13**.

485. *th'Angel:* on the elision, see **11.449**.

486. *Comforter:* "theology. A title of the Holy Spirit" (so *OED* 1b).

487–88. *who shall dwell / His Spirit within them:* Dunster (in Todd) glosses this line as "the Godhead himself shall dwell in them spiritually."

    dwell: "to remain…as in a permanent residence; to have one's abode; to reside, 'live'" (so *OED* 7). Montgomery proclaims Milton's use of *dwell* here to be classical.

487. Wesley omits this line.

488–94. The mood here is "autumnal," even at times approaching weariness; a far cry from the prophetic indignation at the same image in *Lyc* 113–31 (Rajan, "*Paradise Lost:* The Hill" 61).

488–89. *and the Law of Faith / Working through love:* this passage blends phrasing from Rom. 3:27 and Gal. 5:6. "The result is an ethic of freedom, a morality of love, guided from within, and not forced from without" (R. M. Frye 82). Cf. *DocCh* 1.21, where love is one effect of having been "ingrafted in Christ" (Maurice Kelley 169; Patterson, *Works* 16:9).

489. *upon thir hearts shall write:* paraphrases the Old Testament promise, "I will put my law in their inward parts, and write it in their hearts" (see Jer. 31:33), echoed in such New Testament verses as 2 Cor. 3:3 and Heb. 8:10.

490–92. The "whole armour of God" is described piece by piece in Eph. 6:11–17; Milton also alludes to it in *Animad:* "You are not arm'd Remonstrant, nor any of your band, you are not dieted, nor your loynes girt for spirituall valour, and Christian warfare" (Patterson, *Works* 3:110). The armor is a "systatic" or para-doxical union of apparent opposites, typical in the Renaissance, and consonant with Pauline thinking as indicated in the string of paradoxes in 2 Cor. 6:4–10, where the "armour of righteousness" is mentioned in verse 7 (Huntley, "Before and After" 13–14). In the Eph. 6 passage, the most important piece of armor is faith (Fowler).

490. *To guide them in all truth:* cites John 16:13 on one role of the Holy Spirit.

493–95. Milton is willing to pass quickly over martyrdoms, having early demonstrated an emphatic dislike for deliberately shocking presentations of them (Daniells, *Milton* 176).

What man can do against them, not afraid: restates Ps. 56:11.

With inward consolations recompenc't: cf. *SA* 663–64. Milton may also have been thinking of Ps. 94:19: "In the multitude of my thoughts within me thy comforts delight my soul." Even here, Michael must prevent Adam from forcing the question back to materiality (Lawry, *Shadow* 285).

497–502. This passage briefly summarizes the New Testament book of Acts. Wesley reduces it to a single line, "Their proudest persecutors. Thus they win."

497–98. *the Spirit / Powrd first on his Apostles:* described in Acts 2:1–4.

499. *evangelize the Nations:* see Matt. 28:19, Mark 16:15, Acts 1:8.

evangelize: "to preach the Gospel to; to win over to the Gospel or the Christian faith" (so *OED* 3).

504–40. Although he was "too good of a scripturalist" to positively identify the pope as Antichrist, "Milton brought his poem almost to a close by drawing Antichrist according to the lineaments of Popery" (Schultz 125, 127). Milton's historical survey cannot go into an issue at any length, lest his theme be obscured, but Milton will not let the issue of clerical authority and discipline "go without a fight" (Burden 179–80); see *PL* 12.83–101.

505. *Thir Ministry perform'd, and race well run:* cf. 2 Tim. 4:7–8, where St. Paul at his life's end claims to have "finished [his] course [i.e., race]" and therefore expected the "crown," or laurel of victory. Verity identifies St. Paul's fondness for athletic metaphors, as in the races in 1 Cor. 9:24 or Heb. 12:1. See also the "race of glory won" (*SA* 597).

race: "the course of life or some portion of it" (so *OED* 1c).

506. *Thir doctrine and thir story written left:* Keightley thinks that Milton means "more especially the Gospels of Matthew and John, and the Epistles of Paul," but does not specify why.

507–11. *Wolves shall succeed for teachers:* a biblical metaphor drawn from St. Paul's warning in Acts 20:29 but also conflating Christ's reference to ravening wolves dressed in sheep's clothing (Matt. 7:15), his picture of the good shepherd who resists the wolf, unlike the hireling (John 10:12–13), and the general biblical equation of shepherd with church leader, answering to the Latin word for shepherd, *pastor*. Cf. *Hirelings:* "Not long after, as the apostle foretold, hirelings like wolves came in by herds" (Patterson, *Works* 6:49). The image of the false pastor as wolf appears elsewhere in Milton's poetry (*Sonn 16*, 16, *Lyc* 113–31, *PL* 4.183–93) and numerous places in the prose. *Hirelings* itself cites Acts 20:29. *Ref* complains of "these importunate wolves, that . . . devour thy tender Flock"; in *Animad*, a "better confutation of the Pope and masse" includes "wolves driven from the fold"; *RCG* deplores "the havoc of strangers and wolves . . . in the Church of Christ" and characterizes the bishops as those who "sought to cover under sheeps cloathing, ravenous and savage wolves threatning inrodes and bloody incursions upon the flock of Christ"; in *TKM*, he likens those who buy "benefices," or church positions, to "rav'nous Wolves seeking where they may devour the biggest"; *Eikon* points to those who "howle in thir Pulpits, and by thir howling declare themselvs right Wolves" and calls for those to "be driv'n out of the Fold like Wolves, or Theeves, where they sat Fleecing those Flocks which they never fed"; *OAP* complains of the "shamelesse hypocrisie" of "meer wolves in sheeps cloathing"; and *DocCh* insists that "tithes or other stipendary payments . . . is the part of wolves rather than of ministers of the gospel. Acts 20.29" (Patterson, *Works* 3:76, 175, 188, 274–75; 5:44, 88, 205; 6:259; 16:301). Verity devotes half a page of notes to these lines, thinking they are mostly directed at the Church of England, with typical Miltonic charges of avarice and desire for preferment. Barnes (19) and Verity both find a potential parallel in *Purgatorio* 16.106–29, with its evocations of pastures and corruption. Douady, who reads most of the last two books pessimistically, complains that the original apostles had little to be happy about; the audacious imposters to follow will lead the flock into the abyss (206). The entire passage to 12.537 is not an attack on the Church of Rome or of England but rather a general condemnation of anything in the church "not built by faith" (Fowler). This grim passage nevertheless produces new occasion for virtuous deeds rather than lamentation (Radzinowicz 49).

508–41. This description of later church history represents the further gradual "narrowing of the aperture" from heaven to the world described in the heavenly stairs in *PL* 3.526–39 (Robins 707–08).

509–14. As Conklin notes (32), this passage is matched by copious allusions to scriptural sufficiency in the prose works, of which the strongest were in the Epistle to *DocCh;* cf. Patterson, *Works* 14:5–7, where Milton details his Scripture-centered methodology and also 14:15: "For my own part, I adhere to the Holy Scriptures alone." Bailey, looking for similarities between Milton's thought and Jakob Boehme's, notes that Boehme complained about empty religious shows (166).

509–10. *all the sacred mysteries of Heav'n . . . shall turne:* Milton possibly refers to the "mystery of godliness," the narrative of Christ's early life and deeds (1 Tim. 3:16), which angels desire to look into (1 Pet. 1:12). "The very sin of Adam's usurpation upon deity is perennially repeated . . . usurping now upon the Holy Spirit" (R. M. Frye 83).

511. *lucre and ambition:* these ministerial motives are explicitly rejected in 1 Pet. 5:2–3 and echoed in *Hirelings* (Patterson, *Works* 6:43–100). Cf. *DocCh* 1.31, which cautions against financial considerations as important motives in preaching the Gospel, and against exacting tithes or "other stipendiary payments under the gospel," especially with the help of the civil magistrate (Maurice Kelley 181; Patterson, *Works* 16:299–301).

512. *superstitions and traditions:* cf. *DocCh* 1.30, where Scripture forbids paying attention to human tradition, or implicitly to trust the opinions of forefathers or antiquity (Maurice Kelley 180–81; Patterson, *Works* 16:281–83), as well as other statements in Milton's early prose about the sufficiency of Scripture, e.g., in the antiprelatical tracts (Patterson, *Works* 3:34, 81, 123, 245–46, 325–26).

513–14. Wesley omits this passage. Douady interprets it as describing a secret doctrine available to only a few (206–07).

513. *those written Records pure:* "Milton never faltered in his professions of belief in the uniqueness and sufficiency of the Scriptures" (Tillyard, *Studies in Milton* 150). Cf. the Reformation commonplace of the "two books" of the world (nature) and the word (Scripture); here "the Book of knowledg fair" of *PL* 3.47 "is at last subordinated to the revealed will of God" (Patrides, *Milton* 71). Sims (*Bible* 273) cites John 17:17: "Thy word is truth."

514. *not but by the Spirit understood:* cf. similar statements about the Spirit's internal teaching in John 14:26, 1 Cor. 2:14, and 1 John 2:27. Cf. *DocCh* 1.30, that the Scriptures must not be interpreted by individual human intellect, but with the Spirit's help (Maurice Kelley 180; Patterson, *Works* 16:259–61). Cf. also *DocCh* 1.2: "No one, however, can have right thoughts of God, with nature or reason alone as his guide, independent of the word, or message of God" (Patterson, *Works* 14:31). This line is the strongest proof of Milton's enthusiasm (Warburton, in Newton). Keightley finds it an "absurd notion" shared with Spenser (e.g., *Faerie Queene* 1.10.19) and others.

515–16. *seek to avail themselves of names, / Places and titles:* these were forbidden by Christ to his disciples (Matt. 23:6–12); on titles, see **11.158–59**. Cf. *DocCh* 1.29, which rejects the "futility" of the academic title of *doctor* and also of the clergy claiming the exclusive right to preach the Gospel and, even more illogically, the sole right to celebrate weddings and funerals (Maurice Kelley 180; Patterson, *Works* 16:239, 243, 247–49).

    avail: "to benefit oneself or profit by; to take advantage of, turn to account" (so *OED* 5a).

516–17. *and with these to joine / Secular power:* Todd thinks that Milton has been "particularly copious on this subject in *Ref:* "If the life of Christ be hid to this world, much more is his Scepter unoperative, but in spirituall things" (Patterson, *Works* 3:42). "Milton is carrying on the protests he made as a pamphleteer" (Le Comte).

517–25. At the close of his chapter on the Scriptures in *DocCh,* Milton rejects the human imposition of "any kind of sanction or dogma upon believers against their will," because such imposition places "a yoke not only upon man but upon the Holy Spirit itself" (also noted by Maurice Kelley 180); he also glosses Deut. 4:2 as a prohibition against "human traditions, written or unwritten" (*DocCh* 1.30, Patterson, *Works* 16:281). Fowler cites the Protestant belief in the individual conscience as the ultimate arbiter and its rejection of implicit faith, or the unquestioning acceptance of church doctrines on the authority of the higher clergy, as well as Milton's oft-expressed contempt for dependence on patristic and other authorities, said in *Areop* to result in "a muddy pool of conformity and tradition" (Patterson, *Works* 4:333).

517. *Secular:* "belonging to the world and its affairs as distinguished from the church and religion; civil, lay, temporal. Chiefly used as a negative term, with the meaning non-ecclesiastical, non-religious, or non-sacred" (so *OED* 2a).

518–21. *spiritual…Spiritual:* these words "fill only two or three metrical places," although *spiritual* is tetrasyllabic in our day and presumably was in Milton's; *appropriating* is an example of Milton's later style in the last six books, in that the line's unstressed ending is an unvoiced consonant after a stressed vowel (Oras, "Milton's Blank Verse" 152, 166, 518).

519–20. *The Spirit of God…giv'n / To all Beleevers:* cf. the litmus test of Rom. 8:9, in which anyone without the Spirit does not belong to Christ, and also *Hirelings,* which cites the promise that the Spirit would guide believers into all truth (Patterson, *Works* 6:75) and *DocCh* 1.5, "that spiritual illumination which is common to all" (Patterson, *Works* 14:179). In *DocCh* 1.4, Milton judges that "believers" means the same as "elect" (Maurice Kelley 83; Patterson, *Works* 14:117). The nineteenth century French critic Alexandre Rodolphe Vinet included this passage among his proofs of Milton's trinitarian orthodoxy (Redman 214).

521–30. *Spiritual Lawes by carnal power:* cf. *CivP,* passim, and also *DocCh* 1.14, "external force ought never to be employed in the administration of the kingdom of Christ, which is the church" (Patterson, *Works* 15:301); *DocCh* 1.27, which insists that fallible man should not meddle in matters belonging to God (Patterson, *Works* 16:157) and that magistrates have no reason to compel believers to uniformity or deprive them of the privilege of free judgment (Patterson, *Works* 16:163); and *DocCh* 1.30, which repeats this stricture against compulsion by civil or religious power (Patterson, *Works* 16:267) and declares that any such compulsion places "a yoke…upon the Holy Spirit itself" (Maurice Kelley 177, 180; Patterson, *Works* 16:281).

522–30. Wesley omits this passage.

522–25. *finde…binde:* one of the 52 instances of rhyming lines with two intervening nonrhyming lines (Diekhoff, "Rhyme" 541–42); see Purcell for additional instances (172).

522–24. *Laws which none shall finde:* "laws which are neither laid down in the Scripture, nor dictated by the natural instincts of good men toward piety" (Verity). Cf. Matt. 15:9, "teaching for doctrines the commandments of men." In the preface to *DDD,* Milton invokes "a Law not onely writt'n by Moses, but character'd in us by nature" (Patterson, *Works* 3:383).

523. *Left them inrould:* i.e., in the Scriptures, which like other books of the time, were in rolls (Keightley).
  Spirit within: cf. 8.440 and 12.488.

524–51. This crucial passage quite overshadows the vision of eternal bliss at the end: "The comfort is nominal, the fundamental pessimism unmistakable...[Milton's] hopes...were dashed" (Tillyard, *Milton* 286–87). Reesing (102–03) identifies this passage as, successively, an emphatically concentrated *stretta* passage, "laced with fricatives and labials and, especially, aspirates" (524–37), appropriately "weary cadences" similar to those in 105–06 (537–39), and the last, "most ecstatic treatment of the consummation of all things," stretching out grammar and meaning and sound to suggest eternal joy (549–51); see **11.1–21**.

524. *Shall on the heart engrave:* the new covenant will be written in the heart (Jer. 31:33).

525–26. *and bind / His consort Libertie:* cf. 2 Cor. 3:17, "where the Spirit of the Lord is, there is liberty," together with the exhortation to "stand fast" in Christian liberty in Gal. 5:1, and also the long discussion of Christian liberty in *DocCh* 1.27 (Patterson, *Works* 16:113–163), from which Maurice Kelley notes in particular the declaration that "liberty must be considered as belonging in an especial manner to the gospel, and as consorting therewith" (Patterson, *Works* 16:153). Hutchinson (181) cites Milton's description of Christian liberty in *CivP* as "the fundamental privilege of the gospel, the new-birthright of everie true believer" (Patterson, *Works* 6:28), words exactly paralleled in *PL* where Michael foresees the forcers of conscience in the history of the church. Adam's sin continues to replay itself in the last two books; here, "Man's self-assertive spirit eats away at the Church, and 'unbuilds' God's 'living temples'" (R. M. Frye 83).

consort: in the figurative sense, "A partner, companion, mate; a colleague in office or authority" (so *OED* 1, obsolete).

525. *But force the Spirit of Grace it self:* cf. *CivP:* "instead of forcing the Christian, they force the Holy Ghost; and, against the wise forewarning of Gamaliel, fight against God" (Patterson, *Works* 6:26); cf. Gamaliel's counsel in Acts 5:34–39.

527–28. *what, but unbuild / His living Temples:* cf. St. Paul's identification of the believer's body as the temple of the Holy Spirit (1 Cor. 3:16–17, 6:19), and also *PL* 1.17–18 and *Mask* 461.

528. *Thir own Faith not anothers:* cf. the epistle to *DocCh:* "it is only to the individual faith of each that the deity has opened the way of eternal salvation, and...he requires that he who would be saved should have a personal belief of his own" (Patterson, *Works* 14:5).

530. *Infallible:* Fowler holds that "Rome is Milton's main target here," even though the doctrine of papal infallibility was not devised until 1870; cf. Milton's complaint in *CivP* that the pope "assumes to himself...infallabilitie over both the conscience and the scripture" (Patterson, *Works* 6:8).

531–32. *heavie persecution:* cf. 2 Tim. 3:12: "All that will live godly in Christ Jesus shall suffer persecution." Milton insists that "the succession of lonely just men must continue forever....Christ's coming has not changed the nature of things" (Prince 45).

532–33. *the worship...Of Spirit and Truth:* this passage echoes John 4:23.

533. *farr:* 1669 *far*.

534. *Will deem in outward Rites and specious formes:* "Michael reveals himself as a Puritan" (Le Comte). Cf. Adam and Eve's "adoration pure" in 4.737. This passage and others in Milton's later poetry indicate that he hardly overcame his disappointment with the general mass of humanity; Michael in *PL*, Christ in *PR*, and Samson in *SA* are all critical of the populace (Muldrow 237). On interior versus exterior worship, see, e.g., John 4:23, Rom. 2:29, 2 Cor. 5:16, Gal. 5:2, and also cf. *DocCh* 2.4, which proclaims that the two kinds of worship should go hand in hand, never separated "except by the impiety of sinners" (Maurice Kelley 187; Patterson, *Works* 17:73–75).

Will: 1667 has *Will* and 1674 *Well.* Robert M. Adams finds 1667 *Will* clearly superior (78). The Richardsons claimed that *well* in 1674 was an oversight, and Newton similarly that 1667 is "genuine." Bentley and Fenton have *well.* Fletcher (*Complete Poetical Works*) judges that either *Will* or *Well* works with the context; he prints *Well.*

535–43. Milton's silence about the Reformation reflects the difference between the moods "of intense spiritual exaltation" when the epic was originally conceived and that of its actual composition, "when all those high hopes were dead" (Grierson, *Poems* 2:xxvii). Milton refuses to hope for any political progress before the Second Coming, now indefinitely deferred (Lejosne 93). Tillyard asks whether the feeling here relates rather to a general, Puritan pessimism about human affairs (*Studies in Milton* 167). B. A. Wright insists that Milton's faith was in a redeemed world and never in any atheistic hope that humankind would somehow save itself (*Milton's "Paradise Lost"* 201–02). Rajan judges, rather ambivalently, that even though some of Milton's "severities" exceed the poem's demands, severity itself has its own aesthetic virtues and can be as satisfying as a "balanced statement" ("*Paradise Lost:* The Hill" 62). Cf. *DocCh* 1.33, which lists the common or general signs marking the end of the world (Maurice Kelley 182; Patterson, *Works* 16:341). Radzinowicz suggests that the Reformation is absent because Milton considered pre- and post-Restoration conditions to be tyrannical in Nimrod's style (45–46).

535. *Religion satisfi'd; Truth shall retire:* Keightley cites the departure of Aidos and Nemesis (shamefacedness and righteous indignation) in Hesiod's *Works and Days* 199–201; see **11.670–71.**

536–37. *works of Faith / Rarely be found:* cf. Christ's rhetorical question, "When the Son of man cometh, shall he find faith on the earth?" (Luke 18:8).

536. *Bestuck:* "to pierce through, transfix" (so *OED* 2). Montgomery glosses as "stuck all over; copiously assailed," and adds "only used by Milton."
works of Faith: cf. 12.306 and 427.

537–51. Prince, arguing that the last two books are necessary to the poem, emphasizes here the emphatic conclusion that "justice will be for ever persecuted and yet finally triumphant," adding, "It is strange, if it is true, that modern readers should not be able to respond to the heroic faith of these passages" (45–46).

537–42. Criticism of this passage has been historical and/or theological. In 1947, Rajan judges this section an afterthought, since Michael has already described the final victory of Christ over Satan (451–55), which gives history its theological significance (*"Paradise Lost" and the Seventeenth Century* 84). In 1967, however, Rajan finds Milton's "miscalculations" considerably more sophisticated; Adam is not deceived by Michael's pause but rather shows the progress of his education; Rajan also remarks that "almost every comment on Milton's pessimism and his 'abandonment' of history [has] its roots in this passage" (*"Paradise Lost": The Hill* 58). Muldrow disagrees with Rajan's complaint that "the whole scene does nothing"; Adam must hear the entire Gospel, and the passage emphasizes the principle that inward corruption exhibits itself outwardly and also allows Michael to stress the need for self-government (103); cf. Rajan, *"Paradise Lost" and the Seventeenth Century* 84. Milton's statement here is consistent with his youthful poetic argument that "nature does not suffer decay" (*Naturam non pati senium*), since the world suffers no further physical deterioration after the Fall (V. Harris 160–63). As in book 6, where the war in heaven lasts until Christ drives the rebel angels out, the fallen world will proceed in its fallen fashion until Christ shall come at last to end it (Madsen, "Earth" 526). In Milton's distinctive historiography, there is "no general advance toward a discernible goal, no wave-like movement toward the redeemed society," despite the occasional appearance of an Enoch, Noah, Abraham, or Christ, and yet the eternal principles of Truth, Justice, and Righteousness remained unmoved and serene (Fogle 16). Milton does not seem to think it necessary to mention the Reformation; "even Michael, though almost spitefully severe about affairs on earth, has nothing specific to say about the pains of hell" (Empson, *Milton's God* 190–91, 270).

537. *so shall the World goe on:* some copies of 1667 omit the comma after *on.*

538. *To good malignant, to bad men benigne:* Bentley objects to *men* being in the second clause rather than the first, and emends to "To good *men* malignant, to bad benign." Wesley omits this line. Despite Milton's humanistic learning, which undoubtedly helped shape his religious philosophy, "his vision of the future is medieval or Biblical" (Whiting, *Milton* 127–28).

benigne: "of things: favourable, kind, fortunate, salutary, propitious" (so *OED* 3).

539–51. *groaning:* 1667 *groaning,* Cf. the groaning creation in Rom. 8:22.

respiration...vengeance: the Richardsons refer to the "powerful close" of *Ref* (Patterson, *Works* 3:78–79). Newton glosses *respiration* as the "refreshing" of Acts 3:19, claiming that in the Protestant Junius-Tremellius version, the Greek term *anápsuxis* (ἀνάψυξις) is rendered as *respiratio* in Latin. Actually, that version has *tempora tranquilitatis* ("times of refreshing"), and the Protestant Beza New Testament has *tempora refrigerationis* (cf. the *refrigerii* of the Vulgate). In any case, both *anápsuxis* and *respiratio* refer to an intake of breath. Milton cites Acts 3:19 in *DocCh,* but only the first part of the verse ("Repent ye therefore, and be converted, that your sins may be blotted out" [Patterson, *Works* 15:382]), without the mention of refreshing. Wesley glosses *respiration* as "refreshment, ease." Dunster (in Todd) reads the passage as particularly political, along with *PR* 2.42–48; he also notes that the Vulgate translates *anápsuxis* as *refrigerium,* but that in the Septuagint *anápsuxis* has the sense of *respiratio* in Exod. 8:15, i.e., where Pharaoh sees that there is relief (*anápsuxis*) from the plague of frogs. Moody's gloss of *respiration* is "relief, as at the drawing of a deep breath after some constraint." Bush additionally supplies the meaning "reward." Northrop Frye (*Paradise Lost*) glosses *respiration* as "revival." Hughes (*Paradise Lost, A Poem*) reports that Milton interprets St. Paul's "times of refreshing" as the day of Christ's coming "with clouds" (Rev. 1:7) at the Last Judgment when, as he says in *DocCh* 1.33, "Christ with the saints, arrayed in the glory and the power of the Father, shall judge the evil angels, and the whole race of mankind" (Patterson, *Works* 16:355). The Geneva Bible's gloss on John 14:3 may be relevant here: "And in all places of the Scripture the full comfort of the Church is considered to be that day when God will be all in all, and is therefore called the day of redemption." Fowler sees *groaning* as referring back to nature's groans when Adam and Eve fell (*PL* 9.783, 1001), while *respiration* "looks forward to a new breath, like that by which life was first inspired in man" (7.526); he suggests that Milton may also have been thinking of the KJV marginal gloss on "enlargement" (i.e., deliverance) in Esther 4:14 as "respiration," and he concludes that the entire passage should be compared with *PL* 12.446–65 and with 3.321–41, since all three are apocalyptic prophecies drawing on the same biblical texts.

This is Adam's first time to hear about the Resurrection, as he has missed all the preceding hints in 11.365–66, 457–59, 469–70, and 709–10, but has heard clearly that all men are going to die (Reesing 60); cf. 12.434–35, 444–45. Cf. the Son's miraculous vindication on the pinnacle in *PR:* "in a world outwardly given over to Satan the visible re-establishment of justice must be miraculous," and the Son's vindication in the later epic anticipates the eschatological vindication of the just foreseen in *PL* (Fixler 233). Despite complaints from the eighteenth to the twentieth century that Milton's account of post-apostolic history is "bleak," Milton must have found such triumphs as the Reformation to be largely temporary in light of the "respiration" at the end of time, since the Christian faith could never depend upon humans' continued moral or spiritual progress, or any institution of government, or the incorruptibility of any institution, or the earthly fortunes of any believer (Summers, *Muse's Method* 219–20). Milton's vision of history is "unrelieved evil," and the absence of the Reformation shows "how little Protestantism satisfied Milton" (Saurat 164). This passage is one of those about supernal grace identified by Reesing; see **12.111–13**.

542. *aid:* 1667 *aid,*

543–47. *The Womans seed, obscurely then foretold … to dissolve / Satan:* for fruit-seed imagery, see **11.26–29**; for the oft-repeated promise of Gen. 3:15, see **11.115–16**. Michael—or Milton—presumes that Adam has associated *Serpent* with *Satan,* even though they have not been named together; Milton is more concerned that Adam learn the "greater piece of information," that the seed of the woman is the Son of God (Gilbert, *On the Composition* 51–52). The eating of the fruit, which is death, leads to the planting of the seed, which is life, and the image of the seed flowering into harvest is a basic, subdued, but persistent image in book 12; the fruits of repentance are worth more than the fruits of every tree in uncorrupted paradise (Rajan, "*Paradise Lost:* The Hill" 51); see *PL* 11.26–29 and also the discussion of the seed of the woman in **11.115–16**. The good-to-bad movement of the last two books means that history itself is doomed and has become the image of Satan; Christ will return to the world from outside of it (Ross, *Poetry and Dogma* 95); see also **12.586**. The vision in *PL* has reached its climax; prior to the Incarnation, all events are types and shadows of

,his coming, and since his advent, all events refer back to him (Patrides, *Phoenix* 62–65); cf. **12.302–03**.

545–46. *Last in the Clouds from Heav'n to be reveald / In glory of the Father:* the synoptic Gospels report in several places the apocalyptic claim that Christ would return in the clouds with power and great glory (Matt. 24:30, 26:64; Mark 13:26, 14:62; Luke 21:27), a reference to Daniel's apocalyptic arrival of the "Son of Man" (Dan. 7:13); the claim is repeated in Rev. 1:7 and implied in 1 Thess. 4:16–17 and 2 Thess. 1:7. Milton employs the image in *Nat* 163–64, and also *Ref,* "when thou the Eternall and shortly-expected King shalt open the Clouds to judge the severall Kingdomes of the World" (Patterson, *Works* 3:78). Most commentators stressed not only the wrath of God at the Last Judgment, but also the revelation of his glory (Patrides, "Renaissance" 176). Cf. *DocCh* 1.33, in which the Last Judgment follows the coming of Christ in glory (Maurice Kelley 182; Patterson, *Works* 16:355).

546–51. Fowler glosses *dissolve* as "annihilate, destroy," citing from the original *OED* definitions 6 ("release from life") and 7 ("bring to naught, undo, destroy, consume"). Or, given the heat that Milton and his contemporaries expected from the Apocalypse, "to melt or reduce into a liquid condition" (*OED* 2) may be intended. The Richardsons cite black night being dissolved by morning in Apollonius Rhodius, *Argonautica* 4.1170–71. Newton cites *Aeneid* 8.591, where the morning star dissolves the shadowy night, apt indeed if the star is Christ (Rev. 22:16) and not the *Lucifer* supplied by Virgil. For the fiery end of the world, cf. 2 Pet. 3:10, and also *PL* 3.333; 7.160; 10.638–39, 647; 11.65–66, 900–01; 12.463–64; and *DocCh* 1.33 (Patterson, *Works* 16:337–81), as well as the note on two endings of the world in *PL* in **12.458–65**. The fracture between poetic descriptions of sin and doctrinaire statements of theology "cannot be healed; the weight of woe has gradually weakened the epilogue's connection with the poem's center, and here the epilogue at last drops off" (Martz 165). Christian eschatological commentary emphasized both the wrath of God on the Last Day and the glory then to be revealed (Patrides, "Renaissance" 176–77).

547–51. "The 'sum of earthly bliss' which Adam had found in the nuptial bower…is subsumed now into the endless joy which the elect share" (Pecheux, "Second Adam" 183–84). The dregs of creation were likewise "down purg'd" and "like things to like" ordained in *PL* 7.237, 240 (MacCaffrey 138). A pervasive "triumphant attitude" in the epic anticipates humanity's eventual restoration; their purifying sufferings are integral to the eventual millennial event (Lieb, "*Paradise Lost*" 32–33). On conflagration and renewal, see **11.66** and also *DocCh* 1.33: "Our glorification will be accompanied by the renovation of heaven and earth, and of all things therein adapted to our service or delight" (Maurice Kelley 184; Patterson, *Works* 16:379).

548. *purg'd and refin'd:* cf. 11.900.

Conflagrant: "in conflagration, on fire, blazing" (so *OED* 1); "burning" (Wesley). Montgomery claims that Milton is the only authority for the English use of this Latin borrowing, but *OED* cites an earlier use by Blount in 1656.

549. *New Heav'ns, new Earth:* Hughes (*Paradise Lost*) points out that book 11 ends with the promise that fire will "purge all things new, / Both Heav'n and Earth" (900–01). The emphasis is exactly where Michael wants it: since these events are in the future, the only paradise Adam can have is "the paradise within" (Muldrow 104–05); cf. *PL* 12.587. Unlike Plato's eternal and self-sufficient world, Milton's was created in time and will be destroyed in time, one indication that "for all the heterodoxy of [*De doctrina Christiana*], *Paradise Lost* is closer to spirit to Aquinas than to Plato" (Madsen, "Idea" 224). See **12.553–57**.

550–51. *peace and love...fruits...eternal Bliss:* cf. the Father's earlier promise in 3.336–38 of such a blissful outcome, "fruitful of golden deeds," his renewed promise in 11.43, and also the vision of future bliss in *Lyc* 172–81. This passage summarizes such passages as Rom. 14:17 ("the kingdom of God is... righteousness and peace"), Isa. 35:10 ("They shall obtain joy and gladness"), and Gal. 5:22–23 ("The fruit of the Spirit is love, joy, peace,..."). In Milton's treatment of Genesis, humans require community with both God and other humans to realize their destiny, though "the conditions of everlasting life are provided by an act of God alone" (R. M. Frye 88). Mentions of *fruit* are concatenated here and elsewhere (MacCaffrey 86). A contrast is intended with the "Fruit / Of that Forbidden Tree" (*PL* 1.1–2); the implied disunity is dispelled when Man accepts God's providence and makes Death the Gate of Life (Shawcross, "The Son" 396).

love: 1667 *love,*

551–55. *Bliss…abyss:* Purcell notes that these lines rhyme with three intervening lines (172); this rhyme category was also mentioned by Diekhoff but without specific verse numbers ("Rhyme" 542).

552–87. Tillyard calls this passage "Milton's mature, one may say middle-aged, philosophy of life….the inner paradise is the only paradise that matters. It is a different Milton from the one who wrote the *Defensio Secunda*" (*Milton* 292–93). In the original 1667 edition, Abdiel's speech in the end of book 5 would have matched Adam's in the end of book 10 (Reesing 75). The consummation of Adam's earthly regeneration began in book 10; "only now has he the knowledge of Christ…. the great exemplar of obedience and love which he is to follow" (Ogden 18). Dick Taylor Jr., arguing that Milton's epic does not present a fortunate Fall, claims that this passage is a "sounder statement" of both Adam's and Milton's views, maintaining "a proper balance between guilt and hope in the context of true and realistic wisdom" ("Milton" 49).

552. *thus Adam last reply'd:* i.e., thus begins his last speech in the epic.

553–64. Wesley notes this passage as among those particularly excellent.

553–57. Milton has prepared a vast stage for his conflict between good and evil; the space-continuum "contains all emanated and created existences—heaven, hell, chaos, and the world—and is itself 'contained' in that unique Infinity which is God" (Curry 157). This passage sums up a mythic pattern; *abyss* has grown throughout the epic by means of numerous epithets; then its unity is broken and transferred to the soul, where mythic warfare takes place, and it is transmuted into an allegorical image, and finally, when time stands fixed, there is a return to ultimate realities (MacCaffrey 116–18). Milton's structuring of time to order the major characters' experience has here its greatest impact, since time itself will be dissolved in eternity because of the Fall and redemption (Stapleton 746–47); see **11.134–35.** Herschel Baker's published lectures on Renaissance historiography, *The Race of Time,* draws its title from this passage and even some of its argument; Michael's presentation to Adam represents the Christian view of history not as mere record of events, but as "the matrix in which a timeless purpose is attained" (55). Adam's last words here, as well as Michael's in 11.549, are about time and eternity, thus strategically highlighting for Adam and Eve at their departure the relationship between the exercise of free will and of time (Colie 138). This passage demonstrates that Adam has attained true vision and that the reader must "readjust the perspective glass" at the epic's end, where time stretches out before Adam as an all but impenetrable future (Lewalski 34–35); see also **11.368**. Shumaker, tracing the numerous ways by which Milton achieves his effects, points out the "closing off of narrative time" as one signal of the epic's end, along with numerous metaphors of completion, not only *Measur'd* here but also *fill, containe,* and *summe* (*Unpremeditated Verse* 58–59); cf. 12.558–59, 575. This passage changes the perspective of the first ten books, embracing not only the individual recreated psyche but also a future cosmos in which *time stand[s] fixt* (Lieb, *Dialectics* 218).

554. *Measur'd this transient World:* cf. the angel's rod in Rev. 11:1, which is "to measure the temple of God, that is, to comprehend the history of the church" (Himes, *Paradise Lost: A Poem*). "The time measured by the Archangel is that during which this world lasts" (Verity). The self-knowledge demanded by humility means an acceptance of finitude, of God's infinitude, and of the frailty of created things under God (Burke 91).

555. *Till time stand fixt:* cf. the angel's oath in Rev. 10:6 "that there should be time no longer" (Fowler).
    Fixt: some 1667 *fixt* (Fowler).

556. *Eternitie, whose end no eye can reach:* Bentley, objecting to this passage as too absurd for Milton, and also claiming that Milton typically dropped the last syllable of *eternity,* emends to "Eternity, whose *extent* no eye can reach." Pearce points out that *extent* is as objectionable as *end,* and that Milton never had *eternit'* before a consonant.

557–61. Here "the theological paradox of *felix culpa* which Adam has apprehended leads him to understand its ethical counterpart" (Ferry, "Bird" 198).

557–59. *Greatly in peace of thought:* the last four books are "embellished with descriptions of the evil effects of man's disobedience, and his consolation in the promised redemption" (Bayly 194). De Quincey identifies the visionary restoration of lost paradise as the artifice by which the epic can end in the "large sunlight" required by the genre (Wittreich 464). The *parison* of repeated elements at the beginnings of lines in *PL* suggests a "rigid harmonizing principle" or "divine logos" that constructs reality; here "*Greatly...Greatly*" especially suggests that in the earthly paradise Adam is the agent of divine will (Pironon 124). According to Aquinas, "peace of thought" rests in subjection of self to the will of God; man's dignity and uniqueness do not depend upon a more developed mind or will, but upon receiving divine grace (Burke 88, 228). Adam's speech contrasts markedly to the despairing Adam of such earlier hexameral writers as Du Bartas, della Salandra, and Vondel: Milton's Adam leaves the garden "spiritually re-invigorated, soundly hopeful and proclaiming...inner peace and understanding" (D. Taylor, "Milton's Treatment" 80).

fill...containe: on metaphors of completion, see **12.553–57**. Cf. Adam's similar speech to Raphael in *PL* 8.179–97.

559. *what this Vessel can containe:* Hughes (*Paradise Lost*) glosses *this Vessel* as Adam's body, citing 1 Thess. 4:4, but Milton probably meant to include Adam's soul, which had its own limits of satiety. Cf. other biblical uses of *vessel* that indicate human limitations: Jer. 18:4, 48:38, and Rev. 2:27 (Fowler). Milton warns in *DocCh* 1.2 that human comprehension is limited (Patterson, *Works* 14:61). Milton's hierarchical thinking set appropriate bounds to one's knowledge, but in Milton, "overweeningness and humility, egotism and self-abnegation *always* co-existed" (Tillyard, *Studies in Milton* 48, 134). This passage reinforces Milton's theme of "intemperance in knowledge, of pride and presumption" (Bush). Cf. John 16:12: "I have yet many things to say unto you, but ye cannot bear them now." Hall cites *DocCh* 2.2 for Milton's definition of folly as either an ignorance of the will of God, a false conceit of wisdom, or prying into hidden things (173); cf. Patterson, *Works* 17:31–33 and also Maurice Kelley 146.

560–61. Reesing identifies this passage as the first of three final "arias," the others being 12.561–73 and 575–87 (103); see **11.1–21**.

561–73. *to obey is best:* cf. Samuel's rebuke of the temporizing Saul, "To obey is better than sacrifice" (1 Sam. 15:22) and Adam's earlier echo from the same chapter in 11.157–58. Patterson finds a pervasive theme of obedience, "for disobedience is but an excess of will, of self-confidence, and of pride" (*Student's*

Milton). Cf. the promise of *PR* 1.3–4 that paradise will be recovered "By one man's firm obedience fully tried" (Muldrow 162). According to Steadman, Adam learns the virtue of obedience and the nature of true fortitude from Christ, the ideal pattern of the Christian hero (*Milton's Epic Characters* 37).

Critics have identified other themes in this passage. According to Thompson, Adam has finally accepted Michael's advice, "Nor love thy Life, nor hate," and so on, from 11.553–54 ("Theme" 117–18). This passage might signal Milton's own personal growth, the evils described in books 11–12 being merely "the lazy monsters of his own mind's ocean" (Broadbent, *Some Graver Subject* 132). Kurth thinks Adam describes the role of human heroism as if a creed (123–24), and Pecheux identifies "this finished picture of the better fortitude of patience and heroic martyrdom" as Milton's character of the Christian hero ("Abraham" 367). Bush contrasts Adam's "new understanding of truly heroic knowledge" with Satan's opposite creed, as expressed for example at 2.257–62. Eastland finds Milton conflating wisdom with prudence, since he is finally less interested in the intellectual virtues than in the moral ones (49); cf. *DocCh* 2.2: "Wisdom is that whereby we earnestly search after the will of God, learn it with all diligence, and govern all our actions according to its rule"; "Prudence is that virtue by which we discern what is proper to be done under the various circumstances of time and place" (Patterson, *Works* 17:27, 37). "Just as Aeneas embodies the Roman *virtus* and *pietas* that Virgil would set up in the place of the discred-ited military virtues of an earlier age, so the fallen Adam comes eventually to exemplify the Christian ideal of conduct that for Milton constituted the only true heroism" (Harding, *Club of Hercules* 51). Barker ("*Paradise Lost*" 69–71) hears in Adam's affirmation—and Michael's response—an echo of the Father's promise (*PL* 3.173–97) of election, regeneration, and sanctification. Tillyard asserts that the very structure of *PL* ironically exposes the weakness of satanic pride when matched against even the smallest sincere regenerate human feel-ing, and—*pace* critics who associate human actions with satanic motives—that Adam's summary might be describing his own and Eve's repentant acts, their "small" act of reconciliation "accomplishing great things" (*Studies in Milton* 6–7, 44). Babb underscores the Christian theological distinction between merely following the laws of nature, as did the classical philosophers, and having a rev-elation from God (5). Ferry makes this passage the ethical counterpart to the theological paradox of *felix culpa* (*Milton's Epic Voice* 39–40). Whiting links these words with the bottom of the ladder of which each stair "mysteriously was meant" (*Milton* 80); cf. *PL* 3.516. Reesing (103) identifies this passage as the second of three final "arias," the others being 12.560–61 and 575–87; see **11.1–21**. Reesing also stresses the double nature of this conclusion: as Adam sums up what he has learned, "we sense an austere discipline undergirding the ardent joy he is mastering," and Reesing traces the rhetorical pattern of Adam's speech, "very slow at first as he tries to realize the wonders he has seen and heard, then gradually smoothing out into the consummate poise of the third and final sentence" (61). Sasek hears a note of almost stoic resignation to suffering (62, 195). Fish (291) argues that Adam's education or renovation has proceeded much more rapidly than our own; only 1,300 lines after Michael's benign reproof (11.340–41), Adams knows that "all truly meritorious actions are merely expressions of obedience to God." Summers claims that Adam's predominant emotion in this speech is neither "surprised joy" nor sorrow but, rather, peaceful acceptance; he recognizes both the fullness and the limitation of his knowledge and his perception of God's methods (*Muse's Method* 221). Shawcross sees in this passage a potential allusion to Ps. 1:1–2, about the man who shuns various sinful tendencies and instead delights in God's law (*"Paradise Lost"* 17). Mohl sees parallels between this passage and George Fox's Quaker statements on human perfectibility, including its emphasis on love, service, and suffering (*Studies* 111–12). Kogan reads this speech as Adam's reconciling himself within a capitalist economy by talking about his place in the divine scheme of things (31); see **11.531**.

561–64. Rajan distinguishes between servile and filial fear, which he defines as "an indwelling sense of the holy...imperative enough to make one shrink back from the possible violation of that order, " perfectly demonstrated by Christ's obedience (*"Paradise Lost:* The Hill" 54–55); cf. 12.402–04 and also 4.291–94.

562–65. Whaler cites these lines as an example of a pattern he calls "E 1–2," which "stresses or implies an affirmative idea of perfection, absolute completeness, order, truth, harmony, power, or some virtue" (*Counterpoint* 52–53); see **11.2–7**.

562–64. See Baumgartner's comment on patience in **11.111**.

562–63. *to walk / As in his presence:* see **11.315–16**.

562. *And love with fear the onely God:* cf. the exhortation to "rejoice with trembling" in Ps. 2:11, and Christ's words in John 14:15: "If ye love me, keep my commandments." "Milton substituted love for knowledge as the mainspring of human joy, and...the theory of love which he learned from Plato led him to go beyond the Platonic scale of values" (Samuel, *Plato* 167).

563–64. *to observe / His providence:* cf. *DocCh* 2.3: "Patience is that whereby we acquiesce in the promises of God, through a confident reliance on his divine providence, power, and goodness, and bear inevitable evils with equanimity, as the dispensation of the supreme Father, and sent for our good" (Patterson, *Works* 17:67).

564. *on him sole depend:* cf. exhortations to trust God alone in Ps. 62:5 and 1 Pet. 5:7.

565–69. *Mercifull over all his works:* a restatement of Ps. 145:9; cf. the promise of mercy in *PL* 3.134. Summers claims that Adam has finally come—as we must—to see God as "continuously and triumphantly subversive," overturning the ordinary categories of importance by which we judge (*Muse's Method* 20). This passage is a paradox as surely as is the fortunate Fall, the technique being Milton's own but the general method recalling that of other poet-prophets (Isaiah, the Job author, Dante) "to absorb the merely natural into a far more comprehensive vision until all paradoxes merge" (Patrides, *"Paradise Lost"* 112–13).

  with good / Still overcoming evil: cf. similar counsel in Rom. 12:21. Adam finally recognizes God's nature and that "Heav'nly love shall outdo Hellish hate" (Patrides, "Adam's 'Happy Fault'" 243); cf. 3.298.

565. *Mercifull:* 1667 *Merciful.*

566–69. This passage refers to 1 Cor. 1:27: "God hath chosen the weak things of the world to confound the things which are mighty." Cf. *DocCh* 1.15: "[Christ] governs...[men's] minds and consciences, and that not by force and fleshly weapons, but by what the world esteems the weakest of all instruments" (Maurice Kelley 163; Patterson, *Works* 15:299–301). "The regeneration of an individual soul, in other words, is sufficient to defeat the great active force of Satan" (Muldrow 106). This paradox also occurs in the writings of Milton's contemporaries (Patrides, *Milton* 159–61).

569–71. This passage represents the "Protestant ideal" (Whiting, *Milton* 157). Cf. *PL* 9.31–33, *SA* 654. Howard, analyzing *PL* in terms of *ArtLog*, identifies this passage as a "more proximate and less conventional end" than that enunciated in 12.469–78 and one that requires the "greater man" to realize in *PR* (165–66). Because sin has entered human experience, "the true way of life is the way of endurance, of patience under affliction . . . victory itself is always reserved to God" (Reesing 78–79). Burke argues that this passage does not reflect stoical apathy, since Milton says in *DocCh* 2.10 that sensibility to pain and lamentations "are not inconsistent with true patience" (Patterson, *Works* 17:253). The events to occur after Adam and Eve have left Eden are purposefully put before their spiritual awakening so the epic may end hopefully (Shawcross, "Balanced Structure" 705).

And to the faithful Death the Gate of Life: Verity cites the Latin proverb *Mors janua vitae* ("Death is the gate of life"); cf. Rev. 2:10: "Be thou faithful unto death, and I will give thee a crown of life." This assertion is "Death's 'death wound,' for in the face of that assurance, Death is powerless over man" (R. M. Frye 86). This metaphor does not represent the myth of return; the end of the cycle is an eternal resurrection rather than another repetition (Shawcross, *"Paradise Lost"* 3–5). Wesley omits this line.

569. *simply meek:* "very illuminating is Milton's use of the adjective 'meek.' This describes the benign and awful majesty of a personality fully harmonious with God, a calm of surface indicating incalculable depth" (Hall 185–86); cf. Milton's definition of meekness in *DocCh* 2.12, which is "so far from offering or taking offence, that we conduct ourselves mildly and affectionately towards all men, as far as is practicable" (Patterson, *Works* 17:283–85).

simply: "with simplicity (of mind) or sincerity; in an honest or straightforward manner; also, in later use, unaffectedly, artlessly" (so *OED* 1).

572–73. *whom I now / Acknowledge my Redeemer:* the Richardsons identify this passage as Adam's "confession of faith," as does Bush, who calls Adam the first

Christian. According to Lewalski, who traces the development of Adam's faith to perceive the "things not seen" of Heb. 11:1, this passage proves that Adam's faith is fully matured (34); see also **11.368**. Burke underscores the importance of Christ's example: from the humiliation of the Son, Adam has learned to evaluate his own experience by the many demands of humility (89).

> *ever blest:* cf. Romans 9:5: "Christ...over all, God blessed for ever."

574. *th'Angel last repli'd:* both Michael's last speech and Adam's in 12.552 are marked with "last replied" (Newton). On the fluidity of Milton's names for angels, see West's and Gage's comments in **11.101**. On the elision, see **11.449**.

575–87. Cf. Raphael's exhortation in 8.167–78. Herford thinks that Michael's concluding speech was partly influenced by Virgil's farewell to Dante at the brink of the earthly paradise: "Free, sound and upright is thy will, and it were an error not to follow it; wherefore I crown and mitre thee king and bishop of thyself" (229); cf. *Purgatorio* 27.140–42. The reference is also noted by Samuel, though, as she adds, Dante is about to ascend where Virgil cannot follow, whereas Adam must remember what he has learned when he descends into a lower world (*Dante* 222–23). Greenlaw compares Spenser's Redcrosse led by an old man, Contemplation, to the Mount of Vision (*Faerie Queene* 1.10.53–59); the Christian graces mentioned in this passage are part of the preparation of Redcrosse in the House of Coelia (214–16). The speech is "Milton's mature and final conclusion," since "the great reformation can come only when each man rises to the greatest possibilities in himself" (Patterson, *Student's Milton*). To prove that man's state is improved, Gilbert cites the beginning of *DocCh* 1.14: "man...is raised to a far more excellent state of grace and glory than that from which he had fallen" ("Problem" 187); cf. Patterson, *Works* 15:251. In part, Milton is calling for Adam's actions to accord with right reason and conscience, as he equated the two in *DocCh;* that is, for his actions to be both prudent and just (Burke 85); cf. *DocCh* 1.2 (Patterson, *Works* 14:29). Michael identifies the most important of the "more elaborate doctrines" Adam needs in the new world: happiness will be determined by ethical habit, even though purely cognitive expansion is not forbidden (Samuel, "Milton" 712). "They miss the point who think that Milton sets Adam's degenerate state above the state of innocence"; the gain of a paradise within means "this disjoining of the inner and outer state" (Samuel, *Plato* 121). Although Michael stresses moral issues, he still includes such intellectual issues as the knowledge of the stars, which in book 8 was given a unique role, and other realms of universal knowledge necessary for dominion over nature (Burden 122–23). The bare statement of doctrine here is necessary—Milton the poet had to be drawn to the material by Milton the Puritan (Muir 162–63). Reesing (103) identifies this passage as the last of three final "arias," the others being 12.560–61 and 561–73; see **11.1–21**. Martz, who complains that most of the last two books is an unpoetic disequilibrium between sin and grace, nevertheless finds that Michael here "prepares the way for the poem's perfectly tempered finale, by recalling that the promised redemption consists primarily in the renewal of man's inner powers" (166–67). Kogan reads this passage as a statement about how fallen man, the historical man of the seventeenth century must develop confidence in himself and be the independent and virtuous bourgeois entrepreneur (22, 27–28); see **11.531**. Rajan thinks the words "look back irresistibly to the sweep" of *Prol 7* ("*Paradise Lost:* The Hill" 62–63). Wesley notes this passage as among those particularly excellent.

575–76. *the summe / Of wisdome:* the phrasing may echo the biblical words to the king of Tyre, "Thou sealest up the sum, full of wisdom" (Ezek. 28:12), although that message is critical. Cf. Job 28:28: "The fear of the Lord, that is wisdom" (Fowler). This opening sentence is the "glowing climax" of our transformed feelings about loss (Reesing 61). On metaphors of completion, see **12.553–57**. Summers compares this wisdom with lower, instrumental knowledges—later science, the riches of Croesus, the power of Alexander or Augustus (*Muse's Method* 222); cf. **11.551–52**. Similarly, Hoopes claims that Milton held "intuitive reasoning," or the response to impulses from God and a "power that fuses thought and action," was always superior to the discursive reasoning that observed natural phenomena and developed theories and systems (194–95); see also Hoopes's comment in **12.83–101**.

576–79. The continued attraction of scientific lore was felt not only by Milton but reflected on the title pages of dozens of medieval and Renaissance encyclopedias (Svendsen, *Milton and Science* 47).

   hope no higher…All secrets of the deep: because of the shift from the physical universe to the soul, the heights and depths are renamed but still resemble their macrocosmic analogs (MacCaffrey 61–62).

576. For George Coffin Taylor's argument on similarities with a 1640 consolatory text, see **12.587**.

   wisdome: 1667 *wisdom.*

579. *in Heav'n, Aire, Earth, or Sea:* the Richardsons claim Milton is thinking of heaven as fire, listed with the other three elements of air, earth, and water, in imitation of the classical authors, e.g., Ovid's *Metamorphoses* 1.21–22, "Nam caelo terras, & terras abscidit undas, / Et liquidem spisso secrevit ab aere coelum" (Now from sky he cut the lands, and lands from waters, and dense liquid parted from airy heaven), and also 1.26, "Ignea convexi vis & sine pondere coeli" (The fiery arched power and without weight the skies).

   Aire: 1667 *Air.*

580. *enjoydst:* see **12.610** on verb inflections.

581–649. Emma includes this section in his small sample of beginning and ending lines from *Mask, PL, PR, SA, Areop, RCG, Animad,* and *TKM* (159).

581–87. Cf. the similar list of virtues in 2 Pet. 1:5–7. Warburton explains this list excellently (Newton). These virtues are the new heroism Milton offers instead of heroism found in battle or magnificent display (Bowra 210). The list is necessary because paradise will be recovered not merely by man as "contemplator but by man as actor" (Summers, *Muse's Method* 222). Lieb (*"Paradise Lost"* 35–39) supplements the biblical context with lists of virtues from 1 Cor. 13:2, 13 and 2 Pet. 1:8–9; Milton's humanism works comparably with Eliot's use in *The Waste Land* of the Brihadaranyaka Upanishad: he sees solutions to moral dilemmas as so basic that they can be pictured as physical elements. Fowler, looking for Pythagorean numerology, points out that Milton subtracts godliness and brotherly love from the original biblical list, adding *deeds,* resulting in seven conditions of fruitfulness, with *virtue* in the central, most important position. Emma notes the *asyndeton,* or rhetorical omission of conjunctions between coordinate grammatical elements (155). The heroic fortitude of this passage is by no means passive resistance but rather the steady, cumulative effect of the good choices of Adam, Abel, Enoch, Noah, Abraham, and Christ (Radzinowicz 50).

581–82. *onely add / Deeds:* cf. "faith without works is dead" (James 2:20, 26) and also the warning in *DocCh* 1.33 that one will finally be judged by the disparity between words and actions (Maurice Kelley 183; Patterson, *Works* 16:355).

to thy knowledge answerable, add Faith: Bridges believes that the elision should be between *–ble add* rather than eliding the first *e* of *answerable* (31); see a similar case in *PL* 11.92. Sprott, however, insists that it is generally better to elide *–able* words internally rather than with the next word (92–93).

answerable: Verity supplies "corresponding with," as in *Areop:* "a vertue (honour'd Lords and Commons) answerable to Your highest actions" (Patterson, *Works* 4:354). Cf. *OED* 4, "corresponding in quantity of amount; proportional, commensurate."

582–83. Lieb links the poet's initial mention of Sion (*PL* 1.10) and the temple (1.18) to David's plan to build a temple (2 Sam. 7), arguing that Milton "wishes his poem to reveal how man should arrange his temporal affairs" (*Dialectics* 40). See Baumgartner comment on patience in **11.111**.

583. *vertue:* 1667 *Vertue.*

583–85. Charity (Latin, *caritas;* Greek ἀγαπὴ) is the selfless love of 1 Cor. 13:13. Cf. *Tetr,* where Milton cites 1 Tim. 1:5, "the end of the commandment [i.e., all scriptural law] is charity" (Patterson, *Works* 4:197). Love represents the whole "knot of Christian graces," including all practical religion (Patterson, *Student's Milton*); cf. *DocCh* 1.1, "Christian Doctrine is comprehended under two divisions: Faith, or the Knowledge of God; and Love, or the Worship of God" (Patterson, *Works* 14:23). Charity is the last lesson in heroic virtue that Adam needs in order to leave paradise willingly (Hughes, *Paradise Lost*). Charity "is the final and full antithesis to the constricting circle of self-embrace that is Satan" (Di Cesare 25). Cf. *DocCh* 1.16, "Christ fulfilled the law by perfect love to God and his neighbor" (Patterson, *Works* 15:317), and, as noted by Maurice Kelley (169), *DocCh* 1.21, where the source of spontaneously and freely produced good works is love (Patterson, *Works* 16:9). Emma cites *the soul / Of all the rest* as one of Milton's rarer uses of the partitive genitive (39).

587–89. See Lieb on the language of generation in **11.369**.

587. *A paradise within thee, happier farr:* cf. "The mind is its own place" (*PL* 1.254) and the hell within Satan (4.20–23, 75). In the notes to his translation of *Orlando Furioso* 34, Sir John Harington refers to "the comfortable peace of conscience, the only true Paradise of this world" (399). According to Todd, Arminius's motto was "Bona conscientia Paradisus" (A good conscience is Paradise). Todd also cites Henry More's comment, in *Exposition of the… Seven Churches* (6.11), that Philo and other interpreters likewise allegorized a vineyard into something interior. Jakob Boehme claimed that both heaven and hell were within humans (Bailey 158). This line and also 11.547 and 12.576 are linguistically similar to *Paradice within Us, or The Happie Mind* (1640), a consolatory text written by Robert Crofts, a seventeenth century imitator of Du Bartas; the possibility of an inward paradise suggests that Adam's fall was fortunate (G. C. Taylor, "Did Milton Read" 207–10). This passage "is one of those world-thoughts which occur independently to many minds," such as "I Myself am Heav'n and Hell," quatrain 66 of Fitzgerald's *Rubaiyat* (Verity; see Khayyam 121). The greater good is chosen by the " 'right Reason' choosing the 'human mind fully informed' over the 'arbitrary will of God' " (Green 570). Bøgholm thinks that the poem "rises to true dramatic grandeur" in these lines, and recalls the end of *SA:* "calm of mind all passion spent" (50). Milton was able to objectify himself whereas the self-glorifying Byron and the self-pitying Shelley could not; in the world vision at the end of Byron's *Cain*, the title character stops short of Adam's peace, knowledge, and transcendent vision, and a bleaker inner world is proposed at the end of Shelley's *Revolt of Islam* (Siegel 615–17). Milton is disappointed at the failed revolution; because the present world is doomed to dissolution, salvation for man depends on his absolute withdrawal from history (Ross, *Poetry and Dogma* 96); see also Ross's comment in **12.543–47**.

Kermode points to more general poetic difficulties: "poetry cannot say much more about [the new Eden], because the senses do not know it" (121). Ferry compares the new paradise with the better sight proposed in the introduction to book 3; in the same way that the narrator has a truer vision because he is blind, so Adam and Eve are granted the inward paradise only after they have lost their first one (*Milton's Epic Voice* 32–33, 38). Ogden counters the assumption that Adam will be happier after leaving the garden of Eden than he was before the Fall; the line refers to Adam's lament for "this happy place, our sweet / Recess" (11.303–04), when Michael could add only the partial consolation that God is everywhere (18). Sasek also denies that this passage confirms Satan's principle that "the mind is its own place" (1.254); rather, Michael is saying in context that a good conscience is better outside paradise than a bad conscience within (195). It is by successive exodus experiences that faith is renewed throughout the history described in the last two books, advancing in successive stages from the specific (Eden as earthly heaven) to the more general, from local to the universal paradise within (Shawcross, *"Paradise Lost"* 8–9). Joseph, comparing the hell within Satan with the paradise within available for Adam, insists that "it is a false view, based on a false evaluation of self, that sees freedom in rebellion" (284), whereas Mohl cites this passage in her discussion of human perfectibility—"The development of Adam and Eve to greater man and woman involves their becoming moral agents"; Quakers were attacked, among other things, for their similar belief (*Studies* 87, 112); see also **11.681**. Adam is humanized through the experience of history, attaining the sum of wisdom, and is no longer loath to leave paradise; "the Fall therefore becomes fortunate" (Lieb, *"Paradise Lost"* 41). Whereas both Satan and the human couple lost a paradise, hell possesses Satan psychologically while Adam and Eve may create paradise within (Lieb, *Dialectics* 217–28). "The tone which characterizes the narrative voice throughout *Paradise Lost*...derives its complexity from paradox" (Ferry, "Bird" 197). The poem is an epic, because although the tragic hero is a kind of Satan, Milton's Satan is not the hero of *PL,* nor are Adam and Eve, who are instead victors after suffering (Samuels 65, 77). Milton's description of the earthly paradise also included such "unmistakable intangibles as happiness, joy, and bliss" (Ryken 201).

   within thee, happier: some editions of 1667 omit the comma (Fowler).
   paradise: 1667 *Paradise.*

588–94. *top / Of Speculation:* "one from which a wide or extensive view is obtained" (so *OED* 2c), reminiscent of Gregory the Great's *turris speculationis,* or watch tower, in his *Moralium* (Migne, *Patrologiae...Latina* 76:6190). Milton may intend a reference to the watchman of Ezek. 3:17 and 33:2–7 with its attendant idea of a raised vantage point, since as Hume and others note, the Latin equivalent is derived from *specula;* cf. *Oxford Latin Dictionary* 1, "a raised structure or eminence used as a look-out post"; cf. also the "Specular Mount" of *PR* 4.236. The meaning of "theological speculation" is also possible (Fowler). The height is both physical and metaphoric; they have been on a literal mountaintop and "have just attained the highest point of philosophy or speculative wisdom" (Masson). Cf. "upon this mountain...speculation" of *Henry V* 4.2.30–31, though the speculation there is "idle" (Verity 31). Himes

(*Paradise Lost: A Poem*) compares this passage with the disciples' descent from the mount of transfiguration (Matt. 17:9, Mark 9:9, Luke 9:37). Milton frequently uses, at the end of book 12, words and phrases that evoke "an impression of coming back to earth, of settling down, of relaxing from strain" (Shumaker, *Unpremeditated Verse* 58); see also **12.645**.

 the hour precise: precise, from Latin *praecisus,* "cut off" — Chambers Murray (in Richardsons) has "broken off, abrupt." Himes (*Paradise Lost: A Poem*) compares Priam's departure from the Grecian camp before Achilles could no longer have protected him (*Iliad* 24.677–91); Himes also wants to place in the morning three other departures (Lot's from Sodom [Gen. 19:15–16], the disciples from the mount of transfiguration [Matt. 17:9, Mark 9:9, Luke 9:37], and Adam's from paradise [Gen. 3:23–24]). Although the "hour precise" is not specified, the phrase helps us return to a different scale of experience: Milton shifts subtly from a vast temporal perspective back to the immediate kind of time in which Adam has lived and will again be living (Stapleton 747); see **11.134–35**. We are not told the exact time — though the context suggests evening — because Milton does not want to suggest the emotions associated with the postlapsarian evening in the garden when Adam feared God's approach (Gen. 3:8–10); Adam and Eve are no longer afraid, but neither are they tranquil (Knott, "Pastoral Day" 180). Fowler argues that the time now is "noon," since noon terminates the 24–hour period beginning at the noon of the Fall (*PL* 9.739) and thus the "day" mentioned in the prohibition of 8.329–23 is only now accomplished, and also since Hugh of St. Victor identified noon as the hour of the Expulsion, as well as of the Crucifixion, making the Expulsion itself a Janus image that looks both ways (cf. *PL* 11.129).

590. *Guards:* on the fluidity of Milton's names for angels, see West's and Gage's comments in **11.101**.

591–92. *expect / Thir motion:* i.e., watch for a military signal to move.
 motion: cf. the obsolete military sense: "each of the several successive actions of which a prescribed exercise of arms consists" (*OED* 4c).

591. *yonder:* "at or in that place; there; usually implying that the object spoken of is at some distance but within sight" (*OED* 1a).

592–93. *at whose Front a flaming Sword, / In signal of remove:* cf. the original biblical narrative of expulsion in Gen. 3:24, and also the swords of cherubim in *PL* 1.664 and 11.120–22.

    remove: can have the military sense of "departure"—*OED* 1c is "to lift a siege"; it thus sustains the military diction (Fowler).

594–605. The tone of this passage is controlled by the divine injunction in *PL* 11.117 for Michael to "send them forth, though sorrowing, yet in peace" (Ferry, *Milton's Epic Voice* 42).

    one Faith unanimous though sad: the balanced themes of submission and faith are continually reinterpreted and enlarged against each other in the last two books, implying both the growth of Adam's understanding and the mysteriousness of God's providence; Milton also expresses his own faith here, since "The Expulsion is a matter of fact, the bruising of the serpent a matter of faith" (Fowler).

594–97. Until now, Eve's only reported dreams have either had satanic origins or been the after-effects of lust (Allen, *Harmonious Vision* xx). See also **11.366–68** and the vague description of Eve's dream in *PL* 12.610–23.

596. *compos'd:* "to address or dispose (especially the mind, oneself) calmly and collectedly to or for an action or state, or to do something" (so *OED* 13).

600. *The great deliverance by her Seed to come:* the promise of Gen. 3:15 is frequently repeated in Michael's narration; see **11.115–16**.

601. *Womans Seed:* Emma judges this "direct genitive" to be infrequent in Milton's works (36–37).

    Some editions of 1667 have a comma after *mankind* (Fowler).

602–05. Michael's final words enforce the mingled mood of sadness and joy that characterizes not only the last two books but also the opening lines of the poem (Miner 49).

602. *ye may live, which will be many dayes:* according to Gen. 5:5, Adam lived 930 years. Ogden, denying a fortunate Fall, claims that Michael's last words are sobering rather than triumphant (19). Emma cites this line as an instance of "inflected nouns of time" (28).

603–04. *though sad...yet...cheer'd:* cf. 11.117. Despite the desire of Augustan critics that Adam remain in a state of exultation proper to an epic, Milton must also depict Adam's natural sorrow, tempered by the vision, at his departure from Eden (Moore 32–33). This passage is a "very conspicuous toning down" of Michael's speech; "the lines describe the precise shape of human loss" (Reesing 62). This "happy end" is to be achieved only by the Son's labor "above heroic" (Samuel, *Plato* 121).

603. *unanimous:* 1667 *unanimous,* though some editions of 1667 omit the comma (Fowler).

604–05. See Lieb on the language of generation in **11.369.**
    with cause for: because of.

604. *cause:* Wesley changes to *grief.*

605. *meditation on the happie end:* the paradise within is not instantly attained; "tragedy surrenders to Dantean comedy only in the immense perspective of eternity" (Lawry, *Shadow* 286–87). "The poet keeps returning to the language and original promise of the earthly paradise" (Giamatti 350).

606. *He ended, and they both descend the Hill:* Milton here combines the historical present with past tense forms (Emma 92).

607. *Descended:* 1667 *Descended,* though some copies of 1667 omit the comma (Fowler).

608. *but found her wak't:* the Argument says, "Adam wakens Eve" (Newton). Tenderness, noticeable especially since the Fall, now becomes the dominating emotion (Patterson, *Student's Milton*).

609. *not sad:* "perhaps the most pathetic touch in this pathetic passage" (R. C. Browne 1877).

610–23. "Eve's personal, domestic, intimate speech" comprises two sentences, with a simple middle part (614–19) "sheltered" between two passages "rather more exalted in diction" (610–14, 620–23), with high frontal vowels interlaced throughout with sonorous ones (Reesing 104); see **11.1–21**. Northrop Frye, who suggests that Eve's vaguely described dream represents an independent, God-ordained feminine self, concludes lyrically, "far below this rarefied pinnacle of rational vision, there lies a humiliated mother dreaming of the vengeance of her mighty son" ("Revelation" 47); see also **11.366–68**. "Eve's final speech indicates that she has already recovered the inward paradise" (Summers, *Muse's Method* 223).

610. *Whence thou returnst, and whither wentst, I know:* "a journey has been accomplished; it was physical, but it was also a metaphor of search into the future significance of acts performed in the narrative past" (Shumaker, *Unpremeditated Verse* 60). Milton always follows the common inflection *–st* for second-person singular verbs (i.e., with *thou*), even with the past tense *enjoydst* in 12.850 (Emma 89, 93n10); see also **12.617–18**.
    and whither: 1667 *& whither.*

611. *For God is also in sleep, and Dreams advise:* cf. God speaking to biblical prophets in dreams and visions in Num. 12:6, as well as similar sentiments in *Iliad* 1.63 ("A dream is from Zeus"). The biblical reference particularly applies here, since Eve dreamed and Adam had a vision (Montgomery). R. C. Browne (1877, 6:478) refers to Bacon's phrase in "Of Youth and Age": "Vision is a clearer Revelation [i.e., of God] then a Dreame." Addison claims, "the Sleep that fell upon Eve, and the effects it had in quieting the Disorders of her Mind, produces the same kind of Consolation in the Reader" (*Spectator* 3 [3 May 1712]: 388). Cf. *DocCh* 1.27: "the Holy Spirit is to them an equivalent and substitute for prophecy, dreams, and visions" (Barker, "Structural and Doctrinal Pattern" 193–94; Patterson, *Works* 16:119). Milton is careful to encourage and instruct Eve so that she will not have to depend solely upon Adam; it may be significant that this enlightenment comes directly from God (D. Taylor, "Milton's Treatment" 81). Although our will is entirely free, God can and does plant ideas in one's subconscious in the hope that one will choose the eternal good (Boswell 94). The eighteenth century poet James Scott may have been alluding to this passage in his *Ode 9: To Sleep,* about the "auspicious visions" that "sooth'd great Milton's injured age, / When in prophetic dreams he saw / The tribe unborn with pious awe" (Good 71). Fowler identifies the authorities on dream types as Artemidorus (*Oneiorocritica*) and Macrobius (*Commentary* 1.3.2–17); the prophetic vision (Latin, *visio*) is defined as a dream that comes true (1.3.9). Bridges elides *also in* (25).

613. *Presaging:* foretelling supernaturally; cf. *presage* (*OED* 1).
  sorrow and: Bridges elides (25).

614–23. *But now lead on:* this last speech, the "best spoken in paradise," is a good example of Eve's exercise of private virtues in contrast to Adam's public ones (W. A. Raleigh 151–52). Cf. Eve's command to the serpent in 9.631. Eve's speech resembles Adam's declaration of "love" before his fall, but it now expresses continued perseverance in redemptive love on the human level, perfected by its conscious dependence on the promised love of the Redeemer (Summers, "Voice" 1089; *Muse's Method* 184–85). This passage foreshadows redemption, since the Fall occurred when the reciprocal rule of marital love and obedience was broken (Haller 97). Eve has taken to heart Michael's exhortation to go with her husband (11.292); her words resonate with her pleasure in Adam's company in *PL* 4.634–56 (Fowler).

614–19. The epic is continually preparing for the final human condition (Stoll, "From the Superhuman" 14); see **11.138–39**.

615–18. Cf. Ruth's words to Naomi, "Whither thou goest, I will go" (Ruth 1:16), as well as the assurance of Andromache, Hector's wife, that he was all relations to her (*Iliad* 6.429–30). Newton points out that Eve has been brought to agree with Michael's counsel in 11.290–92 and that woman's paradise is in company with her husband, but for man, it is "A paradise within" himself (12.587). Patrides similarly compares Eve's finding her paradise in Adam, and Adam's in God (*Milton* 177), though Lawry claims Eve's so deciding accomplishes part of her "paradise within" (*Shadow* 275). Eve is reconciled to her banishment from the pastoral world, as the speaker-poet is reconciled to his blindness (Ferry, "Bird" 194).

615. *In mee is no delay:* numerous early commentators cite Virgil's "In me mora non erit ulla" (In me will be no delay at all) (*Eclogues* 3.52), though the context of the latter—a singing contest—is considerably different. Cf. the *mora* (delay) in *Aeneid* 2.701 ("Iam iam nulla mora est; sequor et qua ducitis adsum" [Now, now there is no delay; I follow, and where ye lead, there am I!]) and *Aeneid* 12.11 ("Nulla mora in Turno" [with Turnus is no delay]). This moment is the last of three milestones "on the inner journey from innocence to regeneration," echoing the Virgin Mary's words in Luke 1:38: "Be it unto me according to thy word" (Pecheux, "Concept" 366); see **11.162–71.**

617–18. *thou…Art:* see **12.610** on verb inflections.

620–23. Even before Adam and Eve leave the garden, they have both met their Redeemer and seen the working of their future salvation, assisting their redemption through their own spiritual and intellectual growth (D. Taylor, "Milton's Treatment" 80). Reesing praises the "harmonious blending of the many varied feelings with which the two main characters will depart from the garden"; Eve's last words complete the process (63, 67).

623. *By mee the Promis'd Seed shall all restore:* the last spoken words in *PL* are Eve's repetition of the promise of Gen. 3:15, a promise frequently repeated in Michael's narration; see **11.115–16.** The last spoken word of the epic, *restore,* promises that its vision will be translated into history (Patrides, *Phoenix* 65; *Milton* 262). "The story of Eve's creation has become the story of the end of the world" (Pecheux, "Second Adam" 184).

624–49. The atmosphere of ambivalence and paradox of the final verse paragraph can only be understood in terms of medieval and Renaissance pseudoscience (Svendsen, *Milton and Science* 105).

624–32. Tillyard cites this passage as proof that the mature Milton had lost neither the tenderness of *Nat* nor the sensuous opulence of *Mask* (*Miltonic Setting* 116). The syntax of this passage is "mainly loose, partly periodic" (Emma 149).

624–26. Adam's reticence is admirably decorous: in the presence of an angel, he refrains from even spoken endearments to his wife (Hume). The passage shows with dramatic economy how alien the spirit world is now (Broadbent, *Some Graver Subject* 284).

Archangel: two words in some copies of 1667 (Fowler).

624. *so spake:* Emma, citing Charles Fries, calls attention to this archaic past tense form, used despite Milton's accelerated tendency to use the same form for "strong verbs" (i.e., those changing tense in the vowel) in both the past and the past perfect (94–95).

our Mother Eve: Milton's last individual reference is "an appropriate and comprehensive epithet for Eve," emphasizing her relation to us and her future understanding of her children based on her own frailties (Hutcherson 260). This is the last time that Eve is specifically mentioned (Patterson, *Student's Milton*).

625–32. *and from the other Hill:* i.e., the hill where the angels "made halt" in 11.210. Cf. the two allegorical hills of grace and law in Gal. 4:24–26 and also cf. 2 Cor. 3:12–17, about the spiritual darkness of those who seek justification by works of the law, to the *Ev'ning Mist* around the *Labourers heel* (Himes, *Paradise Lost: A Poem*). This passage summarizes books 11 and 12, looking both backward and forward, and in the frightening context of the Expulsion, "a moving evocation of the life of toil and poverty and weariness, and also of homely satisfactions…which Adam and Eve must now undertake" (Prince 52). Knott agrees, but adds that one is more conscious of the threatening mist at the laborer's heel, especially when the passage is compared with the more comforting return from day's labor in Virgil's eclogues ("Pastoral Day" 181).

625. *but answer'd not:* i.e., did not answer. One might suspect that Milton prefers constructions without the auxiliary verb *do;* the now-obsolescent *nigh* was in common use as late as the nineteenth century (Emma 99–100, 121).

627–49. Landor (in Wittreich 318) judged that although most of book 12 was dry and flat, the ending unites the sublime and the pathetic, and answers God's promise to leave the human pair "sorrowing yet in peace"; cf. *PL* 11.117.

627–28. *Station:* "post of watching; Latin, *statio*, a military term = a picket, guard" (Verity).

　　Cherubim: Milton's narration follows Gen. 3:24 in placing cherubim on guard, but on the fluidity of Milton's names for angels, see West's and Gage's comments in **11.101**.

627. *in bright array:* cf. the same phrase in 6.801.

628–40. Cf. Moses' leading the chosen people forth under God's guidance in 12.200–20 (Shawcross, *"Paradise Lost"* 15).

628–29. *on the ground / Gliding meteorous:* in the Greek, *meteorous* (μετήορος) means "lifted off the ground, hanging" (Liddell and Scott). Addison cites Heliodorus's *Æthiopics* as authority that the gods can slide over the surface of the earth (*Spectator* 3 [3 May 1712]: 389). Todd reports that Alexander Pope uses the same words to describe the movement of the gods in his translation of Homer's *Iliad:* "Iris from the skies, / Swift as a whirlwind, on the message flies; / Meteorous the face of ocean sweeps" (24.99–101). Wesley glosses the term as "like a meteor, or vapour." The image opposes the black mist in which Satan travels in *PL* 9.180 (Richardsons), which Ricks finds to be an apt example of "how Milton releases enhancing suggestions from the burial-places of memory" (*Milton's Grand Style* 109). Cf. also 9.74–75, 158–59. Keightley surmises that Milton had observed gliding mist at Horton. Joseph Hunter claims that to the popular mind, mists sometimes do look like horsemen and footmen, "large armies like what we may imagine the cherubim to have been" (71–72). Satan himself is compared to a delusively bright mist in 9.633–41; the mist's suggestion of threat is from fallen man's new perspective (Svendsen, *Milton and Science* 107–10). In the seventeenth century, the term *meteor* was applied to almost any atmospheric phenomenon, but especially to luminous bodies and exhalations such as fireballs, shooting stars, comets, and *ignis fatuus*, or marsh gas (Fowler).

629–32. *as Ev'ning Mist / . . . at the Labourers heel / Homeward returning:* this is the last extended simile in the epic (Ferry, *Milton's Epic Voice* 78). Not only does the simile suggest angelic movement, but *Labourers heel* "unites Adam [i.e., condemned to labor in 10.201–06] with the Woman's Seed, whose heel will be bruised even as he restores all" (Di Cesare 24). Milton wants us to link this simile with the endangered night wanderer (9.634–42) because Adam and Eve will be able to avoid the dangers of delusion by exiting Eden (Lieb, *Dialectics* 219). In this "anticipatory simile," Adam and Eve are henceforth to be day-laborers, and they are "Homeward returning" because the common earth is henceforth to be their home (Whaler, "Miltonic Simile" 1051–52). Sims finds that "it helps to mitigate the sadness of Adam's expulsion from the garden," since his labor has changed little (*Bible* 129). The twilight mood of the ending typifies the twilight in which humans dwell (Stoll, "Was Paradise" 434). Bush likewise calls the passage an "unobtrusive but poignant reminder of the judgment on Adam . . . and the everyday world of history." Stapleton concludes with this reference his survey of Milton's thematic use of time, in which Michael gives Adam a sense both of the outcome of cosmic time and of being in human time (747); see **11.134–35**.

630. *Ris'n from a River o're the marish glides:* Sprott cites this line as an example of Milton's contracting past participles and nouns with a terminal *–n* that then will disappear from the scansion (76).

    marish: i.e., marsh (*OED* 1). Todd cites occurrences of the word in 1 Macc. 9:42 and 45; see also Ezek. 47:11. Also cited is *1 Henry 6* 1.1.50, though the Riverside Shakespeare has "Our isle be made a *nourish* of salt tears," i.e., a *nurse* (French, *nourrice*), and lists no variants. R. C. Browne (1877) reports usage by Spenser, Drayton, and Browne. The word is used often in the translations of Ariosto and Tasso (Verity).

632–49. The ending's power is due to "the double motions and emotions" of the entire poem being present "quietly, indissolubly, and without comment" (Summers, *Muse's Method* 223).

632–40. "The truth is that Adam is both Lear and Edgar, both Hamlet and Fortinbras, and we cannot forget the defeat of the one while we take comfort in the reassertion of order represented by the other. Although Milton affirms the happiness of the saints, he portrays vividly the expulsion of Adam from paradise" (Sasek 195).

632–34. *High in Front advanc't / The brandisht Sword of God…blaz'd / Fierce as a Comet:* cf. Gen. 3:24: "He placed at the east of the garden of Eden Cherubims, and a flaming sword which turned every way, to keep the way of the tree of life." Whiting ("Cherubim" 469–70) recounts Salkeld's 1613 summary of interpretations of the Genesis passage: that the angelic sword represents a purging fire (Ambrose), that Eden is located at the equator (Aquinas), that the sword represents a flaming wall (Abulensis), that the cherubim are allegories for devils who hinder our spiritual life, that the cherubim are visions of terrifying beasts (cf. Milton's "dreadful Faces" in 12.644), or literally cherubim; Milton adopts the literal reading but reinforces it with the others. Di Cesare judges that the final similes reflect ambivalent feelings toward angels, who "however friendly…cannot now guide and protect" (24); see also **12.643–44.** This stage in the epic imaginatively joins two others: "the dismal situation waste and wild" of 1.60 and the first evening on earth in book 4 (Stoll, "From the Superhuman" 11).

advanc't: Verity glosses as "raised aloft, like a flag," as the "Ensigns high advanc'd" of 5.588; he also cites the "swords advanced" of *Coriolanus* 1.6.61 and Marvell's comparison of pre–Civil War England as paradise ("Upon Appleton House," in *Complete Poems* 321–28). Milton's detail that the sword was *High in Front advanc't* seems to be on rabbinical authority (W. B. Hunter, "Two Milton Notes" 91). Cf. Milton's complaint in *DDD* 13 that wrong-headed commentators "would have us re-enter Paradise against the sword that guards it" (Patterson, *Works* 3:469).

Fierce as a Comet: cf. *PL* 2.708–11. Dunster (in Todd) cites Sylvester's translation of Du Bartas: "For the Almightie set before the dore / Of th' holy Parke, a Seraphin, that bore / A waving sword, whose bodie shined bright, / Like flaming Comet in the midst of night"; see Du Bartas 1:356.635–38. Grotius's *Adamus Exul* includes Eve's description of multiple flames, "a gleaming conflagration / That wanders hastily," as if the entire garden were burning without fire (Grotius, in Kirkconnell 219); cf. a similar description by Eve in Vondel's *Adam in Ballingschap* (1613): "O what a fire kindles all the Garden / And browses of the trees" (Vondel, in Kirkconnell 479). Edmundson (122) also cites Vondel's description of the rod of God's judgment as "A comet with a tail, as fairy red / As blood, the token of God's wrath." Svendsen links the comet simile here with the famous "error" of locating the constellation Ophiucus in the north, referred to in *PL* 2.706–11; comets were traditionally located in the north (*Milton and Science* 91). Milton was interested in comets, not only because of the various controversies occasioned by Galileo's theories, but because an appearance of Halley's comet in 1607 occasioned a great number of pamphlets (Nicolson, "Milton and the Telescope" 92). "Swan and Gadbury, among others, report that a comet shaped like a sword 'signifieth warres and destruction of cities'" (Svendsen, *Milton and Science* 92–93).

634–35. *which:* i.e., the sword.

with torrid heat, / And vapour as the Libyan Air adust: the flames are punitive and hellish, but they are also purgative and heavenly, suggesting the tragically heroic phoenix image that closes *SA* (Lawry, *Shadow* 287). Shawcross likens the Expulsion to leaving the amniotic fluid of the womb: "Adam and Eve issue forth to a desiccated world adust (with its obvious pun on mortality)"; "th'Eastern Gate" is another womb symbol (Shawcross, *"Paradise Lost"* 22); cf. **12.196–98**. The torrid features here answer to what Shawcross ("Balanced Structure" 708) calls the "interwoven solstices" of the Fall, the features of rain, ice, hail, snow, and cold winds (*PL* 10.1063–65). Cf. the flaming "Chariot of Paternal Deitie" in 6.750; the previously temperate clime of Eden begins to return to a disordered state (Lieb, *Dialectics* 220). Milton may have read the Jesuit John Salkeld's review of several theories about the swords of the cherubim guarding the entrance of Eden, among them Thomas Aquinas's suggestion that the garden lay under the equator, thought then to be a *torrida Zona,* a burning zone that no one could pass (Hughes, *Paradise Lost, A Poem* 283–85), also cited by Whiting ("Cherubim" 469–70; see **12.632–34**). The "torrid zone" was a common gloss on the cherubim's sword, going back to Tertullian; it depends on the old belief that the torrid zone was uninhabitable (Fowler). Wesley omits these two lines.

adust: "scorched, seared; burnt up, calcined; dried up with heat, parched" (so *OED* 1). Masson has "scorched, burnt: from the Latin *adustus* (*adurere*), Ital. *adusto*," citing uses in Robert Burton and Francis Bacon. Keightley references *l'aria adusta* of Tasso (*Gerusalemme liberata* 7.52)—which Fairfax translates only as "bright heav'n"—and claims that *vapour* is nearly the same as *torrid heat;* R. C. Browne (1877) agrees, citing Horace, *Epodes* 3.15–16: "Nec tantus umquam siderum insedit vapor / Siticulosae Apuliae" (Never did such summer heat sit on dried-out Apulia).

vapour: Bush glosses as "waves of heat," as does Le Comte. Himes (*Paradise Lost: A Poem*) recalls the burning of Mt. Sinai (Exod. 19:18). Hughes (*Paradise Lost*) thinks of the flaming sword as scorching paradise like a blast of heated air blowing from the Libyan desert (i.e., Sahara). The *OED*, however, links all definitions of *vapour* to the action of heat on liquids.

torrid: "intensely hot, burning, scorching" (so *OED* 1).

636–49. Despite modern complaints that the last two books are inferior, this passage is acknowledged to be equal to anything else in the poem, but it would not have its full significance if not preceded by the previous thousand lines of world history (Prince 46–47).

636. *Began:* Wesley changes to *And 'gan.*

parch: cf. *Lyc* 13, *PL* 2.594–95. "Milton uses it of the drying, withering effect of cold or heat" (Verity).

637–47. Hazlitt identifies the pathos in this passage as "that mild contemplative kind which arises from regret for the loss of unspeakable happiness, and resignation to inevitable fate" (Wittreich 387).

637–40. Ibershoff thinks Bodmer's *Noah* echoes these lines (Ibershoff 598). See also **11.118–20**.

637. *In either hand the hastning Angel caught:* in Gen. 3:24, God "drove out the man." As often noted by commentators, the angels so hastened Lot and his family from doomed Sodom (Gen. 19:16). The allusion is hopeful, since Lot was delivered through God's mercy (Sims, *Bible* 128–29). In *The Life of Adam and Eve,* Michael takes Adam by the hand (E. C. Baldwin, "Some Extra-Biblical Semitic Influences" 395). Among Renaissance commentators on the passage, Pareus reports that a Jewish tradition had God taking man by the hand and leading him to the gate of paradise (A. Williams, *Common Expositor* 137). DuBois (551) compares *PL* and *The Glass of Time* (1620) by Thomas Peyton:

> But mild and gently takes them by the hand,
> Shows them the gate that to the east doth stand;
> Leads them along, lamenting of their fall,
> For all their cries sets them without the wall,
> Bars up the door with such an iron lever
> As none alive that once can enter ever.

The destruction of the cities of the plain ("Sodom") and "Adam in Banishment" are possible epic topics listed in the Trinity Manuscript, as is "Josuah [*sic*] in Gibeon" (Patterson, *Works* 18:236); see **12.265–66**.

Adam and Eve are separated from each other by Michael but also joined through him, and as God's messenger he stands in some sense for God (Shumaker, *Unpremeditated Verse* 223). The illustrators often did not consult Milton's text but rather inserted a scene from Genesis, "unaware perhaps that the Scriptures are not a reliable crib to the poem"; Martin's illustration is the most "Miltonian" portrayal of Milton's "paradox of banishment," the same combination of encouraging and discouraging forces (Svendsen, "John Martin" 67–68). Medina's book 12 illustration is disappointing (as is book 2's), because it is negative and tragic, whereas Milton's scene, while unhappy, is also positive and hopeful; the ambivalence of Blake's illustration is far truer to the text (Pointon 157–59). In the iconography of the Fall, the most condensed version features the central tree, the female-headed serpent, and our first parents driven out of an enclosed paradise (Trapp 255). C. H. Collins Baker (3, 4, 19, 112, 113, 116) likewise notes, in illustrations of *PL* up to the year 1800, numerous depictions of an angel driving the outcasts before him with a flaming sword, though Hayman in 1749 has Michael leading Adam and Eve out: Fuseli's single fresh subject in 1802 is Adam and Eve's already standing outside of paradise at the Expulsion; "Adam and Eve Outside Paradise" is also one of four illustrations for book 12 in Tilt's 1843 edition of Milton's *Poetical Works;* the Expulsion scene itself is the most common illustration for book 12 among those from 1688–1850 noted by C. H. Collins Baker. See further lists of Tilt's illustrations in **11.187** and **12.1–5**. "Blake was the first artist to conceive of Milton's Expulsion with hope and love in the faces of Adam and Eve, and an unarmed Michael leading them by the hands, as Milton has him do" (Hughes, "Some Illustrators" 678). Michael's efficient solicitude is in stark contrast to Andreini's Expulsion scene, where the abusive archangel calls his charges "rotted buds" and "putrid worms" (Kirkconnell 259).

Milton most often has an adverb immediately preceding the verb when he engages in syntactic inversion (Emma 145–46).

638. *th'Eastern Gate:* cf. *PL* 4.542–48 and 11.118–20. Though the Expulsion means, for both Satan and the humans, a rejection from a womb into suffering in a netherworld, the eastern exit implies a natural birth and the promise of regeneration (Lieb, *Dialectics* 220).

639–47. *down the Cliff…The World was all before them:* "spaciousness is the natural milieu of disorder and evil"—cf. Satan's first broad prospect of hell in 1.59–60—yet humanity's fall will be worked to his glory, for the pair have Providence as their guide (Cope 59–61).

639. *direct:* an example of Milton's occasional use of a "flat" adverb, i.e., without the *–ly* termination (Emma 114–15).

640. *the subjected Plaine:* the *Antiquitatum* of "Berosus" reports that "Noah…with his family…descended into the subjected plain full of cadavers" (Noa…cum familia…descendit in subjacentem planitatem plenam cadaverum) (76); for "Berosus," see **12:101–04.** The epic traditionally moves either in a linear way on a quest or goes down to the underworld and back, but this epic moves from hell up to the mount of God and then back down to "our own mundane world," the reverse of the traditional mythic journey theme (MacCaffrey 59). Although the delightful topography of Eden has not changed since the Fall, the mount of paradise is now compared with the "subjected Plaine" where the humans dominate their surroundings instead of blending into them, a topography adumbrated by the plain of *PL* 11.671–73 (Knott, "Symbolic Landscape" 53–54).

    subjected: literally "lying beneath," from the Latin (Hughes, *Paradise Lost*); cf. *subjectus, Oxford Latin Dictionary* 1 "situated under or on a lower level." Cf. Spenser's *Faerie Queene* 1.11.19, where the dragon carries Redcrosse "aboue the subiect plaine," and the "subiect" valley of *Faerie Queene* 3.7.4.

641–48. Milton's ending "does not want at this point to commit itself fully to either joy or woe, or to one literary kind" (Burden 200). Milton has fully prepared the "benign and magnanimous ending" of the epic, because ever since Eve's temptation Milton has been gradually humanizing the tone and adjusting his point of view (Stoll, "Was Paradise" 430, 433).

641–42. *all th'Eastern side beheld / Of Paradise:* Empson cites *all,* of which he counts 612 occurrences in *PL,* as an example of Milton's "stylistic and thematic absolutism" ("Emotion" 597; *Structure* 101). Cf. Adam and Eve's view of the total shape of paradise to our remarkable sense of the total structure of the epic at its close (Ferry, *Milton's Epic Voice* 148). The couple leaves by the eastern gate, whereas Satan when apprehended was escorted to the western wall (4.861–64) and fled westward (Robins 709). Milton most often inverts his syntax to subject, object, verb from the normal English pattern of subject, verb, object (Emma 144–45).

642. *happie seat:* cf. 2.347, 3.632, 4.247, and 6.226.

643–44. *Wav'd over by that flaming Brand… / With dreadful Faces throng'd and fierie Armes:* William B. Hunter ("Two Milton Notes" 90–91) traces the tradition of the fiery and terrifying cherubim through Procopius, Theodoret, and at least two seventeenth century commentators, including the Cambridge Platonist Henry More, who followed Milton as a student at Christ's College and whose picture of the cherubim most closely approaches Milton's. It was these lines by Milton rather than Byron's *Cain* that influenced a similar passage by Victor Hugo (Couffignal 256–57). These lines moved De Quincey to proclaim, "Milton was not a writer among writers, not a poet among poets, but a Power among Powers" (De Quincey, in Visiak 15). "Even though Satan uses artillery, the arms and the tactics of the angel-soldiers seem more classical than Cromwellian" (Babb 105). Darbishire (*Milton's "Paradise Lost"*) finds these two lines the most notable place in the last 26 lines of the poem where the sound of long *a* adds to the rich unity of the passage (49–50). Gardner finds disappointing this scene by Milton's first illustrator, Medina; it looks as if Adam and Eve are descending a subway (*Reading* 128). She also notes Michael's "wavy sword," the lack of the "dreadful Faces" and "fierie Armes" at the gate (*PL* 12.644), and the fact that Adam and Eve are not even "hand in hand" (12.648); see also **11.182–90** and **11.239–40**. The threatening angels of the last book recall the fallen ones of the first; Adam and Eve suffer a like expulsion except for grace and the promised Redeemer (Svendsen, *Milton and Science* 107).

Brand: "a sword. (Cf. the poetical use of 'blade.') A poetical use, though in the present century writers of romance have used it in prose as an archaism" (so *OED* 8b), but *OED* also cites this line in its definition for 3d, "*Jove's* or *God's brand:* the lightning. *Phoebus' brand:* the burning rays of the sun. With a blending of the sense 'weapon': (cf. Milton's 'flaming brand' of the archangel in *PL* 12.643)," also citing Thomas Peyton's *Glass of Time* (1620): "A smoky hill, which sends forth fiery brands / Of burning oyle, from hel's infernall deepe, / Much like the sword the tree of life did keepe" (18–20). The Richardsons see a large, heroic sword, *brando* in Italian, as in Spenser's *Faerie Queene* 5.1.9;

cf. the "flaming brand" of *Godfrey of Bulloigne* 11.81 (Tasso). Warton (in Todd) references Norse ideas about swords, e.g., that "the hall of Odin is said to be illuminated by drawn swords only," and also the claim by N. Salanus West-mannus in *Gladius Scythicus*, his 1691 philological dissertation at Uppsala, that the ancients formed their swords in imitation of a flaming fire so that we thus *brandish* a sword. *Brand* derives properly from a word meaning *torch* because of the gleam of the metal; cf. *flamberge* (French), *tizona* (Italian), and the "burning brond" of *Faerie Queene* 2.3.18 (Keightley). *Brand* for "fire-brand" appears nowhere in Milton's work except in the manuscript of *Mask*, where the "noontyde brand" (384) is a synonym for the midday sun, afterward substituted (Verity); cf. nevertheless "shake the brand of Civill Discord" in *Ref* (Patterson, *Works* 3:76).

dreadful Faces: cf. Virgil, *Aeneid* 2.622 (*dirae facies*) and Tasso, *Gerusalemme liberata* 13.28 (*terribil faccia*), and also the monstrous form guarding the ves-tibule of Hades in *Aeneid* 6.575. "Milton has here improved upon the opinion of some commentators (cited by Moses Bar-Cepha), that God placed 'spectrum quoddam vehemens et terribile' ['a spectre that could be called fiery and frighten-ing'] before the gates of paradise" (R. C. Browne [1877]). Di Cesare here also finds ambivalent feelings toward angels (24); see **12.634**. Milton, here and in 11.120–21 ("of a sword the flame / Wide waving"), is following the Chaldee Paraphrast in understanding it to be a literal sword; despite interpretations that claim the *dreadful faces* are reminiscent of Satan and his cohort, "guilt is not an uncommon cause of fear," and even a truly fearful appearance would not necessarily make them evil (Fowler).

645–49. These last "very affecting lines . . . paint the human pair leaving paradise with pensiveness and a degree of reluctance, yet represent them rather joyous and full of hope than despondent and miserable" (Bayly 194). The tone of these closing lines is controlled by the paradox of the *felix culpa* (Ferry, *Milton's Epic Voice* 40–41). In these five lines, the iambic stresses are absolutely regular (Beum 344). The Expulsion is not as dreadful as it could have been, because Milton "could not quite accomplish what his severe piety intended" (Ransom, "Idea" 133).

645. *Som natural tears they drop'd:* cf. the "sorrowing, yet in peace" of 11.117. "The Scene which our first Parents are surprised with upon their looking back on

Paradise, wonderfully strikes the Reader's Imagination, as nothing can be more natural than the Tears they shed on that Occasion" (Addison, *Spectator* 3 [3 May 1712]: 390). Cf. the tears of exiled Aeneas (Virgil *Aeneid* 3.10–12), leaving the coast of Troy with his companions but accompanied by gods (Himes, *Paradise Lost: A Poem*). Milton's contemporary readers, sharing Adam's expectations about the world, must have felt for their own errors in life (Colie 132–33). The word *drop'd* "adds almost imperceptibly" to the other indications of descent in this passage (Shumaker, *Unpremeditated Verse* 58); see also **12.588–94**.

646–49. "This exquisite quiet close, a conclusion in which nothing is concluded, takes its touching pathos from the word 'solitarie,'" since Adam and Eve are in fact not solitary if Milton has succeeded in reaffirming God's constant care for humankind (Gardner, *Reading* 23). This passage demonstrates how well Adam and Eve have been indoctrinated in the bourgeois ethic (Kogan 31); see **11.531**. The closing lines are thoroughly appropriate to the human condition: "We must weep and we must dry our tears. We have all that Alexander desired—the world—and we have, moreover, the assurance that Providence will guide. But with the memory of the past immediate presence of God, our steps must be at our first entrance into the world 'wand'ring' and 'slow'" (Summers, *Muse's Method* 224). The ending is not "quiet"; it is quite unlike the quiet close of a Virgilian eclogue—it does not feel complete or calm, and we sense instead Adam and Eve's uncertainty as they set out (Knott, "Pastoral Day" 180). The poem's end, revealing Adam leaving the garden to face his destiny without dismay, indicates that the "poet's real story" is the regaining of paradise (Thompson, "Theme" 119). The last four lines can be heard variously—depending on the reader's temperament and background—as concerned by the end of direct intercourse with God, as flippant and congratulatory over the disappearance of the unnecessary angelic escort, as resolute with self-confidence, as intelligently responding to the challenge of life, or as recognizing the fulfillment of God's declaration in *PL* 3.196–97 that they would "safe arrive"; the interpretation depends on one's view of the *felix culpa* (Hughes, "Some Illustrators" 672). Peck silently rearranges the last four lines (W. A. Wright).

646–47. *The World was all before them, where to choose / Thir place of rest:* some early commentators hear Shakespearean echoes, such as the Friar's speech to Romeo urging patience: "Here from our Verona art thou banished: / Be patient, for the world is wide" (*Romeo and Juliet* 3.3.15–16), or banished Mowbray's parting words, "Save back to England, all the world's my way" (*Richard II*, 1.3.207). "Adam in Banishment" is one of the epic topics listed in the Trinity Manuscript (Verity); cf. Patterson, *Works* 18:232. The movement from vision to narration in books 11–12 signals a shift from physical stasis to the temporal stasis of consciousness; hence, Adam and Eve's choice of resting place becomes a "weighted option" (Brisman 259). "No painter or engraver has yet succeeded in picturing all that Milton in these last few lines describes" (Patterson, *Student's Milton*). "The mingling of sorrow and joy in the last four lines, as in the whole of the last two books, is no mere mechanical paradox but a triumphant reconciliation of opposites (Pecheux, "Abraham" 371). *Providence* can be the object of *choose*, indicating that "decisions of faith lie ahead" (Fowler).

648–49. Addison found these last two lines inferior to the two preceding ones (*PL* 12.646–47) because they are too reminiscent of Adam and Eve's anguish (*Spectator* 3 [3 May 1712]: 390). Walter Savage Landor counters that "we are not willing to lose sight…of our first parents" (Landor, in Wittreich 320). Masson decries Addison's comment, finding Milton's ending to be "consummately beautiful." Verity defends the lines for "entirely Miltonic style" and their calm beauty, which mingles resignation and reluctance, similar to the quiet ending note of Shakespearean tragedy. Morris reports that one Reverend Richard Jago attempted a libretto of *PL*, posthumously published in 1784, that deleted these last two lines; Morris thinks the lines unbearably underscore humanity's estrangement from God (157). Wesley also omits the two lines. Bentley famously emends the last two lines to read: "*Then* hand in hand with *social steps their way* / Through Eden took, *with heav'nly comfort cheer'd*," reasoning that the last distich seems cut off from and inferior to the foregoing, and especially that it overlooked various expressions of joy and comfort (12.372, 463, 475, 558, 620); he complains that the couple should not be wandering if they are guided by Providence, that they should not be moving slowly when Eve has eschewed delay, and that their way cannot be any more solitary than during any of their walks in paradise. Pearce objects, among other things, that *wandr'ing* is prepared by Eve's comment in 11.282–83 and *solitary* by Adam's comment in 11.305 that they will face unfamiliar territory, and that all the consolation regards promises for the distant future; moreover, God said they would leave "sorrowing" (11.117). An epic is not required to end happily, and the subject matter of *PL* requires that its ending inspire fear and commiseration; the last two lines also indicate the pair's acceptance of their new life, as the first line moves slowly but the second picks up in pace (Newton). Lawry similarly cautions against being misled by the pathos of *solitary,* since the world is no mean gift (*Shadow* 288); cf. 11.339–40. Stebbing's answer to the various critics occasions one of his longest comments: "The conclusion of this wonderful poem is not inferior in beauty to its progress. Ceasing from the calm and unadorned narrative which occupies the former part of the last book, the author rises again into his accustomed sublimity, and then with the most admirable skill closes the poem with an appeal, deep and powerful, to all the feelings of awe and tenderness which its subject can awaken. Never, I think, has worst taste been shewn than by the critics who would have had the last two lines omitted."

Broadbent complains that Bentley converts sad resignation to "anguish" and "melancholy" (*Some Graver Subject* 285–86). The various arguments for and against including the last two lines turn on the impossible task of correctly identifying its mood; Milton's artistic and philosophical achievement in the closing can best be understood in the iconographic context (Hughes, "Some Illustrators" 673–77). Bentley's insistence that he knew Milton's intention is like modern critics' attempts to make the epic about the *felix culpa* (Kermode 102). Peter, in fact, says that the final two lines provide the climax that the *felix culpa* failed to do: (158). Himes (*Paradise Lost: A Poem*) thinks that Milton's conclusion to Adam's long vision is appropriate, since at the end of a similar experience, the prophet Daniel is told, "Go thou thy way till the end be" (Dan. 12:13). Bentley's omission of these lines coarsens, flattens, and sentimentalizes the "marvelous complexity of attitude, the fine adjustment of tone, the beautiful appropriateness of feeling of the original," along with the "richness of mood and meaning" that the epic's conclusion requires (Ferry, "Bird" 183–84). The poem "rises to true dramatic grandeur" in these lines, and recalls the end of *SA:* "calm of mind, all passion spent" (Bøgholm 50). Münch's response to the last lines possibly reflects the cultured European one: "In simple final notes the powerful poem fades away. The close no longer strikes one as high tragedy, leaving behind rather the impression of melancholy resignation as brought forth—in contrast to a paradisal ideal—by the reality of human life. And this impression reflects the intention of the poet and the idea of his poetry" (156 [trans. William Odom]). John Crowe Ransom represents much modern interpretation about God "deliberately and knowingly" endowing Adam and Eve "with a prodigious adventurousness" so as to be pioneers of a happiness that only strength can win in a world of pain, sickness, and death ("Idea" 137); their mood is better represented, however, by Michael's commission (11.117) to "send them forth, though sorrowing, yet in peace" (Hughes, *Paradise Lost, A Poem*). Todd compares Petrarch's *Rime sparse* 306.5–8: "ond' io son fatto un animal silvestro / che co' pio vaghi, solitari, et lassi, / porto 'l cor grave, e gli occhi humidi e bassi / al mondo ch'è per me un deserto alpestro" [so that I have become an animal of the woods, and with wandering, solitary, and weary feet I carry about a heavy heart and eyes wet and cast down in the world, which is for me a mountainous desert"]. In his 1839 translation of Grotius's *Adamus exul,* Barham renders Grotius's closing lines as, "my eye, / Wet with its many-gushing tears, looks back / To take its long, its last farewell of Eden. / Where shall we wander? Whither shall we bend / Our weary steps? Where choose our place of rest / And find a home in exile, and a hope?" (51). B. A. Wright (*Milton's Paradise Lost* 204–05) finds the strongest note to be of mutual affection and trust, symbolized by "hand in hand"; he argues against T. S. Eliot's claim that Adam and Eve were not individuals ("Milton II" 269) by claiming that they are indeed individualized at the poem's end, because "there is a poignancy in the farewell such as can only be felt for persons." The ending's subtle mood is a mixture of poignant sadness, stoic resignation to the human lot, and triumphant Christian hope (Parish, "Pre-Miltonic Representations" 2). "The story simply stops, but it does not end.... Their story cannot end so long as place and time are the dimensions of human history" (Colie 132). Madsen, who argues that the final vision is a human rather than an angelic one, judges that "the twilight mood" of the poem's closing is foreshadowed by the description of the evening that ends Adam and Eve's first day and is reflected in such phrases as "though sorrowing, yet in peace" (11.117), "though in fall'n state, content" (11.180), "Quiet though sad" (11.272), and the last lines of the poem ("Idea" 267). The ending continues to present problems; whereas the eighteenth century wanted a happy ending, modern readers "are suspiciously attached to our visions of a catastrophic or meaningless one" (Summers, *Muse's Method* 188–89).

648. *hand in hand:* hands signify Adam and Eve's obedience; they are "hand in hand" when Satan first sees them (4.321), and also go that way to the bower (4.689) and into it (4.738–39), but just before their disobedience, Eve withdraws her hand (9.385–86), and fallen Adam seizes Eve's hand in a parody of the nuptial rites (9.1037); here they are once again "hand in hand," i.e., properly obedient (Reiter). The phrase signals that they are "born united into the fallen world"; their way is *solitarie* because "they now become authors of their own fate" (Lieb, *Dialectics* 220).

The dislocated syntax of this line perfectly expresses the lingering, slow, and wandering movement of Adam and Eve (Di Cesare 24). Bush also references 4.488–89 and 8.510–11. Our last sight of Adam and Eve matches their passing out of our first sight of them (4.319–21): in both scenes, two figures are viewed as one in the distance, but in the second view the location is no longer indeterminate but located "in the dimension of time between a past already realized and a future promised in vision" (Stein, *Answerable Style* 131). Terror would be the last passion left in the reader's mind, were it not for the hopefulness of the clasped hands (Fowler).

wandring: Fish (140–41) argues that this action is transformed in book 12; see **11.281**.

649. *solitary:* Sims (*Bible* 273) and Fowler cite Job 30:3, "For want and famine they were solitary; fleeing into the wilderness in former time desolate and waste," and Ps. 107:4, "They wandered in the wilderness in a solitary way; they found no city to dwell in." Shawcross also claims that the last line derives from Ps. 107:4 and reinforces both God's deliverance and the Exodus ("*Paradise Lost*" 17).

Works Cited

EDITIONS

Beeching, H. C., ed. *The Poetical Works of John Milton*. Oxford: Clarendon Press, 1900.

Bentley, Richard, ed. *Milton's "Paradise Lost": A New Edition*. London: Jacob Tonson, 1732.

Browne, R. C., ed. *English Poems by John Milton*. 2 vols. Oxford: Clarendon Press, 1877–78.

———. *English Poems by John Milton. New Edition, with the Etymological Notes Revised by Henry Bradley*. 2 vols. Oxford: Clarendon Press, 1894.

Bush, Douglas, ed. *Milton: Poetical Works*. London: Oxford University Press, 1966.

Darbishire, Helen, ed. *Poetical Works*. 2 vols. Oxford: Clarendon Press, 1952–55.

Fletcher, Harris Francis, ed. *The Complete Poetical Works of John Milton: A New Text Edited with Introduction and Notes*. Boston: Houghton Mifflin, 1941.

Fowler, Alastair, ed. *Paradise Lost*. Corrected from *Complete Poems of Milton* (1968). London: Longman, 1971.

Frye, Northrop, ed. *"Paradise Lost" and Selected Poetry and Prose*. New York: Holt, Rinehart and Winston, 1951.

Gillies, John, ed. *Milton's "Paradise Lost," Illustrated with Texts of Scripture*. London: Rivington, 1788.

Grierson, H. J. C., ed. *The Poems of John Milton*. 2 vols. New York: Brentano's, 1925.

Hawkey, John, ed. *Paradise Lost, a Poem in Twelve Books*. Dublin: S. Powell, 1747.

Himes, John A., ed. *Paradise Lost: A Poem in Twelve Books*. New York: Harper, 1898.

Hughes, Merritt Y., ed. *Complete Poems and Major Prose*. New York: Odyssey Press, 1957.

———. *Paradise Lost*. New York: Odyssey Press, 1935.

349

———. *Paradise Lost, A Poem in Twelve Books. A New Edition.* New York: Odyssey Press, 1962.

Hume, Patrick, ed. *Paradise Lost.* London: Jacob Tonson, 1695.

Keightley, Thomas, ed. *The Poems of John Milton.* 2 vols. London: Chapman and Hall, 1859.

Le Comte, Edward, ed. *"Paradise Lost" and Other Poems.* New York: New American Library, 1961.

Marchant, John, ed. *Paradise Lost.* London: R. Walker, 1751.

Masson, David, ed. *The Poetical Works of John Milton.* 3 vols. London: Macmillan, 1874.

Milton, John. *Paradise Lost: A Poem in Ten Books.* London: Peter Parker, 1667.

———. *Paradise Lost: A Poem in Ten Books.* London: Peter Parker, 1668.

———. *Paradise Lost: A Poem in Ten Books.* London: S. Simmons, 1669.

———. *Paradise Lost: A Poem in Twelve Books. The Second Edition, Revised and Augmented by the Same Author.* London: S. Simmons, 1674.

———. *Paradise Lost: A Poem in Twelve Books. The Twelfth edition, to Which Is Prefix'd an Account of His Life [by Elijah Fenton].* London: Jacob Tonson, 1725.

Montgomery, James, ed. *Poetical Works.* London: Henry G. Bohn, 1861.

Moody, William Vaughan, ed. *The Complete Poetical Works of John Milton.* Cambridge, MA: Riverside Press, 1899.

Newton, Thomas, ed. *Paradise Lost. A Poem in Twelve Books.* London: J. and R. Tonson, 1749.

Paterson, James, ed. *A Complete Commentary, with Etymological, Explanatory, Critical, and Classical Notes on Milton's "Paradise Lost."* London: R. Walker, 1744.

Patterson, Frank Allen, ed. *The Student's Milton.* 1930. Rev. ed., New York: F. S. Crofts, 1933.

———, gen. ed. *The Works of John Milton.* 18 vols. in 21. New York: Columbia University Press, 1931–38.

Pearce, Zachary, ed. *A Review of the Text of the Twelve Books of Milton's "Paradise Lost."* London: John Shuckburgh, 1733.

Richardson, Jonathan, Father and Son, eds. *Explanatory Notes and Remarks on Milton's "Paradise Lost."* London: James, John, and Paul Knapton, 1734. Facsimile reprint, New York: Garland, 1970.

Ricks, Christopher, ed. *"Paradise Lost" and "Paradise Regained."* New York: Signet, 1968.

Shawcross, John T., ed. *The Complete Poetry of John Milton.* 1963. Rev. ed., New York: Anchor Books, 1971.

St. Maur, Raymond de, ed. *The State of Innocence, and Fall of Man.* London: T. Osborne, 1745.

Stebbing, H., ed. *The Complete Poetical Works of John Milton.* London: Scott, Webster, and Geary, 1839.

Todd, Henry John, ed. *The Poetical Works of John Milton*. 1801. 2nd ed. 7 vols. London, 1809. New York: AMS Press, 1970.

Vaughan, Robert, ed. *Milton's "Paradise Lost."* London: Cassell, Petter, and Galpin, 1866.

Verity, A. W., ed. *Milton's "Paradise Lost."* 1892–96. Rev. ed., Cambridge: Cambridge University Press, 1910.

Warton, Thomas, ed. *Poems upon Several Occasions*. London: J. Dodsley, 1785. 2nd ed. London: G. G. J. and J. Robinson, 1791.

Weidner, Paul R., ed. "John Milton: *Notes on Paradise Lost*." Charleston: The College of Charleston, 1939.

Wesley, John, ed. *An Extract from Milton's "Paradise Lost."* 1763. Reprint, London, 1791.

Wolfe, Don M., gen. ed. *Complete Prose Works of John Milton*. 8 vols. in 10. New Haven: Yale University Press, 1953–82.

Wright, B. A., ed. *Milton's Poems*. London: J. M. Dent and Sons, 1956.

Wright, William Aldis, ed. *The Poetical Works of John Milton*. Cambridge: Cambridge University Press, 1903.

COMMENTARIES AND REFERENCE WORKS

Adams, John R. "The Theism of *Paradise Lost*." *Personalist* 22 (1941): 174–80.

Adams, Robert M. *Ikon: John Milton and the Modern Critics*. Ithaca, NY: Cornell University Press, 1955.

Addison, Joseph. *The Spectator*. 5 vols. Ed. Donald F. Bond. Oxford: Clarendon Press, 1965.

Agar, Herbert. *Milton and Plato*. Princeton, NJ: Princeton University Press, 1928.

Allen, Don Cameron. *The Harmonious Vision: Studies in Milton's Poetry*. 1954. Enlarged ed. Baltimore: Johns Hopkins University Press, 1970.

———. *The Legend of Noah: Renaissance Rationalism in Art, Science, and Letters*. Urbana: University of Illinois Press, 1949.

———. "Milton and the Descent to Light." *Journal of English and Germanic Philology* 60 (1961): 614–30.

———. "Milton and the Sons of God." *Modern Language Notes* 61 (1946): 73–79.

———. "Milton's Amarant." *Modern Language Notes* 72 (1957): 256–58.

———. *Mysteriously Meant: The Rediscovery of Pagan Symbolism and Allegorical Interpretation in the Renaissance*. Baltimore: Johns Hopkins University Press, 1970.

———. "Some Theories of the Growth and Origin of Language in Milton's Age." *Philological Quarterly* 28 (1949): 5–16.

Andreini, Giovanni Battista. *L'Adamo, con un saggio sull' "Adamo" e "Il Paradiso perduto."* Ed. Ettore Allidolo. Lanciano: R. Carabba, 1913.

Apollodorus. *The Library [Bibliotheca]*. 2 vols. Trans. J. G. Frazer. London: Heinemann, 1921.

Apollonius Rhodius. *Argonautica*. Ed. Johann Gottlob Schneider. Jena: Frommann, 1803.

Aquinas, Thomas. *Summa Theologicae*. Trans. Fathers of the English Dominican Province. New York: Benziger Brothers, 1948.

Ariosto, Ludovico. *Orlando Furioso*. Ed. Robert McNulty. Trans. Sir John Harington. Oxford: Clarendon Press, 1972.

Aristotle. *The Nichomachean Ethics*. Trans. H. Rackham. 1926. Reprint, London: Heinemann, 1968.

———. *On the Soul. Parva Naturalia. On Breath*. Trans. W. S. Hett. London: Heinemann, 1957.

Assman, K. *Miltons epische Technik nach "Paradise Lost."* Berlin: Hermann Blankes, 1913.

Augustine. *City of God*. 7 vols. Trans. W. C. Greene. London: Heinemann, 1960.

Austin, William. *Haec Homo, Wherein the Excellency of the Creation of Woman Is Described*. London: Richard Olton for Ralph Mabb, 1637.

Avery, Christine. "*Paradise Lost* and the Power of Language." *English* 19 (1970): 79–84.

Babb, Lawrence. *The Moral Cosmos of "Paradise Lost."* East Lansing: Michigan State University Press, 1970.

Bacon, Sir Francis. *Works of Francis Bacon*. 14 vols. Ed. James Spedding et al. London: Longman, 1857–74. Reprint, New York: Garrett Press, 1968.

Bailey, Margaret L. *Milton and Jakob Boehme: A Study of German Mysticism in Seventeenth-Century England*. New York: Oxford University Press, 1914. Reprint, New York: Haskell House, 1964.

Baker, C. H. Collins. "Some Illustrators of Milton's *Paradise Lost* (1688–1850)." *Library*, 5th ser., 3 (1948): 1–21, 101–19.

Baker, Herschel. *The Race of Time: Three Lectures on Renaissance Historiography*. Toronto: University of Toronto Press, 1967.

Baldwin, Edward Chauncey. "*Paradise Lost* and the Apocalypse of Moses." *Journal of English and Germanic Philology* 24 (1925): 383–486.

———. "Some Extra-Biblical Semitic Influences upon Milton's Story of the Fall of Man." *Journal of English and Germanic Philology* 28 (1929): 366–401.

Baldwin, T. W. "A Double Janus." *PMLA* 56 (1941): 583–85.

Bamberger, Bernard Jacob. *Fallen Angels*. Philadelphia: Jewish Publication Society of America, 1952.

Banks, Theodore. "The Meaning of 'Gods' in *Paradise Lost*." *Modern Language Notes* 54 (1939): 450–54.

———. *Milton's Imagery*. New York: Columbia University Press, 1950.

Barker, Arthur. "*Paradise Lost:* The Relevance of Regeneration." In *"Paradise Lost": A Tercentenary Tribute,* ed. Balachandra Rajan, 48–78. Toronto: University of Toronto Press, 1969.

———. "Structural and Doctrinal Pattern in Milton's Later Poems." In *Essays in English Literature from the Renaissance to the Victorian Age, Presented to A. S. P. Woodhouse,* ed. Millar MacLure and F. W. Watt, 169–94. Toronto: University of Toronto Press, 1964.

Barnes, C. L. "Parallels in Milton and Dante." *Papers of the Manchester Literary Club* 43 (1917): 8–29.

Barrett, James A. S. "Ambiguities in *Paradise Lost.*" *Times Literary Supplement,* Oct. 8, 1925, 656.

Baumgarten, A. *John Milton und das "Verlorene Paradies."* Coburg: George Sendelbach, [1875].

Baumgartner, Paul R. "Milton and Patience." *Studies in Philology* 60 (1963): 203–13.

Bayly, Anselm. *The Alliance of Musick, Poetry and Oratory.* London: John Stockdale, 1789.

Bell, Millicent. "The Fallacy of the Fall in *Paradise Lost.*" *PMLA* 68 (1953): 863–83.

Bell, Millicent, and Wayne Shumaker. "Notes, Documents, and Critical Comments: The Fallacy of the Fall in *Paradise Lost.*" *PMLA* 70 (1955): 1185–1203.

Benson, William. *Letters concerning Poetical Translations, and Virgil's and Milton's Arts of Verse.* London: J. Roberts, 1739.

Berger, Harry, Jr. "Archaism, Vision, and Revision: Studies in Virgil, Plato, and Milton." *Centennial Review* 11 (1967): 24–52.

Berkeley, David S. "Thematic Implications of Milton's Paradise of Fools." In *Papers on Milton,* ed. Philip Mahone Griffith and Lester F. Zimmerman, 3–8. Tulsa, OK: University of Tulsa Press, 1969.

"Berosus" [Giovanni Nanni (1432?–1502)]. *Antiquitatum Italiae ac totius orbis libri quinque.* 1498. Reprint, Antwerp: John Stelsius, 1552.

Beum, Robert. "So Much Gravity and Ease." In *Language and Style in Milton: A Symposium on the Tercentenary of "Paradise Lost,"* ed. Ronald David Emma and John T. Shawcross, 333–68. New York: Frederick Ungar, 1967.

Bible. *The Bible: Authorized King James Version with Apocrypha.* Introduction and notes by Robert Carroll and Stephen Prickett. New York: Oxford University Press, 1998.

———. *Biblia sacra iuxta vulgatam versionem.* Ed. Bonifatius Fischer and Robert Weber. 1969. 3rd ed., Stuttgart: Deutsches Bibelgesellschaft, 1983.

———. *The Holy Bible, Translated from the Latin Vulgate* [Douay-Rheims Version]. Baltimore: John Murphy, 1899.

———. *Jesu Christi Domini Nostri Novum Testamentum.* Trans. Immanuel Tremellius and Franciscus Junius. London: Henry Middleton, 1585.

———. *Jesu Christi D. N. Novum Testamentum.* Trans. Theodore Beza. London: Thomas Vautrollerius, 1587.

———. *The Old Testament of the Jerusalem Bible*. Ed. Alexander Jones. Garden City, NY: Doubleday, 1966.

Blondel, Jacques. "Milton et l'Éden." In *Le "Paradis perdu," 1667–1967*, ed. Jacques Blondel, 49–85. Paris: Minard, 1967.

Bøgholm, N. *Milton and "Paradise Lost."* Copenhagen: Levin & Munksgaard, 1932.

Boswell, Jackson C. "Milton and Prevenient Grace." *SEL* 7 (1967): 83–94.

Bowra, C. M. *From Virgil to Milton*. London: Macmillan, 1945.

Boyer, Carl. B. *The Rainbow from Myth to Mathematics*. New York: Thomas Yoseloff, 1959.

Boys, John. "Sermon for the Second Sunday in Lent." In *The Works of John Boys*, 238–50. [London]: Imprinted [by George Miller] for William Aspley, 1629 [1638].

Brennecke, Ernest. *John Milton the Elder and His Music*. New York: Columbia University Press, 1938.

Bridges, Robert. *Milton's Prosody, with a Chapter on Accentual Verse, & Notes*. Oxford, 1901. Rev. ed., Oxford: Clarendon Press, 1921.

Briggs, Samson. "When Common Souls Break from Their Courser Clay." In *Justo Edovardo King naufrago, ab amicis moerentibus, amoris et μνείας χάριν*, 14–15. Cambridge: Thomas Buck and Roger Daniel, 1638.

Brisman, Leslie. "Milton's Options." Ph.D. diss., Cornell University, 1969.

Broadbent, J. B. "Milton's 'Mortal Voice' and His 'Omnific Word.'" In *Approaches to "Paradise Lost,"* ed. C. A. Patrides, 99–117. London: Edward Arnold, 1968.

———. "Milton's Paradise." *Modern Philology* 51 (1954): 160–76.

———. "Milton's Rhetoric." *Modern Philology* 56 (1959): 224–42.

———. *Some Graver Subject: An Essay on "Paradise Lost."* London: Chatto & Windus, 1960.

Brockbank, Philip. "'Within the Visible Diurnal Spheare': The Moving World of *Paradise Lost*." In *Approaches to "Paradise Lost,"* ed. C. A. Patrides, 199–221. London: Edward Arnold, 1968.

Brooks, Cleanth. "Eve's Awakening." In *Essays in Honor of Walter Clyde Curry*, 281–98. Nashville: Vanderbilt University Press, 1954.

———. "Milton and Critical Re-Estimates." *PMLA* 66 (1951): 1045–54.

Brown, J. R. "Some Notes on the Native Elements in the Diction of *Paradise Lost*." *Notes & Queries* 196 (1951): 424–28.

Browne, Sir Thomas. *Works*. 4 vols. Ed. Sir Geoffrey Keynes. London: Faber & Faber, 1964.

Browne, William. *Britannia's Pastorals*. London: George Norton, 1616.

Bryan, Robert A. "Adam's Tragic Vision in *Paradise Lost*." *Studies in Philology* 62 (1965): 197–214.

Buff, Friedrich. *Miltons "Paradise Lost" in seinem Verhältnis zur "Aeneide," "Ilias," und "Odyssee."* Hof a. S.: Mintzel, 1904.

Bundy, Murray W. "Milton's View of Education in *Paradise Lost.*" *Journal of English and Germanic Philology* 21 (1922): 127–52.

Burden, Dennis H. *The Logical Epic: A Study of the Argument of "Paradise Lost."* Cambridge, MA: Harvard University Press, 1967.

Burke, Herbert C. "The Poles of Pride and Humility in the *Paradise Lost* of John Milton." Ph.D. diss., Stanford University, 1954.

Burton, Robert. *The Anatomy of Melancholy.* 6 vols. Ed. Thomas C. Faulkner, Nicolas K. Kiessling, and Rhonda L. Blair. Oxford: Clarendon Press, 1989–2000.

Butler, A. Z. "The Pathetic Fallacy in *Paradise Lost.*" In *Essays in Honor of W. C. Curry,* 269–79. Nashville: Vanderbilt University Press, 1954.

Buxton, Charles R. "Milton's *Paradise Lost:* A Politician Plays Truant." *A Politician Plays Truant: Essays on English Literature,* 60–82. London: Christophers, 1929.

Calvin, John. *Commentaries on the First Book of Moses called Genesis.* 2 vols. Ed. John King. Grand Rapids, MI: Eerdmans, 1948.

Camoëns, Luis de. *Os Lusiadas.* Ed. Frank Pierce. Oxford: Clarendon Press, 1973.

Cann, Christian. *A Scriptural and Allegorical Glossary to Milton's "Paradise Lost."* London: C. and J. Rivington, 1828.

Carnes, Valerie. "Time and Language in Milton's *Paradise Lost.*" *ELH* 3 (1970): 517–39.

Castiglione, Baldassare. *The Book of the Courtier.* Trans. Sir Thomas Hoby. London: J. M. Dent, 1948.

Cato [the Elder]. *Cato and Varro: On Agriculture.* London: Heinemann, 1934.

Cawley, Robert Ralston. *Milton and the Literature of Travel.* Princeton, NJ: Princeton University Press, 1951.

Champion, Larry S. "The Conclusion of *Paradise Lost*—A Reconsideration." *College English* 27 (1966): 384–94.

Chang, Y. Z. "Why Did Milton Err on Two Chinas?" *Modern Language Review* 65 (1970): 493–98.

Chapman, George. *Chapman's Homer: The Iliad.* Ed. Allardyce Nichol. New York: Pantheon, 1956. Reprint, Princeton, NJ: Princeton University Press, 1998.

Chappell, William. *The Preacher; or, The Art and Method of Preaching.* London: Edward Farnham, 1656.

Charles, R. H., ed. *The Apocrypha and Pseudepigrapha of the Old Testament.* 2 vols. Oxford: Clarendon Press, 1913.

Chaucer, Geoffrey. *The Riverside Chaucer.* Ed. Larry D. Benson. Boston: Houghton Mifflin, 1987.

Cicero. *De re publica. De legibus.* Trans. Clinton Walker Keyes. London: Heinemann, 1928. Reprint, London: Heinemann, 1976.

———. [*De senectute*]. *On Old Age. On Friendship. On Divination.* Trans. W. A. Falconer. Cambridge, MA: Harvard University Press, 1923.

———, as supposed author. *Rhetorica ad Herennium.* Trans. Harry Caplan. London: Heinemann, 1981.

Ciris: A Poem Attributed to Vergil. Ed. R. O. A. M. Lyne. Cambridge: Cambridge University Press, 1978.

Claudian Claudianus. *Claudian.* 2 vols. Trans. Maurice Platnauer. Cambridge, MA: Harvard University Press, 1922. Reprint, London: Heinemann, 1963.

Clements, Rex. "The Angels in *Paradise Lost.*" *Quarterly Review* 264 (1935): 284–93.

Colie, Rosalie L. "Time and Eternity: Paradox and Structure in *Paradise Lost.*" *Journal of the Warburg and Courtauld Institutes* 23 (1960): 127–38.

Collett, Jonathan H. "Milton's Use of Classical Mythology in *Paradise Lost.*" *PMLA* 85 (1970): 88–96.

Conklin, G. N. *Biblical Criticism and Heresy in Milton.* New York: King's Crown Press of Columbia University, 1949.

Conti, Natale. *Natale Conti's "Mythologiae."* 2 vols. Trans. John Mulryan and Steven Brown. Tempe: Arizona Center for Medieval and Renaissance Studies, 2006.

Cope, Jackson I. *The Metaphoric Structure of "Paradise Lost."* Baltimore: Johns Hopkins University Press, 1962.

Corcoran, Mary I. *Milton's Paradise with Reference to the Hexameral Background.* Washington, DC: Catholic University of America Press, 1945.

Couffignal, Robert. "Le *Paradis perdu* de Victor Hugo et Pierre-Jean Jouve." In *Le "Paradis perdu," 1667–1967,* ed. Jacques Blondel, 251–74. Paris: Minard, 1967.

Cowley, Abraham. *Poems: Miscellanies, the Mistress, Pindarique Odes, Davideis, Verses Written on Several Occasions.* Ed. A. R. Waller. Cambridge: Cambridge University Press, 1905. Reprint, [London?]: Elibron Classics, 2001.

Crashaw, Richard. *The Poems, English, Latin and Greek.* Ed. L. C. Martin. Oxford: Clarendon Press, 1957.

Curry, Walter Clyde. *Milton's Ontology, Cosmology and Physics.* Lexington: University of Kentucky Press, 1957.

Daiches, David. "The Opening of *Paradise Lost.*" In *The Living Milton: Essays by Various Hands,* ed. Frank Kermode, 55–69. London: Routledge & Kegan Paul, 1960.

Daniells, Roy. "'A Happy Rural Seat of Various View.'" In *"Paradise Lost": A Tercentenary Tribute,* ed. Balachandra Rajan, 3–17. Toronto: University of Toronto Press, 1967.

———. *Milton, Mannerism and Baroque.* Toronto: University of Toronto Press, 1963.

Darbishire, Helen. *Milton's "Paradise Lost."* London: Oxford University Press, 1951.

Dennis, John. *Letters concerning Poetical Translations, and Virgil's and Milton's Arts of Verse, &c.* London: Printed for the author, 1739.

Dhabar, E. B. N. "The Modern Avista of Milton." In *Essays on Iranian Subjects Written by Various Scholars in Honour of Mr. Kharshedji Rustamji Cama,* 79–97. Bombay: Fort, 1900.

Di Cesare, Mario. "Adventr'ous Song: The Texture of Milton's Epic." In *Language and Style in Milton: A Symposium on the Tercentenary of "Paradise Lost,"* ed. Ronald David Emma and John T. Shawcross, 1–29. New York: Frederick Ungar, 1967.

Diekhoff, John. *Milton's "Paradise Lost": A Commentary on the Argument.* New York: Columbia University Press, 1946. Reprint, New York: Humanities Press, 1963.

———. "Rhyme in *Paradise Lost." PMLA* 41 (1934): 539–43.

Dobson, E. J. "Milton's Pronunciation." In *Language and Style in Milton: A Symposium on the Tercentenary of "Paradise Lost,"* ed. Ronald David Emma and John T. Shawcross, 154–92. New York: Frederick Ungar, 1967.

Donne, John. *Devotions upon Emergent Occasions.* Ed. Anthony Raspa. New York: Oxford University Press, 1987.

Douady, Jules. *La création et le fruit défendu selon Milton.* Paris: Hachette, 1923.

Douglas, John. *Milton No Plagiary; or, A Detection of the Forgeries Contained in Lauder's Essay.* London: A. Millar, 1756.

Draper, John W. "Milton's Ormus." *Modern Language Review* 20 (1925): 323–27.

Drayton, Michael. *Moses His Birth and Miracles. The Muses Elizium,* 121–84. London: Thomas Harper for John Waterson, 1630.

Drummond, William. *The Poetical Works of William Drummond of Hawthornden. With "A Cypresse Grove."* 2 vols. Ed. L. E. Kastner. 1856 [1913?]. Reprint, New York: Haskell House, 1968.

Dryden, John. *The Works of John Dryden.* 20 vols. Ed. Edward Niles Hooker, H. T. Swedenberg, and Vinton A. Dearing. Berkeley and Los Angeles: University of California Press, 1956–2000.

Du Bartas, Sieur de. *The Divine Weeks and Works of Guillaume de Saluste, Sieur du Bartas.* 2 vols. Ed. Susan Snyder. Trans. Josuah Sylvester. Oxford: Clarendon Press, 1979.

DuBois, L. E. "An Inglorious Milton." *North American Review* 91 (Oct. 1860): 539–55.

Dunster, Charles. *Considerations of Milton's Early Reading, and the Prima Stamina of His "Paradise Lost."* London: John Nichols, 1800.

Eastland, Elizabeth W. *Milton's Ethics.* Nashville: Joint University Libraries, 1942.

Edmundson, George. *Milton and Vondel: A Curiosity of Literature.* London: Trübner, 1885.

Eliot, Sir John. *The Monarchie of Man. Manuscript 2,228, Harleian Collection.* 2 vols. Ed. Alexander B. Grosart. [London]: Privately printed, 1879.

Eliot, T. S. "Milton II." 1947. In *Selected Prose of T. S. Eliot,* ed. Frank Kermode, 265–74. New York: Farrar, Straus and Giroux, 1975.

———. "A Note on the Verse of John Milton." *Essays and Studies* 21 (1936): 32–40.

Emma, Ronald David. *Milton's Grammar*. The Hague: Mouton, 1964.

Empson, William. "Emotion in Words Again." *Kenyon Review* 10 (1948): 579–601.

———. *Milton's God*. 1961. Rev. ed., London: Chatto & Windus, 1965.

———. *Some Versions of Pastoral*. London: Chatto & Windus, 1935. Reprint, Norfolk, CT: New Directions, 1950.

———. *The Structure of Complex Words*. London: Chatto & Windus, 1951.

Erskine, John. "The Theme of Death in *Paradise Lost*." *PMLA* 32 (1917): 573–82.

Euripides. *Ion, Hippolytus, Medea, Alcestis*. Trans. Arthur S. Way. London: Heinemann, 1964.

Eusebius of Caesarea. *Praeparatio evangelicae*. Trans. Edwin Hamilton Gifford. Oxford: Oxford University Press, 1903.

Evans, J. M. *"Paradise Lost" and the Genesis Tradition*. Oxford: Clarendon Press, 1968.

Ferry, Anne Davidson. "The Bird, the Blind Bard, and the Fortunate Fall." In *Reason and the Imagination: Studies in the History of Ideas, 1600–1800*, ed. J. A. Mazzeo, 183–200. New York: Columbia University Press, 1962.

———. *Milton's Epic Voice: The Narrator in "Paradise Lost."* Cambridge, MA: Harvard University Press, 1963.

Fisch, Harold. "Hebraic Style and Motifs in *Paradise Lost*." In *Language and Style in Milton: A Symposium on the Tercentenary of "Paradise Lost,"* ed. Ronald David Emma and John T. Shawcross, 30–64. New York: Frederick Ungar, 1967.

Fish, Stanley E. *Surprised by Sin: The Reader in "Paradise Lost."* London: Macmillan, 1967.

Fixler, Michael. *Milton and the Kingdoms of God*. Chicago: Northwestern University Press, 1964.

Flaccus, Valerius. *Argonautica*. Trans. J. H. Mozley. Cambridge, MA: Harvard University Press, 1963.

Fletcher, Harris F. *Milton's Rabbinical Readings*. Urbana: University of Illinois Press, 1930.

Fogle, French R. "Milton as Historian." In *Milton and Clarendon: Two Papers on Seventeenth Century English Historiography Presented at a Seminar Held at the Clark Library on December 12, 1964 by French R. Fogle and H. R. Trevor-Roper*, 1–18. Los Angeles: Clark Library, 1965.

Fortescue, Sir John. *De natura legis naturae*. Trans. Chichester Fortescue. In *The Works of Sir John Fortescue, Knight*. 2 vols. London: Privately printed, 1869. Reprint, New York: Garland, 1980.

Fox, Robert C. "The Seven Deadly Sins in *Paradise Lost*." Ph.D. diss., Columbia University, 1957.

Frye, Northrop. "The Revelation to Eve." In *"Paradise Lost": A Tercentenary Tribute*, ed. Balachandra Rajan, 18–47. Toronto: University of Toronto Press, 1969.

———. "The Typology of *Paradise Regained*." *Modern Philology* 53 (1956): 227–38.

Frye, Roland Mushat. *God, Man and Satan: Patterns of Christian Thought and Life in "Paradise Lost," "Pilgrim's Progress" and the Great Theologians.* Princeton, NJ: Princeton University Press, 1960.

Fulke, William. *A Goodly Gallerye.* London: William Griffith, 1563.

Gage, Clara S. "The Sources of Milton's Concepts of Angels and the Angelic World." Ph.D. diss., Cornell University, 1936.

Gardner, Helen. "Milton's First Illustrator." *Essays and Studies,* n.s., 9 (1956): 27–38.

———. *A Reading of "Paradise Lost."* Oxford: Clarendon Press, 1965.

Giamatti, A. Bartlett. *The Earthly Paradise and the Renaissance Epic.* Princeton, NJ: Princeton University Press, 1966.

Gilbert, Allan H. "A Double Janus (*Paradise Lost* XI, 129)." *PMLA* 54 (1939): 1027–30.

———. *A Geographical Dictionary of Milton.* Ithaca, NY: Cornell University Press, 1919.

———. "Milton and the Mysteries." *Studies in Philology* 17 (1920): 147–69.

———. *On the Composition of "Paradise Lost": A Study of the Ordering and Insertion of Material.* Chapel Hill: University of North Carolina Press, 1947.

———. "A Parallel between Milton and Seneca." *Modern Language Notes* 34 (1919): 120–21.

———. "The Problem of Evil in *Paradise Lost*." *Journal of English and Germanic Philology* 22 (1923): 175–94.

Gill, John. *Exposition of the Old Testament.* 6 vols. 1748–63. Philadelphia: Woodward, 1817–19.

Ginzberg, Louis. *The Legends of the Jews.* 7 vols. Trans. Henrietta Szold. Philadelphia: Jewish Publication Society of America, 1909–38.

Glanvill, Joseph. *Catholick Charity Recommended in a Sermon.* London: Henry Eversden, 1669.

———. *The Vanity of Dogmatizing.* London: Henry Eversden, 1661.

Godwin, William. *The Life of Geoffrey Chaucer, the Early English Poet.* 4 vols. 2nd ed. London: T. Davison, 1804.

Good, John W. *Studies in the Milton Tradition.* Urbana: University of Illinois, 1915.

Grandsen, K. W. "*Paradise Lost* and the *Aeneid*." *Essays in Criticism* 17 (1967): 281–303.

Graves, Robert, and Raphael Patai. *Hebrew Myths: The Book of Genesis.* Garden City, NY: Doubleday, 1964. Reprint, New York: McGraw-Hill, 1966.

Green, Clarence C. "The Paradox of the Fall in *Paradise Lost*." *Modern Language Notes* 53 (1938): 557–71.

Greenlaw, Edwin. "'A Better Teacher Than Aquinas.'" *Studies in Philology* 14 (1917): 196–217.

Gregory the Great. *Moralium libri sive expositio in librum beati Job.* In *Patrologiae cursus completus...Series Latina,* 221 vols., ed. Jacques Paul Migne, 75:509–1162B, 76:9–782A. Paris: Garnier, 1844–64.

Grierson, Herbert J. C. *Milton and Wordsworth, Poets and Prophets: A Study of Their Reactions to Political Events.* New York: Macmillan, 1937.

Grotius, Hugo. *The Adamus Exul of Grotius; or, The Prototype of "Paradise Lost."* Trans. Francis Barham. London: Sherwood, Gilbert & Piper, 1839.

———. *Sophompaneas; or, Joseph, a Tragedy. With Annotations.* Trans. Francis Goldsmith. London: W. H. for John Hardesty, [1634].

Hagenbüchle, Roland. *Sündenfall und Wahlfreiheit in Miltons "Paradise Lost."* Bern: Franke, 1967.

Hakluyt, Richard. *Principal Navigations, Voyages, Traffiques and Discoveries of the English Nation.* 3 vols. London: George Bishop, Ralph Newbery, and Robert Barker, [1598–1600].

Hall, Amy V. "Milton and the City of God." Ph.D. diss., University of Washington, 1941.

Haller, William. "'Hail wedded love.'" *ELH* 13 (1946): 79–97.

Hamilton, G. Rostrevor. *Hero or Fool? A Study of Milton's Satan.* London: George Allen and Unwin, 1944.

Harding, Davis P. *The Club of Hercules: Studies in the Classical Background of "Paradise Lost."* Urbana: University of Illinois Press, 1962.

———. *Milton and the Renaissance Ovid.* Urbana: University of Illinois Press, 1946.

Harrington, James. *The Commonwealth of Oceana.* London: J. Streater, 1656.

Harris, James. *Hermes.* London: H. Woodfall for J. Nourse and P. Vaillant, 1751.

Harris, Victor. *All Coherence Gone.* Chicago: University of Chicago Press, 1949. London: Frank Cass, 1966.

Hartwell, Kathleen E. *Lactantius and Milton.* Cambridge, MA: Harvard University Press, 1929.

Haworth, Helen E. "The Titans, Apollo, and the Fortunate Fall in Keat's Poetry." *SEL* 10 (1970): 637–49.

Herford, C. H. "Dante and Milton." *Bulletin of the John Rylands Library* 8 (1924): 191–235.

Hesiod. *The Works and Days. Theogony. The Shield of Herakles.* Trans. Richmond Lattimore. Ann Arbor: University of Michigan Press, 1959.

Heylyn, Peter. *Cosmographie in Four Books.* Oxford, 1621. Rev. ed., London: A. C. for P. Chetwind and A. Seile et al., 1677.

Heywood, John. *The Proverbs of John Heywood.* Ed. Julian Sharman. London: George Bell and Sons, 1874.

Himes, John A. "The Plan of *Paradise Lost.*" *New Englander* 42 (1883): 196–211.

———. *A Study of Milton's "Paradise Lost."* Philadelphia: J. B. Lippincott, 1878.

Hobbes, Thomas. *The English Works of Thomas Hobbes of Malmebury.* 11 vols. Ed. Sir William Molesworth. London: John Bohn, 1839. Reprint, Darmstadt: Scientia Verlag Aalen, 1966.

Homer. *The Iliad.* 2 vols. Trans. A. T. Murray. London: Heinemann, 1925. Reprint, London: Heinemann, 1967.

———. *The Odyssey.* 2 vols. Trans. A. T. Murray. Cambridge, MA: Harvard University Press, 1919. Reprint, London: Heinemann, 1966.

Homeric Hymns. Works of Hesiod and the Homeric Hymns. Trans. Daryl Hine. Chicago: University of Chicago Press, 2005.

Hoopes, Robert. *Right Reason in the English Renaissance.* Cambridge, MA: Harvard University Press, 1962.

Horace. *Odes [Carmina] and Epodes.* Trans. Niall Rudd. Cambridge, MA: Harvard University Press, 2004.

Howard, Leon. "The Invention of Milton's Great Argument: A Study of the Logic of God's Ways to Men." *Huntington Library Quarterly* 9 (1946): 149–73.

Hughes, Merritt Y. "Beyond Disobedience." In *Approaches to "Paradise Lost,"* ed. C. A. Patrides, 181–98. London: Edward Arnold, 1968.

———. "Milton's Limbo of Vanity." In *Th'Upright Heart and Pure: Essays on John Milton Commemorating the Tercentenary of the Publication of "Paradise Lost,"* ed. Amadeus P. Fiore, 7–24. Pittsburgh: Duquesne University Press, 1967.

———. "Some Illustrators of Milton: The Expulsion from Paradise." *Journal of English and Germanic Philology* 60 (1961): 670–79.

———. "Three Final Issues of Principle: Law of Nature, the Covenant, the Charge of Tyranny." In *Complete Prose Works of John Milton,* 8 vols. in 10, gen. ed. Don M. Wolfe, 3:65–100. New Haven: Yale University Press, 1962.

———. "Variorum Notes and Commentary." Unpublished annotations, Department of English, University of Wisconsin–Madison.

Hulme, Hilda M. "On the Language of *Paradise Lost.*" In *Language and Style in Milton: A Symposium on the Tercentenary of "Paradise Lost,"* ed. Ronald David Emma and John T. Shawcross, 65–101. New York: Frederick Ungar, 1967.

Hunter, Joseph. *Milton: A Sheaf of Gleanings after His Biographers and Annotators.* London: John Russell Smith, 1850.

Hunter, William B. "Prophetic Dreams and Visions in *Paradise Lost.*" *Modern Language Quarterly* 9 (1948): 277–86.

———. "Two Milton Notes." *Modern Language Review* 44 (1949): 89–91.

Huntley, Frank L. "Before and After the Fall: Some Miltonic Patterns of Systasis." In *Approaches to "Paradise Lost,"* ed. C. A. Patrides, 1–14. London: Edward Arnold, 1968.

———. "A Justification of Milton's 'Paradise of Fools' (*P.L.* III, 431–499)." *ELH* 21 (1954): 107–13.

Hutcherson, Dudley R. "Milton's Epithets for Eve." *University of Virginia Studies,* n.s., 4 (1951): 253–60.

Hutchinson, F. E. *Milton and the English Mind.* London: Houghton and Stoughton, 1946.

Ibershoff, C. H. "Bodmer and Milton." *Journal of English and Germanic Philology* 17 (1918): 589–601.

Jerome. *Commentariorum in epistolam Beati Pauli ad Philemonem liber unus.* In *Patrologiae cursus completus...Series Latina,* 221 vols., ed. Jacques Paul Migne, 26:599–618. Paris: Garnier, 1844–64.

Jewish Encyclopedia, The. 12 vols. New York: Funk and Wagnalls, 1901–06.

Johnson, Samuel. "Milton." In *The Lives of the Poets,* ed. Stephen Fix, 21:99–205. New Haven: Yale University Press, 2010.

———. *The Rambler.* Ed. W. J. Bate and Albrecht B. Strauss. New Haven: Yale University Press, 1969.

Jonson, Ben. *Works.* 11 vols. Ed. C. H. Herford et al. Oxford: Clarendon Press, 1925–52.

Joseph, Sister Miriam. *Orthodoxy in "Paradise Lost."* Quebec: Les Presses Universitaires Laval, 1954.

Josephus, Flavius. *Complete Works.* Trans. William Whiston. 1867. Reprint, London: Pickering and Inglis, 1960.

Justa Edovardo King, naufrago, ab amicis mœrentibus, amoris et μνείας χάριν. Cambridge: Thomas Buck and Roger Daniel, 1638.

Juvenal. *Juvenal and Persius.* Trans. G. G. Ramsey. London: Heinemann, 1918. Rev. ed., 1940. London: Heinemann, 1965.

Keith, A. L. "Personification in Milton's *Paradise Lost.*" *English Journal* 17 (1929): 399–409.

Kelley, Sister Margaret Teresa. "The Influence of Dante's *Paradiso* upon Milton." Ph.D. diss., Cornell University, 1938.

Kelley, Maurice. *This Great Argument: A Study of Milton's "De doctrina christiana" as a Gloss upon "Paradise Lost."* Princeton, NJ: Princeton University Press, 1941. Reprint, Gloucester, MA: Peter Smith, 1962.

Kermode, Frank. "Adam Unparadised." In *The Living Milton: Essays by Various Hands,* ed. Frank Kermode, 85–123. London: Routledge & Kegan Paul, 1960.

Khayyam, Omar. *The "Rubaiyat" of Omar Khayyam...with Notes Indicating the Minor Variants.* Ed. Nathan Haskell Dole. Trans. Edward Fitzgerald. Boston: L. C. Page, 1899.

Kirkconnell, Watson. *The Celestial Cycle: The Theme of "Paradise Lost" in World Literature with Translations of the Major Analogues.* Toronto: University of Toronto Press, 1952.

Klibansky, Raymond, Erwin Panofsky, and Fritz Saxl. *Saturn and Melancholy: Studies in the History of Natural Philosophy, Religion and Art.* New York: Basic Books, 1964.

Knott, John R. "The Pastoral Day in *Paradise Lost*." *Modern Language Quarterly* 29 (1968): 168–82.

———. "Symbolic Landscape in *Paradise Lost*." In *Milton Studies,* vol. 2, ed. James D. Simmonds, 37–58. Pittsburgh: University of Pittsburgh Press, 1970.

Knowlson, James. *Universal Language Schemes in England and France: 1600–1800.* Toronto: University of Toronto Press, 1975.

Koehler, Ludwig, and Walter Baumgartner. *The Hebrew and Aramaic Lexicon of the Old Testament.* 5 vols. (English translation of *Hebräisches und aramäisches Lexicon zum Alten Testament.*) Ed. and trans. M. E. J. Richardson et al. Leiden: Brill, 1994–2000.

Kogan, Pauline. "The Political Theme of Milton's *Paradise Lost*." *Literature and Ideology* 4 (1969): 21–41.

Kurth, Burton O. *Milton and Christian Heroism: Biblical Epic Themes and Forms in Seventeenth Century England.* Berkeley and Los Angeles: University of California Press, 1959.

Lauder, William. *An Essay on Milton's Use and Imitation of the Moderns in His "Paradise Lost."* London: J. Payne and J. Bouquet, 1750.

Lawry, Jon S. " 'Euphrasy and Rue': Books XI and XII, *Paradise Lost*." *Ball State University Forum* 8, no. 3 (1967): 3–10.

———. *The Shadow of Heaven: Matter and Stance in Milton's Poetry.* Ithaca, NY: Cornell University Press, 1968.

Lejosne, René. "Satan républicain." In *Le "Paradis perdu," 1667–1967,* ed. Jacques Blondel, 87–103. Paris: Minard, 1967.

Lerner, J. D. "The Miltonic Simile." *Essays in Criticism* 4 (1954): 297–308.

Lewalski, Barbara Kiefer. "Structure and Symbolism of Vision in Michael's Prophecy, *Paradise Lost,* Books XI–XII." *Philological Quarterly* 42 (1963): 25–35.

Lewis, C. S. *Perelandra.* 1943. Reprint, New York: Macmillan, 1944.

———. *A Preface to "Paradise Lost."* London: Oxford University Press, 1942.

Liddell, H. G., and R. Scott. *Greek-English Lexicon, with a Revised Supplement.* 9th ed. Rev. Sir Henry Stuart Jones and Roderick McKenzie. Oxford: Clarendon Press, 1996.

Lieb, Michael. *The Dialectics of Creation: Patterns of Birth and Regeneration in "Paradise Lost."* Amherst: University of Massachusetts Press, 1970.

———. "*Paradise Lost* and the Twentieth Century Reader." *Cithara* 9 (1969): 27–42.

Loane, George G. "Milton and Chapman." *Notes & Queries* 175 (1938): 456–57.

———. "Milton and the Brute Creation." *Spectator* 101 (1908): 291–93.

Lovejoy, Arthur O. "Milton and the Paradox of the Fortunate Fall." *ELH* 4 (1937): 161–79.

Low, Anthony. "The Image of the Tower in *Paradise Lost*." *SEL* 10 (1970): 171–81.

Lowth, Robert. *A Short Introduction to English Grammar.* London: A. Miller & R. & J. Dodsby, 1762. Reprint, Menston: Scolar, 1967.

Lucretius. *De rerum natura.* Trans. W. H. D. Rouse. London: Heinemann, 1924. Rev. Martin Ferguson Smith. 1937. Cambridge, MA: Harvard University Press, 1975.

Luther, Martin. *Lectures on Genesis.* In *Luther's Works,* ed. Jaroslav Pelikan, vols. 1–8. St. Louis: Concordia, 1958–66.

MacCaffrey, Isabel Gamble. *"Paradise Lost" as Myth.* Cambridge, MA: Harvard University Press, 1959.

MacCallum, Hugh. "Milton and Figurative Interpretation of the Bible." *University of Toronto Quarterly* 31 (1961–62): 397–415.

———. "Milton and Sacred History: Books XI and XII of *Paradise Lost.*" In *Essays in English Literature from the Renaissance to the Victorian Age,* ed. Millar MacLure and F. W. Watt, 149–68. Toronto: University of Toronto Press, 1964.

MacKellar, Walter. "Milton and Grotius." *Times Literary Supplement,* Dec. 15, 1932, 963.

Macrobius. *Commentary on the Dream of Scipio.* Trans. William Harris Stahl. New York: Columbia University Press, 1952.

———. *The Saturnalia.* Trans. Percival Vaughan Davies. New York: Columbia University Press, 1969.

Madsen, William G. "Earth the Shadow of Heaven: Typological Symbolism in *Paradise Lost.*" *PMLA* 75 (1960): 519–26.

———. "The Fortunate Fall in *Paradise Lost.*" *Modern Language Notes* 74 (1959): 103–05.

———. *From Shadowy Types to Truth: Studies in Milton's Symbolism.* New Haven: Yale University Press, 1968.

———. "The Idea of Nature in Milton's Poetry." In *Three Studies in the Renaissance,* 181–283. New Haven: Yale University Press, 1958. Reprint, [Hamden, CT]: Archon, 1969.

Mahood, M. M. *Poetry and Humanism.* New Haven: Yale University Press, 1950.

Mariana, Juan de. *De rege et regis institutione libri III.* Toledo, 1599. Reprint, Darmstadt: Scientia Verlag Aalen, 1969.

Marino, Giambattista. *Gierusalemme distrutta e altri teatri di guerra.* Ed. Marzio Pieri. Parma: Università di Parma, 1985.

Marshall, William H. "*Paradise Lost:* Felix Culpa and the Problem of Structure." *Modern Language Notes* 76 (1961): 15–20. Reprinted in *Modern Essays in Criticism,* ed. Arthur E. Barker, 336–41. London: Oxford University Press, 1965.

Martz, Louis L. *The Paradise Within: Studies in Vaughan, Traherne, and Milton.* New Haven: Yale University Press, 1964.

Marvell, Andrew. *The Complete Poems.* Ed. Elizabeth Story Donno. Harmondsworth, Middlesex: Penguin, 1976.

McColley, Grant. "The Book of Enoch and *Paradise Lost.*" *Harvard Theological Review* 31 (1938): 21–39.

———. *"Paradise Lost." Harvard Theological Review* 32 (1939): 181–235.

———. *"Paradise Lost": An Account of Its Growth and Major Origins, with a Discussion of Milton's Use of Sources and Literary Patterns.* Chicago: Packard, 1940.

Mede, Joseph. *Diatribae. Discourses on Divers Texts of Scripture: Delivered upon Severall Occasions.* London: M. F. for John Clark, 1642.

Migne, Jacques Paul, ed. *Patrologiae cursus completus…Series Graeca.* 166 vols. Paris: Imprimerie Catholique, 1857–66.

———. *Patrologiae cursus completus…Series Latina.* 221 vols. Paris: Garnier, 1844–65.

Miner, Earl. "Felix Culpa in the Redemptive Order of *Paradise Lost.*" *Philological Quarterly* 47 (1968): 43–54.

Mohl, Ruth. "Milton's *Commonplace Book:* Translation, Preface, and Notes." In *Complete Prose Works of John Milton,* 8 vols. in 10, gen. ed. Don M. Wolfe, 1:344–59. New Haven: Yale University Press, 1953.

———. *Studies in Spenser, Milton, and the Theory of Monarchy.* New York: King's Crown Press, 1949. Reprint, New York: Columbia University Press, 1962.

Mollenkott, Virginia R. "The Cycle of Sins of *Paradise Lost,* Book XI." *Modern Language Quarterly* 27 (1966): 33–40.

Moore, C. A. "The Conclusion of Paradise Lost." *PMLA* 36 (1921): 1–34.

Moorman, Charles. "Melville's *Pierre* and the Fortunate Fall." *American Literature* 25 (1953): 13–30.

More, Henry. *Antipsychopannychia; or, A Confutation of the Sleep of the Soul after Death.* Cambridge: Roger Daniel, 1642.

Morris, Brian. " 'Not without Song': Milton and the Composers." In *Approaches to "Paradise Lost,"* ed. C. A. Patrides, 137–61. London: Edward Arnold, 1968.

Mörs, Ferdinandus Joseph. *De fontibus "Paradisi amissi" Miltoniani.* Publicly defended philological dissertation. Bonn: Charles Georg, [1865].

Moss, Sidney P. "The Problem of Theme in *The Marble Faun.*" *Nineteenth-Century Fiction* 18 (1964): 393–99.

———. "The Symbolism of the Italian Background in *The Marble Faun.*" *Nineteenth-Century Fiction* 23 (1968): 332–36.

Muir, Kenneth. *John Milton.* London: Longmans, 1955.

Muldrow, George M. *Milton and the Drama of the Soul.* The Hague: Mouton, 1970.

Münch, W. *Milton's "Verlorenes Paradies": Eine Auswahl aus dem Text mit Erklärenden Anmerkungen.* Salzwedel: Gustav Klingenstein, [1874].

N. O. "Annotations on *Paradise Lost.*" *General Repository* [Cambridge, MA] 2 (1812): 66–84.

Nanni, Giovanni. *See* "Berosus."

Neal, Daniel. *The History of the Puritans.* 2 vols. Ed. Joshua Toulmin. New York: Harper, 1844.

Nelson, James G. *The Sublime Puritan: Milton and the Victorians.* Westport, CT: Greenwood Press, 1963.

Nicolson, Marjorie H. "Milton and Hobbes." *Studies in Philology* 23 (1926): 405–33.

———. "Milton and the Telescope." *Science and Imagination,* 80–109. Ithaca, NY: Cornell University Press, 1956.

Ogden, H. V. S. "The Crisis of *Paradise Lost* Reconsidered." *Philological Quarterly* 36 (1957): 1–19. Reprinted in *Milton: Modern Essays in Criticism,* ed. Arthur E. Barker, 308–27. London: Oxford University Press, 1965.

Oras, Ants. "Milton's Blank Verse and the Chronology of His Major Poems." In *SAMLA Studies in Milton: Essays on John Milton and His Works,* ed. J. Max Patrick, 128–95. Gainesville: University of Florida Press, 1953.

———. *Milton's Editors and Commentators from Patrick Hume to Henry John Todd (1695–1801): A Study in Critical Views and Methods.* London: Oxford University Press, 1931. Reprint, New York: Haskell House, 1964.

Osgood, Charles Grosvenor. *The Classical Mythology of Milton's English Poems.* New York: Holt, 1900.

Otten, Charlotte. "Homer's Moly and Milton's Rue." *Huntington Library Quarterly* 33 (1970): 361–72.

Ovid. *Fasti.* Trans. Sir James George Frazer. Cambridge, MA: Harvard University Press, 1967.

———. *Metamorphoses.* 2 vols. Trans. Frank Justus Miller. London: Heinemann, 1916. Rev. G. P. Goold. New York: G. P. Putnam's Sons, 1977. Reprint, London: Heinemann, 1999.

———. *Tristia. Ex Ponto.* Trans. Arthur Leslie Wheeler. Cambridge, MA: Harvard University Press, 1965.

Oxford English Dictionary. 2nd ed. 1989. OED Online. Oxford University Press. Apr. 4, 2000. http://dictionary.oed.com/cgi/entry/00181778.

Oxford Latin Dictionary. Ed. P. G. W. Glare. Oxford: Clarendon Press, 1996. Oxford: Clarendon Press, 2004.

Parish, John E. "Milton and God's Curse on the Serpent." *Journal of English and Germanic Philology* 58 (1959): 241–47.

———. "Pre-Miltonic Representations of Adam as a Christian." *Rice Institute Pamphlet* 40, no. 3 (1953): 1–24.

———. "Standing Prostrate: The Paradox in *Paradise Lost,* X, 1099 and XI, 1." *English Miscellany* 15 (1964): 89–101.

Patrick, John M. *Milton's Conception of Sin as Developed in "Paradise Lost."* Logan: Utah State University Press, 1960.

Patrides, C. A. "Adam's 'Happy Fault' and Seventeenth Century Apologetics." *Franciscan Studies* 23 (1963): 238–43.

———. *Milton and the Christian Tradition.* Oxford: Clarendon Press, 1966.

————. "Milton and the Protestant Theory of the Atonement." *PMLA* 74 (1959): 7–13.

————. "*Paradise Lost* and the Language of Theology." In *Language and Style in Milton: A Symposium on the Tercentenary of "Paradise Lost,"* ed. Ronald David Emma and John T. Shawcross, 102–19. New York: Frederick Ungar, 1967.

————. *The Phoenix and the Ladder: The Rise and Decline of the Christian View of History.* Berkeley and Los Angeles: University of California Press, 1964. Reprinted as *The Grand Design of God: The Literary Form of the Christian View of History.* London: Routledge & Kegan Paul, 1972.

————. "The 'Protoevangelium' in Renaissance Theology and *Paradise Lost.*" *SEL* 3 (1963): 19–30.

————. "Renaissance and Modern Thought on the Last Things: A Study in Changing Conceptions." *Harvard Theological Review* 51 (1958): 169–85.

Pecheux, Mother Mary Christopher. "Abraham, Adam, and the Theme of Exile in *Paradise Lost.*" *PMLA* 80 (1965): 365–71.

————. "The Concept of the Second Eve in *Paradise Lost.*" *PMLA* 75 (1960): 359–66.

————. "The Second Adam and the Church in *Paradise Lost.*" *ELH* 34 (1967): 173–87.

Peck, Francis. *Memoirs of the Life and Actions of Oliver Cromwell.* London, 1740.

————. *New Memoirs of the Life and Poetical Works.* London, 1740.

Peter, John. *A Critique of "Paradise Lost."* New York: Columbia University Press, 1960.

Petrarch, Francesco. *Petrarch's Lyric Poems: The "Rime sparse" and Other Lyrics.* Trans. Robert M. Durling. Cambridge, MA: Harvard University Press, 1976.

Peyton, Thomas. "Lines from *The Glass of Time in the First Age.*" In *Select Poetry, Chiefly Sacred, of the Reign of King James the First,* ed. Edward Farr, 177–80. Cambridge: Cambridge University Press, 1847.

P[hillips], E[dward]. *The New World of English Words.* London, 1658, 1662, 1663.

Phillips, Edward. *The New World of Words.* London, 1671, 1678, 1696, 1700.

Philo Judaeus. *Philo in Ten Volumes.* Trans. F. H. Colson and G. H. Whitaker. London: Heinemann, 1929. Reprint, London: Heinemann, 1968.

————. *Questions and Answers on Exodus.* 2 vols. Trans. Ralph Marcus. Cambridge, MA: Harvard University Press, 1929. Reprint, London: Heinemann, 1953.

Pironon, Jean. "La rhétorique dans les discours d'Adam et d'Eve (*Paradis Perdu* de Milton): Description et fonction." In *Rhétorique et communication: Actes du Congrès de Rouen* (1976). Paris: Didier-Erudition, 1976. 117–28.

Pliny [the Elder]. *Natural History.* 10 vols. Trans. H. Rackham. London: Heinemann, 1938–63.

Pliny [the Younger]. *Letters and Panegyrics.* 2 vols. Trans. Betty Radice. London: Heinemann, 1969.

Pointon, Marcia R. *Milton and English Art.* Toronto: University of Toronto Press, 1970.

Pope, Alexander. *The Twickenham Edition of the Poems of Alexander Pope.* 11 vols. Ed. John Butt. London: Methuen, 1939–69. Reprint, New Haven: Yale University Press, 1961–69.

Pope, Elizabeth Marie. *"Paradise Regained": The Tradition and the Poem.* Baltimore: Johns Hopkins, 1947.

"Precursor of Milton, A." *Atlantic Monthly* 65 (1890): 33–43.

Prince, F. T. "On the Last Two Books of *Paradise Lost.*" *Essays and Studies* 11 (1958): 38–52.

Purcell, J. M. "Rime in *Paradise Lost.*" *Modern Language Notes* 59 (1944): 171–72.

Purchas, Samuel. *Purchas His Pilgrimes.* 5 vols. London: William Stansby for Henrie Fetherstone, 1625–26.

Radzinowicz, Mary Ann. "'Man as a Probationer of Immortality': *Paradise Lost* XI–XII." In *Approaches to "Paradise Lost,"* ed. C. A. Patrides, 31–51. London: Edward Arnold, 1968.

Rajan, Balachandra. "Jerusalem and Athens: The Temptation of Learning in *Paradise Regained.*" In *Th'Upright Heart and Pure: Essays on John Milton Commemorating the Tercentenary of the Publication of "Paradise Lost,"* ed. Amadeus P. Fiore, 61–74. Pittsburgh: Duquesne University Press, 1967.

———. *"Paradise Lost:* The Hill of History." *Huntington Library Quarterly* 31 (1967): 43–63.

———. *"Paradise Lost" and the Seventeenth Century Reader.* London: Chatto & Windus, 1947.

Raleigh, Sir Walter. *Works.* 8 vols. Oxford: Oxford University Press, 1829.

Raleigh, Walter A. *Milton.* London: E. Arnold, 1900. Reprint, New York: Benjamin Bloom, 1967.

Ransom, John Crowe. *God without Thunder: An Orthodox Defense of Orthodoxy.* London: Howe, 1931.

———. "The Idea of a Literary Anthropologist and What He Might Say of the *Paradise Lost* of Milton: A Speech with a Prologue." *Kenyon Review* 21 (1959): 121–40.

Redman, Harry, Jr. *Major French Milton Critics of the Nineteenth Century.* Pittsburgh: Duquesne University Press, 1994.

Reesing, John. *Milton's Poetic Art.* Cambridge, MA: Harvard University Press, 1968.

Reiter, Robert. "Milton's *Paradise Lost,* XII, 648." *Explicator* 28, no. 1 (1969): item 2.

Ricks, Christopher. *Milton's Grand Style.* Oxford: Clarendon Press, 1963.

Robins, Harry. "Satan's Journey: Direction in *Paradise Lost.*" *Journal of English and Germanic Philology* 60 (1961): 699–711.

Ross, Malcolm Mackenzie. *Milton's Royalism: A Study of the Conflict of Symbol and Idea in the Poems.* Ithaca, NY: Cornell University Press, 1943. New York: Russell and Russell, 1970.

———. *Poetry and Dogma: The Transfiguration of Eucharist Symbols in Seventeenth-Century England.* New Brunswick, NJ: Rutgers University Press, 1954.

Rozenberg, Paul. "Don, amour, et sujéton dans le *Paradis perdu*." In *Le "Paradis perdu,"* *1667–1967,* ed. Jacques Blondel, 105–40. Paris: Minard, 1967.

Ryken, Leland. *The Apocalyptic Vision in "Paradise Lost."* Ithaca, NY: Cornell University Press, 1970.

Sackville, Thomas. "Mr. Sackville's Induction." In *A Mirour for Magistrates,* ed. John Higgins, 255–71. London: Felix Kyngston, 1610.

Salkeld, John. *A Treatise of Angels.* London: Nathaniel Butter, 1613.

Samuel, Irene. *Dante and Milton: "The Commedia" and "Paradise Lost."* Ithaca, NY: Cornell University Press, 1966.

———. "Milton on Learning and Wisdom." *PMLA* 64 (1949): 708–23.

———. "*Paradise Lost* as Mimesis." In *Approaches to "Paradise Lost,"* ed. C. A. Patrides, 15–29. London: Edward Arnold, 1968.

———. *Plato and Milton.* Ithaca, NY: Cornell University Press, 1947.

Samuels, Charles T. "The Tragic Vision in *Paradise Lost.*" *University of Kansas City Review* 27 (1960): 65–78.

Sasek, Lawrence A. "The Drama of *Paradise Lost,* Books XI and XII." *Studies in English Renaissance Literature,* ed. W. F. McNeir, 181–96. Baton Rouge: Louisiana State University Press, 1962.

Saurat, Denis. *Milton, Man and Thinker.* New York: Dial Press, 1925. Rev. ed., London: J. M. Dent, 1944.

Schultz, Howard. *Milton and Forbidden Knowledge.* New York: Modern Language Association, 1955.

Seneca. *Moral Essays.* 3 vols. Trans. John W. Basore. London: Heinemann, 1928–35. Reprint, London: Heinemann, 1975–85.

———. *Tragedies: Hercules Furens, Troades, Medea, Hippolytus, Oedipus.* Trans. Frank Justus Miller. London: Heinemann, 1979.

Shakespeare, William. *The Riverside Shakespeare.* Ed. G. Blakemore Evans. Boston: Houghton Mifflin, 1974.

Shawcross, John T. "The Balanced Structure of *Paradise Lost.*" *Studies in Philology* 62 (1965): 696–718.

———. "The Metaphor of Inspiration in *Paradise Lost.*" In *Th'Upright Heart and Pure: Essays on John Milton Commemorating the Tercentenary of the Publication of "Paradise Lost."* Ed. Amadeus P. Fiore, 75–85. Pittsburgh: Duquesne University Press, 1967.

———. "Orthography and the Text of *Paradise Lost.*" In *Language and Style in Milton: A Symposium on the Tercentenary of "Paradise Lost,"* ed. Ronald David Emma and John T. Shawcross, 120–53. New York: Frederick Ungar, 1967.

———. "*Paradise Lost* and the Theme of Exodus." In *Milton Studies,* vol. 2, ed. James D. Simmonds, 2–26. Pittsburgh: University of Pittsburgh Press, 1970.

———. "The Son in His Ascendance: A Reading of *Paradise Lost.*" *Modern Language Quarterly* 27 (1966): 388–401.

————, ed. *Milton, 1732–1801: The Critical Heritage*. London: Routledge & Kegan Paul, 1972.

Shumaker, Wayne. "The Fallacy of the Fall in *Paradise Lost*." *See* Bell, Millicent.

————. *Unpremeditated Verse: Feeling and Premeditation in "Paradise Lost."* Princeton, NJ: Princeton University Press, 1967.

Sidney, Sir Philip. *The Countess of Pembroke's Arcadia*. Ed. Maurice Evans. 1977. Reprint, New York: Penguin, 1984.

Siegel, Paul. "'A Paradise within Thee' in Milton, Byron, and Shelley." *Modern Language Notes* 56 (1941): 615–17.

Sims, James H. *The Bible in Milton's Epics*. Gainesville: University of Florida Press, 1962.

————. "Camoëns' *Lusiads* and Milton's *Paradise Lost:* Satan's Voyage to Eden." In *Papers on Milton*, ed. Philip Mahone Griffith and Lester F. Zimmerman, 36–46. Tulsa, OK: University of Tulsa Press, 1969.

Sophocles. *Sophocles in Two Volumes*. Trans. F. Storr. 1912–13. Reprint, London: Heinemann, 1967–68.

Spenser, Edmund. *The Faerie Queene*. Ed. A. C. Hamilton et al. London: Longman, 2001.

————. *The Shepheardes Calender*. In *Spenser's Minor Poems,* 3 vols., ed. Ernest de Sélincourt, 1:1–121. Oxford: Clarendon Press, 1910.

Sprott, S. Ernest. *Milton's Art of Prosody*. Oxford: Basil Blackwell, 1953.

Stainer, J., and W. A. Barrett. *A Dictionary of Musical Terms*. London: Novello, Ewer, [1876].

Stapleton, Laurence. "Perspectives of Time in *Paradise Lost*." *Philological Quarterly* 45 (1966): 734–48.

Starnes, DeWitt T., and Ernest William Talbert. "Milton and the Dictionaries." *Classical Myth and Legend in Renaissance Dictionaries: A Study of Renaissance Dictionaries in Their Relation to the Classical Learning of Contemporary English Writers*. Chapel Hill: University of North Carolina Press, 1955. 226–339.

Steadman, John M. "Adam and the Prophesied Redeemer (*Paradise Lost,* XII, 359–623)." *Studies in Philology* 56 (1959): 214–25.

————. *Milton and the Renaissance Hero*. Oxford: Clarendon Press, 1967.

————. *Milton's Epic Characters: Image and Idol*. Chapel Hill: University of North Carolina Press, 1968.

Stein, Arnold. *Answerable Style: Essays on "Paradise Lost."* Minneapolis: University of Minnesota Press, 1953.

————. *Heroic Knowledge*. Minneapolis: University of Minnesota Press, 1957.

Stoll, Elmer Edgar. "From the Superhuman to the Human in *Paradise Lost*." *University of Toronto Quarterly* 3 (1933): 3–16.

————. "Was Paradise Well Lost?" *PMLA* 33 (1918): 429–35.

Strong, James. *A Concise Dictionary of the Words in the Hebrew Bible; with Their Renderings in the Authorized English Version.* New York: Eaton & Mains, 1890. Reprinted in *The New Strong's Exhaustive Concordance of the Bible,* 3–126. Nashville: Thomas Nelson, 1984.

Stroup, Thomas B. *"Paradise Lost." Religious Rite and Ceremony in Milton's Poetry.* Lexington: University of Kentucky Press, 1968. 15–47

Summers, Joseph H. "The Embarrassments of *Paradise Lost.*" In *Approaches to "Paradise Lost,"* ed. C. A. Patrides, 65–79. London: Edward Arnold, 1968.

———. "Grateful Vicissitude in *Paradise Lost.*" *PMLA* 69 (1954): 251–64.

———. "Milton and the Cult of Conformity." *Yale Review* 46 (1956–57): 511–27. Reprinted in *Milton: Modern Judgements,* ed. Alan Rudrum, 29–43. London: Macmillan, 1969.

———. *The Muse's Method: An Introduction to "Paradise Lost."* London: Chatto & Windus, 1962.

———. "The Voice of the Redeemer in *Paradise Lost.*" *PMLA* 70 (1955): 1082–89.

Svendsen, Kester. "Epic Address and Reference and the Principle of Decorum in *Paradise Lost.*" *Philological Quarterly* 28 (1949): 185–206.

———. "John Martin and the Expulsion Scene of *Paradise Lost.*" *SEL* 1 (1961): 63–73.

———. *Milton and Science.* Cambridge, MA: Harvard University Press, 1956.

Swan, John, D. *Speculum mundi.* Cambridge: Printers to the University of Cambridge, 1635.

Tasso, Torquato. *Gerusalemme liberata. Godfrey of Bulloigne. A Critical Edition of Edward Fairfax's Translation of Tasso's "Gerusalemme liberata," together with Fairfax's Original Poems.* Ed. Kathleen M. Lea and T. M. Gang. Oxford: Clarendon Press, 1981.

Taylor, Dick, Jr. "The Battle in Heaven in *Paradise Lost.*" *Tulane Studies in English* 3 (1952): 69–92.

———. "Grace as a Means of Poetry: Milton's Pattern for Salvation." *Tulane Studies in English* 4 (1954): 57–90.

———. "Milton and the Paradox of the Fortunate Fall Once More." *Tulane Studies in English* 9 (1959): 35–51.

———. "Milton's Treatment of the Judgment and the Expulsion in *Paradise Lost.*" *Tulane Studies in English* 10 (1960): 51–82.

Taylor, George Coffin. "Did Milton Read Robert Crofts' *A Paradice within Us or The Happie Mind?*" *Philological Quarterly* 28 (1949): 207–10.

———. *Milton's Use of Du Bartas.* Cambridge, MA: Harvard University Press, 1934. Reprint, New York: Octagon Books, 1968.

Thompson, E. N. S. "For *Paradise Lost,* XI–XII." *Philological Quarterly* 22 (1943): 376–82.

———. "Milton's Knowledge of Geography." *Studies in Philology* 16 (1919): 148–71.

———. "The Theme of *Paradise Lost*." *PMLA* 28 (1913): 106–20.

Tibullus. *Tibullus: A Commentary.* Ed. Michael C. J. Putnam. Norman: University of Oklahoma Press, 1973.

Tillyard, E. M. W. *Milton.* London: Chatto & Windus, 1949.

———. "Milton and Sidney's *Arcadia*." *Times Literary Supplement,* Mar. 6, 1953, 153.

———. *The Miltonic Setting: Past and Present.* New York: Macmillan, 1949.

———. *Studies in Milton.* London: Chatto & Windus, 1951.

Toole, William B. " 'The Attractions of the Journey': A Comment on the Structure of *Paradise Lost*." *Arlington Quarterly* 1 (1968): 18–37.

Trapp, J. B. "The Iconography of the Fall of Man." In *Approaches to "Paradise Lost,"* ed. C. A. Patrides, 223–65. London: Edward Arnold, 1968.

Tschumi, Raymond. "De Dante à Milton." In *Le "Paradis perdu," 1667–1967,* ed. Jacques Blondel, 141–76. Paris: Minard, 1967.

Tuve, Rosemond. *Images and Themes in Five Poems by Milton.* Cambridge, MA: Harvard University Press, 1967.

Ussher, James. *Annals of the World.* London: E. Tyler for J. Crook and G. Bedell, 1658.

———. *A Body of Divinity.* London: M. F. for Thomas Downes and George Badger, 1649.

Vida, Marcus Hieronymus. *The Christiad, a Poem in Six Books.* Trans. J. Cranwell. Cambridge, 1768.

Virgil. *Eclogues, Georgics, Aeneid I–VI, and Aeneid Books 7–12, Appendix Vergiliana.* 2 vols. Trans. H. Rushton Fairclough. Rev. ed. Cambridge, MA: Harvard University Press, 1986.

Visiak, E. H. *The Portent of Milton: Some Aspects of His Genius.* New York: Humanities Press, 1968.

Vitruvius. *Vitruvius on Architecture.* 2 vols. Trans. Fred Granger. London: Heinemann, 1931, 1934.

Waddington, Raymond B. "The Death of Adam: Vision and Voice in Books XI and XII of *Paradise Lost*." *Modern Philology* 70 (1972): 9–21.

Watson, J. R. "Divine Providence and the Structure of *Paradise Lost*." *Essays in Criticism* 14 (1964): 148–55.

Webb, Daniel. *Remarks on the Beauties of Poetry.* London: R. and J. Dodsley, 1762.

Weisinger, Herbert. "Ideas of History during the Renaissance." *Journal of the History of Ideas* 6 (1945): 415–35.

———. *Tragedy and the Paradox of the Fortunate Fall.* London: Routledge & Kegan Paul, 1953.

West, Robert H. *Milton and the Angels.* Athens: University of Georgia Press, 1955.

———. "Milton's Sons of God." *Modern Language Notes* 65 (1950): 187–91.

Whaler, James. "Animal Simile in *Paradise Lost.*" *PMLA* 47 (1932): 534–53.

———. "The Compounding and Distribution of Similes in *Paradise Lost.*" *Modern Philology* 28 (1931): 313–27.

———. *Counterpoint and Symbol: An Inquiry into the Rhythm of Milton's Epic Style.* Copenhagen: Rosenkilde and Bagger, 1956.

———. "The Miltonic Simile." *PMLA* 46 (1931): 1034–74.

Whiting, George Wesley. "Before the Flood: *Paradise Lost* and the Geneva Bible." *Notes & Queries* 194 (1949): 74–75.

———. "Cherubim and Sword." *Notes & Queries* 192 (1947): 469–70.

———. *Milton and This Pendant World.* Austin: University of Texas Press, 1958.

Wickert, Maria. "Miltons Entwürfe zu einem Drama vom Sündenfall." *Anglia* 73 (1955): 171–206.

Willet, Andrew. *Hexapla in Genesis, that is, A Sixfold Commentary upon Genesis.* London: Felix Kyngston, 1608.

Willey, Basil. *The Seventeenth-Century Background: Studies in the Thought of the Age in Relation to Poetry and Religion.* London: Chatto & Windus, 1934. Reprint, London: Chatto & Windus, 1950.

Williams, Arnold. *The Common Expositor: An Account of the Commentaries on Genesis, 1527–1633.* Chapel Hill: University of North Carolina Press, 1948.

———. "Conservative Critics of Milton." *Sewanee Review* 49 (1941): 90–106.

Williams, Norman Powell. *Ideas of the Fall and of Original Sin: A Historical and Critical Study.* London: Longmans, Green, 1927.

Williamson, George. "The Education of Adam." *Modern Philology* 61 (1963): 96–109.

Wittreich, Joseph Anthony, Jr. *The Romantics on Milton: Formal Essays and Critical Asides.* Cleveland: The Press of Case Western Reserve University, 1970.

Woodhouse, A. S. P. "Pattern in *Paradise Lost.*" *University of Toronto Quarterly* 22 (1953): 109–27.

———. Review of Hoopes, *Right Reason in the English Renaissance. Modern Language Review* 59 (1964): 102–03.

Woods, M. A. *The Characters of "Paradise Lost."* London: Ouseley, 1908.

Wright, B. A. "'Mainly': *Paradise Lost*, XI, 519." *Review of English Studies*, n.s., 4 (1953): 143.

———. *Milton's "Paradise Lost."* London: Methuen, 1962.

———. "A Note on Milton's Diction." In *Th'Upright Heart and Pure: Essays on John Milton Commemorating the Tercentenary of the Publication of "Paradise Lost,"* ed. Amadeus P. Fiore, 143–49. Pittsburgh: Duquesne University Press, 1967.

———. "Stressing of the Preposition 'Without' in the Verse of *Paradise Lost*," *Notes & Queries* 203 (1958): 202–03.

Yerkes, R. K. *Sacrifice in Greek and Roman Religions and Early Judaism.* New York: Scribner, 1952.

Zanchius, Hieronymus. *De operibus Dei intra spacium sex dierum creatis.* Neustadt: Nicholas Schramm for Wilhelm Harnisius, 1602.

Zeno. *Tractatus.* In *Patrologiae cursus completus...Series Latina,* 221 vols., ed. Jacques Paul Migne, 11:253–528. Paris: Garnier, 1844–64.

Index